SCIPIO AFRICANUS

OTHER BOOKS BY RICHARD A. GABRIEL

The Battle Atlas of Ancient Military History (2008)
The Warrior's Way: A Treatise on Military Ethics (2008)
Muhammad: Islam's First Great General (2007)
Soldiers' Lives Through History (2006)
*Jesus the Egyptian: The Origins of Christianity and the Psychology
    of Christ (2005)*
Empires at War: A Chronological Encyclopedia, 3 volumes (2005)
Subotai the Valiant: Genghis Khan's Greatest General (2004)
*Lion of the Sun: A Chronicle of the Wars, Battles and Great Deeds of
    Pharaoh Thutmose III, Great Lion of Egypt, as Told to Thaneni
    the Scribe (2003)*
The Military History of Ancient Israel (2003)
The Great Armies of Antiquity (2002)
Sebastian's Cross (2002)
*Gods of Our Fathers: The Memory of Egypt in Judaism and
    Christianity (2001)*
*Warrior Pharaoh: A Chronicle of the Life and Deeds of Thutmose III,
    Great Lion of Egypt, Told in His Own Words to Thaneni the
    Scribe (2001)*
Great Captains of Antiquity (2000)
The Culture of War: Invention and Early Development (1990)
The Painful Field: Psychiatric Dimensions of Modern War (1988)
No More Heroes: Madness and Psychiatry in War (1987)
Military Incompetence: Why the U.S. Military Doesn't Win (1985)
*To Serve With Honor: A Treatise on Military Ethics and the Way
    of the Soldier (1982)*

With Donald W. Boose Jr.

*Great Battles of Antiquity: A Strategic and Tactical Guide to Great
    Battles That Shaped the Development of War*

With Karen S. Metz

A Short History of War: The Evolution of Warfare and Weapons
*History of Military Medicine, Vol. 1, From Ancient Times to the
    Middle Ages*
*History of Military Medicine, Vol. 2, From the Renaissance Through
    Modern Times*
From Sumer to Rome: The Military Capabilities of Ancient Armies

SCIPIO AFRICANUS

Rome's Greatest General

RICHARD A. GABRIEL

POTOMAC BOOKS, INC.
WASHINGTON, D.C.

Library of Congress Cataloging-in-Publication Data

Gabriel, Richard A.
  Scipio Africanus : Rome's greatest general / Richard A. Gabriel.
     p. cm.
  Includes bibliographical references and index.
  ISBN-13: 978-1-59797-205-5 (hardcover : alk. paper)
  1. Scipio, Africanus, ca. 236–183 B.C. 2. Rome—History, Military—265–30 B.C. 3. Generals—Rome—Biography. 4. Consuls, Roman—Biography. I. Title.
  DG248.S3G33 2008
  937'.04092—dc22

                                           2007048961

Potomac Books, Inc.
22841 Quicksilver Drive
Dulles, Virginia 20166

First Edition

10 9 8 7 6 5 4 3 2

For
Katherine Anna Nurik
and
Clara Rosemarie Kaufman, little miracles,
and, of course, for Suzi

Contents

Contents

Illustrations

Preface

THE WORLD often misunderstands its greatest men while neglecting others entirely. Scipio Africanus, surely the greatest soldier that Rome produced, suffered both these fates. The man who stood like a beacon above his contemporaries on the strength of his brilliance and character during the Republic's darkest hour; who revolutionized Roman military tactics; who set Rome on its imperial course by propounding a wider strategic view of Rome's mission than the Roman aristocracy of his time was capable of comprehending; who extended Roman power into Spain, Africa, and Asia; who defeated the great Hannibal and won the Second Punic War; who was the central figure of his time; and who, after all his accomplishments, turned away from the temptation of personal ambition, retired from public life, and preserved the institutions of Roman republicanism remains almost unknown to modern readers. In a cruel paradox one of the men Scipio defeated, Hannibal Barca, captivated the imagination of scholars and laymen over the centuries while the greater soldier and statesman of the two remained unrecognized for his achievements.

The state of modern scholarship regarding Scipio still reflects this undeserved obscurity. No scholarly biography of this great man is in print. Only one book, Basil Liddell-Hart's *Scipio Africanus: Greater Than Napoleon*, remains available, but it is not a scholarly or accurate account of Scipio's life and fails on the grounds of comprehensiveness as well. First published in 1926, Liddell-Hart wrote the book as a response to the anti-Scipionic biographies of Hannibal that were popular at the time. Propagandistic and almost without footnotes and documentation, contemporary historians criticized Liddell-Hart's book as a popular and unbalanced work. Although he later became a renowned historian, Liddell-Hart was a journalist when he published this book and was seen as lacking in scholarly credentials, a deficiency manifested in the book's pro-Scipio bias and its paucity of documentation. Liddell-Hart read neither German nor Italian, languages in which much of the scholarly research on Scipio was published at the time, forcing him to ignore some of the best available information regarding his subject.

The book's shortcomings led two young scholars, Howard Scullard and Richard Haywood, to attempt their own works on Scipio. Scullard's work was published in 1929 as part of his doctoral dissertation, and Haywood's was published three years later. A response to the German school of literary *Quellenkritik*, Scullard's work is a typical British academic tome of the period. He attempts in minute detail to resolve the difficulties among the various literary accounts of the "original" sources. It is more a work of classics than of military history, but it remains a valuable source for the military biographer. Haywood's monograph is a collection of essays on various aspects of Scipio's life, and while valuable, it cannot be regarded as a comprehensive attempt at a biography of Scipio. Scullard later rewrote parts of his earlier work, stressing the source materials for Scipio's political life and trial. Published in 1970, it has been out of print for thirty years.

It is regrettable that the least scholarly and complete work on Scipio has been the only book on the great general available to modern scholars and general readers. My purpose is to correct this and write a new military biography of Scipio Africanus, one based on more detailed and complete source materials than Liddell-Hart had at his disposal. Scullard's and Haywood's works were both written after Liddell-Hart's and provide much information on which the military historian can draw. Most of the significant archival material, which Liddell-Hart could not draw on, is in the form of academic monographs and journal articles written in German and Italian between 1890 and 1933 and is readily available to me because of my ability to read both languages.

Of great importance in this regard are two works in German by Johannes Kromayer and George Veith written in 1912 and 1922, respectively. Kromayer was a professor of ancient military history at Leipzig, and Veith was the director of the Military Archive in Vienna and a colonel in the Austrian army. The first of their works (1912) is *Antike Schlachtfelder* in three volumes and provides detailed and technical descriptions of many ancient battlefields, including those relevant to this work: New Carthage, Baecula, Ilipa, Utica, the Great Plains, and Zama. The second work, *Schlachten-Atlas zur antiken Kriegsgeschichte* (1922) is the result of military cartographic survey teams visiting the ancient battle sites and preparing color topographic maps of more than 170 ancient battlefields on which were superimposed the troop dispositions and tactical maneuvers. Included are topographic and battle maps of Scipio's battles at New Carthage, Baecula, Ilipa, Utica, the Great Plains, and Zama. These materials are rare, and I am fortunate to have acquired them. The maps and descriptions provide a richly detailed portrait of the terrain and obstacles relevant to Scipio's battlefields, permitting a more empirical analysis of events than would otherwise be possible if solely relying on the historical accounts.

While no comprehensive military biography of Scipio exists, there has been some relevant and valuable scholarly research on various aspects of his life in the last seventy years. I have tried to consult it in what I believe is its entirety. This book's bibliography attempts to present a complete and current listing of all the source material relevant to any further study of Scipio Africanus and includes all relevant materials published between 1890 and 2007 in English, German, French, and Italian.

I also consulted material from the original literary sources—Polybius, Livy (Titus Livius), Appian, Cassius Dio, Diodorus Siculus, Plutarch, Silius Italicus, and Frontinus—but always with an eye toward the biases that afflict them. Diodorus Siculus's history, for example, is valuable for its sources, now lost to us. Despite its unreliable chronology, this Sicilian-centered compendium of Mediterranean history makes use of many firsthand sources on various topics that are important for understanding Scipio's life and still offer an "un-Roman" perspective on events. The *Punica* of Silius Italicus is a more valuable source of anecdotal information about Scipio. The longest epic poem in the Latin language, twelve thousand verses, was written in the first century CE and is strongly rooted in the then extant literary sources. It provides a good compendium of most of the material concerning Scipio's life available to a Roman writer of the time. The geographical sources Italicus used are also accurate. Although the *Punica* is poetry, not history, it presents its facts accurately when measured against the known historical record and preserves the spirit of Punic times while avoiding rhetorical artifice. In consequence, it offers useful details about Scipio's life not available elsewhere.[1]

It became clear while researching this book that in addition to the common fault of exaggerating the numbers of combatants, the ancient accounts are often not consistent with the details of terrain and distance provided by topographical analysis of the battlefields. For example, Polybius's claim that Scipio marched his army from Tarraco to New Carthage, a distance of more than four hundred miles across two rivers and five major streams swollen with spring rains, in seven days cannot be accepted.[2] Whenever I have encountered such difficulties, I have attempted to resolve them by emphasizing the empirical realities of ground warfare over the historical accounts. In this effort I have followed N. Whatley's advice and utilized deductions drawn from the study of geography and topography, general tactical and strategic principles, the application of logic, critical analysis of the sources, the study of the armies, and the biological data regarding the physiological and psychological limits of human endurance.[3] In addition, I have brought to bear my own research in "experimental archaeology" to assess the lethality of ancient weapons.[4] The result as presented in these pages is, I hope, a more comprehensive and accurate account of the life and accomplishments of the greatest Roman general, Scipio Africanus, made available to general readers and scholars for the first time in many years.[5]

Roman generals did not begin their tradition of writing their memoirs until almost a century after Scipio died. The only account of Scipio's military exploits that can be traced to his own hand is his letter to King Philip V of Macedon, written in Greek, in which he explains his campaigns. The letter has not survived, but we can be confident that Polybius had access to it. Cicero tells us that in his day no literary work by Scipio had survived. Our knowledge of Scipio's life in the original sources must of necessity rely more heavily on the works of Polybius and Livy, with the latter writing 150 years after Polybius did and basing his accounts of Scipio's exploits almost entirely on Polybius's earlier work. In addition, Livy was one of the first Roman historians to come from the rural country of Italy rather than from Rome and its governing classes, and much of his information comes from the traditional narratives and opinions found in the provinces outside Rome. He often provides color, context, and details that are difficult to find elsewhere. I have relied on Livy as a supplementary source and as a primary source in those areas where Polybius is silent. The remainder of the original sources is often untrustworthy and too far removed from the events they purport to describe, and I use them sparingly and with caution.

Polybius, therefore, is the earliest and most important extant source for Scipio's life. Born in 208 BCE, Polybius received political, diplomatic, and military training at the hands of his father, who was a leading statesman of the Achaean League. Polybius was a soldier and commanded men in battle. After the battle of Pydna in 168 BCE, along with other hostages he was taken to Rome and held for sixteen years. As a Greek diplomat, he had earlier established a friendship with General Aemilius Paullus in the campaign against King Perseus. Polybius became a tutor to the general's two sons, the younger of which the general had adopted and was named Publius Scipio Aemilianus. These circumstances brought Polybius into the Scipionie family and allowed him access to the written and oral materials concerning Scipio's life, including Scipio's account of his campaigns written for Philip V of Macedon. Polybius is the only extant source who had access to these materials.

Polybius claims to have traveled extensively in Spain and North Africa and to have walked the very ground on which Scipio fought some of his battles. He conducted extensive interviews with Scipio's best friend and second-in-command, Gaius Laelius, who was with Scipio at all the important battles and events of his career. Polybius also interviewed Massinissa, the Numidian chief who was Scipio's ally in the North African campaign and who fought by his side in every major battle there. Polybius also had access to the diplomats and generals of Carthage itself when he served on the Roman commission to Carthage in 146 BCE. This said, Polybius is not beyond criticism, and his shortcomings as a military historian, as Hans Delbrück and others have outlined, are always to be borne in mind. Finally, Polybius had access to the works of two important Greek historians, Sosylus and Silenus. Both these "war correspondents" traveled with Hannibal's army for many years and wrote extensive accounts of the Carthaginian war with Rome. Sosylus is said to have taught Hannibal Greek. These sources are lost except through Polybius.

In examining the original accounts of ancient battles it must always be kept in mind that war has a dynamic all its own that imposes limitations and affords possibilities on its conduct. Terrain, weather, distance, logistics, the endurance of men and animals, and human psychology all put constraints on war that cannot be ignored. The military historian must possess a deep appreciation for these limits to accurately assess the veracity of the ancient accounts. Without this experience as a tool of contextual assessment, there is a danger that the historical accounts will be too easily accepted. I have been a ground soldier and have written several books on the subject of ancient warfare. These experiences hopefully afford me a critical eye for the truth and falsity of the events portrayed in the original accounts.

All this said, it must be remembered that the single biggest obstacle to our understanding of Punic War battles is a lack of reliable evidence. For later battles, and even for earlier hoplite battles, historians have been able to draw on archaeological evidence, representations, reliefs, battle poetry, and accounts by men like Thucyidides and Xenophon, who had firsthand experience with the events and fighting they described. For Punic War battles, archaeological evidence is much thinner, and we are forced to rely heavily on literary accounts written between fifty and four hundred years after the events themselves took place.[6]

Publius Cornelius Scipio (236–183 BCE) stood at the center of the history of Republican Rome. Before Scipio few Romans would have dreamed of empire, and Scipio himself would have regarded such an ambition as a danger to his beloved Republic. And yet, paradoxically, Scipio's victories in Spain and Africa enabled Rome to consolidate its hold over all of Italy and to become the dominant power in the western Mediterranean, achievements that virtually ensured a future confrontation with the Greco-Macedonian kingdoms to the east as well as future Roman expansion into North Africa and the Levant. Scipio lived at a pivotal point in Roman history, when the Republic was at its most vibrant even as it was transitioning from a powerful city-state to become the center of the Western civilized world within a century. The Roman imperium was being born, and Scipio had sired it.

Scipio was one of Rome's greatest generals, if not the greatest of them all. Some scholars regard him as the greatest general in all antiquity. He ranks with the Duke of Marlborough as one of history's few commanders who never suffered defeat. Napoleon remarked that "in war, it is not men, but the man that counts." This description surely fits Scipio, for few generals have displayed such daring, imagination, and innovation in war as he did. He fought against some of the best commanders of the ancient world and defeated every one of them, including Hannibal Barca. Hannibal himself is supposed to have said that if he had defeated Scipio at Zama, he would have considered himself a general even greater than Alexander.

The man's character, evident when commanding his men in battle, revealed itself even more clearly once he relinquished the sword and returned to civic life. Because of his great victories, the people of Rome clamored to make him consul for life. Some suggested he become dictator, so convinced were they that he would rule justly; however, Scipio was a Republican to his core and loathed regal power for the threat it presented to liberty and the rule of law. Polybius tells us that Scipio refused all these honors, rebuking those who offered them as creating a threat to their own liberties. Later, he put a stop to efforts to raise statues to him. Like Cincinnatus before him, Scipio refused all these honors as dangerous to the Republic. Few men in history have resisted these temptations.

In an unfortunate quirk of history Hannibal is remembered as the greater of the two men, but Scipio, not Hannibal, possessed a vision of the future that eventually shaped the West. Scipio was a creative spirit, a combination of the dreamer and a man of action, who seems to have been the first to grasp a sense of Rome's destiny and shaped it into a strategic vision for future generations of Romans. Scipio did not make war to destroy but to create a new Roman world order in which Rome stood as civilizer of the world, ruling justly and fairly as first among other states. Scipio's defeat of Hannibal and his refusal to destroy Carthage were the opening moves in this larger strategic plan. Hannibal, in contrast, despite his military brilliance and resolve, came only to destroy, not to build. His life's work was his attempt to destroy Rome. But what would he have put in its place? What had Carthage to offer the world that might have arisen from the ashes of Rome's destruction? The military glory of the Barca family, Hannibal's ultimate motivation, was hardly the stuff of which imperial dreams and realms could have been fashioned. Had Hannibal triumphed, the world would have been the worse for it. It is Scipio who stands as the greater man.

Acknowledgments

NO SCHOLAR STANDS alone in his efforts. I am deeply grateful to the following individuals and institutions who aided me in accomplishing this work: Professor David George, senior fellow of the American School of Classical Studies at Athens, Greece; Professor Linda Rulman, professor of classics and an expert in the Republican period; Silvia Shannon, professor of Roman history; Matthew Gonzales, professor of classics; Joel Klein, an expert in oriental languages; and Steve Weingartner, military historian and editor. I wish to also acknowledge the encouragement and support of my colleagues in the Department of History and War Studies at the Royal Military College of Canada at Kingston, Ontario, and my colleagues at the Department of Defence Studies, Canadian Forces College, Toronto, where I hold a joint appointment. Thanks are also owed to Angelo Caravaggio of the Department of Defence Studies, who used parts of this book in his courses on ancient commanders. I could not have written his book without the aid and comfort of all these fine people, and in gratitude I absolve them of blame for any and all errors that may have made their way into the manuscript. Finally, there is my wife, Suzi, without whose love nothing I do would really be worth doing.

Chronology

236 BCE   Born Publius Cornelius Scipio the Younger; learns Greek; studies the campaigns of Alexander; becomes a Hellenophile

218   Accompanies his father on the campaign against Hannibal in northern Italy as a cavalry officer; rescues his wounded father at the battle of the Ticinus River

217–16   Continues to serve in Italy against Hannibal; fights at the battle of Cannae and escapes to Canusium, where he takes command of the four thousand survivors; stops the fainthearted from deserting

213   Elected as *curule aedile* at the age of twenty-two, three years younger than the legal minimum-age requirement

212   Learns his father and uncle are killed at a battle near Castulo, Spain, on the banks of the Guadalquivir River in the Baetius Valley

211   Offers himself as a candidate to command the armies in Spain; is appointed *imperio privatus* and given command of Roman armies in Spain

210   Arrives in Spain in the summer and sets about training and provisioning his army

209   Attacks New Carthage, the main Carthaginian base in Spain, and occupies it; reorganizes the Roman army with heavier maniples; equips it with the new Spanish steel sword, later to become the *gladius*; and trains his army in new tactics

208   Defeats Hasdrubal, Hannibal's brother, at the battle of Baecula

207   Convinces the Spanish tribes to change sides and support Rome

206   Faces Carthage, which reinforced its army in Spain, in a pitched battle; defeats Hasdrubal's army at the battle of Ilipa; crushes rebellious Spanish tribal chiefs at the battle of the Ebro

205   Is elected consul; convinces Roman Senate to permit him to attack Africa; retakes the southern Italian town of Locri from the Carthaginians

204	Assembles a large army in Sicily and sails to Africa; lands near Utica; wins a strategic victory when Carthage, fearing attack, recalls Hannibal's army from Italy
204–203	Tries to draw Hasdrubal to battle; defeats Hanno at the battle of the Tower of Agathocles; attacks and burns a Carthaginian encampment; defeats Carthaginian Numidian ally, Syphax, and Hasdrubal at the battle of the Great Plains; negotiates a truce with Carthage
202	After the truce collapses, maneuvers to force Hannibal into battle; defeats Hannibal at the battle of Zama, causing Carthage to sue for peace; presses Rome to sign the treaty
201	Returns to Italy in triumph; angers political enemies as he attempts to influence the peace terms with Carthage; is elected *princeps senatus*
194	Elected consul for a second time
189	Selected as *princeps senatus* for the third time; accompanies his brother, Lucius, who, with overall command of the army, defeats Antiochus at the battle of Magnesia
187	Responds to his enemies' attempts to discredit him by putting his brother on trial for misappropriating funds by tearing up the charges and refusing to answer them; however, after a second attempt succeeds, his brother is heavily fined
185	Faces second attempt to discredit him, this time charges of granting Antiochus generous peace terms in return for a bribe and of committing treason; refuses to answer; goes into exile at Liternum, ending his civic life
184	Dies at age fifty-three in self-imposed exile and is buried at Liternum

1

The Man

PUBLIUS CORNELIUS SCIPIO was born in Rome in 236/235 BCE, 517 years after the city's founding, a scion of the Cornelii family, one of the five great families of Rome. The Cornelii were of Etruscan stock and one of the oldest Roman families.[1] In a common Roman practice that resulted from the original tribal nature of his society, Scipio was given the same name as his father, Publius (P.) Cornelius. Every Roman had the name of his gens or tribe (*nomen*), his personal name (*praenomen*), and his family name (*cognomen*), or in this case, Publius (praenomen), Cornelius (nomen), Scipio (cognomen). Only after his great victories in Africa did the Romans, and later historians, commonly refer to him as Scipio Africanus. Among the other great Roman families—the Fabian, Claudian, Aemilian, and Valerian—the Scipiones were most closely allied with the Aemilii. Scipio later married the daughter of Aemilius Paullus, one of the consuls who fell at Cannae.

The Scipiones had played an important role in Roman politics for more than a century before Publius was born. They had held key political and military positions during the First Punic War (264–241 BCE) and during the First Illyrian War (229–228 BCE). Of the ten consuls elected between 222 and 218 BCE, three came from the Scipio family: Gnaeus Cornelius Scipio was consul in 222 BCE, P. Cornelius Scipio Asina was consul in 221 BCE and oversaw the establishment of a Roman naval arm, and Publius's father, P. Cornelius Scipio, was elected consul in 218 BCE to deal with the threat of Hannibal's invasion of Italy. Scipio's father and his uncle, Gnaeus, led a Roman army into Spain and attacked Hannibal's line of communications. Thus, as the oldest of the younger generation of this illustrious family, no doubt people expected much of young Publius.

Except for a few images on Roman coins and signet rings, no certain physical portrayal of Scipio has survived.[2] The absence of any comment in the ancient sources regarding his physical appearance reasonably suggests that he was probably a typical Roman and not physically remarkable. If so, we could expect that he looked like a Roman of his day, with an average height between five foot five and five foot eight and probably a stocky muscular build. He weighed perhaps between 145 and 150 pounds. Although Scipio relished Greek culture and art, we may safely assume there was nothing Greek about his physical appearance. In Scipio's time conservative Romans thought Greek features were effeminate and a sign of moral decadence. Had Scipio possessed any such features, his enemies would surely have mentioned them.

As a young man, Scipio's likeness on coins shows his hair cut long in Greek fashion.[3] Later, he is portrayed as bald with a thick ring of hair running around his neck and ears. His facial features, marked by a high forehead, thick eyebrows, and deep-set eyes protected by prominent brows and high cheekbones, create the appearance of strength and determination. The seriousness—or most Roman of virtues, gravitas—in his face reflects his character and shows a self-confident man willing to endure and, if need be, to suffer to achieve his ends. Beneath his large and prominent nose, a true Italian proboscis similar to those seen on any Roman to this day, is a spacious ridge of flesh that leads to thick, prominent lips; a forceful mouth; and a strong and protruding chin. Worry lines mark his neck and cheeks, drawing the viewer's eye to his large ears, which befit the man of whom it was said made a habit of listening to others before deciding on a course of action. The *Punica* says that Scipio "had a martial brow and flowing hair; nor was the hair at the back of his head shorter. His eyes burned bright, but their regard was mild; and those who looked upon him were at once awed and pleased."[4]

While all his features suggest strength, Scipio may have been in chronic ill health from childhood, and serious ailments sometimes afflicted him on campaign. He reacted slowly, for example, to the mutiny at the Sucro River because he was ill and confined to his quarters. At the battle of Magnesia, when he was in his forties, he was forced to relinquish command of the army because of illness. Scipio, however, appears to have generally been capable of performing physically on the battlefield. At Cannae, tasked with training the Campanian allied troops, he impressed them with a display of physical agility and spear throwing.[5] At New Carthage he personally led the assault on the city gate, and at the battle of Baecula he led the Roman right wing up a steep incline and attacked the Carthaginian flank. Given Scipio's sensitivity to the effect that even his minor actions might have on troop morale, he likely hid his ailments from his officers and men in all but the most pressing circumstances.

Roman historians credit Scipio with being the first man in Rome to shave daily,[6] and he may have introduced the practice to the Roman army. The *Iliad*'s heroes were all bearded men, and Plutarch tells us that not until Alexander's time did military men in Greece go clean shaven and thus prevent their adversaries from grabbing their beards in battle. Romans wore beards until Scipio's day, when it became the custom to shave regularly or to keep one's beard trimmed. If Scipio was the first Roman to shave every day, one might reasonably assume he was following the fashion of Greek warriors, for the beardless Alexander was held as the example by almost all military men of the day. Daily shaving became the Roman habit, and until the end of the Empire, Roman soldiers shaved daily.

By Scipio's day upper-class Romans were taking greater cognizance of the outside world. The First Punic War had brought them into contact with the Hellenistic culture of the larger Mediterranean world, and Greek practices and values had begun to penetrate Roman society. One aspect in particular was Greek education, which some aristocratic families saw as superior to traditional Roman education. Some even built small additions on their villas to serve as gymnasiums and hired itinerant Greek tutors who traveled from place to place in the Hellenistic world, educating the wealthy and politically powerful. Even Cato, who was famous for his rants against Greek habits and values, educated his son in the Greek fashion.[7]

The upper class's hired tutors taught a curriculum that included philosophy (logic, ethics, cosmology), science (astronomy, geometry, mathematics, and biological curiosities), literature (including the study of Greek military heroes), physical education in the gymnasiums, and the Greek language.[8] The Greek method provided a much broader, empirical, and intellectually challenging education than did the traditional Roman method with its emphasis on tradition, law, ritual, and physical military prowess. A Greek education would likely have equipped Scipio with a much more empirical and rationally oriented mind capable of adapting to new ideas and situations and of quickly solving problems and giving him confidence in his own thinking. No historian tells us whether Scipio received a Greek education, but his ability to read and write Greek; his admiration of Greek habits, virtues, and fashions (he insisted his daughters learn Greek); and his political enemies' criticism that he was more Greek than Italian led to the conclusion that he had.

Ancient historians tried to discover what was in Scipio's personality that led him to such great achievements. Polybius notes, for example, "the fact that he won greater fame than almost anyone before him makes the whole world curious to know what kind of man he was, and what were the natural gifts and training which enabled him to succeed in so many greater enterprises."[9] By Polybius's day a rich legend had already grown up around Scipio that made it difficult to separate the man from the myth. Legend had it that the gods had chosen Scipio to achieve great things and even that he was the son of Jupiter. Some said Scipio's mother had been barren until a snake appeared in her bedroom and sired the child. Part of the later legend held that when the infant Scipio was lying in a basket in a courtyard, a large snake crawled over him but did him no harm. The tales imply that Scipio was of divine birth or at least had the gods' protection. The story is strongly similar to that told about Alexander's birth and in both cases was likely to have been invented by Greek chroniclers more interested in myth and the glorification of heroes than in actually recounting events. We cannot be certain if the legend of Scipio's divine birth was extant during his lifetime. What seems likely, however, is that Greek and Roman chroniclers invented the version involving the snake well after his death.[10]

Other elements of the Scipio legend that appear in the early sources present Scipio as a devoutly religious man, even a mystic, who regularly called on the gods for divine favor. Scipio was said to spend long hours in the temples deep in contemplation before making his decisions. These sources also said that the gods arranged miracles for him, like the tide's ebb at New Carthage, to bring him victory on the battlefield.[11] This view of a religiously devout Scipio, a mystic and favorite of the gods, was certainly extant during Polybius's day, and he set out to debunk it. Polybius's attempt to debunk the myth led him to the position that Scipio was not a mystic but a hypocrite; that is, Scipio used the legend's claims to motivate his troops and later gain political advantage with the Roman people. Polybius seems to have replaced one caricature of Scipio with another.

In all likelihood Scipio was a pious man by Roman standards or at least was as pious as the average Roman of his day.[12] Later in his life he became a Salian priest of Mars, but this position by no means justifies the conclusion that Scipio was a mystic. Certainly the tales of his long contemplative vigils in the temples before going into battle or making important decisions are false. Most of Scipio's deeds took place on foreign battlefields, far from Rome and its temples.[13] Moreover, going before the gods in search of moral insight and self-contemplation was a Greek habit, not a Roman one. If Scipio went to the temple, he did so for the same reason that all Romans did: to ask for material help. As W. W. Fowler observed, "The idea of Scipio conforming his life to the will of any of these *numina* would, of course, be absolutely strange to him; the expression would have no meaning whatever for him. The help which he sought from them was not moral help, but material."[14] No evidence exists that, as is sometimes claimed, Scipio arranged miracles to convince his troops that he was divinely favored.[15]

There is, of course, no contradiction between being religiously observant and praying for help and luck on the battlefield. Many of history's generals were religious men, and it is commonly said that "there are no atheists in foxholes." Religious faith need not prohibit one from being a good soldier or commander.[16] If Scipio's soldiers regarded him as religiously observant and as likely to earn the gods' favor, Scipio would have been foolish not to encourage their beliefs. Perhaps his soldiers thought him not only competent but lucky as well. Napoleon himself believed strongly in luck and once opined that he preferred lucky generals to merely competent ones. Cicero remarked that luck was an essential quality of a successful general, and an old military axiom says that "fortune favors the brave." Soldiers everywhere have always believed in luck and the Roman soldier no less so in *Fortuna*. That Scipio, too, may have done so is hardly surprising.

The question of religious hypocrisy aside, Polybius's assessment of Scipio's character seems sound when he says, "It is generally agreed that Scipio was beneficent and magnanimous, but that he was also shrewd and discreet with a mind always concentrated on the object he had in view."[17] In other words, Scipio possessed a disciplined mind and focused on the objective. Polybius says Scipio's two finest qualities, those "most worthy of respect, were cleverness and laboriousness."[18] These are, of course, typical Roman virtues, and Polybius may have stressed them to counter charges that Scipio was "too Greek." It is, perhaps, also revealing that Polybius says that "no one will admit" that Scipio possessed these qualities "except those who have lived with him and contemplated his character, so to speak, in broad daylight."[19] His assessment suggests Scipio may have cultivated a public persona somewhat different from the private self that he revealed only to his closest friends. Given command of an army at such a young age may have required Scipio to cultivate a somewhat sterner and more military image than was natural to his own personality.

In this regard Scipio may have possessed a more compassionate side than is revealed in the texts. The *Punica* tells us that he wept uncontrollably after receiving the news that his father had been killed. "Though it was not his wont to yield to misfortune, he beat his breast now and rent his garments in the violence of his grief. No efforts of his friends, no regard for his high military station and military command, could restrain him . . . he refused all consolation."[20] He was twenty-four years old at the time and already an experienced combat veteran. Moreover, the Romans of Scipio's time would have regarded such displays of grief as weakness. Even more revealing was his behavior after he became a successful general. After he had driven the Carthaginians from Spain, Scipio held funeral games in celebration during which "Scipio, with tears in his eyes, led the semblance of a funeral procession with due rites of burial." He then "with tears recited the glories of the dead."[21] This combat-hardened general's public display of emotion must have struck those present as very unusual.

Scipio's troops held him in high regard perhaps because, as Livy says, "he understood men sympathetically." The fighting men's esteem for their commander, who, after all, is the man who places them in harm's way, is not easily earned, for battle has an uncanny way of turning a commander's best intentions and plans to ruin. Scipio was always among his soldiers, checking on their quarters, seeing to their rations, and being generous with pay and booty. He dispensed justice fairly, as when he put down a mutiny among his troops, who had not been paid, and took care to execute the leaders and pardon the rest after asking sorrowfully, "Shouldn't you have come and talked to me about it?"[22] Scipio seems not to have possessed the brutal streak so often found among ancient military men, but he could be brutal when it served his military objectives. He once ordered the slaughter of New Carthage's civilian population until the enemy commander saw the futility of further resistance and surrendered. But this killing, too, was done as a lesson and to avoid greater brutality by convincing the enemy to surrender sooner. To his men Scipio never appeared petty or jealous. He praised his officers for their actions in front of their men. When Scipio assumed command in Spain, he assembled his army and publicly praised the heroic Marcus Marcius, the commander he was replacing. He always justified his orders to his troops on the grounds of their duty and service to Rome and never to himself. If Scipio fought for personal glory instead of for Rome's, he was at least wise enough to conceal it. He seems to have learned what all successful commanders understand: no soldier will die willingly for his commander's career.

As we shall see in the analysis of Scipio's campaigns, Scipio possessed a strongly empirical intellect that searched for and made connections between means and ends. He always had a plan to follow, and he did not permit prior assumptions to degenerate into rigidity. The plan itself was usually innovative in concept and always inextricably linked to specific means for execution. Scipio was a brilliant tactical thinker and a problem solver of the first order, and he never relied on hope as a method. If at times the means to achieve an objective did not exist, Scipio invented them, as when he revolutionized the legion's tactical capabilities by introducing the first significant tactical change in the Roman army in more than a century.[23] No Roman general introduced more tactical innovations to the Roman army than Scipio did.

Besides a brilliant intellect, Scipio possessed great confidence in his own abilities, the character trait Livy stressed above all others. Confidence in one's self to the point of recklessness was not something Romans of Scipio's day would have regarded as a virtue; instead, it would have seemed to them untraditional and risky. Scipio's confidence led some of his enemies to claim he was high-handed and conceited.[24] Whatever else, Scipio was a confident commander who, as Napoleon's maxim goes, "never took counsel of his own fears," and if he did, he took pains to hide it from those around him. Many of Scipio's personality traits—confidence, brashness, a sense of being lucky, faith in one's own thinking, and so on—are, of course, the traits of a young man. When he took command of the Roman armies in Spain, he was only twenty-six years old, or the same age Hannibal was when he took command of the Carthaginian armies. It is difficult not to imagine that it might have been their youth that made both Scipio and Hannibal such daring commanders.

BAPTISM BY FIRE

As it had been for centuries, the Roman army of Scipio's day was a militia army comprised of property-owning citizens who were called to arms when needed. No formal system of military training existed; instead, fathers and uncles trained their sons and nephews in military skills and provided them with weapons and armor. Assigning young men to the various military branches—infantry, cavalry, and navy—was done on the basis of wealth. The wealthy usually served in the cavalry, and it is a fair guess that Scipio was trained as a cavalryman. At the Ticinus River his father placed him in command of a troop of cavalry, albeit for his own protection. Even so, this position required a degree of horsemanship and familiarity with weapons that a young man of seventeen years of age could not have acquired anywhere else except in cavalry training. Once the legion was called to assemble, military tribunes trained their respective new recruits, including cavalry, in a conscript encampment before deploying for war. Scipio, too, must have trained in this manner in his father's army before accompanying him on campaign.

Military training is one thing, military education another. Scipio came from a military family. His father, uncle, and grandfather had all fought in the First Punic War. His father had served in at least ten campaigns; otherwise he could not have been elected consul. Similar to the sons and daughters of general officers today, Scipio likely grew up listening to discussions of military matters, tactics, logistics, and strategy. Here he would have acquired practical lessons about the conduct of war and leadership of men in battle. Moreover, his Greek education would have acquainted him with the histories of the famous Greek generals, including Alexander, Epaminondas, Philip, Pyrrhus, and Xenophon, as well as of those great generals they defeated, such as Darius and Xerxes. It is often forgotten that until the second half of the twentieth century, modern military education centered around the study of previous campaigns in much the same manner that Scipio studied them. By the time of his military service at age seventeen, Scipio was a well-educated, well-trained, and intellectually capable junior officer.

Scipio's first taste of war came at the battle of the Ticinus River, a tributary of the Po in northern Italy, in the autumn of 218 BCE. That summer, Hannibal began crossing the Alps to invade Italy. The Romans sent an army under Publius Scipio, Scipio's father, to Massilia (modern Marseilles) to intercept and block Hannibal's advance, but the Romans arrived too late. Publius then sent the army to Spain under the command of his brother, Gnaeus, while he returned to Rome to raise another army and prepared to meet Hannibal on the northern Italian plain. A Roman army under Tiberius Sempronius Longus that was preparing to invade Sicily was recalled and redeployed northward, where it linked up with Publius Scipio's army. Staging from Pisa, Publius Scipio's advance scouts skirmished with some of Hannibal's Numidian cavalry near the Rhône River and drove the Numidians off.

The Romans then knew that Hannibal's main force was somewhere close. Publius assembled a reconnaissance force of four thousand Roman light infantry (*velites*) and twenty-five hundred Roman and Celtic cavalry and undertook a wide reconnaissance sweep, hoping to locate Hannibal.[25] The two forces met on the banks of the Ticinus River. Taken while still in column of march, the Romans were quickly surrounded. According to the *Punica,*

> The Carthaginian spearmen made a ring around the Roman general; they sought to give Hannibal what he had never got before—the dripping head of a consul, and his armor as booty. Scipio stood firm, resolved never to yield to Fortune; made fiercer by the slaughter, he hurled back spear for spear with vehement effort. By now his limbs were drenched with his own blood and the enemy's.[26]

And then he was struck by a spear.

Polybius records what happened next:

> He [the son] was then, as it seems, eighteen years old and on his
> first campaign. His father had given him a squadron of hand-picked
> cavalry for his protection; but when in the course of the battle he
> saw his father surrounded by the enemy, with only two or three
> horsemen near him, and dangerously wounded, he first tried to
> cheer on his own squadron to go to his father's assistance, but when
> he found them considerably cowed by the numbers of the enemy
> surrounding them, he appears to have plunged by himself with reck-
> less courage into the midst of the enemy; whereupon his comrades
> being forced to charge also, the enemy were overawed and divided
> their ranks to let them pass; and Publius the elder, being thus un-
> expectedly saved, was the first to address his son as his preserver in
> the hearing of the enemy.[27]

Publius Scipio ordered that his son be awarded the *corona civica,* or civic crown,
Rome's highest military decoration for bravery. Polybius tells us that young Scipio
refused the award, however, saying, "The action was one that rewarded itself."

There is no good reason to doubt Polybius's account of Scipio's bravery.[28]
Scipio was already of military age (seventeen years old), and it was common for
Roman commanders to take their sons to war when they reached military age.
Under the Republic all property owners of military age, and certainly the sons of
the aristocracy, were expected to perform military service. The Republic's highest
political and military offices were reserved for those who had seen no fewer than
ten tours of military service. Further, any attempt to fabricate the story would
have been immediately discovered given the number of people involved. Finally,
Laelius, Scipio's boyhood friend and eyewitness to every important event in Scipio's
life, told Polybius the story when Laelius was an old man and with little reason
not to tell the truth.

Whatever the facts of the matter, Scipio acquired a reputation with soldiers
and citizens alike for personal bravery after his courage at the Ticinus. It is interesting, however, that later in life his political enemies attacked his valorous reputation, circulating the story that it was not Scipio but a slave who had rescued his
father at the Ticinus. They also criticized Scipio for his behavior during the assault on New Carthage, when he moved around the battlefield closely guarded by

three men carrying large shields for his protection. In this regard Scipio may have been the first to establish the *praetoriani*, the field commander's personal body-guard who was charged with protecting his life.[29] Though Livy suggests that Roman generals were sometimes attended by a select troop for their protection in the Republic's early days,[30] Scipio may well have institutionalized the practice.

Philip of Macedon at the battle of Chaeronea (338 BCE) was the first Western general to command his troops from nearby rather than in the thick of the fighting, a practice Scipio later adopted.[31] Until Scipio's time, Roman generals fought in the midst of their troops, displaying personal courage and sharing the risk. During the war against Hannibal, this practice produced dire results. So many of Rome's experienced commanders were killed and wounded that the army faced a serious shortage of competent military leaders, forcing Rome to rely on young and sometimes untested men to command its armies. Scipio himself was one of these young commanders when he received his commission to command the Roman army in Spain.[32] Scipio was aware of the criticism of his battlefield performance. According to Frontinus, Scipio answered those who criticized his valor by saying, "My mother bore me a general, not a warrior!"[33]

Scipio seems to have been the first Roman commander whose style of command was more akin to that of a "battle manager" than to that of the Homeric warrior general so characteristic of earlier Greek and Roman warfare. Caesar imitated Scipio's command style, and it became the model for the imperial commanders who followed. These commanders sometimes ventured into the thick of the fighting, but they were cautious about exposing themselves to the dangers of the battlefield. They spent their time much more productively, moving about the battlefield with a small bodyguard, rallying stragglers, turning back those who tried to retreat, encouraging the faint-hearted, regrouping units, and leading support to threatened points. Whereas their influence on the flow of events was usually limited to the immediate area in which they found themselves, the general as battle manager was still able to affect events to a far greater degree than before.[34] Hannibal also employed this style of command, but Scipio seems to have been the first Roman general to do so.

CANNAE

We do not hear again of Scipio's military service until the battle of Cannae in 216 BCE. According to Livy, Scipio was a military tribune with one of the legions that fought at Cannae.[35] The military tribune was a legion staff officer, somewhat equivalent to the modern-day staff lieutenant colonel. An appointment to this post represented a rapid rise for a young man who was not yet twenty years old and raises a number of questions.

After the ambush at the Ticinus, the wounded elder Scipio withdrew across the Trebia, assumed a safe position, and waited for Sempronius and his legions to arrive. Scipio's son must have been with him. With Scipio wounded, command of both forces passed to Sempronius, and we may reasonably assume the young Scipio and his cavalry troop also came under Sempronius's command. After his courageous performance at the Ticinus, the young Scipio could hardly have refused or offered to remain with his wounded father. If so, then young Scipio must have taken part in the battle at the Trebia. As a cavalryman, he would have been posted on one of the wings of Sempronius's army. The initial clash of cavalry forces resulted in the Roman cavalry being driven from the battlefield, a circumstance that presumably permitted the young Scipio to escape the infantry slaughter that ensued.[36] Sempronius's defeat had opened the western road to Rome, and the Romans quickly sent another army under Gaius Flaminius to close it. Given the panic that Hannibal's victory at the Trebia provoked, one would think that the defeated Roman army's remnants would have been attached to Flaminius's blocking force. If so, then Scipio and his cavalry troop, which would have survived mostly intact after being driven off by the Carthaginian cavalry, might have been attached to Flaminius's army. It was destroyed at Lake Trasimene in 217 BCE, but more likely than not Scipio was there.

That Scipio did not accompany his father to Spain is curious. Further, while neither Livy nor Polybius suggest that Scipio fought at the battles of the Trebia or Lake Trasimene, no account exists of Scipio's role in the battle of Cannae itself. We are forced to assume he was at the battle because he was present at subsequent events.[37] The *Punica* offers the only literary evidence that Scipio might have fought at both Trebia and Trasimene. The epic tells how, after his father's death (in 211 BCE), Scipio was torn between continuing military life or retreating into private solace. The spirits Pleasure and Virtue came to him in a dream and debated his choices. Pleasure tried to convince Scipio to give up war. "This is madness, my son, to use up all the flower of your age in war. . . . Have you forgotten Cannae and the river Po [a reference to the Trebia] and the Lydian Lake [a reference to Lake Trasimene]. How long will you persist in defying fortune on the battlefield?"[38] Silius Italicus seems to be telling us that Scipio fought at Trebia and Trasimene as well as at Cannae, all sites of Roman defeats. Perhaps Livy and

Polybius did not mention Scipio's presence at any of these battles precisely because they were defeats that Scipio had somehow survived. It would, of course, be much easier for a cavalryman than for an infantryman to have escaped from these infantry battles.

If Scipio had been present at these three disasters and acquitted himself reasonably well, it would help explain why he did not accompany his father to Spain and, more important, how he had been promoted to tribune at such a young age. The Popular Assembly elected the military tribunes, and later the army commander appointed two of every six,[39] although we are uncertain when army commanders were given the authority to make such appointments. Thus, it is possible that Scipio's reputation for bravery and his now extensive military experience would have contributed to his election as tribune. Though not yet twenty, Scipio would have been one of the most combat-experienced junior officers in all of Rome, and his reputation would have played well with the Roman crowd. If, however, the power to appoint tribunes had already been granted to army commanders, then another possibility suggests itself. When the battle of Cannae occurred, Scipio was either engaged or already married to Amelia, the daughter of Lucius Aemilius Paullus, who had been elected consul in 216 BCE and was one of the consuls in command at Cannae. Given the close relationship between the Scipione and Aemiliani families and that Paullus was Scipio's father-in-law, Scipio's promotion to military tribune is more understandable on these grounds.

After Trasimene, the Romans decided to meet Hannibal head-on and raised an army of eighty thousand men, the largest Roman army ever put into the field until that time. Caught in a double envelopment by Hannibal's cavalry, the Romans were slaughtered at the battle of Cannae. Scipio and some forty-two hundred stragglers fled the battlefield and took refuge in the nearby Roman camp. The exhausted Roman troops were stunned and awaited the coming of Hannibal's troops to meet their deaths. Along with Scipio, a small group of officers (probably cavalry) and men under the command of a tribune left the camp at night. Evading Hannibal's cavalry patrols, the group made its way to Canusium, six or seven miles from the battlefield and still within easy reach of Hannibal's patrols. This small remnant of the army gathered to elect a leader. The men chose as co-commanders two officers—Appius Claudius and Scipio, who was picked over the more experienced Fabius Maximus the Younger.

Soon afterward a group of young nobles began to despair that Rome was finished. They agreed among themselves to leave Italy and go into service overseas with foreign kings. When news of these events reached Scipio, he immediately moved against the conspirators. Livy recounts what happened next:

> But young Scipio—the man who was destined to command the Roman armies in this war, said that this was no matter for debate; the crisis had come, and what was needed was not words but bold action. "Come with me," he cried, "instantly, sword in hand, if you wish to save our country. The enemy's camp is nowhere more truly than where such thoughts can arise!" With a few followers he went straight to where Metellus was staying. Assembled in the house were the men of whom Philus had spoken, still discussing their plans. Scipio burst in, and holding his sword over their heads, "I swear," he cried, "with all the passion of my heart that I shall never desert our country, or permit any other citizen of Rome to leave her in the lurch. If I willfully break my oath, may Jupiter, Greatest and Best, bring me to a shameful death, with my house, my family, and all I possess! Swear the same oath, Caecilius; and all the rest of you, swear it too. If anyone refuse, know that against him this sword is drawn." They could not have been more scared had they been looking into the face of their conqueror Hannibal. Every man took the oath and gave himself into the custody of Scipio.[40]

Learning that Gaius Terentius Varro, the Roman commander at Cannae, was rallying what was left of his legions at Venusia, Scipio led his men there and placed himself under Varro's command. Later, historians reviled Varro for the defeat at Cannae, attributing the catastrophe to various problems: a disagreement between him and his co-consul, Paullus, as to whether to offer battle; the nature of the terrain; and Varro's general competence. The Senate, however, never held Varro responsible for the disaster at Cannae. The Senate voted to thank him for rallying and saving the remnants of the army and appointed him to other commands later in the war.

After the catastrophe at Cannae, Rome returned to the Fabian strategy it had abandoned before the battle. As a young officer looking to make a reputation for himself, Scipio might have headed for the sound of clashing swords and shields and might have seen service in the various Roman armies that were dogging Hannibal's heels as he maneuvered around southern Italy. During this time Scipio might have taken part in any number of skirmishes between the Romans and Carthaginians, but no ancient historian left an account of his actions in them.

PUBLIC OFFICE

Scipio reappears in the ancient accounts of 213 BCE, when he is recorded as standing for election as an aedile in Rome. An aedileship was the lowest and usually the first elective office for which candidates competed in the Republic. Four aediles were elected annually. They were responsible for overseeing maintenance in the city of Rome itself, such as repairing the roads and public buildings, ensuring the water supply, and maintaining the grain supply to feed the city's populace. The aediles also had powers of legal jurisdiction in some minor matters.[41] We may safely disregard the story Livy told that Scipio was drawn into the race to lend his popularity to his brother, who was also running for one of the four positions. But why was Scipio as well known at this time as Livy and Polybius suggest? It is unlikely that his bravery at the Ticinus, having occurred more than five years earlier, was by itself still the reason for his fame. If, however, he had indeed seen combat at Trebia and Lake Trasimene, served as a tribune at Cannae, and continued his military service against Hannibal between 216 and 213, thereby compiling a relatively long and more recent record of military achievement, the assumption that his reputation was a contributing factor to his successful election makes more sense.

Scipio was also heir to the leadership of a politically powerful family, so his entrance into politics on that account alone would not have been entirely unexpected. Moreover, gaining an appointment to a high-level military command in Republican Rome was through elective office, namely, the consulship. If Scipio hoped for such a command in the future, he would have been wise to begin his political career when he did. Finally, while the war against Hannibal had degenerated into a stalemate in Italy, Scipio's father and uncle had won an impressive string of victories in Spain, further enhancing the Scipio family's reputation. For all these reasons it was probably an opportune time to bring the next generation of Scipioni into the political arena. Scipio was twenty-two years old at the time, however, and the legal minimum-age requirement for the office was twenty-five. Scipio's youth provoked opposition from two of the People's Tribunes, but, Livy tells us, the popular acclamation of the people overrode them. Scipio is supposed to have replied to his opponents, "If all the Roman people want to make me aedile, well then . . . I am old enough."[42]

Within a year of Scipio's election, disaster struck the Scipio family. After almost seven years of war, a series of Roman victories had successfully blocked the Carthaginians in Spain from reinforcing Hannibal in Italy; however, in 212 BCE the armies of Publius and Gnaeus Scipio were betrayed by their Spanish allies and the Carthaginians annihilated them near Castulo.[43] The Roman armies fled north and back across the Ebro River, where they gathered their forces and held a thin defensive line. Seven years of military effort were reversed in a single afternoon, and the Roman cause in Spain seemed lost. Fear swept Italy that the Carthaginians would invade the country a second time. If the Carthaginian armies invaded Italy from the north and linked up with Hannibal in the south, Rome would be in mortal danger. And Scipio was not yet twenty-four years old when he suddenly found himself the head, or the paterfamilias, of the Scipio family.

SELECTION FOR COMMAND

Scipio received news of his father's death sometime in 211 BCE while he was at Puteoli. According to the *Punica,* "while Capua thus atoned with blood for her fatal error . . . it chanced that young Scipio was then resting in the city of Puteoli. Fighting was over, and he was revisiting his home, when rumor brought him bitter tears to shed for the untimely death of his kinsmen." The text clearly implies that Scipio had taken part in the nearly yearlong siege of Capua, which ended in 211. Moreover, the *Punica* continues, "no efforts of his friends, no regard for his high military station and military command could restrain him . . . he refused all consolation," indicating that Scipio already held an important military command at this time, perhaps as commander of a legion at Capua.[44] Thus, once more we find Scipio on the battlefield and engaged in one of that year's major military operations. Of the seven years that had passed from the incident on the Ticinus (218 BCE) to the end of the siege of Capua (211 BCE), Scipio seems to have been engaged in active military service for six years. Only in 213 BCE, when he served as an aedile, did Scipio enjoy a respite from the rigors of war. Scipio was probably among the most combat hardened of all Rome's younger officers.

We next hear of Scipio in 210 BCE, when he was given command of the Roman armies in Spain and succeeded his father and uncle in prosecuting the war against the Carthaginians. After the Roman defeat near Castulo, Gaius Claudius Nero, one of Rome's most experienced senior officers, had been sent to take command in Spain and stabilize the Roman defense along the Ebro River. With this feat accomplished, Rome recalled Nero to command the armies facing Hannibal in Italy. The Senate then assigned the command in Spain to Scipio, who was just twenty-six years old.

The appointment of such a young officer to a high-level command is remarkable. The youngest age at which a person could usually hold the power of *imperium* during the Republic was thirty-nine, which was also the youngest age at which one could become *praetor*.[45] In light of the legal requirements, Scipio was appointed *privatus cum imperio*, that is, a private citizen with military powers. In this sense, he was not formally a government official. Scipio, however, was the first private Roman citizen to be invested with the proconsular imperium, and the emperor's later claim to military rights and power rested on Scipio's precedent. Scipio's appointment thus foreshadowed the emergence of the legal basis of private military command that came later in the empire. And so it was that "Scipio cast a shadow across the Republic" for here was the first use of the private military power of the *condottieri*, or mercenary, commanders who ultimately destroyed the Republic.[46]

Why was young Scipio given such an important command? Again we may disregard Livy's explanation: with events going so badly in Spain no one except Scipio dared to assume responsibility for such a situation.[47] Even in this time of war and danger, the Senate—not the consuls—governed the Republic. While the consuls' political and family connections were important, these ties alone were not sufficient to obtain military commands.[48] Nero could have been left in command in Spain, but the Senate recalled him because it needed his experience to confront the greater danger of Hannibal in Italy. Moreover, Nero was an insensitive man whose lack of nuance would almost certainly have alienated the Spanish tribes on which the Romans' success in Spain ultimately depended.[49] Another possibility is that the Senate was again becoming dissatisfied with the Fabian policy and wanted to resume the offensive in Spain even if it was not possible in Italy. Scipio's father and uncle had pursued the latter policy in Spain, and the Senate perhaps thought that the Scipio legacy's heir might also.[50] Scipio also might have wanted the command and pressed for it with the aid of his family and political allies. The Scipiones may have held the balance of political power between the Claudian and Fabian blocs in the Senate at that time and were able to secure Scipio's appointment.[51] All these factors probably influenced the decision to appoint Scipio.

The most likely important reason Scipio received the appointment was that Rome was suffering from a shortage of experienced military commanders. Rome had been at war for almost a decade, and many consuls and senior commanders who had taken the field had been killed, wounded, or grown too old. While Rome usually elected two consuls each year and only rarely permitted a second consulship for the same man, this process changed after the defeats at Trebia, Trasimene, and Cannae. In the nine years from 215 to 207 BCE, only seven new men were elevated to consul, and in 214 and 209 BCE both consuls were re-elected. Both Fabius and Marcellus were elected consul five times and Fulvius four times. Thus, the prorogation of offices enabled small groups of commanders to fill most of Rome's other commands with their clients.[52] If, as has been suggested, Scipio was an experienced combat soldier who had fought in some of the most critical battles of the war, it would explain why the Senate might have taken seriously his request for command in Spain. Rome needed experienced field commanders, and Scipio's aristocratic background or the single incident of his courage at the Ticinus would unlikely have been sufficient reason to award him the Spanish command. Having been a tribune at Cannae, he would have probably risen to legion command by the time he saw action at Capua. His long, solid record of military competence is probably what weighed most heavily in awarding Scipio the Spanish command.

Suspending the usual consular system of annual rotation permitted some commanders to remain in place for several years at a time. The two Scipios, for example, held command in Spain for almost seven consecutive years. The usual system of annually rotating commanders that was employed earlier in the war made it difficult for commanders to train their armies sufficiently before taking them into the field. Further, older veteran commanders were often resistant to new methods and tactics, and followed a tradition of highly aggressive, impatient, and often reckless conduct of war.[53] The result was that regardless of who was in command, a Roman army almost always fought in the same tactical manner, a shortcoming that Hannibal exploited time and again. The reforms Scipio later introduced in organization, tactics, and weapons were possible only because commanders then enjoyed longer tours of duty during which they could fashion their armies into instruments of their will. The longer the war went on, the more proficient the Roman armies became.

That Scipio came from a powerful family, wished to avenge the deaths of his father and uncle, had considerable military experience, and probably pressed for the assignment likely influenced his selection. At the same time, however, none of Rome's best and most-experienced commanders could be spared for assignment to an overseas theater of operations, at least not as long as Hannibal was encamped on Italian soil and threatened Rome itself. Scipio was selected as the best qualified of the lesser men and candidates who were available. Richard M. Haywood's study of Scipio's competitors convincingly concludes, "In fact, none of the group was a better man than Scipio. Scipio did not gain preference over a group of tried and brilliant soldiers, but over a group who were only moderately competent. He was the best man available, so he received the appointment."[54] Scipio assumed command of the Roman armies in Spain.[55]

MILITARY COMPETENCY

Scipio excelled in six key areas of military competency: strategy, tactics, the appreciation of war's moral dimension, the use of tactical and strategic intelligence, logistics and administration, and leadership. As a strategist, Scipio had few equals in his ability to see the application of force within a larger context. He saw clearly that Hannibal's weakness was strategic not tactical, and as long as the tactically inferior Roman armies engaged Hannibal only in Italy, they could not bring about a strategic decision. Scipio understood that Hannibal's weakness was his inability to replace lost manpower and sustain his army. Hannibal recruited impressive but still insufficient manpower from the rebel tribes of southern Italy; consequently, unless he could resupply with manpower from Spain, his cause was ultimately lost. The most he could achieve under these circumstances was a stalemate. Even so, Scipio saw that it was unlikely that military pressure alone could drive Hannibal from Italy. The key to forcing Hannibal to leave Italy was to threaten Carthage itself. When Scipio did so, Hannibal was recalled to protect the city and forced to abandon Italy. Although Liddell-Hart called Hannibal the "father of strategy," in fact Scipio was the better strategist.[56]

Scipio was also a brilliant tactical commander and very much the military reformer. He recognized the Roman legions' weaknesses and reformed their organization, tactics, weaponry, and training. Under his hand a Roman army was fashioned as an instrument of a commander's will for the first time. The charges some historians made—that Scipio's military experience led him to study Hannibal and to copy his tactics as well as the insinuation that Scipio copied Alexander's tactics—were untrue. Instead, Hannibal admired Alexander and imitated his operational-level tactics by employing cavalry as his arm of decision and by using elephants. Hannibal was also an admirer of Pyrrhus's, whom he called his "master in battlefield tactics." Hannibal understood that the phalanx alone was not decisive and that it needed cavalry and light infantry support to exploit the gaps it made in the enemy line.[57] Scipio, in contrast, understood that the strength of Roman arms lay in its heavy infantry and its problem was the legion's tactical inflexibility. To correct this deficiency Scipio may have been most influenced by the infantry tactics of Epaminondas and Philip of Macedon, with the latter being a student of the former's. Just as Philip drilled the Macedonian phalanx in numerous tactical maneuvers to increase its flexibility in battle, Scipio also trained the legion in a number of innovative maneuvers. After training the maniples to maneuver on command, Scipio then made them heavier by adding more troops and reforming them into cohorts, which made them more resistant to the shock of barbarian infantry and cavalry attack. Scipio's victories over the Carthaginians were in no small measure because of these tactical reforms.

There is no more deadly defect in a military commander than to see war as an exercise in military technique. This fatal flaw often appears to afflict modern-day military men to an excessive degree. Warfare always occurs within a political, cultural, and moral context, which, if ignored, can result in defeat no matter how proficiently military force is applied. Scipio always and clearly saw the larger context in which he fought. He realized that the key to success in Spain was to win the allegiance of the Spanish tribes, which were the Carthaginian armies' major source of manpower. Without this allegiance, no number of Roman legions would have been able to subdue the country. The Carthaginian commanders, however, failed to appreciate the context of their occupation of Spain and routinely treated the tribes harshly, taking hostages and carrying out executions. Even Hannibal failed to take into consideration the political context of his campaign in Italy. Its success depended heavily on convincing large numbers of Rome's Italian allies to support him. Some southern tribes did go over to Hannibal but not in sufficient numbers to meet his manpower requirements. Meanwhile, Scipio's military campaign in Spain succeeded largely because he first won the Spanish to his side with fair and honorable treatment. During his later North African campaign, Scipio showed the same appreciation for political and social factors by winning the allegiance of Massinissa, the chief of the Numidians, and convincing him to support Rome. Scipio achieved this by supporting Massinissa's claim to the throne against his rival and by kindly treating the prince's nephew once Scipio captured him in battle and then returning him unharmed. In conducting his campaigns, Scipio anticipated Carl von Clausewitz's maxim that "war is always the continuation of policy by other means."[58]

Scipio was almost alone among Roman commanders in his understanding of the role of intelligence in war. His use of strategic and tactical intelligence "underlines the spectacular originality of Scipio in the Republican military context."[59] Scipio's campaigns provide the best documented use of intelligence by a Roman commander in the Second Punic War.[60] Until the war's last years, Roman strategic and tactical intelligence capabilities had been generally poor. From the strategic perspective, Rome failed to anticipate Hannibal's invasion (218–217 BCE), the crisis in Sicily (216–215 BCE), the rebellion of Sardinia (215 BCE), the threat from Macedonia (215–214 BCE), and the defections of the southern Italian tribes to Hannibal (216–215 BCE). In each case the Romans were taken by surprise. Rome's tactical intelligence was just as poor and was reflected in the number of ambushes inflicted on Roman armies: in a little more than three years, the Carthaginians destroyed no fewer than six Roman armies by ambush.[61] Other Roman units, including the army of Scipio's father and uncle at Castulo, were badly mauled if not destroyed completely because of tactical intelligence failures.

One cannot point to a single strategic or tactical intelligence failure during Scipio's eight years of war. The Spanish tribes' betrayal of his father likely gave Scipio an acute appreciation for strategic intelligence. Before taking command in Spain, Scipio gathered information on the political and geographic conditions of the Spanish area of operations, specific operational intelligence on the three Carthaginian armies' strength and location, the significance of the city of New Carthage as the main logistics base for the entire Carthaginian effort in Spain, and detailed tactical intelligence about the city itself, including its topography, defenses, and the depth of the lagoon that surrounded it. This information helped Scipio successfully attack and capture the city, completely altering the strategic and military balance in Spain to Rome's advantage in a single blow. Scipio made similar strategic intelligence preparations for his invasion of North Africa, sending naval units to reconnoiter the coast and using landing parties to discern the conditions in Numidia. He sent his trusted friend, Gaius Laelius, to Africa to discern the political situation, and at great personal risk Scipio secretly visited Syphax, an important tribal chief, and attempted to convince him to support the Romans.

Roman failures of tactical intelligence can be attributed, in part, to the legion not having a permanent organic element to conduct reconnaissance. Thus, any given Roman commander's collection effort was haphazard at best.[62] Most Roman commanders used the velites (or light infantry) for reconnaissance missions, sometimes augmenting them with small troops of cavalry.[63] Other times they employed horsemen from the *extraordinarii*. Scipio's father may have used these elite troops as a reconnaissance force in his skirmish against the Numidians on the Rhône River. Scipio appears to have been the first Roman commander to establish a permanent unit within the legion tasked with collecting tactical field intelligence. This unit was assembled from one-third of the cavalry normally assigned to the extraordinarii and one-fifth of the light infantry. Together the new unit might comprise almost two thousand men.[64] Also, Scipio's bodyguard, the praetoriani, may have occasionally performed intelligence tasks.

"An army," Napoleon once remarked, "travels on its stomach." One of Scipio's greatest talents as a logistician and administrator was ensuring that his army was adequately supplied. Moreover, he always oversaw logistical preparations personally. The night before the invasion of Africa, Scipio met with each captain of the supply transports to make certain that all was in order. He never undertook a campaign or even a single battle without adequate supplies, and he took great care never to sever his supply lines when engaged in extended tactical operations. Ancient historians record not a single instance of Scipio being required to change his operational plans because of a supply shortage. In this regard Scipio was not only a brilliant operational planner and commander but an excellent logistician as well.

As a leader of men at war Scipio has few equals. He led the Roman army for eight years in two major campaigns, Spain and North Africa; fought six major battles and numerous skirmishes; and won them all. In every engagement Scipio fought against an opponent who was much more experienced in war than he, and yet he triumphed. At Zama he faced the most experienced and talented general of his age, Hannibal Barca, and defeated him. Why was Scipio able to achieve such success? A study of the ancient world's great commanders suggests that they shared certain traits and abilities that contributed to their greatness.[65] All, for example, were educated men, products of formal intellectual training in the use of the mind. Such training provides a leader with the confidence to trust his intellect to make reasonable sense of the world. Mentally disciplined commanders think in terms of cause and effect, that is, of one thing leading to another or of chains of actions where one might bring about expected results with some degree of certainty by setting in motion events yet far removed from those ends. These leaders are far less likely to accept the world or immediate situations as they present themselves and to permit culture, tradition, or habit to determine their actions. These leaders are far more likely than others to see themselves as controlling their own fate and as being able to change the course of events rather than acquiescing in it. Scipio's sometimes excessive self-confidence surely suggests this ability. Great commanders like Scipio are linear thinkers who always move from cause to effect and seek ways to control the causes.

A great commander must be able to adjust quickly to changing circumstances, and this ability requires receptivity to new ideas. Scipio's reform of the legion's organization, tactics, and weaponry in order to deal with the combat capabilities of the highly flexible Carthaginian armies shows his willingness to entertain and adopt new ideas. Before Scipio, the Roman legion had not changed significantly in more than a hundred years. Receptivity to new ideas is often employed by great leaders to challenge existing assumptions about their environment and generate new assumptions to direct their thinking so as to succeed in a new environment. Scipio challenged the basic strategic assumptions about the war with Hannibal when he concluded that the war could never be won in Italy and that the key to victory lay in Spain and ultimately in North Africa. All the great captains of antiquity were superb strategic thinkers, and Scipio was no exception.

As a regular habit of mind, great leaders possess imagination, or the ability to conceptualize alternative sets of circumstances that might be brought about by their actions. It encompasses the ability to foresee what may happen under reasonable conditions of knowledge. Imagination is closely connected to extrapolation and is a highly pragmatic intellectual tool for dealing with situational complexity. Great commanders like Scipio often succeed because they can imagine circumstances that do not yet exist but could exist if events could be directed in certain ways. These intellectual traits together constitute what might be called imaginative reasoning, where all relevant aspects of problem solving come together to make reasonable sense of the world outside the mind. To substitute formulas, technologies, traditions, or rituals for imaginative thought—that is, to do what has always been done because it always has been done—is to court disaster on the battlefield. The Roman armies that fought against Hannibal were defeated repeatedly because their commanders used them again and again precisely as they were designed to be used. Scipio saw the need to change the legion's structure and tactics and ultimately defeated the Carthaginians.

These habits of mind are insufficient by themselves, however, to produce a great leader. Great commanders are first and foremost men of action. It is one thing to conceive of great deeds, but quite another to attempt them, especially in wartime, when the consequences of failure are often destruction and death. All the great captains of antiquity, including Scipio, possessed great self-confidence. Trusting one's thoughts and experiences is central to the strength of personality and character required to lend sound thinking to the force of action. The roots of self-confidence lie in character, not intellect; in experience, not study; and in the ability to endure the fear of failure without worrying about it.

A great leader must also be willing to take great risks. The great commander must possess the riskiness of the professional gambler, not the enthusiastic amateur, for he knows that knowledge of circumstances and events alone are insufficient to master them. The world can never be completely known or turned completely to one's will in the turmoil of battle. The terrible "ifs" always accumulate. Uncertainty and the unknown always need to be confronted. Great commanders like Scipio and Hannibal faced uncertainty with the willingness to take risks and to reduce the threat of the unknown by plunging into it and thereby making it known. Only great gamblers would have dared to invade Italy across the Alps or to strike at the main Carthaginian logistics base at New Carthage. Without the ability to gamble on a large scale, no commander can reduce or master the uncertainty of the battlefield that always threatens to frustrate his will. Scipio possessed all the intellectual and character traits of a great leader that together produced a degree of military competency that no other general of his time, and few since, have equally demonstrated.

Scipio was a talented field commander who achieved great success by incorporating all aspects of warfare into his thinking. His intellect made him an innovative commander, but his personality made him a daring one. Perhaps it was a youth spent in the presence of his warrior father and uncle or perhaps it was the endless conversations with these role models, first as a young man only listening to his more experienced elders and then, later, as a soldier himself, that provided him with a good example. Perhaps, too, his early study of Greek history led him to appreciate the campaigns of Epaminondas, Philip, Alexander, and Pyrrhus and stimulated him to seek command of men in war as an expression of his own manhood. Whatever his early influences, Publius Scipio emerged at a young age with a brilliant, integrated mind harnessed to a personality marked by self-confidence and a willingness to risk everything on a single bold stroke when circumstances required. He was one of those rare military men who never ceased learning from his own experiences and constantly reassessed the lessons of the past against the experiences of the present in order to anticipate the future. He was a general the likes of which Rome never saw again.

2

The Strategic Setting

THE CONFLICT BETWEEN Rome and Carthage known as the Punic Wars was the first one in history to demonstrate a defining characteristic of modern war: strategic endurance. Prior to this development, wars were largely settled in one or two major battles in which the combatant states obtained or failed to obtain their strategic objectives. Battles between antagonists represented all-or-nothing affairs, and empires sometimes changed shape as the consequence of a single military engagement. The Punic Wars lasted more than forty years, during which Rome lost battle after battle without collapsing. Drawing on a larger pool of strategic resources than any Western state had heretofore had available, Rome fought on until it achieved victory. Its strategic endurance stemmed as much from its political will and social organization as from its material resources. Rome's eventual victory signaled a new era in which political will and the ability to marshall sufficient strategic resources in pursuit of military and political objectives became the most important characteristics of the state at war.

From approximately the eighth to the third century BCE, Rome and Carthage developed independently and without conflict as the major regional powers in the western Mediterranean. The small Roman city-state on the Tiber's banks gradually grew into the major power in Italy but had few overseas contacts and no colonies or possessions outside the Italian Peninsula. Rome developed as a classic continental, albeit peninsular, power. Founded by Phoenicians from the city-state of Tyre sometime in the seventh century BCE, Carthage began as a trading colony. By the fifth century, Carthage had gained its independence from Tyre and had become the richest and most powerful trading state in the western Mediterranean. Carthage's power was based on its ability to secure almost monopolistic access to markets and resources in Sicily, Corsica, Sardinia, the Balearic Islands, and coastal Spain. It also enjoyed a rich trade with Greece and the eastern

Mediterranean states. While Rome developed as a land power, Carthage necessarily sought its role at sea. With access to overseas areas as its most important element of national power, Carthage developed a large commercial fleet and a navy to protect its vital sea-lanes. Treaties regulated the meager contacts between Rome and Carthage at the time, and Carthage granted Rome a free hand on the Italian mainland in return for a Carthaginian trading monopoly in the western Mediterranean. As long as Carthage did not encroach on Roman ports and Rome did not seek to expand into overseas areas of Carthaginian interest, the two states lived in relative harmony.

Rome required almost three centuries to extend its control throughout Italy. Through incorporation or alliances, Rome eventually controlled most of the territory from the Strait of Messina in the south to the Po Valley in the north. With the exception of a few remaining Greek colonies in the south, Rome controlled most of the Italian Peninsula by 264 BCE and was positioned to expand beyond it. Rome's conflict with Carthage came over Sicily.

Carthage and Greek city-states had long occupied Sicily, and the Carthaginians had constructed fortifications and established garrisons on the island's western side. The eastern side was under the influence of Greek colonies and independent city-states. The Carthaginians saw Sicily as a strategic platform from which an invasion of Carthage itself could be launched, and for centuries a major goal of Carthaginian policy was to retain control of the island's western side. Having achieved a degree of hegemony over most of Italy, however, Rome regarded the continued presence of Carthage and the Greeks in Sicily as an obstacle to its further expansion. Extending its territories to the north was difficult because of the region's harsh terrain and warlike Gallic tribes. Sicily, however, offered the double prize of expanding into a rich and developed area of considerable commercial value while reducing the presence of a major power on Italy's border. Under the press of Roman expansion, in Rome's view, it could not permit the continued Carthaginian presence on the strategic platform of Sicily. In 264 BCE Rome encroached upon Sicily and the First Punic War broke out.

Lasting more than twenty years, the war was fundamentally fought at sea, with some ground engagements undertaken in Sicily to expel Carthaginian garrisons. After several defeats at the hands of superior Carthaginian seamanship, Rome embarked on a program of naval expansion. The Romans had never before established a naval arm and lacked the technical expertise to design ships. Using a captured Rhodian *quinquereme* as a template, the Romans built hundreds of fighting ships. Men recruited into the army were trained in rowing and tactics on land and then deployed shipboard. Despite Rome's numerical advantage in ships, Carthage defeated the Roman navy in battle after battle. At one point Roman naval casualties and losses from storms amounted to approximately 15 percent of the total number of able-bodied men of military age in Italy.[1]

The problem of Carthaginian superiority at sea was finally solved by the introduction of new technology. The Romans' strong suit was infantry combat. The military planners' problem was how to bring this advantage to bear at sea. The answer was the grappling hook and the *corvus*, or "raven." A century earlier the Celts had defeated the Romans in a naval engagement in the mouth of the Seine River. While Roman ships attempted to ram, the Celts used grappling hooks on ropes to bring the two ships together, rushed its infantry aboard, and killed the Roman crews. The Romans seem to have copied the iron grappling hook (*manus ferreae*), but the corvus seems to have been a Roman invention. The corvus was a large wooden bridge with a spike at one end. The bridge was mounted at the front of the ship and rotated outward. As an enemy ship was caught with the grappling irons and brought into contact with the Roman ship, the Romans swung the corvus out and down so that the spike stuck in the enemy's deck. Roman marines could then rush across the wooden bridge to the enemy ship and attack its crew. But the corvus had a drawback: it made the boats top heavy and uncontrollable in a heavy sea, resulting in thousands of sailors and soldiers lost in storms when the unwieldy vessels turned over and sank. The Roman navy abandoned the corvus sometime between 255 and 250 BCE.[2]

Polybius called the First Punic War the bloodiest in history. Rome alone lost more than four hundred thousand men. Both sides were exhausted and in 241 BCE concluded a peace treaty. Carthage surrendered its claims and garrisons in Sicily and to all the islands between the city of Rome and Sicily. Because it was an independent city-state, Syracuse remained outside Roman control of Sicily, but Corsica was occupied. The indemnity levied on Carthage was so high that it could not pay its mercenary armies, leading to a three-year war between Carthage and its own mercenaries.[3] Near the war's end the Romans seized Sardinia on the pretext that Carthaginian garrisons there were targeted at Rome.

Exhausted from war, Carthage was deprived of its most important markets and trading stations and faced economic ruin. Its navy was destroyed and the trading fleet reduced. Its economic basis of power was severely eroded. For more than a century Carthage had maintained a small trading port at Gades (modern Cádiz). Under Hamilcar Barca's urging, Carthage sought to rebuild its power by expanding its influence in Spain and establish a new source of markets and resources. The last holdout against Roman arms on Sicily and an accomplished general, Hamilcar spent the next nine years conquering the rugged people of southern and central Spain. His son-in-law, Hasdrubal the Splendid, continued the campaign. With force, diplomacy, and diplomatic marriages, Hasdrubal secured Carthaginian hegemony over southern Spain. Following Hasdrubal's assassination in 221 BCE, the army chose Hannibal, Hamilcar Barca's oldest son, as the commander of the Carthaginian army in Spain.

Hasdrubal had concluded a treaty with Rome in which both recognized the Ebro River as the northern limit of Carthaginian influence in Spain. South of that line, only the city of Saguntum remained independent. The treaty's purpose was to allay Roman suspicions. Rome had watched for almost two decades as Carthage increased its power in Spain and staged a remarkable economic and military recovery. The Romans began to see the growing Carthaginian power and wealth in Spain as a possible new strategic platform from which to strike at Corsica and Sardinia or, perhaps, even Italy itself. The Romans, never ones to forget a defeat, suspected that Carthage was preparing for a war of revenge.

In 219 BCE Saguntum revolted against Carthage, perhaps stimulated by a pro-Roman faction within the city. Despite the city's pleas for Roman aid, Rome did not react. In the absence of Roman pronouncements to the contrary, Hannibal assumed he had a free hand to deal with the revolt. Saguntum, after all, was south of the Ebro, and Rome had conceded that sphere of influence to Carthage by treaty. Hannibal attacked the city and destroyed it after an eight-month siege. This action was the casus belli that Rome had sought. It reacted immediately. Roman ambassadors arrived in Carthage with an ultimatum: either Hannibal and his officers were to be tried and punished for their actions at Saguntum or Rome would hold Carthage responsible and declare war. Saguntum was merely an excuse. Rome had already concluded that Carthaginian power was a threat and had to be reduced by military action. Roman diplomacy was serving these strategic ends.[4] The Roman ambassador, Quintus Fabius, held out two folds of his toga and said, "Here I bring you peace and war, chose what you will."

Carthage chose to fight. The result was the Second Punic War (218–201 BCE).

CARTHAGINIAN STRATEGY

To understand the Carthaginian strategy, one must understand the constraints under which it developed. In any war with Rome, Carthage faced three major strategic constraints that greatly affected its military strategy's chances of

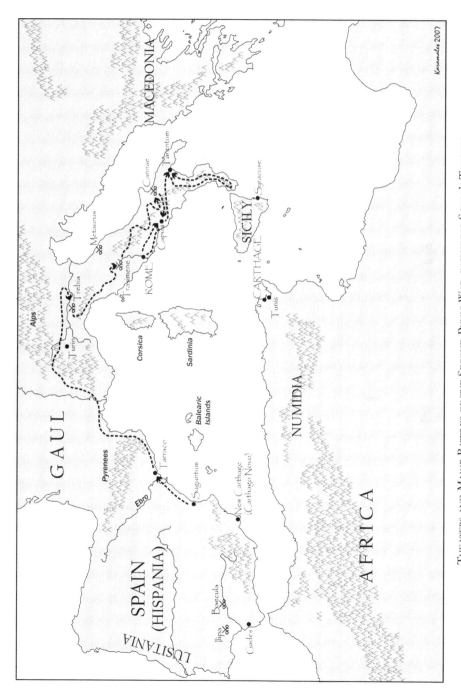

Theaters and Major Battles of the Second Punic War, including Scipio's Theater of Operations in Spain and North Africa, and Hannibal's Route of Invasion

succeeding. The first constraint was its lack of an adequate manpower base from which to recruit and sustain the Carthaginian armies. If we can believe the historian Strabo that Carthage's population at this time was approximately seven hundred thousand people, we can use Yigael Yadin's method of measuring ancient city-states' abilities to raise forces from their respective manpower bases and estimate the manpower pool available to Carthage for military use.[5] Approximately 20 to 25 percent of the population, at maximum, could be put to military use. A maximum military effort, therefore, could produce only about 150,000 men for service in the Carthaginian armies *and* the fleet along with somewhere in the vicinity of thirty thousand to thirty-five thousand horse cavalry.

While these resources were not unsubstantial, they were not sufficient in light of the strategic force deployments Carthage had to anticipate. From its general manpower pool Carthage had to deploy substantial contingents to Spain to retain control of the only partially pacified tribes that the Romans were rigorously stirring to revolt. Failure here would have placed the rear of Hannibal's armies and his major recruitment pool at risk. Moreover, Carthage needed continued access to trade with Spain and its rich silver mines throughout the war if Carthage was going to raise the money needed to sustain the war. Another drain on manpower resources was the need to protect Libya-Phoenicia on the African coast. This area provided the bulk of Carthage's grain supply as well as a large surplus to export for the hard currency needed to pay for the war. Finally, manpower reserves had to be committed to defend the African coast and Carthage itself against a Roman seaborne attack launched from Sicily. Taken together these requirements stretched Carthaginian manpower resources to their limits. Under these circumstances Hannibal could not count on Carthage to provide more than forty thousand men and eight thousand to ten thousand cavalry for the war. Carthage would have to find an additional source of manpower if it were to have any chance of success.

The Roman manpower situation was considerably better. Drawing only on its own resources and that of allied Campanian city-states, Rome could deploy 250,000 foot and 23,000 horse cavalry within a year of the outbreak of the war. With contingents drawn from other allied states on the Italian Peninsula, Rome had a strategic manpower pool of seven hundred thousand foot soldiers and seventy thousand horse cavalry.[6] Any attempt by Carthage to fight a war of attrition or to engage in multiple theaters of operations had to eventually fail. The Romans, however, possessed enough manpower to engage on multiple fronts. To draw off Roman forces, Carthage enticed Philip V of Macedon to declare war on Rome, but the Romans met the challenge. They continued the war without any significant effect on their force levels deployed against Hannibal.

The second strategic factor limiting Carthaginian fighting power in the Second Punic War was Carthage's inability to control the sea-lanes. Carthage was about to engage in a war far from its shores while conceding control of the sea to Rome. Thus, Carthage had to pursue a different policy from the First Punic War. Then it had deployed more than three hundred warships, or quinqueremes, each of which required 270 oarsmen and 120 marines.[7] After that first war Carthage had continued to maintain and expand its commercial fleet but had invested little in its naval fleet.[8] Reasons for this change might have stemmed from its manpower shortage and the cost required to maintain a sizable naval arm. After all, rowers were not slaves but hired skilled labor, and thirty-five thousand rowers were needed to man the fleet. Also, while the Barcids, who had controlled Carthaginian strategic policy for more than twenty years, certainly produced great generals well versed in land warfare, these men lacked any significant naval experience. This background may have led Hannibal to undervalue sea power's role in his strategic thinking.[9] In the meantime, Rome had maintained a large navy after the first war and possessed sufficient naval combatants to take control of the sea.

In antiquity a country's effective use of naval resources in war depended primarily on the number of ships it possessed. While transports could move by sail across the open sea for days at a time uninterrupted, oarsmen powered quinquereme warships, and they needed rest, food, and water at regular intervals. Quinqueremes had only limited space and weight for crew provisions, forcing the warships to put into shore each evening to rest and feed the crews. Without such periodic stops, an oarsman would have lasted no more than a single day before succumbing to thirst and fatigue. Going to shore then depended on finding a friendly coast, one free from hostile forces that could attack the crews. Thus, Hannibal was forced to come overland because the only possible sea route from Spain to northern Italy was along the coast, and the Romans controlled the entire coast from the Ebro to northern Italy. In addition, Hannibal would have had to sail past Massilia, a staunch Roman ally with its own fleet of warships. Had Hannibal attempted this sea route, he would have likely encountered a Roman fleet coming along the same route in the opposite direction, its warships ready to pounce on the Carthaginian convoy. Rome also controlled Sicily, Sardinia, and the Bruttian coast, the key stepping stones naval transports needed to stop and replenish. Hence Rome controlled the sea by controlling the land.

Carthage's inability to protect its sea-lanes placed severe limits on its strategic capability. First, Carthage could not transport its troops to key areas, making strategic surprise from the sea impossible. Also, resupplying, reinforcing, and evacuating troops already deployed by ship were difficult tasks and fraught with risk. Next, with Roman naval combatants roaming at will, they could easily disrupt the Carthaginian trade, which was its main source of funding for the war. Finally, without an adequate covering naval force, Carthage and the coast of Africa were open to Roman raids and invasion. Unlike the first war, where most of the action occurred at sea, this time Carthage would have to play against the Roman advantage in ground forces. Once committed, Carthaginian ground units would have to be self-sustaining for the war's duration. Its navy could provide little logistical help.

The requirement for self-sufficiency brought into focus the third element limiting the Carthaginian strategy, that is, the nature of its political rule over its colonies. Carthaginian colonial rule was based on cruelty and force, with disputes settled by fire and crucifixion. The loyalty of Carthage's colonial subjects in Spain never went very deep, because Carthage took few pains to gain their genuine allegiance. At the same time Carthage heavily depended on these overseas possessions for recruiting its mercenary armies. Carthage's general manpower shortage meant that if the war dragged on, it would have to find some way to continue the flow of manpower from the colonial areas to the Carthaginian armies. The subjected people's questionable loyalty, however, meant that Roman gains in these areas would not only deprive Carthage of territory but would also cut off its manpower recruitment system.

Hannibal's experience with the tenuous loyalty of Carthaginian allies in Spain might have led him to conclude that he could possibly draw off the support of Rome's allies once he invaded Italy. If so, he failed to comprehend the political sociology of Roman rule in Italy. Rome made great efforts to treat its allied states fairly, in some cases to the point of extending Roman citizenship and law to them in return for troop contingents under the command of Roman officers. The situation in Italy was much more stable than in Carthaginian domains, and the Roman allies' loyalty had already been tested during the first war and more recently in 225 BCE, when Italy was subjected to the great Gallic invasion. Before that, Pyrrhus's invasion of Italy had failed because of the strength of the Roman colonial system and the weak support Pyrrhus was able to obtain from his Italian allies. The only rebellious area Hannibal could be somewhat certain of winning over was the newly subdued areas of northern Italy, which were inhabited by Gauls. With a few important exceptions, Capua and Tarentum, Rome's Italian allies remained loyal throughout the war.

The constraints of manpower, control of the sea, and harsh Carthaginian rule placed significant limits on the Carthaginian military strategy. These main strategic constraints generated numerous other limiting consequences that further limited Carthage's strategic planning.

1. By necessity, Carthage would have to fight a ground war and require little support by sea. Unlike in the first war, Carthage could not hope to weaken Rome's will by destroying large contingents of Roman manpower at sea. Carthage would have to exact every casualty with close combat.

2. The war would have to be fought on the Italian mainland. A war anywhere else would not sufficiently threaten Rome into a political settlement. In any case Carthage could not sustain a war elsewhere in light of Rome's control of the sea-lanes.

3. Hannibal would have to insert his army overland from his strategic platform in Spain since naval transport was impossible. To minimize losses during deployment, he would need strategic surprise.

4. Once in Italy, Hannibal would have to find some way to replace Carthaginian combat losses or risk a war of attrition against the Romans that he could not win.

5. Once in Italy, Hannibal would have to reduce Rome's manpower advantage either through battlefield defeats or political defection.

6. Rome had to be prevented from striking directly at Carthage or Spain with sufficient force to bring the war to an end while Carthaginian armies were in the field.

7. Roman armies could not be defeated in their entirety. Rome's center of gravity was the political will of the Roman Senate and the loyalty of its Italian colonies and allies. For Carthage, the war's purpose was to break that will and forge an advantageous treaty that would restore Corsica, Sardinia, and Sicily to Carthaginian control.

Hannibal formulated a high-risk strategy for defeating Rome that was designed to carry out military operations within these strategic constraints while attaining Carthage's political objectives. Had he succeeded, the history of the West might have been considerably different.

Hannibal knew his adversary well enough to know that Rome would not have declared war against Carthage without first a plan having in place for its prosecution. He surmised that Rome was already planning to move militarily and that its strategy would probably involve a two-pronged assault on the Carthaginian position. Rome would likely mount an invasion of Spain to engage and pin down Hannibal's forces there while it launched a second invasion from Sicily and fell on Carthage itself. With no way to interdict Roman transports at sea, the key to Hannibal's plan was to strike first. The plan was to move a large army through northeastern Spain, skirt the Pyrenees along the coast, cross the Alps, and debouch on the northern Italian plain near the Po River. The shock of this deployment was aimed at paralyzing the Roman decision-making structure and disrupting Roman plans to invade Carthage from Sicily. Hannibal figured Rome would likely shift its forces scheduled for the invasion north to meet his invading troops.

Hannibal's route of march was difficult, but it had the advantage of making it equally difficult for Roman armies to interfere with it. The march over the Alps could be expected to take a heavy toll on Hannibal's army, as indeed it did. Without possible reinforcement from Carthage, Hannibal's plan required recruiting large numbers of Gallic tribesmen living on both sides of the Alps and as far south as the Po Valley. Given the long history of mutual hatred between the Gauls and Romans and the frequency of their slaughterous conflicts, Carthaginian recruitment officers reasonably expected to replace the manpower lost during Hannibal's passage of the Alps. If he was successful, Hannibal could place a large and replenished army on the northern Italian plain before Rome could react.

Hannibal expected Rome to react quickly to his army once it arrived on Roman territory. The Carthaginian plan was to draw the Roman army far from its base, engage it as quickly as possible, and defeat it in a series of battles. If the Roman army could be defeated on its own soil, the Roman Senate might move toward a quick political settlement. If Rome was not quick to settle the conflict, Hannibal hoped to live off the land for as long as possible, courting Roman allied states with kind treatment and promises of freedom. Significant numbers of defections to the Carthaginian cause would deprive Rome of critical manpower assets and war supplies. More important, it would demoralize Rome's will and confront it with the choice of accepting a peace treaty or taking the risk of having its alliances come apart one by one until the entire Roman dominion in Italy was threatened.

After assessing the opposing forces' comparative strength, it was vital that Hannibal not be drawn into a war of attrition. A series of bloody Roman defeats would be meaningless if his own army also suffered high costs. If Rome did not panic and quickly settle the war after a series of battlefield defeats and political defections, it could recover its balance and mobilize its full strategic resources. Under these circumstances Hannibal risked being isolated in Italy while Rome struck unhindered at Spain and Carthage. The risk was high that Carthage's political leaders themselves might make peace to save what they could. Hannibal and his army would then become a strategic irrelevancy.

The basic assumption of Hannibal's grand strategy was fatally flawed. Hannibal was a Hellene in his thinking, training, and understanding of history. In the Hellenic world, grand strategy at the highest level was relatively straightforward. If one power could invade another's heartland territory, win a few battles, and cause sufficient disruption, it could reasonably expect its enemy to collapse and seek terms. This sequence was the norm in Hellenic warfare, and Hannibal's study of Alexander's campaigns clearly demonstrated its validity. Further, the Carthaginians themselves had seen some of their Sicilian adventures come to naught in a single day's fighting. This strategic perspective remained unchanged even after the Punic Wars, and it was how Rome later overthrew Macedon, Syria, and Achaea. Hannibal thus assumed Rome would behave in the conventional Hellenistic manner.

But the Romans were not Hellenes, and their response to Hannibal's victories was unconventional: they kept on fighting.[10] Given that Carthage never had the resources to defeat Rome militarily, once Rome refused to behave like the Hellenistic states, Hannibal's war degenerated into a war of attrition and a stalemate that he could not win. Ultimately, Hannibal would be penned in an area that was a little larger than Bruttium and become a mere nuisance as the Romans overran Spain, reconquered Sicily, neutralized Philip's threat from Macedon, and then invaded Africa by striking at Carthage itself. In a terrible irony, the genius of bold, swift, unpredictable warfare would spend most of his years frustrated and wandering the hills of southern Italy. Hannibal would no longer be the master of events but their prisoner.[11]

In the summer of 218 BCE Hannibal put his plan into operation and began to move an army of fifty thousand infantrymen, nine thousand cavalry, and thirty-seven elephants through the Pyrenees toward the Rhône Valley.[12] Bypassing Massilia, Hannibal avoided Roman cavalry patrols and moved across southern Gaul. Hannibal's delay in suppressing a tribal revolt north of the Ebro River forced him to attempt crossing the Alps too late in the season and made it more difficult. Once into Cisalpine Gaul, the tribes began to rally to his standard. By

November Hannibal had replenished much of his army lost in the crossing and began to search for the Roman army. The Romans reacted as he had predicted. An army under Publius Scipio had moved to Massilia in late summer to intercept Hannibal. Arriving too late, Scipio dispatched the army's main body under his brother, Gnaeus, to Spain to restore Roman power north of the Ebro River.[13] Although the Carthaginians controlled the area south of the Ebro and the interior, Roman forces were generally successful, and within a year Hannibal's line of retreat and reinforcement from Spain was severed. Publius Scipio himself returned to Rome and raised a new army to engage Hannibal on the northern Italian plain. The Roman army under Sempronius that had been poised in Sicily to invade Africa abandoned its planned invasion and marched north, where it linked up with Scipio's army. In November the Romans went hunting for Hannibal and found him waiting on the banks of the Trebia River.

THE BATTLE OF THE TREBIA RIVER, 218 BCE

Publius Scipio had failed to catch Hannibal north of Massilia that summer. He then took command of the new army at Pisa and moved north into the Po Valley. He marched east along the river as Hannibal moved his army down from the foothills and into the valley. Probably by accident, the two armies met on the banks of the Ticinus, a northern tributary of the Po. Hannibal struck the Roman army while it was still in line of march. After a brief but heavy skirmish in which Scipio was wounded and his cavalry destroyed, the Romans retreated behind the Po to wait for Sempronius's army to link up. Hannibal broke contact and disappeared. He made no attempt to prevent the two Roman armies from linking up. If he was to extract the maximum political effect from a Roman defeat, the larger the Roman force he could destroy the better. Moreover, with Scipio wounded, Hannibal knew that Sempronius would command the consular army, and Sempronius was an impetuous man. The trick was to draw him into battle under unfavorable conditions.

Polybius notes that Hannibal chose "a place between the two camps, flat indeed and treeless, but well adapted for an ambuscade, as it was traversed by a water-course with steep banks densely overgrown with brambles and other thorny plants, and here he proposed to lay a stratagem to surprise the enemy."[14] Hannibal used his youngest brother, Mago, a dashing and sometimes reckless cavalry commander, to set the trap. Under cover of night an elite force of two thousand cavalry and infantry took up positions on the stream's banks and concealed their mounts and weapons in the thick brush. The Carthaginian horses had been trained to lie prone on command. As dawn broke, the view from the Roman camp over the Trebia River was clear of enemy troops.

Shortly before dawn Numidian cavalry attacked the Roman camp, penetrating the encampment from all sides, wheeling about, and striking again and again. Roman officers drove their troops from their sleep, hastily forming them into battle lines. Having awakened the Roman camp, the Numidians withdrew, seeking to draw the Romans out toward a position Hannibal chose for an ambush. Sempronius took the bait. The Roman commander hastily assembled his legion. Cold and wet after a night of soaking rain and without breakfast, the Roman army moved out across the sodden plain. Between them and Hannibal was the swollen Trebia River, running swiftly in the cold, gray November dawn. Snow began to fall. Hannibal's troops were huddled around their campfires. Having consumed a hearty breakfast, they covered their bodies with oil as protection against the snow and sleet. Hannibal had chosen the sloping ground on the Carthaginian side of the river as the place of battle. If the Romans wanted a fight, they would first have to cross the river. Once they did, they would have Mago, still hidden from sight, at their backs.

Sempronius ordered his troops to wade across the river. An army of forty thousand slowly made its way into the cold waters and up the sloping ground on the other side. The Roman army was comprised of sixteen thousand Roman infantry, twenty thousand allied infantry, and four thousand cavalry that protected the wings in typical Roman battle formation. Arrayed in the long Carthaginian battle line were twenty thousand Celts, Africans, and Spanish infantry and ten thousand cavalry deployed to anchor the wings.[15] In front of the regular force were the light infantry skirmishers. The elephants were positioned in front of each cavalry wing to help protect the Carthaginian flanks.[16] The battle began with the usual Roman attack in the center.

As the Romans pressed the Carthaginian center, Hannibal struck directly at the cavalry formations protecting the Roman flanks. Outnumbered almost two to one by the Spanish and Numidian cavalry, the Roman cavalry gave ground and exposed the infantry's flanks. As the infantry battle raged in the center, with neither side giving much ground, the Numidian cavalry broke contact with the Roman cavalry, left them in disarray, and wheeled to attack the Roman infantry's flanks. With the Romans now pressed in the center and on the flanks, Mago, who waited in ambush with his men and horses below the stream's banks, attacked the Roman rear.

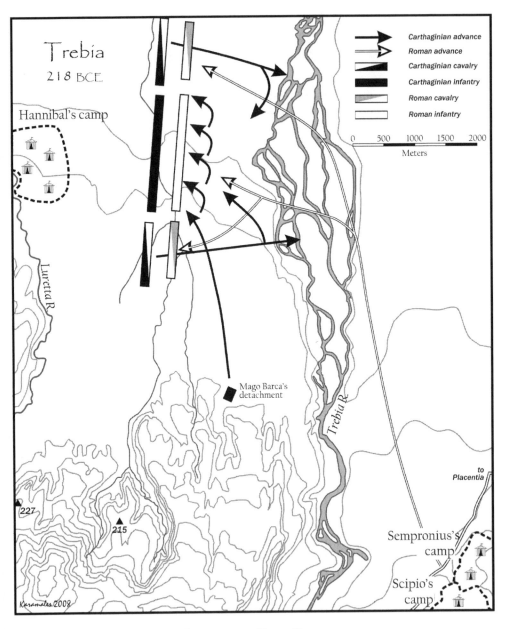

Trebia
218 BCE

Hannibal's camp

Luretta R.

Mago Barca's
detachment

227

215

Trebia R.

to
Placentia

Sempronius's
camp

Scipio's
camp

Karamales 2008

| Carthaginian advance |
| Roman advance |
| Carthaginian cavalry |
| Carthaginian infantry |
| Roman cavalry |
| Roman infantry |

0   500   1000   1500   2000
Meters

BATTLE OF THE TREBIA RIVER

Each of Mago's two thousand cavalry riders carried another infantryman with him on his horse. As the cavalry crashed into the Roman rear, the horse-borne infantrymen jumped from the horses and waded into the battle while the cavalry continued to fight on horseback. With the Roman flanks already perilously close to collapse, the shock and surprise of a new assault from yet another direction broke the Roman formation. A rout commenced, and the pursuing Carthaginians slaughtered thousands of Roman soldiers. Many more drowned attempting to recross the Trebia and reach the safety of the Roman camp. Only the Roman center held. Unable to retreat and pressed from both flanks, the Roman units in the center continued to fight their way through the Carthaginians. Punching through at last, they continued forward in good order and protected their rear until they reached a nearby Roman fortress town. The rest of the Roman army was destroyed. Of the forty thousand Roman troops committed that day, fewer than ten thousand reached safety. Hannibal had drawn first blood.[17]

THE BATTLE OF LAKE TRASIMENE, 217 BCE

The Romans met the defeat at the Trebia with gravitas. They raised four new legions, chose commanders, and deployed fresh troops to block Hannibal moving any farther south. A Roman army under Gaius Flaminius was sent to Arretium (modern Arezzo) on the Apennines' western side to block the road to Tuscany, and another force under Gaius Servilius Germinus took up positions at Arminium (modern Rimini) to block the eastern road. It was winter, and no one expected Hannibal to attempt to move his army over the Apennines in the cold weather, but he did exactly that. Harsh weather conditions forced him back, and the Carthaginians went into winter quarters with the Gauls.

Springtime found the Roman armies blocking Hannibal's advance to the south. Hannibal moved his army through the marshes of the lower Arno River valley in an effort to slip between the Roman armies. He lost numerous troops and animals in the difficult crossing and contracted an eye infection that cost him his sight in one eye. By early spring, however, the Carthaginians had slipped between the blockading Roman forces and moved into the rich agricultural area of Tuscany. If the Romans wanted to do battle with Hannibal, they would have to catch him first.

Hannibal had studied his adversary, Flaminius, and, as both Polybius and Livy note, knew his reputation as a man given to anger and impetuous acts. The trick was to irritate Flaminius and provoke him into a foolish move. As Hannibal approached Tuscany, he deliberately passed within sight of the Roman army at

Arretium but did not pause to fight. Instead, he began to ravage the countryside, burning crops, towns, and villages and slaughtering livestock. Hannibal knew that devastating the lands of a Roman ally would signal to other allies that Rome could not protect them. Perhaps they would see it to their advantage to join the successful invader's ranks. Day after day Flaminius watched smoke rise over the Tuscan plain as Hannibal's army ravished the countryside. Unable to contain his anger any longer, Flaminius marched out of Arretium to engage Hannibal.

Hannibal's route took him through the small village of Passignano along the road that skirted Lake Trasimene's northern shore. Beyond the village the terrain narrowed into a defile with the lakeshore on one side and tall cliffs on the other. Past the narrow passageway the terrain opened on a narrow valley with hills on one side and the lake on the other. Straight ahead the road ran up a steep hill at the far end of the valley. As Hannibal moved his army over this route, he noticed that thick morning lake fog made visibility very difficult. Hannibal moved his army to the hilltop at the valley's end, pitched camp, and waited for Flaminius.

Flaminius moved his army into Passignano. His analysis of the terrain made him wary of an ambush in the narrow defile, but he concluded that the hills were too steep to conceal any large number of men.[18] He camped for the night but failed to send reconnaissance parties into the valley. Flaminius assumed Hannibal was moving away from him. He planned to catch Hannibal's army in line of march, engage and defeat the rear guard, and then attack the main body before it could turn and face the Roman assault. At dawn the next day Flaminius marched his army through the narrow defile onto the widening plain. The thick morning mist from the lake made visibility to the right and left difficult. Straight ahead and above the mist, however, Flaminius could see Hannibal's encampment on the hill at the valley's exit. It was the rear guard of Hannibal's army, and Flaminius ordered his vanguard to assume battle formation and move quickly to engage it. With the rest of the Roman column still in line of march, six thousand Roman legionnaires rushed up the hill to engage Hannibal's army. It must have appeared to Flaminius that he had taken Hannibal by surprise.

At the top of the hill the Carthaginians turned and met the Roman charge. The fighting was furious, but gradually the Carthaginians gave ground, turned, and fled. The Roman advance guard seeking the main body of Hannibal's army marched off in disciplined pursuit of the fleeing Carthaginians. On the valley floor Flaminius's army was now entirely through the narrow defile and its head moved up the hill at the valley's exit. The gap between the Roman advance guard and the rest of the army had widened as the Romans pursued the fleeing Carthaginians. Then, Hannibal sprang the trap.

The figure on page 42 shows the disposition of the Carthaginian and Roman forces at Trasimene. Always a gambler, Hannibal had bet that on the morning of the battle the lake would produce an early morning fog to cover his deployed troops waiting in ambush. The night before he had positioned thirty thousand men on the flank of the Roman line of march. The force on the hill that Flaminius's vanguard had engaged was a ruse designed to convince Flaminius that Hannibal's army was straight ahead in column of march when in fact the bulk of his forces were hidden in the fog on the Roman flank. Polybius notes that the morning stillness was broken by three trumpet blasts to signal the attack. Hannibal's army struck the Roman flank with overwhelming force.

The Spanish and African heavy infantry smashed into the front of the Roman column at an acute angle while the light infantry struck the center. Within minutes the Celts and Spanish were within the Roman column and hacking from the inside. Then the Numidian cavalry smashed into the rear of the column. The surprise was total and the Roman units could not form their battle formations to meet the attacks. Livy described the confusion:

> In that enveloping mist ears were a better guide than eyes: it was sounds, not sights, they turned to face—the groans of wounded men, the thud or ring of blows on body or shield, the shout of onslaught, the cry of fear. Some, fleeing for their lives, found themselves caught in a jam of their own men still standing their ground; others, trying to return to the fight, were forced back again by a crowd of fugitives. In every direction attempts to break out failed.[19]

The Numidian cavalry made retreat along the road impossible, and the lake precluded any depth to withdraw and form units for battle. It was a wild melee, the kind at which the Celts and Spanish infantry excelled.

The battle raged "for three long and bloody hours" until the Roman army was slaughtered. Flaminius himself was struck by an Insubrian cavalryman's lance and killed. Far to the front the Roman advance guard found itself alone as the Carthaginian forces they had been pursuing melted away into the hills. Turning back toward the valley, they came over the hill to see fifteen thousand Roman legionnaires lying dead on the ground. Carthaginian soldiers were stripping the dead of their weapons and armor. On the lakeshore the cavalry was cutting down

Lake Trasimene
217 BCE

0	1000	2000	3000	4000

Meters

Kassandra 2008

Carthaginian advance
Roman advance
Carthaginian cavalry
Carthaginian infantry
Roman infantry

Borghetto

Tuoro

Hannibal's camp

Passignum

Monte del Lago

Torricella

Magione

BATTLE OF LAKE TRASIMENE: HANNIBAL'S AMBUSH

the remnants of the Roman infantry that had tried to flee into the water. Hannibal had killed fifteen thousand Roman soldiers and destroyed another Roman army at a cost of only fifteen hundred of his own men.

THE BATTLE OF CANNAE, 216 BCE

In less than two years Hannibal had met the best of the Roman legions and dealt them one defeat after another. Ticinus had cost the Romans upward of two thousand men. The engagement at the Trebia destroyed thirty thousand Roman and allied soldiers. And now, at Trasimene, Hannibal destroyed fifteen thousand more Roman troops and took a major Roman commander's life. The Roman relief force, which came late to the battle of Lake Trasimene, had also been ambushed at a cost of four thousand more men. Hannibal had inflicted fifty-one thousand Roman casualties, a number equal to ten legions. Worse, with Flaminius's army destroyed and Servilius's army still at Arminium on the Adriatic coast, the road to Rome was open. If he wished, Hannibal could strike at the capital itself.

Rome went into mourning as news of the defeat reached the city. Rome itself was in danger, and the Senate, according to Polybius, "abandoning therefore the system of government by magistrates elected annually, . . . decided to deal with the present situation more radically." Rome put the safety of its city in the hands of a dictator, Quintus Fabius, a competent general of keen intellect. Rome could afford no more rash commanders who squandered armies.

Fabius's brilliance was evident in his strategic assessment of the problem. He knew that Rome's superior manpower, naval, and economic resources would, in the end, carry the day against Hannibal. Time worked to Rome's advantage, not Hannibal's. The real threat then was to Rome's resource base, which depended heavily on Rome maintaining the loyalty of its colonies and allies on the Italian mainland. Despite the quick succession of Roman defeats, no ally had yet gone over to Hannibal. More Carthaginian victories, however, might tempt them to defect. Rome's primary strategic objective, therefore, was not military at all but political. Roman military forces had to be used in such a way as to maintain the loyalty of its allies. Sooner or later Fabius knew Roman arms and naval power would destroy the Carthaginian base in Spain and make an attack against Carthage itself possible. His military strategy, then, was not aimed at destroying Hannibal but at containing him and keeping him on the move. Should an ally defect, Rome had the military capacity to punish it severely as an example to others who might be similarly tempted, as Rome proved when it severely punished Capua in 211 BCE for its treachery.

Fabius had discerned correctly that Hannibal's strategy ultimately depended on securing the defection of Rome's allies as a prelude to breaking Rome's will. To foster this political objective, Hannibal freed the allied soldiers captured at Trasimene and the Trebia and permitted them to return to their homes.[20]

The Roman Senate authorized a new army of eight legions accompanied by a similar number of allied contingents. The total force was almost seventy thousand men, making it the largest army that Rome had ever fielded. Hannibal himself had scarcely fifty thousand men. Under Fabius's direction, the city of Rome's defenses were strengthened. Next, Fabius marched his army from the city and found Hannibal. For almost six months Fabius followed in Hannibal's route of march, keeping to the high ground and maintaining contact with him. On several occasions Hannibal attempted to draw Fabius into battle but never succeeded. While the Roman army had secure logistics lines, Hannibal had to forage continually for food and supplies. Occasionally Fabius would attack these foraging detachments, but he refused to fight Hannibal's main force. Hannibal's army was now encumbered with thousands of prisoners, cattle herds, and war booty, all of which slowed its rate of movement. Hannibal continued to court Rome's Italian allies, however. A favorite tactic was to occupy a small town or estate, kill all the Roman men of military age, carry off their wives and children, and leave the allied population unharmed. But the allied townspeople knew the Roman army was not far away and that if they defected to Hannibal, once his army moved on the Romans would extract a terrible revenge. Rome continued to win the political battle for the allied populations' allegiance. Fabius's strategy was effective, but its ultimate success depended on maintaining the political will of the Senate and Roman people. Doing so was difficult in a society accustomed to destroying its enemies by decisive victories. For his efforts Fabius earned the nickname Cunctator (the Delayer), and people did not always use it affectionately. Ultimately he would win the name Fabius Maximus (the Greatest), and his strategy of delay passed into military history as the Fabian strategy.

Fabius's term as dictator expired after six months, and he dutifully resigned his post. Senatorial politics determined the choice of a successor, and a faction rose to power on the platform of directly confronting Hannibal. The Senate abandoned dictatorial rule and reverted to the traditional Roman system of divided military command. The elections produced two new consuls to lead the army—Lucius Aemilius Paullus and Gaius Terentius Varro. The latter was no more talented than Rome's previous commanders who had tried to defeat Hannibal, and he was hotheaded and took things personally. As summer approached,

Hannibal moved from his base in Apulia and attacked a small Roman garrison in the town of Cannae. His goal was to draw the Roman army into a fight. Varro obliged, and on August 2, 216 BCE, the armies met in southeastern Italy at the battle of Cannae.

Shortly after sunrise, Varro moved his army across from the Carthaginian camp and took up a position with the Aufidus River on his right flank. Varro's army comprised nearly seventy thousand Roman and allied foot soldiers and six thousand horse cavalry. Hannibal's army numbered thirty-five thousand infantry, eleven thousand horse cavalry, and a few thousand light infantry, skirmishers, and slingers.[21] The legion's cavalry under the command of the co-consul, Aemilius Paullus, anchored the Romans' right wing. The left wing was comprised of four thousand allied cavalry. The Roman center arranged itself in double formation, and the maniples deployed with a smaller front but with deeper ranks. Varro intended to carry out a traditional Roman infantry attack and cut straight through the Carthaginian center. He acted almost as if the enemy cavalry did not exist.

Hannibal formed up opposite the Roman mass. In front of the Roman cavalry on the right wing he placed his Spanish and Celtic heavy cavalry, some seven thousand strong. Opposite the legion cavalry on the Roman left were four thousand Numidian horsemen. In the center of the line Hannibal deployed his weakest troops, Celtic and Spanish light infantry. Anchoring the ends of the infantry line were large phalanxes of heavy African infantry. After forming his infantry in a straight line, Hannibal redeployed his center units outward and facing the Roman center. The Carthaginian line bowed outward toward the Roman line, forming a crescent. Hasdrubal commanded the Spanish and Celtic cavalry while Maharbal, perhaps the greatest cavalry commander of the war, commanded the Numidians. Hannibal and Mago commanded the center. On the trumpet's sound, both armies' skirmishers moved into position and began throwing their javelins. The Balearic slingers on the Carthaginian side rained down stone and lead shot on the Roman formations, wounding Aemilius Paullus. The armies moved toward one another with a great roar.

The Spanish and Celtic cavalry, outnumbering the Roman horsemen by more than two to one, smashed into the Roman right wing. Polybius notes that the Roman cavalry force immediately came apart. During the wild melee, many were slaughtered or driven into the river. Those who fled were cut down without mercy. On the other wing the Numidians and the allied cavalry were locked in a deadly struggle, and neither side was able to gain a decisive advantage. In the center the

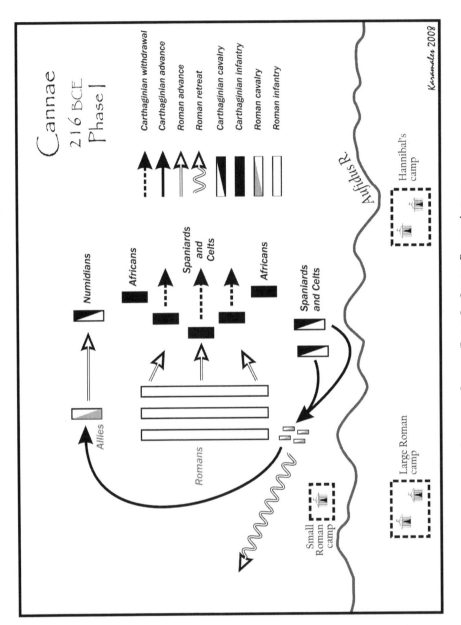

BATTLE OF CANNAE: PHASE I—INITIAL ROMAN ATTACK

46

Roman infantry gradually drove the crescent bulge of the Carthaginian line back. First the line was hammered even with the African phalanxes that anchored it. Then it was pressed back farther. As the Carthaginian center gradually flexed under the pressure of the Roman assault, Roman units were drawn deeper and deeper into the V-shaped line. The Romans fought up a slight incline, and the more forward their units progressed, the more compressed they became. After some time, almost the entire Roman infantry was pressed into the interior of the V. Still the Carthaginian center gave ground.

Having driven the Roman cavalry from the field, Hasdrubal reformed his units and rode completely around and behind the Roman line to join the battle between the Roman allied and Numidian cavalry. There the allied cavalry was crushed between the two Carthaginian cavalry forces and fled the field. Hasdrubal reformed his cavalry again, this time sending the Numidians in pursuit of the allied units so they could not rejoin the battle. The Roman infantry was now totally committed into the V that Hannibal's retreating infantry had created. The Romans were so tightly compressed that they could no longer maneuver in any direction but forward. They continued to cut their way through the Carthaginian center, which, under the command of Hannibal himself, still held. At this critical moment the African phalanxes that had been anchoring the infantry line turned obliquely inward and attacked the compacted Roman formations' flanks. The Romans found themselves jammed together like packed cattle. In Polybius's words, "They were caught between the two divisions of the enemy, and they no longer kept their compact formations but turned singly or in companies to deal with the enemy who was falling on their flanks."[22]

All that was left was to block the Roman retreat and completely envelop the packed Roman infantry. Having assured himself that the allied cavalry was clear of the field, Hasdrubal's heavy cavalry attacked the Roman rear with tremendous shock. Unable to move in any direction, the Roman army was massacred where it stood. Within a few hours, it was over.

Livy tells us that of the original Roman force of 70,000 men, 45,000 infantry and 2,700 cavalry were killed.[23] From other passages in Livy it emerges that 19,300 were taken prisoner,[24] some men having reached the Roman camp and surrendered later. Many senators, sons of prominent families, and government officials had gone to war at Cannae. When the Senate next convened, 177 vacancies had to be filled after the casualties suffered at Cannae.[25] The Carthaginians lost 6,000 men, most (4,000) of whom were Celtic infantry fighting in the center of the line. Another 1,500 Africans and Spanish infantry died as well as about

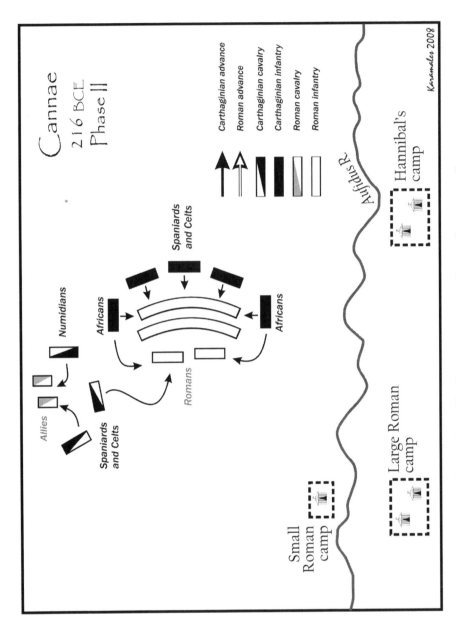

Cannae
216 BCE
Phase II

Carthaginian advance
Roman advance
Carthaginian cavalry
Carthaginian infantry
Roman cavalry
Roman infantry

Kerander 2008

Spaniards and Celts

Numidians

Africans

Africans

Romans

Spaniards and Celts

Allies

Spaniards and Celts

Aufidus R.

Hannibal's camp

Small Roman camp

Large Roman camp

BATTLE OF CANNAE: PHASE II—DESTRUCTION OF THE ROMAN CAVALRY AND ENVELOPMENT

48

500 cavalrymen. The total butcher's bill was 54,200 men heaped in an area roughly the size of Central Park. Few men, before or since, have witnessed such a sight.[26] Livy described the battlefield after the fighting ended:

> On the following day, as soon as it dawned, they set about gathering the spoils and viewing the carnage, which was shocking, even to enemies. So many thousands of Romans were lying, foot and horse promiscuously, according as accident had brought them together, either in battle or flight. Some, whom their wounds, pinched by the morning cold, had roused, as they were rousing up, covered with blood, from the midst of the heaps of slain, were overpowered by the enemy.
>
> Some too they found lying alive with their thighs and hams cut, laying bare their necks and throats, bid them drain the blood that remained in them. Some were found with their heads plunged into the earth, which they had excavated; having thus, as it appeared, made pits for themselves, and having suffocated themselves by overwhelming their faces with the earth which they threw over them.
>
> A living Numidian, with lacerated nose and ears, stretched beneath a lifeless Roman who lay upon him, principally attracted the attention of all; for when the Roman's hands were powerless to grasp his weapon, turning from rage to madness, he had died in the act of tearing his antagonist with his teeth.[27]

Hannibal had achieved his great victory over the Romans. In the three battles of Trebia, Trasimene, and Cannae, the Romans' cost in military manpower had been horrendous. No less than 20 percent of the entire Roman population of military age had been killed, captured, or wounded.[28] Hannibal's army, meanwhile, was intact and capable of further offensive action. Polybius says that while Hannibal and Maharbal were looking out over the blood-soaked plain, Maharbal pressed his commander to strike at Rome itself. "You follow," Maharbal said, "I'll go ahead with the cavalry—they'll know I've come, before they know I'm coming." Maharbal said he could be in Rome in five days. Hannibal, perhaps moved by the magnitude of the slaughter he had inflicted, refused. In frustration Maharbal shouted, "So the gods haven't given everything to one man: you know how to win, Hannibal, but you don't know how to use a victory."[29] Although the war continued for another fifteen years, Hannibal never attacked Rome.

Choosing not to strike directly at the heart of the Roman political establishment and decapitate its leadership remains one of the more puzzling aspects of Hannibal's campaign. The usual answer is that Hannibal had left behind his siege machinery in Spain, and after the Scipios, who were operating south of the Ebro River, had cut that route of supply, he had no chance of getting the equipment. This excuse is hardly convincing. The siege machinery of the day was relatively simple and could have been easily fabricated from the resources within Hannibal's zone of operations. As for technical expertise, captured military and civilian experts were surely available.[30] Why, then, did Hannibal not attack Rome?

First, even if Maharbal's cavalry could have reached Rome in five days, as he said, Hannibal's main army was still more than 250 miles from the city. His army was tired and needed reprovisioning and repair before it could begin the march. Moreover, the towns and populations along the route were not friendly, and they would encounter more unfriendly towns the closer he was to Rome. Second, once Hannibal arrived outside the city's walls, sufficient Roman forces within and near the city would defend it. There were the two *legiones urbanae* raised at the beginning of the year, Marcellus's fifteen hundred men at Ostia and the marines he had sent to Teanum Sidicinum, and all the able-bodied men of the city who could be pressed into service, including slaves, some of whom were already armed. These circumstances made it unlikely that Hannibal could have taken the city by a coup de main.[31] The last possibility was a siege of the city, but Hannibal dared not place Rome under siege. A siege would have tied him down in a single place. Every army in Italy would head for Rome and Hannibal's army. With his movement and tactical flexibility lost, he would be forced into a battle of attrition against a numerically superior force, again a battle he would eventually lose. His decision not to attack Rome made sound military sense. Still, Maharbal may have been right. The defeat at Cannae sent the Roman political leadership into shock. Although the Roman manpower base was nowhere near depletion, it took considerable time to raise, equip, and train new armies. Had Hannibal moved on Rome immediately after Cannae, the Senate's political will might have broken.[32] Hannibal, the daring gambler, refused to roll the dice.

These were dark days for Rome, but darker days lay ahead. It is sometimes forgotten that despite the renewed Fabian strategy's success in preventing Hannibal from destroying any more Roman armies on such a magnitude, Hannibal continued to inflict defeats on the Roman army. In 212 BCE he cost the Romans sixteen thousand casualties at Herdonea. A year later at the second battle of Herdonea,

Hannibal killed the Roman commander and eleven of his twelve military tribunes as well as thirteen thousand troops. He won again at Numistro in 210 BCE, and in 209 BCE twice defeated Marcellus at Canusium. In 208 Hannibal ambushed a Roman army and killed both consuls.[33] In addition, Roman historians have tended to minimize the number of Italian allies that defected to Hannibal. In 216 BCE Capua went over to Hannibal, and by 212 BCE more than 40 percent of Rome's Italian allies, including the Campanians, could no longer supply troops to Rome. But a more important indication that Hannibal's strategy may have been succeeding was that in 209 BCE twelve of the thirty Latin colonies refused to supply their troop contingents for the Roman army on the grounds that their men were mistreated by Roman commanders.[34] By 210 BCE Rome was on the verge of losing the political war.

SPAIN

While Italy suffered under Hannibal's campaign, the military operations of the Scipio brothers—*duo fulmina belli*—met with success. In the summer of 218 BCE, Gnaeus Scipio landed in Spain at Emporiae at the head of a Roman army. He immediately began moving south to occupy the territory north of the Ebro River. He captured a few small towns along the route and recruited some Spanish tribes to join the Roman effort. Hanno, the Carthaginian general in command of the district north of the Ebro, was occupied putting down a revolt in the interior and made no effort to interfere. When Scipio moved farther south and reached Cissa near Tarraco, Hanno marched to intercept him. The Romans defeated the Carthaginians in a pitched battle, and the main Carthaginian base at Tarraco north of the Ebro fell to the Romans. A Carthaginian counterattack to drive the Romans off failed, and Gnaeus Scipio went into winter quarters at Tarraco. With the capture of Tarraco, the territory north of the Ebro River was securely in Roman hands, effectively preventing any reinforcements getting through to Hannibal.

In the spring of 217 BCE the Carthaginians attempted to dislodge the Romans. Hasdrubal approached the mouth of the Ebro with a large army supported by his fleet. Gnaeus Scipio crushed the Carthaginians in a great victory that also broke the Carthaginian naval hold on the Spanish coast.[35] The way was now open for the Romans to advance farther south, using their fleet to protect their line of communications along the coast. Shortly thereafter Publius Scipio arrived with reinforcements to support his brother. With the Roman armies now at full strength, the Scipios advanced on Saguntum, which they captured with the help of a Spanish chieftain who betrayed the Carthaginians. Then the armies went into winter quarters.

The next year Hasdrubal was reenforced by the arrival of Himilco with an army from Carthage. The combined armies maneuvered on the Ebro's south bank to attack Dertosa, an important town controlling the coastal road, the passage of the river, and the entrance to the valley leading to the interior. If Hasdrubal drove the Romans from the town, he would be able to cross the Ebro and pursue them northward, opening the way for Carthaginian reinforcements to reach Hannibal in Italy. The Roman armies held, however, and halted the Carthaginian advance. The Carthaginian defeat provoked an uprising against them by the Spanish tribes, and many came over to the Romans. The Scipios quickly reestablished their control over the coastal road as far south as Saguntum. Lacking sufficient manpower to move farther south and denied reinforcements from Rome, the Scipios held their position for the next two years. The Carthaginians were also stretched thin as they were forced to put down another series of revolts among the tribes.

In North Africa a revolt led by the powerful tribal chief Syphax had prevented Carthage from sending any reinforcements to Spain. In 213 BCE the revolt ended, freeing manpower for the Spanish theater. Two armies—one under the command of Hasdrubal, son of Gisgo, and the other under Mago—arrived in Spain to support Hasdrubal Barca. The Scipios had not received any reinforcements since 217 BCE. The need to garrison the captured towns had forced the Romans to rely heavily on mercenaries their tribal allies supplied. In 212 BCE the Scipios took the offensive and divided their army. Two-thirds of the Roman force under Publius Scipio moved toward Castulo to engage the armies of Mago and Hasdrubal, son of Gisgo. The remaining Roman forces under Gnaeus Scipio moved toward the army of Hasdrubal Barca.[36] The Roman armies were cut off and decimated when their tribal allies proved unreliable, with some defecting to the Carthaginians just before the fighting began. The Scipio brothers were killed, and the remnants of the Roman army fled, finally stopping on the Ebro River's north bank. The road to Italy was open once again.

Why didn't the Carthaginian generals mass their armies, cross the Alps, and reinforce Hannibal? Had they done so they might have been able to deal Rome a fatal blow. The answer probably lies in an old quarrel that had broken out between the Barca family and the government representatives who were sent along with the Carthaginian army. Or the three generals may have wanted to exploit the success for their own advantage and refused to cooperate with Hannibal's colleagues.[37] Perhaps the Iberian allies were becoming restless and their loyalty was in doubt. While the generals argued among themselves, the Roman army's remnants, some nine thousand men, reestablished the line at the Ebro and held it against Carthaginian probing attacks until Gaius Nero and Roman reinforcements arrived. The experienced Roman commander took command and stabilized the Roman line of defense. The Carthaginians' chance to reinforce Hannibal slipped away. Scipio arrived the following spring with ten thousand infantry, a thousand cavalry, and thirty ships to take command in Spain. The road to Italy was blocked, and it would never be open again.

The war with Hannibal continued for fifteen more years. After Cannae, Rome mobilized its large manpower reserves and placed two hundred thousand men under arms, with half of them facing Hannibal and the rest committed in Spain, Sicily, and Greece. Hannibal roamed Italy, slashing at any Roman army that came within reach, but Rome persisted in its Fabian strategy in Italy while Roman armies struck at Spain and Sicily. Two major attempts to reinforce Hannibal's army by land and sea failed. By 210 BCE Hannibal had been contained in southern Italy, Hasdrubal was being pressed back in Spain, and Hannibal's Greek allies were checkmated. For eight years Rome had successfully fought a defensive war on three fronts to a stalemate. Now the counteroffensive began.

3

The Armies

AT THE CONCLUSION of the Third Punic War the Roman army destroyed Carthage so completely that few Carthaginian records survived. What we know of the Carthaginian armies comes mostly from their Roman enemies' accounts. Carthage usually maintained no standing army at all, although it seems probable a small band of armed citizens, about fifteen hundred men, might have been permanently organized for military service. By law this force could not be deployed outside the *chora* (urban district) of Carthage, suggesting it might have been only a civil guard to guarantee the authority of Carthage's civilian government. When arms were needed, the Carthaginians used their vast wealth to raise a mercenary force under the direction of Carthaginian commanders. It is unlikely that the Carthaginian armies in Spain and under Hannibal had more than thirty thousand troops drawn from Carthage itself.

THE CARTHAGINIAN ARMY

Before their wars with the Romans, Carthaginian troops fought in an infantry phalanx supported by chariots.[1] During the Punic Wars the infantry phalanx remained the basic combat formation and used armor and weapons similar to those of the Greeks. Metal helmets, greaves, linen cuirasses, round shields, two-handed pikes, and short swords, all typical of the Greek infantry of Alexander and Pyrrhus, were the Carthaginian infantry's standard kit. When the texts refer to Hannibal's or Hasdrubal's African infantry, it is the Carthaginian infantry that is meant. When deployed with a line of elephants, the African infantry phalanxes were a formidable force. The African infantry phalanxes trapped the Roman army at Cannae. They were an elite force, and Hannibal and others depended on them greatly. After the battle of Trasimene, the Africans were reequipped with captured Roman weapons and armor. The Carthaginians replaced the long pike with the Roman *pilum* (javelin) and retrained the infantry in Roman tactics. With Carthage unable to replace its battle losses, the African-Carthaginian elite infantry units gradually disappeared from the Carthaginian armies through sickness and battlefield attrition.

Carthaginian light troops were recruited from among the Libyans and the Moors. Moorish bowmen served at Zama, and the Carthaginians themselves fielded troops of archers armed with the composite bow characteristic of Near Eastern armies for centuries. The Carthaginians were also well equipped with an artillery arm organized along similar lines found in the Hellenic armies of the Successors. Some idea of the numbers and type of artillery available to the Carthaginian armies can be gained from what Scipio found when he captured the arsenal in New Carthage: 120 large catapults, 281 smaller catapults, 23 large ballistae, and 52 smaller ballistae. At the end of the Second Punic War, Carthage surrendered 2,000 pieces of artillery.

Hannibal's army was comprised of a mix of soldiers from many lands and cultures, a characteristic of Carthaginian mercenary armies for almost a century. Carthage made no attempt to organize these different troops into a uniform force that used the same weapons and tactics; instead, each native group fought in its own way under the command of its own chief. To a great degree any Carthaginian army's success depended on the general's talent and his ability to hold these various forces together and to find their most effective uses. A Carthaginian army included Carthaginians, Liby-Phoenicians, Numidians, Spaniards, and Celts, whom the Romans called "Gauls."[2] As the war in Italy wore on, significant contingents of Italians, including Samnites, Lucanians, and Bruttians, composed Hannibal's army. When Hannibal was forced to withdraw from Italy in 203 BCE, eighteen thousand Italians went with him. At the battle of Zama, these Italian troops formed Hannibal's third and most reliable line and stood fast until the end.[3] Greek troops also formed part of the Carthaginian armies near the end. Four thousand Macedonians fought at Zama.[4]

Without the tribal manpower of the Spanish, Gallic, and Apennine tribes, Hannibal's war against Rome would have been impossible. The Romans also employed tribal contingents in large numbers, first in Spain and then in Africa when Scipio used contingents of Numidian cavalry and infantry at the battles of the Tower of Agathocles, the Great Plains, and Zama. Sometimes these tribes fought out of loyalty to the commander, as when Scipio succeeded in gaining the Spanish tribes' loyalty through fair treatment and respect, and sometimes they fought as mercenaries for one side or the other for pay. Tribal mercenary contingents played a much larger role in the Carthaginian armies. The danger of mercenaries was brought home to the Romans in 212 BCE, however, when the Scipio brothers hired twenty thousand Celtiberians to augment their army. With this new manpower the Scipios moved to engage the Carthaginians. Hasdrubal Barca, the Carthaginian commander, paid the Celtiberians to do nothing and go home, leaving the Scipios stranded on the battlefield with insufficient troops. Both Scipios were killed and six years of Roman gains were wiped out in a single day.[5]

SPANIARDS

Hannibal's Spanish infantry was recruited from the Celtiberian tribes, a people descended from Iberians and Celts who, by the time of the Punic Wars, had formed a distinct culture. The Celtiberians occupied Spain's central plateau. They supplied units of light and heavy infantry and cavalry. These soldiers wore a short white tunic gathered at the waist by a wide leather belt. Nobles used bronze helmets of Greek design while the average soldier made due with a simple helmet of leather or bronze with attached neck and cheek guards. Spanish heavy infantry wore the scale armor, lamellar armor, or chain mail of the day, with the latter being an innovation of the Celts and standard issue in the Roman armies of the period. A large oblong shield similar to the Roman scutum afforded personal protection. Light infantry used the *caetra*, a light, round buckler shield of distinct Spanish design. Made of leather, wicker, or wood, it was slightly convex with a metal boss and handgrip. Spanish light infantry relied on speed and agility in sword-and-buckler combat. One important characteristic of the Spanish infantry was its tradition of operating in close concert with the cavalry, allowing the Spanish cavalry to quickly exploit any gaps the infantry opened in the enemy line.[6]

The Spanish heavy infantry had strong and courageous fighters who were every bit a match for Roman infantry. These infantrymen carried a throwing javelin similar to the Roman pilum called a *soliferreum*. Made entirely of iron, it was about 180 to 190 centimeters in length and had a leaf-shaped barbed blade. Iberian infantry also carried the *falarica*, a shaft of pine with a long iron head around which pitch or tow was wrapped and lit aflame to create an incendiary weapon. Both types of Spanish infantry carried the *falcata*, the Iberians' main weapon. Made of fine Spanish iron (almost steel), the slightly curved sword had a single-edged blade for the first two-thirds of its 55- to 63-centimeter length and was 5 centimeters wide at its broadest point. The remainder of the blade was double edged and sharply pointed at the tip. The hilt and blade were forged in a single piece, giving the falcata great strength. Its design was perfect for both cutting and thrusting. Hannibal was sufficiently impressed with the weapon to equip his own Carthaginian troops with it. To some extent his victory at Cannae may have stemmed from the Spanish sword's superiority in close combat over the short sword of Greek origin that the Romans used at the time. Scipio, too, was impressed with the Spanish sword, and after capturing New Carthage, he ordered the Spanish blacksmiths to equip his army with them. With some design changes, it became the *gladius hispanicus*, the Roman army's basic infantry weapon.

Carthaginian armies also employed military specialists like Balearic slingers, who carried two slings, one for long distances and one for short. The long-range sling could cast a stone the size of a tennis ball almost three hundred yards. Smaller plumb-shaped lead shot could be fired along a flat trajectory like a modern bullet and easily hit and kill its target at a hundred yards. These slingers were the finest in the ancient world, and for almost six hundred years one army after another hired them as mercenaries. Diodorus mentions Mauritanian archers and Numidian cavalry as other military mechanics found in Carthaginian armies.[7]

Perhaps the most powerful arm of the Carthaginian armies was the Spanish heavy cavalry, or *jinetes*. The Spanish cavalryman was armed with a long lance fitted with a leaf-shaped socketed head and an iron ferrule fixed to the butt. For close combat he also carried the falcata sword and the caetra buckler shield for defense. Spain was excellent horse-breeding country, and the Spanish mounts were strong and accustomed to traversing mountainous terrain, traits that made Spanish cavalry extremely flexible in deployment. The jinete did not use a saddle, making do with a blanket and girth, and he controlled the animal with a bridle and bit. A particularly useful practice of the Spanish tribal cavalry was carrying a second infantryman into battle on the horse's back. The extra infantryman would then dismount and fight on foot. Mago's cavalry used this trick when he ambushed the Romans at the Trebia River, and the Spanish cavalry broke the Roman cavalry at Cannae. One reason Scipio sought to gain the tribes' loyalty during the Spanish campaign was to persuade the Spanish cavalry to change sides. The jinetes made a powerful and effective combat arm.

GAULS AND CELTS

Hannibal recruited large cohorts of Celtic infantry from the Gallic tribes north of the Po River. The Gauls first attacked Rome in 390 BCE and sacked the city. Over the next century they invaded central Italy repeatedly. Only seven years before Hannibal invaded Italy an army of seventy thousand Gauls had crossed the Apennines in an attempt to bloc Roman expansion. Given their history of conflict with Rome, that the Gauls made willing allies for Hannibal is not surprising. They composed 40 percent of Hannibal's army when it arrived in Italy. Organized into clans, these tribal warriors lived for war, glory, and plunder. The Gaul was a heavy infantryman, equipped with a helmet, large shield, and long sword. Although the Gauls manufactured the best chain mail of the day, some fought in the traditional Celtic fashion, naked and without armor. These large people terrified the Romans with their long lime-washed hair, war dances, and frightening battle cries. Their attacks were wild and ferocious, and they had the unnerving habit of taking heads.[8] Roman historians record the Gauls' weaknesses as not having endurance, being prone to panic, and quitting the battle once they had taken an enemy's head or acquired enough booty.[9]

The Celts fought in bodies of heavy infantry and rarely as skirmishers. Their basic weapon was a seventy-five- to eighty-centimeter-long double-edged sword with a rounded point. They employed it as a slashing weapon, swinging it round the head and bringing it down like an ax. Used in this manner the Celtic sword required considerable space to wield, and the Celtic warrior fought mostly as an individual combatant, relying on agility for his defense. The Celtic shield was a large oblong device made of oak planks that were reinforced by a felt or hide covering. The shield's large size was necessary because many Celts fought without armor. The Celtic spear was not usually used in war, but the Celts were quick to adopt the Roman pilum. Celtic cavalry was comprised of the nobility, and except for a smaller round shield, the men were equipped with the same weapons as the infantry. At Cannae four thousand Celtic nobles fought as heavy cavalry. Celtic troops were difficult to control once engaged; consequently, Carthaginian generals often used them as shock troops to strike the enemy's center. This deployment, of course, produced heavy casualties. As the war wore on, they gradually replaced their traditional weapons from captured Roman stocks.

NUMIDIANS

Among the best and most reliable cavalry were the Numidian light cavalry. These sometime enemies of Carthage, who at other times served out of common interests but mostly as paid mercenaries, came from Numidia, or approximately the area of present-day Morocco. Living on horseback from an early age, Numidian cavalrymen rode bareback with only a neck strap of plaited rope for a harness. Without a bit or bridle, they relied on voice commands, heel pressure, and a stick to control their mounts. The Numidians' main weapons were thrown short javelins and light spears. Normally armed with small round shields, they sometimes wore an animal skin over their arms in the shield's place. They seem as well to have been experts with the sling. They were specialists in maneuver warfare, often attacking, retreating, maneuvering, and attacking again at a different place on the battlefield. They were particularly useful in reconnaissance, raiding, and ambush. Numidian cavalry lacked the weight of heavy cavalry and were less useful as shock troops. At Cannae they were unable to drive off the Roman cavalry on their own and needed the Spanish heavy cavalry's aid. Once the enemy was broken, however, the Numidians were the perfect force to conduct the pursuit.

ELEPHANTS

The first Western military commander to encounter the elephant as an instrument of war was Alexander, who discovered them in his wars against the Persians, and they, in turn, probably obtained the animals from the Indians. The elephants of the Indian general Porus caused Alexander's army great problems at the battle of the Hydaspes River. During the wars of Alexander's successors, using the elephant in battle became common among the armies of the eastern Mediterranean states. The Carthaginians encountered the elephant in their wars with Greece and took to capturing and training the African forest elephant for their own armies. Once native to Morocco, Algeria, and the edge of the Sahara Desert, the now-extinct African forest elephant was smaller (two and a half meters at the shoulder) than the famed African bush elephant or Indian elephant (both three and a half meters).

Elephants rarely breed in captivity and must be captured in the wild before being trained for war. They are usually captured at ages younger than five, but they are not large enough to train for combat until in their teens. Elephants reach their full size in their twenties and are in their prime for war duty while in their thirties and forties. In the wild the animal lives into its sixties but rarely survives its forties in captivity. The elephant is surefooted, not prone to falls, and can easily negotiate a one-to-six gradient with little effort. They walk at three miles per hour and can easily cover fifteen to twenty miles a day while carrying a heavy load. Without loads, the animal can average forty miles per day for a week. They love water and are good swimmers. Hannibal had difficulty in getting his elephants across the Rhône River because they had been raised in captivity and had forgotten how to swim.

The Carthaginians first encountered the war elephant in their conflict with Pyrrhus in Sicily from 278 to 276 BCE. Carthage immediately established an elephant corps, which replaced the horse-drawn chariot as the primary instrument for delivering shock. During the First Punic War, Carthage maintained an elephant corps of three hundred animals that were housed in stables in the city's casement walls. Hannibal took thirty-seven elephants with him when he crossed the Alps, all of which survived the journey. At the battle of the Trebia River he used his elephants to anchor his infantry's wings, and the Roman auxiliaries collapsed under their attack. When the battle was over, twenty-nine of the elephants had died either of battle wounds or exposure. Of the remaining eight, only one, Surus, survived the winter. When Hannibal lost his sight in one eye to infection during the Arno marshes crossing, his officers convinced him that he would see better while atop the elephant. In 215–214 BCE the Carthaginians smuggled forty elephants past the Roman naval blockade to aid Hannibal in southern Italy. In 209 BCE Hannibal used these animals to break the Roman lines in his battle with Marcellus.

The elephant was an important combat asset and played an important tactical role. It frightened those soldiers who had never seen the animal, and unless a horse had been trained around them, elephants spooked the cavalry mounts. In Claudius's reign, the Romans took them to Britain to impress and cower the local chieftains. Under the control of their handlers, or *mahouts*, a charge of rampaging elephants against an infantry formation could have tremendous shock effect. Persia, India, and Greece used them as platforms for archers and javelin throwers, as anchors for the center or ends of infantry lines, and because of their height, as screens behind which to shift cavalry units. Perched atop a twelve-foot-tall animal, a commander had an excellent view of the battlefield.

Like all implements of war, however, using the elephant had its disadvantages. Experienced light infantry skirmishers could meet the elephants ahead of the infantry line and strike them with darts, swords, and javelins, wounding them into a rage. Once enraged, an elephant became uncontrollable and had a tendency to turn back in the direction from which it came, running over the very formations that had launched it. An out-of-control elephant would rumble around the battlefield and disrupt everyone's plans. Dio Cassius says that to prevent their rampages, Carthaginian mahouts carried a large iron spike and a hammer. If the elephant could not be brought under control by normal means, the mahout would drive the spike into the elephant's brain, killing it instantly. An effective defensive tactic was to move behind the elephant and cut its hamstring tendon.

Why did Hannibal take elephants along on his difficult march? Certainly the Romans were familiar with the elephant and knew how to deal with it. The

Romans had first been routed by an elephant charge in 280 BCE during the war with Pyrrhus. Five years later at the battle of Beneventum, the Romans killed two and captured eight of the elephants used against them. Although the elephant was an expensive and prestigious weapon, it represented no significant military advantage against the legions. Most probably Hannibal used them as propaganda instruments. He took them along to impress the Gauls and convince them to join his campaign. Possibly he also displayed them before Roman allied towns to convince their inhabitants that Hannibal's army was a modern fighting force bent on serious business and that it would be in their interest to join him.

The Carthaginians' use of elephants in the Spanish theater of operations is easier to understand. Elephants were simply an important part of the Carthaginian army and were well integrated into the Carthaginian field commanders' tactical thinking and designs. Thus, Scipio had to contend with Carthaginian elephants in every major battle he fought there. One reason for Scipio's attack on the Carthaginian flanks at Ilipa was to avoid Hasdrubal's thirty-two war elephants that anchored the center line. At Zama, Scipio also faced an army equipped with war elephants. So seriously did Scipio take their possible use that he rearranged his infantry formations and created lanes between units through which the attacking elephants could pass without disrupting the Roman formations. Eleven elephants died at Zama. Scipio gave the rest to Massinissa and took some to Rome for his triumph.

TACTICS

The Carthaginian armies were such a mixture of groups, weapons, and languages that they could not be disciplined to a standard set of tactics. It is testimony to the brilliance of Carthaginian commanders that for more than a century they were able to field these kinds of armies and wield them effectively in war. Carthaginian field commanders were known for their personal bravery and courage, traits that often endeared them to tribal and clan units. Similarly, Scipio gained the respect of the Spanish chiefs but did so through a combination of military success, clemency, and fair treatment. Scipio was hailed by some Spanish tribes as their king, and they adopted him as their patron and chief.[10] But Carthaginian commanders could also be ruthless in disciplining their troops with beatings and death sentences, hardly surprising for an officer corps well acquainted with seeing comrades who failed in battle crucified in the public square of Carthage. Truly the soldiers of the Carthaginian armies often had more to fear from their commanders than from the enemy.

Because the nature of the Carthaginian armies made following a standard tactical system impossible, their combat effectiveness depended heavily on the tactical imagination their Carthaginian commanders, who had to employ their different types of units creatively to obtain maximum collective effect. At the same time they had to weave the battlefield tapestry into some sort of tactical whole to achieve victory. This task was not easy, and modern commanders might well ponder the difficulties involved. By contrast, the Roman allied contingents—Latins, Etruscans, Campanians, and Italian Greeks—were already organized along Roman military lines and could be more easily integrated within Roman tactical doctrine and practice.[11]

Although the Carthaginian infantry was superb, Carthaginian armies in general, and Hannibal's in particular, relied more on cavalry as the combat arm of decision and on infantry as a platform of maneuver. This emphasis is not surprising. Close contacts with the Greeks in the eastern Mediterranean made the Carthaginians thoroughly familiar with Alexander's and Pyrrhus's military systems, which also used cavalry as the arm of decision and infantry as a platform of maneuver. Their experience with Pyrrhus had taught Carthaginian commanders that a strong infantry phalanx was not decisive by itself and had to be made more mobile and flexible to defend against attack. It was Carthaginian military genius to reform its infantry in this manner and then use it as a platform for cavalry maneuver.[12]

Another factor led the Carthaginians to stress cavalry in their tactical doctrine. Because Numidia bordered Libya-Phoenicia, Carthage was frequently forced to defend Libya and its valued grain crop against Numidian cavalry raids. The border's length made fixed fortifications expensive and impractical against the nomadic Numidians. Thus, Carthage developed its own cavalry to deal with the problem. Consequently, Carthage developed a tactical doctrine that stressed using the horse over infantry, or exactly the reverse of the Roman tactical doctrine. All things considered, however, Carthaginian armies were fragile entities subject to indiscipline and sudden fragmentation if events escalated beyond their commanders' control. The Carthaginian commanders who faced Scipio and other Roman generals, however, rarely let this happen.

Because Carthaginian commanders could not employ a standard tactical system, their trick was to use the various units in roles that maximized their effectiveness while sustaining an overall tactical plan specific to each battle situation. It is possible, however, to discern some tactical constants or general rules that appear to have governed Carthaginian tactics. The first rule was always to maximize shock and surprise. The ambush at Trasimene is an excellent example. Commanders frequently engaged while the enemy was still in column of march. Another rule was to engage the enemy only after he had worked hard to transit such obstacles as a river, stream, or forest, as the Romans were forced to do at the Trebia. A third rule was to use the terrain to their advantage and always tempt the enemy to fight uphill. Carthaginian generals often anchored their infantry lines with heavy formations of dependable phalanx infantry on the wings that could swing against the pivot points of an extended infantry line, forcing the enemy into a smaller and smaller area. Sometimes elephants supported by either infantry or cavalry were used to carry out this maneuver. Cavalry tactics centered on consistently using horsemen to drive the enemy cavalry from the field as a prelude to returning and staging a shock attack against the enemy infantry's rear or exposed flank. The final rule seems to have been that if none of these advantages could be obtained, then they avoided the battle. If the Carthaginian commander could not fight on his terms, he would usually not fight at all.

THE ROMAN ARMY

From the beginning Rome's army was always called the *legio* (legion). The term originally referred to the armed band Romulus led against Amulius and for which Romulus recruited a thousand men from each tribe.[13] Even at this early date the legion was divided into centuries, which, in turn, formed combat companies called "maniples." The original meaning of the word *maniple* is derived from the word *manus,* meaning a "handful," and refers to the wisp of hay that according to tradition was affixed to the end of a pole and served as the military standard of Romulus's legion.[14] The legion was not the equivalent of a modern regiment in that it contained troops of all arms and was therefore regarded as a complete combined arms army. For centuries the legion was comprised exclusively of Roman citizens called to arms as a part-time militia. Any male citizen whose net worth was at least four thousand asses was eligible for military service from age seventeen to forty-six and remained subject to calls for military service for twenty years in the infantry and ten years in the cavalry. The poorest citizens served in the navy. It was not until around 100 BCE, when Gaius Marius reformed the army, that non-Roman citizens were permitted to serve with regular troops. Military training was haphazard. Boys received their first instruction in arms from their fathers. Once called to active service, the legion was assembled in a conscript camp under the command of veteran military tribunes who then trained the troops in unit combat for several weeks before taking the legion into the field. The legion commander was responsible for further training. Citizen-soldiers expected to be called to arms in times of emergency, to remain on active duty for a short period, and then to return to their farms. Under these circumstances the Romans never developed a professional officer or noncommissioned officer corps during the Republican period.

From the time of the Republic's founding (circa 500 BCE), the earliest Roman military formation was modeled on the Greek hoplite phalanx. The Roman citizen-soldier's weaponry was also Greek and included the short spear, round shield, helmet, armor, greaves, and sword.[15] In the usual case of set-piece battles on level ground against armies using similar formations, the phalanx worked well enough; however, on uneven terrain, the phalanx could not maneuver and tended to break apart. In Rome's wars against the Samnites (340–290 BCE), which were fought in the rugged Apennine hills, valleys, and glens against mobile infantry and competent cavalry, the phalanx proved unworkable and too brittle when struck by surprise attack. In the wars with the Gauls at about the same time, the Gallic armies' highly mobile formations easily enveloped the phalanx's open flanks and crushed it from all sides once the accompanying cavalry was driven from the field. Given that the Roman cavalry was never very good, driving it from the field prior to surrounding the phalanx was not usually difficult.

During and after the Samnite Wars, the Romans gradually replaced the phalanx legion with the manipular legion. During this time the Romans also replaced their heavy Argive shields with the Samnites' larger but lighter wooden scutum shields. The Romans may also have adopted the famous pilum from the Samnites along with the *ciocciara* military boot. This equipment remained standard Roman issue until the end of the imperial period. The manipular legion usually comprised forty-two hundred infantrymen and ten cavalry troops (*turmae*) of thirty horses each. During times of crisis the legion's strength was sometimes increased to fifty-two hundred infantry, although the number of cavalry and *triarii* (the men in the legion's third line) remained the same.[16] The two legions that crossed to Africa under Scipio were even larger, with sixty-two hundred men each.

The manipular legion was the Roman army's basic fighting formation throughout the Punic Wars. However, when Scipio discovered that the legion was too fragile to withstand the massed attacks of the Carthaginian Spanish heavy infantry, he strengthened them by increasing their number to 5,200 men and combining three maniples of infantry (360 men) and 60 velites, or light infantry, into a new combat formation. These new cohorts gradually replaced the maniples until the cohortal legion became their basic fighting formation. The transition from

Manipular Legion

c. 300 ~ 100 BCE

4200 infantry total
(3000 heavy infantry, 1200 light infantry)
300 cavalry

Direction of Attack

Hastati
Principes
Triarii

Frontage approx. 400 - 900 yards

Gap approx.
80 yards

Gap approx.
80 yards

Cavalry Turmae
(Squadron)
10 horses wide x 3 deep

Maniple of Triarii
(armed with Hasta)
10 men wide x 6 deep

Velites (light infantry)
(position after falling
back from skirmishing)

Maniple of Hastati or Principes
(armed with Pilum)
20 men wide x 3 deep

1 century (60 men)

1 century (60 men)

1 maniple (120 men)

Karamandes 2008

THE MANIPULAR LEGION

66

the manipular legion to the cohortal legion seems to have begun during the later stages of the Second Punic War, and it may have originated with Scipio seeking a solution to the maniples' fragility in the face of the ferocious Spanish and Celtic infantry and heavy cavalry. The Roman legion usually deployed with a counterpart force of the same size and organization drawn from Italian allies. Some allied legions had a heavier cavalry section of 600 horses, and the combined legions had 9,000 to 10,000 men. Two Roman legions and two allied legions under the same command made up a consular army of 20,000 men and deployed across a combat front of one and a half miles.

When the manipular legion was introduced, the army also reorganized on the basis of age. The youngest, most agile, and least trained men served as light infantry (velites). Protected by a small circular buckler shield and armed with a sword and a small javelin (*hasta velitaris*), the velites acted as a skirmisher. There were a thousand velites to a legion. A second class of fighting men, the *hastati,* who were older and more experienced, occupied the legion's front line. The hastati, from the word *hasta* (spear), wore protective body armor—a helmet, a breastplate, and greaves—and carried a scutum shield. Over the breastplate they sometimes wore a nine-inch square brass plate called the "heart preserver." They were later equipped with chain mail. Armed with a sword, two *pila*, and the scutum shield, the hastati formed the first line of heavy infantry. The center line was comprised of the best and most experienced soldiers (*principes*). Averaging thirty years old, these battle-hardened veterans were equipped in the same manner as the hastati. The third line was comprised of older men, or *triarii*, and constituted the last line of resistance. Armed with the long spear, they lent stability to the formation, and in times of retreat they remained in place and covered the other ranks as they passed through their lines. A legion of forty-two hundred men had a thousand velites, twelve hundred hastati, twelve hundred principes, six hundred triarii, and a hundred or so officers, staff, and noncommissioned officers.

TACTICS

The Roman army's basic tactical unit was the 120-man maniple, comprised of two centuries, or platoons, of 60 soldiers each. An administrative unit without any tactical function, a century originally had 100 men. That number probably proved too large for a single centurion to control, so the army reduced the numbers to between 60 to 80 men but retained the name "century," meaning "one hundred." The army assigned a total of 30 maniples to a legion. The Roman army used this type of organization at the outbreak of the Second Punic War and in the legions Scipio took to Spain.

The key to the legion's flexibility was the relationship between the maniples within each line and the lines of heavy infantry. Each maniple deployed as a small independent phalanx covered by a screen of velite light infantry. The spacing between each soldier allowed independent movement and room for sword fighting within an area of about five square yards. Each maniple was laterally separated from the next by about fifty yards, a distance equal to the maniple's frontage itself. Arranged in line, the maniples were staggered, with the second and third lines covering the gaps in the lines to their front. Each line of infantry maniples was separated from the next by an interval of a hundred yards. The result was the quincunx, or checkerboard formation that permitted flexibility for each maniple and for each soldier to maneuver within it.

The relationship between the infantry lines increased tactical flexibility. After the first line engaged, if it was unable to break the enemy formation or grew tired or completed a battle pulse, it could retire in good order through the gaps left in the second line. The second line then moved forward and continued to press the attack while the first rank rested and regrouped. They could repeat this maneuver several times, resulting usually in a Roman front line of rested fighting men. How this passage of lines was accomplished will be addressed later, but suffice it to say this ability gave the legion an important advantage over its adversaries. Modern studies demonstrate that men engaged in close phalanx combat could sustain the effort no more than ten to fifteen minutes before collapsing from exhaustion. Gaining a respite from the exertion of fighting was vital to sustaining the legion infantry's fighting power over time.[17] The triarii remained in place in the last rank, resting on one knee with their spears angled upward, ready to act as the last line of defense and cover the legion's withdrawal if circumstances required.

Passing through the infantry lines in a planned fashion offered another advantage. In most armies of the period, defeat in the front ranks often turned a battle into a rout. Until the Romans no army had learned how to break contact and conduct a tactical retreat in good order. The manipular formation solved this problem. On command, the maniples of the infantry's first line turned and withdrew through the gaps left in the other two lines. The second rank followed. The triarii covered the retreat with their spears, and the velite light infantry deployed to the front to delay the enemy while the main body withdrew in good order. The ability of each maniple to fight and maneuver independently once the battle had begun further enhanced its tactical flexibility. Scipio seems to have been the first Roman commander to train his men to operate in this manner. In several of Scipio's battles, the maniples' ability to operate independently of the main force by moving to the wings or by extending into a line to overlap the enemy's flanks was critical to victory.

The Roman soldier was the first soldier in history to fight within a combat formation while at the same time remaining somewhat independent of its movements as a unit. He was also the first soldier to rely primarily on the sword instead of the spear. The Roman sword of this period was a short slashing sword of Italian or Greek origin. During the Punic Wars, the legions gradually adopted the Spanish falcata, which they later modified and called the gladius hispanicus. The Roman model was twenty inches long and approximately three inches wide and was made of tough Spanish steel. Because it was stronger in composition than any existing sword and would not break, it provided a psychological advantage to the Roman soldier. To use it well, however, required skill and high-level training. The gladius was primarily a stabbing weapon, so Roman soldiers were trained not to use it as a slashing weapon, the common method of sword use in most armies of the day. The shield parry followed by a sharp underthrust to the chest became the Roman infantry's lethal trademark. In the hands of a disciplined Roman soldier, the gladius became one of the most destructive weapons of all time prior to the invention of the firearm.

The Roman legion had several tactical weaknesses that the Carthaginian generals repeatedly exploited. The first was its lack of a professional senior officer corps. Roman senior officers were civilians—magistrates and politicians—appointed to command the legions during wartime. Worse, the Roman consular system required that a field army have *two* appointed senior commanders who changed command each day. The practice of divided command often made it difficult for the legions to maintain good command direction and made it impossible for the army to become the instrument of a single commander's will, thus also inhibiting tactical innovation. This consular system of selecting Roman generals often produced incompetent or only marginally competent field commanders. Hannibal often studied his adversaries, and thus he frequently chose the day of battle when, in his opinion, his adversary's lesser general had daily command. Moreover, the difficulty of attempting tactical innovation forced Roman commanders to utilize the legion in the same manner over and over again. Carthaginian commanders knew this Roman habit and took great advantage of it.

The Roman army's second weakness was the poor quality of its cavalry. Comprised mostly of the nobility, who could afford the necessary horse, weapons, and equipment, it was the most poorly trained of the combat arms. During the Punic Wars, Roman cavalrymen retained their old habit of using their mounts to arrive at the battlefield, only to dismount and join the fray as infantry in classic Homeric fashion. Roman cavalry seemed ill suited to maintain the charge's direction and tended to break up into clusters of loose formations and wander all over the battlefield. The cavalry used no special armament, preferring instead to carry infantry weapons in addition to the lance. Roman commanders seem to have had little use for the cavalry, resulting in this arm being frequently untrained to function in concert with the infantry. The Romans also seemed to neglect the cavalry's obvious role in reconnaissance and intelligence gathering, rarely employing it in this capacity.

Carthaginian cavalry, by contrast, was the arm of decision, superbly trained, and always used in concert with infantry. In battle after battle, Carthaginian commanders drove the Roman cavalry from the field almost effortlessly, turned, and massacred the Roman infantry, whose flanks were now exposed. Even Scipio was unable to overcome the Roman cavalry's bad habits. He eventually gave up trying to develop the Roman cavalry and simply hired it from allied Spanish and Numidian tribes.

The legion's combat power was not in its tactical brilliance but in the determination, courage, and discipline of its heavy infantry. The legion's greatest strength, however, was also its greatest tactical weakness. Once engaged, the infantry could only maneuver straight ahead or retreat through its own ranks to the rear. Until Scipio's tactical innovations, it could not maneuver in any other manner. It could not turn to face an attack on its flanks, nor could it move to the oblique or form a line to prevent its front from being overlapped. At the Trebia, for example, although the Roman flanks and rear were destroyed, the legion's front line continued to attack forward, eventually cutting through the Carthaginian line and reaching safety. That Roman field commanders were often amateurs or simply lacked the tactical imagination of a leader like Scipio resulted in employing the legion in the same straight-ahead manner time after time.

Because the organizational structures of the Carthaginian and Roman armies were vastly different, the tactical dynamics of their combat units were also different. The Roman arm of decision was its heavy infantry—indeed, the infantry was all it had—and in this sense it was a one-arm army. The Romans' idea was to commit the infantry to the center of the line and let it hack away until the enemy's center formation broke. Given adequate room to swing their swords and if they maintained their organizational integrity, the Roman infantry would eventually hack its way through any infantry formation in the world. Against the Gauls' and Spaniards' open formations, however, combat was often man on man. But whereas the Gallic and other tribal warriors fought as individuals, the Roman soldier could depend on the man to his left or right for help in warding off an attack. Against the Greek phalanx with their long spears, the Romans simply hacked off the spear points of the *sarissae* and moved inside the spear shafts to close with the enemy. Once inside the phalanx, the individual spearman was defenseless, and the Roman buzz saw could do its deadly work. Since the Carthaginians often used Gallic units in open formations as shock troops and Spanish infantry arrayed in traditional phalanx formation to anchor the center line, the Roman infantry usually had the advantage in the heavy fighting there.

Unlike the manner in which Gallic and Spanish troops used the sword, the Roman soldier was trained to stab with his weapon and not slash. Moreover, the legionnaire was trained not to engage the man directly in front of him but the opponent to his immediate right. Using the sword as a slashing weapon required the Carthaginian soldier to raise it above his head and away from his body, exposing his body's entire right side as a target. His shield, held in the left hand, became a useless protective device. Under these circumstances, the Roman soldier striking to his right would cut down the enemy soldier as he raised his slashing sword against the opponent directly to his front. At the battle of Culloden Moor in 1746, the British army rediscovered this technique after the warriors of the highland Scottish clans hacked them to pieces in two successive battles. The British infantry employed the bayonet instead of the sword.

Stabbing to the right provided yet another advantage in close combat. Having struck a target to his right, the Roman infantryman stepped back to pull out the sword. As he did, he moved slightly to his right to get new footing for the next assault. As a result the Roman line tended to move to the right and slightly to the rear. This "inchworming" forced the enemy line to move to the left and forward and to step over the bodies of the dead and wounded. The dynamics of the two lines moving in reaction to one another left the Roman soldier always prepared to meet his next opponent who had to stumble over the dead while watching his footing. Hannibal eliminated this Roman tactical advantage at the battle of Cannae, when he placed his troops on a slight rise and forced the Romans to attack uphill.

SCIPIO AFRICANUS

BATTLE MECHANICS

The battles of the Punic Wars, especially the Second Punic War, were very different in form and dynamics from the military engagements of the classical period that preceded it.[18] Armies of the Punic period were genuine combined arms armies in which different types of troops fought in concert while directed by competent generals who usually did not fight in the midst of their troops but moved about the battle area issuing orders in an attempt to influence the battle. Whereas earlier classical battles had been soldiers' battles, the battles of the Second Punic War were more "generals' battles" in which the abilities of field commanders like Scipio and Hannibal primarily determined victory or defeat.[19] As in all wars, such factors as numbers, fighting, spirit, equipment, and supply still played important roles in deciding the war's outcome, but more than ever in history the quality of generalship now mattered most.

As armies became more complex, their tactical capabilities became more varied, and deciding and directing what tactics to employ and when became vital to their success or failure. Only the commander's decisions before, during, and after the battle could affect events in such magnitude. A good general could avoid battle except on favorable terms, attract allies and suborn those of his opponent, train and motivate his men to fight well and in certain ways, lay ambushes, seize the initiative and strike while his adversary was unprepared, attack at night, plan operational-level maneuvers before the battle, choose competent subordinates to execute them on command, and react quickly to changes in the battle dynamic by ordering his troops to shift tactics or change formations.[20] None of these actions, of course, guaranteed victory, but they would increase the chances of success. The days of a general fighting at the head of his troops were over. War had become too complex.

Three characteristics mark the battles of the Second Punic War as different from preceding battles: symmetry, infantry maneuver, and an emphasis on rear and flank attacks. Earlier battles were asymmetrical in that the opposing infantry forces deployed in an unbalanced fashion; that is, one wing or end of the line was much heavier and deeper than the other. The object was to mass one's forces opposite the enemy line's weakest point. The ensuing attack was designed to unbalance the enemy by prevailing quickly on one end of his line, turning his formation, and forcing the rest of his troops to retreat. Under these tactical conditions, hoplite and phalanx battles were often settled quickly. During the Punic period, however, opposing forces tended to form up symmetrically, with both sides deploying in equal strength along the entire battle line and their different elements positioned directly across from the enemy's elements. Thus, infantry faced infantry, cavalry faced cavalry, and so on. Why this development occurred is unclear.[21] One possibility is that commanders had realized that with the cavalry's increased role, it was imperative to keep the center infantry formations more stable than ever if they were to function as platforms of maneuver. Under these circumstances, turning a flank would unlikely result in the infantry breaking and running. Instead, the infantry was more likely to be cut off, trapped, pressed together, and unable to defend themselves. This new formation explains why Punic battles lasted longer than earlier ones and also why the casualty rates were much higher. Many of the Punic battles were battles of annihilation in which one side was completely destroyed.[22]

A second characteristic of Punic battles was an emphasis on infantry maneuver. Unlike the earlier phalanx that could maneuver only forward and back, the armies of the Punic period were much more tactically sophisticated and capable of maneuver even when under pressure. Hannibal, of course, was an excellent tactical commander, but Scipio was a true master at tactical maneuver, having trained his army in a new tactical array.[23] Scipio's tactical repertoire included the use of flanking infantry columns, fixing attacks, cavalry flank attacks, envelopment, double envelopment, and aggressive pursuit. While these maneuvers were used in earlier times, Scipio developed them to high art and employed them with a brilliance and effectiveness unparalleled in Roman history.

The third characteristic of Punic battles was the decided emphasis on flank, rear, and surprise attack. Earlier battles had almost always been decided by infantry engagements in which one side drove the other from the field.[24] Punic battles were more often decided by some maneuver in which the adversary's infantry forces were not driven off but trapped and killed. Mago's ambush shattered the Roman army at the Trebia, and Hannibal's surprise attack at Trasimene trapped and slaughtered the Roman army. Scipio's cavalry was decisive at Great Plains and again at Zama. The new battle manager generals of the Punic period were professional commanders who could train their troops in sophisticated tactical maneuvers and turn their armies into instruments of their own will.

As the armies were equipped with new tactical capabilities, the Punic battles' dynamics, what Sabin calls "battle mechanics," were also different from those of previous battles. It is probably wise at the outset to note that the common conceptions of ancient military engagements as involving either prolonged shoving matches or melees in which both sides were closely entangled in hand-to-hand combat are false.[25] Either of these circumstances would have produced horrendous casualties on both sides and would have required a level of physical and psychological endurance beyond most human beings' abilities.[26] Moreover, many of the new tactical maneuvers characteristic of the Punic armies simply could not have been performed if both armies were shoving or killing face-to-face for prolonged periods. The armies could have accomplished them only during lulls in the fighting. This observation being true, what did a "typical" battle of the Second Punic War look like?

As they approached one another, the armies would encamp somewhere between one and seven miles apart, depending on the advantages the terrain offered and the availability of water. Cavalry and light infantry, sometimes performing reconnaissance, harassment, or movements to contact, would engage in skirmishing. This scrapping might go on for days until one side deployed its main force to offer battle and the other accepted. Sometimes the armies remained facing one another for days without further action until one side went into the attack. The main force's initial encounter usually involved an infantry charge preceded (at least in the Roman case) by a discharge of missiles, namely, pila or javelins. The opening charge might occur all along the battle line or in just one segment of it. If the charge was ferocious enough, the other side might quickly lose its nerve, turn tail, and run. More often, however, the enemy would meet the charge, and hand-to-hand combat would ensue. The engagement would last probably no longer than a few minutes, with the lines remaining in contact, hacking at one another, until one side tried to break off the fighting and move back a short distance out of harm's way. The attackers, too, would either break off the fight, eager to be out of danger, or move forward for a few yards, take up the positions the adversary had previously occupied, and remain a few yards apart but without fighting. The point is that the attackers usually would not press the attack once the adversary gave ground. Sheer exhaustion, fear, and high casualties would mitigate against continuous contact.[27]

A few yards apart, the two sides would continue facing each other, yelling, waving their weapons, and daring the other side to attack. As the tension and noise rose, perhaps a few brave individuals might sally forth and engage in individual combats. Then the lines, or perhaps only a segment of a line, would clash again and fight for a few minutes until one side would fall back and the other would advance into the once contested space before breaking off the fighting again. And so this back-and-forth might go on for one or two hours. A superior force might succeed over time in pressing its opposition back for several hundred yards but only in bursts and pulses of combat action.[28] During the lulls between pulses, the wounded would be recovered, reinforcements from the rear moved into their places, the Roman principes might move up to replace the entire hastati battle line, and commanders might take the opportunity to completely rearrange their formations by altering their depth or length.

Then the battle would begin again until one side broke from exhaustion, fear, or, as was often the case in Punic battles, some tactical maneuver—a flank or rear cavalry attack or flanking maneuver by the infantry—destroyed the enemy formation's cohesion, causing its troops to lose their will to fight and to stop resisting or take flight. Safety lay in retaining the fighting formation's integrity. Once it was lost, the soldier's psychological will to resist dropped off rapidly.

> This kind of dynamic stand-off punctuated by episodes of hand-to-hand fighting could continue for some time until one side finally lost its ability to resist, thereby breaking the bonds of mutual deterrence and encouraging the opposing troops to surge forward and begin killing in earnest, their gnawing tension and fear now released and converted into an orgy of blood lust.[29]

The presence of disciplined cavalry in Punic armies made it almost impossible for a soldier to flee the battlefield alive. Cavalry could easily ride down and kill these hapless men, many of whom had thrown away their arms and shields. A rear or flank attack was more likely to force the defeated enemy into the center line, where the attacking infantry would continue to press it from the front. Under these circumstances, the defeated soldiers would find themselves closely packed together without any formational integrity with which to resist. At some point the press of humanity would become so great that they would be unable to use their weapons to defend themselves. As with the Romans at Cannae and the Carthaginians at Great Plains, surrounded and packed together, they would be slaughtered.

LOGISTICS

The armies of the Second Punic War had to master the task of supporting large contingents in the field over great distances and for long time periods. These ancient armies' logistical feats were often more difficult and achieved more proficiently than those accomplished by the nineteenth-century armies, which had the railroad, mass production of supplies, standard packaging, and tinned and condensed food to ease their supply problems. Of all the achievements of the armies of antiquity, modern military planners least appreciate those in the area of logistics.

Ancient armies had to transport more than food and weapons, both of which could be carried by the soldiers themselves. Technological advances increased logistical burdens. Advances in siege craft, for instance, required armies to transport all kinds of siege equipment: ropes, picks, levers, scaling ladders, shovels for tunneling, and covered battering rams. Without siege equipment to reduce enemy cities, an army risked leaving large garrisons across its line of supply and communications. Although the siege machines could be dismantled for transport, they required many pack animals and wagons to carry the parts. Also, Roman armies sometimes carried construction materials in anticipation of having to build bridges. The need to repair tools and weapons brought into existence the military blacksmith with his traveling forge. Livy tells us that a Roman army of eight legions (approximately forty thousand men) required sixteen hundred smiths and craftsmen (fabri) to keep its equipment prepared for battle.[30] Also, much of the new war-fighting technology was too heavy or oddly shaped to be carried by pack animal, forcing ancient armies to use wagons in ever greater numbers. Wagons, of course, also needed animals, often oxen, to pull them as well as repairmen and extra parts to keep the wagons operational. In the Roman army wagons eventually made up 20 to 30 percent of the supply train relative to pack animals.[31]

The most important supplies were, of course, food and water for the soldiers and the pack animals. Scipio's army of 28,000 men and 1,000 cavalry that marched on New Carthage required 61,000 pounds of grain and rations per day to feed the troops. The mules required another 16.8 tons of hard fodder (oats or barley) per day, and the horses ate another 11,000 pounds to keep them fit. In addition, the 8,400 mules in Scipio's army needed 201,600 pounds of green pasturage a day and the horses another 44,000 pounds. Scipio's troops required 58,000 gallons of water per day to sustain themselves, while the mules took 33,600 gallons and the horses 7,500 gallons of water per day.[32] Without sufficient water, the army's animals would die within days, so providing water for them was just as important as it was for the troops. Soldiers carried canteens, but they used them only between the springs and rivers that provided the army's major source of water on the march. Campaigns in desert environments required armies to carry water supplies with them. The Roman general Pompey, campaigning against the Albanians in the Caspian Sea region, ordered water for his troops to be carried in 10,000 water skins so his army could cross the waterless waste.[33]

The number of animals in the ancient armies' baggage trains was substantial. A Roman legion of Scipio's time had fourteen hundred mules, or one animal for 3.4 men.[34] This number is based on Jonathan Roth's analysis that each *contubernium* (eight-man squad) had two mules to carry its equipment, a reasonable assumption for a Roman Republican army.[35] This number of mules equaled the carrying capacity of 175 tons, or 350 wagons.[36] Scipio's army of six legions had eighty-four hundred mules and a thousand horses, or almost ten thousand animals, along with it. For any army of the ancient period, finding fodder for the animals was its largest logistical requirement. The fodder could be either rough fodder—grasses and hay cut from fields or grazed by the animals themselves—or hard or dry fodder, which is a grain, usually barley or oats.[37] Ten thousand animals required 247 acres of land per day to obtain sufficient fodder,[38] and an army would quickly consume its supply of fodder in a few days if it didn't move. Livy tells us that armies often waited "until there was an abundance of pasture in the fields" before undertaking a campaign.[39] One reason why ancient armies broke off campaigns to go into winter quarters was that there was insufficient fodder to feed the army's animals.[40] The army could carry dry fodder—oats and barley—in sufficient quantities to sustain the animals for a few days across desert or rocky terrain, but no army could carry enough grain to feed both its troops and the animals. Finding sufficient fodder, therefore, was an important concern in planning the route of march.

Even a well-supplied and logistically sophisticated army could not carry all the supplies it required to sustain itself in fighting condition for very long. In this sense all armies had to "live off the land." At the minimum, this situation meant finding sufficient daily supplies of water, fodder for the animals, and firewood for cooking, light, and warmth. Armies routinely augmented their transported food supplies with what they could obtain on the march. "Living off the land" entailed foraging, requisitioning, and plundering to supply the army. Foraging meant sending out soldiers to find and bring back fodder or firewood while requisitioning involved obtaining supplies from friendly authorities or individuals, often by paying for them and at other times simply by taking them with a promise to pay. Plundering, however, resulted in seizing others' provisions or property without compensating them. Scipio needed the Spanish tribes' support, so we hear nothing in the texts of his army plundering or requisitioning supplies without compensation from the local population. Foragers did dangerous work and were often subject to attack; consequently, foraging parties usually had security forces with them to provide protection. Foraging parties gathered only as much as the army's supply train could reasonably carry, or usually not more than four or five days' provisions at a time.[41] Foraging took time and slowed the army's rate of advance.

As long as the army moved within the borders of its own country or the imperial realm, it could get supplies from prepositioned stocks at supply depots and forts along its route. Once in enemy territory, however, the supply problem became more pressing. Almost all armies of antiquity used a system of operational bases, tactical bases, and depots to keep their armies supplied in enemy territory. An operational base might be a port or a large city located in or close to enemy territory that could be used to collect large amounts of food and supplies. Livy described the Carthaginians' operational base at New Carthage as "a citadel, treasury, arsenal, and storehouse for everything."[42] The advantage of establishing a base in a port over an inland city was that greater amounts of supplies could be moved faster and cheaper by ship than overland. Water transport during Roman times was forty times less expensive than overland transport.[43]

The army would move from its operational base and establish a tactical base, usually a fortified encampment like the Roman marching camp, when it was close to or in contact with the enemy. A tactical base served as the main resupply facility. While the forward tactical base advanced with the army, previous tactical bases were converted into depots.[44] Supplies were then moved from the operational base to a series of depots positioned behind the army's line of march. A succession of rotating pack animal and wagon convoys shuttled supplies forward to the army via a series of intermediate supply storage depots. These convoys could be used repeatedly because they traveled relatively short distances, perhaps twenty miles between depots.[45] If the army were forced to retreat, it could do so along its previous line of communications, finding stores at each depot to replenish its supplies and maintain its integrity. This system made it possible for ancient armies to project their forces over long distances. This or some minor variation in the supply system of bases, depots, and pack convoys was found among most armies of antiquity, including the Carthaginian army, about whose logistics we know practically nothing.

The main means of moving supplies in antiquity was the animal pack train, which was comprised of donkeys, mules, horses, oxen, camels, and elephants in some appropriate mix. These animals were used either as draft animals (load pullers) or pack animals (load bearers). Regardless of the animal, damaged hooves or feet were a major cause of pack animals going lame. Logistics trains were further burdened by having to take along spare animals or finding some way to acquire them along the way. Ancient armies used hipposandals, or a leather or cloth bag tied over the animal's hooves, to reduce damage to the animals' feet.[46]

In the ancient period's civilian and military economies, donkeys and mules were the most common transporters of goods. Properly equipped with pack saddles, panniers, or wooden frames, a donkey can carry a 220-pound load.[47] Able to carry 450 pounds or more, mules are stronger and more surefooted than donkeys and cheaper to feed than horses;[48] however, mules were more expensive. Although a relatively slow traveler, averaging four to five miles per hour, the mule has incredible endurance and can march continuously for ten to twelve hours.[49] A mule can easily travel forty miles a day. In the nineteenth century, U.S. Army mule trains could make eighty to a hundred miles a day under forced-march conditions.[50] Carrying heavy and bulky loads, an ox-drawn wagon could move a 1,000-pound load nine miles per day, while five horses could carry the same load thirty-two miles a day at twice the speed and on half the forage.[51] Oxen also moved more slowly than mule-drawn wagons, again usually unable to make more than nine miles a day,[52] while a mule-drawn wagon can make nineteen miles a day.[53] Lacking brakes, a pivoting front axle, and axle bearings significantly reduced the wagon's efficiency on the march. Still, wagons were the basic form of transport for most tribal armies in the West, and they could be turned quickly to military advantage by forming them into a laager for defensive purposes.

Hired or conscripted human porters and the soldiers themselves were an important part of the carrying capacity of the logistics train. The Roman soldier of the imperial period carried seventy to eighty pounds,[54] and in an emergency, he could carry a hundred pounds.[55] The soldier's ability to carry his own load drastically reduced the army's overall logistical burden. With soldiers carrying one-third of the load that would normally have been hauled by animals, an army of fifty thousand men required 6,000 fewer pack animals and 240 fewer pack animals to haul feed for the others.[56] Armies at times also drove large cattle and sheep herds with them to provide fresh meat for their troops. Livy tells us that at one point Hannibal had more than 2,000 head of cattle with his army of thirty thousand men.[57]

The ancient armies' logistical apparatus was remarkable for what it could accomplish in an age without mechanical transport. It is worth remembering that no army of the modern period equaled or exceeded the ancient armies' rates of movement until the American Civil War, when the introduction of the railroad made faster troop movement possible. Supported by a sound logistical system, ancient armies could easily conduct operations twenty to forty miles beyond their last tactical base and remain well supplied.[58] Only in the modern era of mechanical transport have armies been able to better this performance.

RATES OF MOVEMENT

One cannot study the Punic Wars without noticing that the Roman armies appear to have moved faster than the Carthaginian armies did. In trying to determine if "Maharbal was right" when he told Hannibal that he could reach Rome in five days, John Lazenby notes that the rate of march for Hannibal's armies in Italy was, on average, only nine miles per day. Occasionally, however, Hannibal could make ten to fifteen miles per day.[59] It is noteworthy as well that in his Spanish campaign Scipio was almost always able to move more rapidly than his Carthaginian adversaries. Once he even caught up to a retreating army and destroyed it. Since we know so little about the Carthaginian logistics system, an attempt to answer whether Maharbal was right would be little more than a guess but, I think, one worth hazarding.

Peter Connolly notes that a Roman army could easily cover eighteen miles a day and still have time to spend four hours constructing a fortified camp each night.[60] On a forced march, the legion could cover twenty-five to thirty miles a day. At the extreme, Marcus Junklemann's experiments show that a soldier might be pressed to do even a hundred miles a day.[61] But such rates of march could not be sustained for very long, perhaps a day or two, and would exert such wear and tear on the army that it would not arrive at its destination in fighting condition. For a Roman army that hoped to move quickly into the attack after arriving at its objective, as Scipio's army at New Carthage was required to do, eighteen to twenty miles a day seems an acceptable average. Even this rate of movement would require between nine to ten hours of *marching time* a day, since troops marching on unpaved ground could make no more than two miles per hour.

But this rate of march is still twice what the Carthaginian armies managed. What slowed down the Carthaginian armies fighting Scipio in Spain? In short, the tribal contingents did. The bulk of the Carthaginian armies in Spain was comprised of tribal contingents that fought either for pay or out of loyalty to the commanders. Many of these tribes were pastoral and kept large herds to supply their diet of meat and milk.[62] If these tribes insisted on taking along their herds on campaign, as Livy notes, then the Carthaginian armies' rate of movement would have been slowed accordingly. The Roman military diet was mostly grain, thereby eliminating the need for large animal herds to accompany the army. Another factor slowing down the Carthaginian armies was the tribes' practice of moving their families and possessions in wagons, which also served as their basic form of transport when they went to war. While the tribes' wagons offered the advantage of being able to quickly form into defensive laager for protection, they were slow. Drawn by oxen, they can make no more than eight or nine miles a day,[63] or about the same rate of movement that Lazenby attributes to Hannibal's army in Italy. Finally, the Carthaginian armies in Spain were often encumbered with elephants, and their forage also had to be transported, further reducing the rate of movement.[64]

4

Scipio's Spanish Campaign

IN THE SUMMER of 210 BCE Scipio set sail from the mouth of the Tiber to take command of the Roman armies in Spain. He was accompanied by an army of ten thousand infantry, a thousand cavalry, and a fleet of thirty quinquereme warships.[1] He made port just inside the Spanish frontier, perhaps at Emporiae, where he assembled his army and marched to Tarraco, the main Roman base north of the Ebro River. There he found the remnants of his father's army under the command of Lucius Marcius, the officer who had conducted the Roman retreat after the Scipios' defeat at Castulo. Marcius's remnant numbered nine thousand men.[2] The other Roman force in Tarraco was the army the Senate sent after the Scipios died. Under the command of Gaius Claudius Nero, this force had six thousand Roman infantry and three hundred cavalry reinforced by another six thousand allied infantry and eight hundred horse cavalry.[3] Marcius remained behind while Nero returned to Rome, and command of the combined forces passed to Scipio as commander in chief of all forces in Spain. The total forces at Scipio's command were thirty-one thousand infantry and twenty-one hundred cavalry. The three Carthaginian armies in Spain that Scipio would have to confront totaled nearly seventy thousand men.

Except for Scipio's troops, about which we have no information, the rest of the army was comprised of combat veterans. They were, however, in three separate armies and accustomed to different commanders. Scipio would have to forge them into a unified fighting force before he could take them into battle. He spent that winter conducting inspections, getting to know the troops, letting them become accustomed to his methods of command, building their confidence and morale, and ensuring their equipment and supplies were in good repair for the coming spring campaign. Gaining the trust and confidence of men who have fought under a previous commander is difficult, and it must have been especially so for the young Scipio. Both Marcius and Nero were older, more experienced generals whose men admired them a great deal. Further, Marcius was a hero to his men for he had saved them from annihilation after the elder Scipios' catastrophe at Castulo. They had elected Marcius their commander and may well have expected him to remain in command. To Scipio's great credit he treated Marcius with respect and praised him in front of the troops. The well-known Gaius Nero, meanwhile, had arrived in Spain with his veterans fresh from the siege of Capua. Only twenty-six years old and with little experience as an operational-level field commander (although with experience as a tactical commander), Scipio must have faced a daunting task in gaining the confidence of his men. Neither Livy nor Polybius mention troop training at Tarraco, and it is unlikely that Scipio attempted to introduce new methods or tactics there as he did later. Instead, he probably drilled his troops in the familiar Roman method of close infantry combat, leaving innovation to another day after his troops had tasted victory and gained confidence in themselves and him.

Scipio had prepared himself for his command by studying the political circumstances that surrounded the war in Spain.[4] He must have been pleasantly surprised to learn that most of the Spanish allies north of the Ebro were still loyal to Rome. Scipio appreciated war's political dimension perhaps more than any other Roman commander of his time. He grasped immediately that without these allies' genuine loyalty to secure his rear and line of communications, no military operation against the Carthaginian army was likely to succeed. Scipio spent much of the winter visiting the friendly tribes, treating them with respect and dignity, and determining their loyalties.[5] He also began to collect intelligence and "to question everybody and to explore all sources of information."[6] While appreciation for the value of intelligence was a new idea for most Roman commanders, Scipio had acquired it early.

Scipio spent considerable time preparing Tarraco as his main base of operations for the coming campaign. Establishing a secure logistical base from which to launch and sustain field operations was another characteristic of Scipio's campaigns. He was an effective organizer and administrator of commissary matters in every respect, and his Spanish campaign surpasses the Spanish campaigns of Napoleon and the Duke of Wellington, who found to their great regret that Spain is a terrible place to fight if an army has to live off the land. Moving overland without planning for adequate food and water forces an army to disperse into small groups to find them, making it impossible to sustain a significant rate of advance or to maintain strategic direction. A secure base of operations also afforded Scipio a place to fall back on should retreat become necessary and should the army need to repair itself.

Terrain and distance are two important factors for any army conducting military operations in Spain. The country's interior is mountainous with few large towns from which to draw supplies or within which to winter. Hostile tribes fighting from ambush could make campaigning very difficult. Later, it took the Romans almost forty years of guerrilla fighting to finally subdue the interior. But in Scipio's day the interior was mostly not relevant. The area that the Carthaginians occupied and where Scipio's battles were fought was along the fertile Guadalquivir River in the Baetius Valley in the south, rich with farms and mines that contributed greatly to Carthaginian wealth, and along the fertile delta of the Ebro River valley in the north. A single road running along the coast linked the two regions. The areas of most immediate military concern to Scipio were around the cities of Saguntum and New Carthage.

An examination of the figure on page 29 reveals why an attack against the southern area of Carthaginian control was unlikely to succeed unless Scipio addressed several problems. First, the north-south coastal road was the only avenue of advance, and gaining its control was imperative. Second, a main logistics base from which the Romans could use supply convoys to sustain their forces in the field had to be established and protected.[7] Achieving either of these conditions was impossible without a fleet to control the coast. Without control of the sea, Carthaginian seaborne forces could slip behind the Roman armies and cut their line of communications and retreat. Finally, the route from the Ebro River, the staging and assembly point for Scipio's offensive, to New Carthage ran through territory inhabited by hostile tribes. The Edetani lived between the Ebro and Saguntum, and the Laecetani occupied the area north of Tarraco as well as some territory between Tarraco and the Ebro. Both were allies of the Carthaginians, although the Edetani's loyalty seems to have been secured by hostages kept in New Carthage. Thus, movement of a substantial Roman force down the coastal road would be easily detected and reported to the Carthaginians in New Carthage. Operational surprise was almost impossible under these circumstances.

THE ATTACK ON NEW CARTHAGE, 209 BCE

By early spring Scipio's army was ready, and he had devised a plan to engage the Carthaginians by attacking New Carthage, the largest Carthaginian logistics base in Spain. But how did such a young commander come by such a daring idea? Neither Polybius nor Livy tells us. The *Punica* attributes the plan to a dream in which Scipio's father comes to him to warn him off what might have been his original plan, to attack the Carthaginian armies directly. Scipio's father tells him,

> Abandon that dangerous enterprise; but bestir yourself and adopt a better plan. There is a city here. . . . [New] Carthage is its name and the population is Punic. This Carthage in Spain is a famous capital. Attack this city, my son, while the [Carthaginian] generals' backs are turned. No victory in the field could bring you as much glory and as much booty.[8]

If Scipio did conceive the plan himself, as both Livy and Polybius suggest, it was probably only after a number of planning discussions with Marcius and Nero, both experienced soldiers who had been in the country for a while and knew the Carthaginian situation in Spain intimately. The suggestion in the *Punica* that Scipio had originally thought about attacking the Carthaginian armies rather than New Carthage is not beyond possibility. Maybe better heads prevailed and Scipio took the more experienced Roman commanders' advice before formulating his final plan.

The Carthaginian forces in Spain outnumbered Scipio's. To risk battle with an army he was not yet certain of and to lose so early in the game would remove the last obstacle to a second Carthaginian invasion of Italy and the reinforcement of Hannibal's army. Finding the three Carthaginian armies was, therefore, of supreme importance. Polybius tells us that Scipio learned the Carthaginian force was divided into three armies positioned at different locations. One army under the command of Hannibal's youngest brother, Mago, was garrisoned near Gades (modern Cádiz). A second army commanded by Hasdrubal, son of Gisgo, operated near the mouth of the Tagus River close to the Atlantic coast of Portugal. Under the command of Hasdrubal Barca, Hannibal's younger brother, the third army was besieging a city in central Spain somewhere near modern Madrid.[9] According to Polybius, all three armies were within ten days' march of New Carthage. The figure on page 87 shows the locations of the three Carthaginian armies relative to New Carthage.

The Carthaginians had surely received news of Scipio's arrival the previous summer. Why, then, were their armies so far from New Carthage and even farther from the Ebro River? Why was there no covering force between New Carthage and the Ebro? Why were no Carthaginian forces stationed around Saguntum? Why was New Carthage itself so lightly garrisoned? Why hadn't the Carthaginians

THE STORMING OF NEW CARTHAGE

begun to redeploy their forces to intercept any Roman movement to the south? The usual explanation is that the Carthaginians had dispersed during the winter because the land would not logistically support such a large concentration of troops in one location. Moreover, to keep the tribes obedient the Carthaginians relied on the use of hostages and demonstrations of force and punishment. To garrison just the most important tribal areas with something approaching a credible force meant that the army had to be spread over a wide area. Except for Hasdrubal's army, which was engaged in operations in the area around modern

Toledo, the Carthaginian armies were dispersed into small detachments. Still, the Carthaginians could have afforded to station at least some small detachments around and to the north of New Carthage to act as trip wires and to warn of any Roman movement. Their failure to do so must be counted as a major mistake.

The Carthaginian armies' dispersal did little to solve Scipio's problem. The Carthaginians could still reconcentrate at New Carthage within ten days if we are to believe Polybius.[10] If so, they were much closer to New Carthage than Scipio was. Scipio could not cover the distance from the Ebro to New Carthage in anywhere near that time. Polybius's claim that Scipio moved his army from Tarraco to New Carthage, a distance of more than four hundred miles, in seven days clearly cannot be true.[11] The road from the Ebro to New Carthage was little more than a beaten track, and in the spring the two rivers and five streams that crossed the track were swollen with the mountain runoff. Scipio's fleet might have covered the distance in ten days, making the average speed of five miles per hour for a quinquereme; however, the fleet was comprised of quinqueremes, which could not serve as troop transports. On a paved Roman road during the imperial period, a Roman legion of military professionals at forced-march pace could cover, perhaps, twenty-five to thirty miles a day, providing that it did not stop to construct a fortified camp each night. Scipio's movement down the coastal road was through uncertain and at times hostile territory, so it is unlikely that he would have permitted his army to move without a secure camp. Under these conditions, Scipio would have been fortunate indeed to make even eighteen to twenty miles a day.[12] At this pace, it would still have taken Scipio's army at least twenty days to arrive outside New Carthage, and even then the army would have been in no condition to fight. They would have required at least three days to recover and repair before going into combat.[13]

There are also problems with Polybius's Spanish geography. While he seems to have possessed some "personal knowledge of the southern part of the peninsula from New Carthage to Gades . . . about the rest there is no plain evidence."[14] Polybius appears to have gotten the distances between the Carthaginian armies and New Carthage wrong. He says that the distance from the Pillars of Hercules (near modern-day Strait of Gibraltar) to New Carthage is 3,000 *stades,* or some 324 miles at 200 yards per stade, and that the distance from New Carthage to the Ebro River is 2,600 stades, or 280 miles.[15] In fact it is approximately 400 English miles from New Carthage to the Ebro and about 300 miles from New Carthage to Gades. Mago's army at Gades was closer to New Carthage than Scipio was. Hasdrubal Barca's army, located somewhere near modern Toledo, or about 240 miles from New Carthage, was also closer than Scipio to New Carthage. Six hundred miles away at the mouth of the Tagus River in modern Portugal, only Hasdrubal, son of Gisgo, was too far distant from New Carthage.

The proximity of two of the three Carthaginian armies to New Carthage may explain why they did not deploy trip wires north of the city or maintain a larger garrison there. Mago could easily have reached New Carthage along the coastal road while traversing about the same type of terrain Scipio faced. Hasdrubal Barca was closest. His march would have taken him along high plateau pasture and through forests and would have required some climbing and a steep descent into New Carthage, but it was by no means impossible. Although Hasdrubal Gisgonis was the farthest distant, his route of march through some of Spain's most fertile lands was the easiest. At least two of the three Carthaginian armies could arrive in New Carthage before Scipio could.

If the distance Scipio had to travel to reach New Carthage was more than a hundred miles farther than the distance Mago had to travel to reach there, then Scipio could not reasonably have planned a surprise attack on the city, at least not how Polybius and Livy represent it, as a bold strategic maneuver that caught the Carthaginians completely unaware and in which speed of march was vital to Scipio's success. Scipio could not rely on his army remaining undetected as it moved down the coastal road. Common sense would have forced him to assume that allied tribes living in the area would report his movements to the Carthaginians. The Carthaginians had occupied the land between the Ebro and north of Saguntum since they had chased Marcius's remnants there after the Scipios' defeat. Even if the Carthaginians had withdrawn the winter before Scipio arrived, surely agents were also left behind to keep watch on the Romans across the river. At the very least allied tribes living in the area might be relied on to report the Roman movements. This suggests that Polybius's and Livy's story of Scipio's rapid march on New Carthage to capture the city before the Carthaginian armies could arrive is not accurate.

The logistics of Scipio's march from Tarraco to New Carthage also make it unlikely that he could have covered the distance in the time Polybius allots. Scipio probably crossed the Ebro at Dertosa, a town on the river's southern bank that controlled the road south, the river crossing, and access to the valley entrance that led to the interior. Marcius had apparently held Dertosa against the Carthaginian attacks until Nero arrived, thus securing the important crossing point for Scipio's army. Polybius says that Scipio left three thousand infantry and five hundred cavalry under Marcus Silanus's command to guard the ford and protect the allies north of the river.[16] Scipio crossed the Ebro with twenty-eight thousand troops and sixteen hundred cavalry. Livy says some of his men also were sent aboard his thirty ships. In all probability, these were his artillerymen and their siege equipment. The artillery for a single legion required 70 wagons and 160 animals to transport overland.[17] Scipio's six legions would have required 420 wagons and 960 animals to move their artillery overland, slowing the rate of march considerably. If Scipio was attempting a rapid march, putting his artillery aboard ship was one way to achieve it.

The Roman soldier in Scipio's army received two *sextari,* or about 1.87 pounds, of wheat a day for his basic ration, which was supplemented by beans (50 grams), cheese (30 grams), oil (40 grams), and salt (30 grams). A day's rations weighed 2.2 pounds.[18] Scipio's 29,600 soldiers required 65,120 pounds, or about 32 tons, of rations per day. Scipio's 8,400 mules required 4.4 pounds of oats or barley a day each, or 36,960 pounds, or 18.5 tons of grain. Sixteen hundred horses required 8,800 pounds of grain, at 5.5 pounds per day per animal, or another 4.4 tons. The logistical burden for human and animal rations alone was 110,880 pounds a day, or 55 tons. The Roman legion of Scipio's day had 1,400 mules for logistical purposes, representing a carrying capacity of 175 metric tons or the equivalent of 350 wagons.[19] Scipio's army of six-plus legions had approximately 8,400 mules, providing a carrying capacity of almost 1,200 metric tons or the equivalent of more than 2,400 wagons.[20] A horse can easily carry 250 pounds, so the cavalry horses could carry their own grain rations for at least twenty days. After the Marian reforms, the Roman soldier himself carried between 80 and 100 pounds on the march to compensate for the fewer mules allotted to each squad.[21] If we assume that Scipio's soldiers carried only half that load, say 45 pounds, the soldiers themselves provided more than 600 tons of additional load-carrying capacity. The logistical transport capacity of Scipio's army was approximately 1,800 tons, enough to sustain the army in the field for more than a month, or some thirty-six days. The area through which Scipio's army traveled was settled with some agriculture and fields, affording adequate fodder for the animals. Also, two major rivers and five streams crossed the route, providing the men and animals with a supply of water.

If, as Polybius says, Scipio was attempting a rapid march to take New Carthage before the Carthaginian armies could react, he might have taken other steps to increase his rate of movement. He could, for example, have left most of his wagons behind. Sending the artillery and siege machinery by ship would have already reduced the number of wagons he needed. He could have put his troops on "iron rations"—that is, *buccelatum,* or hard biscuits—that could have been cooked in large quantities in advance. Unlike bread, which spoils in four or five days, buccelatum easily lasts a month without spoiling. Although cheese, oil, dried fruit, and, perhaps, salt pork or bacon could have supplemented the diet, using precooked biscuits would have made cooking and foraging for firewood unnecessary and freed more time for marching. Then Scipio could have forgone constructing the marching camp each night and saved another four hours a day. There is no evidence in the texts that Scipio did any of these things, however.

Scipio's route of march along the coastal road did not offer many opportunities for speed. As noted, the route was not a proper road at all but only a rough track across the countryside. Because the march took place in "early spring," the streams would have been in full spate and had to be forged, probably by rope lines, taking more time. Further, the uncertain loyalties of the tribes along the route made ambush a real possibility, so security elements would have had to take proper care. All these factors would have slowed Scipio's march. Even if we allow for all relevant factors, it is difficult to see how Scipio's army might have made more than eighteen to twenty miles a day. Moreover, this rate still would have required nine to ten hours of marching time a day at a sustained rate of two miles per hour. In practical terms it is unlikely that Scipio could have reached New Carthage in seven days, as Polybius claims.

Given the city's importance as a major logistical base, Scipio would have probably assumed that the garrison was substantial and would require prolonged fighting to subdue it. As far as we know, he had no knowledge of the Carthaginian garrison's size. It is puzzling how Scipio could have learned about the depth of the lagoon around the city, as Polybius claims, but not about the size of the city's garrison, which, in military terms, was far more important. It is possible, however, that Scipio knew the city was only lightly defended, and this information might have convinced him to strike quickly against it.

Once there, however, how did Scipio intend to sustain himself if he had to lay siege to the city? To some extent he could have lived off the surrounding countryside, if only for a short time, but then troops foraging for food, water, firewood, and fodder would not be available for fighting. Perhaps Scipio sent supplies by sea. If he utilized, say, ten ships to transport his artillery, he would still have had twenty to transport supplies. At 120 feet long, 14 feet wide, and 10 feet high below deck, the quinquereme was only slightly larger than the trireme, and with a draft of 4.5 feet, it displaced close to fifty tons.[22] The quinquereme had only 420 cubic meters of space below deck, in which was squeezed 270 rowers and the equipment for the 120 marines aboard, and some 1,680 square feet of deck space. With the weight of the crew and provisions, the boat probably could not carry more than another fifteen tons of cargo, providing space could be found for it and it was not stacked too high (perhaps not more than a meter and a half) on the deck. Assuming twenty ships at fifteen tons' burden each would have permitted Scipio to transport some three hundred tons of supplies, or about enough to sustain the army for six days, by ship to New Carthage. If Livy is correct when he tells us that all of Scipio's ships were quinqueremes and he did not use transports, then Scipio would have had about fifteen days' worth of supplies—not counting what he could forage in the area—to sustain his army *after* he reached New Carthage.

But was New Carthage Scipio's ultimate objective or was the threat of its capture a means to another end? New Carthage was the most important Carthaginian supply base in Spain. It was certainly a reasonable expectation that once the Romans threatened it, the Carthaginian armies would rush to its defense or to recover it if it fell. Scipio may have concluded that the Carthaginian advantage in troop strength could be offset by his fleet's firepower and ability to land troops to his tactical advantage anywhere along the coast, including behind the Carthaginians. Further, if the three armies did not arrive together but piecemeal, one after the other, Scipio could deal with them one at a time. None of the Carthaginian armies numbered more than 25,000 men.[23] If Scipio could engage them one at a time, Scipio's 27,500 troops would hold the numerical advantage. If things went badly, however, Scipio's command of the sea and the coast meant he could evacuate his army. Even if he found himself trapped against the sea in a defensive cordon, his fleet and transports could still shuttle supplies and reinforcements from the Roman base at Tarraco. Given these military realities, he might not have intended to attack New Carthage at all but only to *feint* toward it and draw the Carthaginian armies toward the city, where he could engage them in a series of great battles that would decide Spain's future. The *Punica* suggests that this course of action had been in his mind, and if Scipio were victorious, Spain would be his. It was the kind of scenario a twenty-six year old might imagine.

Scipio did nothing to stop the rumors that ran through Tarraco as his army prepared to march. He trusted no one with his plans but his old friend, Gaius Laelius, and did not even inform his field commanders until the march was well under way. But Scipio could not have realistically expected that the movement of such a large body of Roman troops would remain undetected for long. He left three thousand infantry and five hundred cavalry under Marcus Silanus's command to guard the Ebro crossing and embarked some of his army aboard ship under the command of Gaius Laelius. Scipio led the remainder of the army overland. Sometime later, perhaps in twenty days or so, Scipio arrived before New Carthage. Perhaps he expected to engage the Carthaginians in decisive battle, but he found his only adversary was the city's small garrison of Carthaginian regulars.

The Carthaginians had already committed major strategic errors by not deploying a covering force between Scipio and New Carthage and by not strengthening the city's garrison as soon as they learned of Scipio's arrival in Spain. This said, why did the Carthaginian commanders fail to react to Scipio's movement? Polybius, Livy, and some modern historians conclude dissention among the Carthaginian generals prevented them from taking concerted action.[24] This supposition, of course, does not explain why at least one of them did not react. It is difficult to believe that the same Carthaginian commanders who had been fighting the Romans in Spain for almost a decade decided not to engage Scipio's army out of personal pique and at the same time place their main position from which to launch another invasion of Italy at risk by refusing to defend their largest logistics base. Surely the answer is simpler. The Carthaginians did not react immediately because they did not know that Scipio's army was moving toward New Carthage until it had almost reached the city itself.

It defies common sense that Carthaginian agents did not detect Scipio's troop movement. But even if they detected it at the Ebro crossing, a rider would have had to cover 750 miles to reach Mago's army in Gades and almost 400 miles to Hasdrubal's army in Toledo, a journey of twenty-five days or fifteen days, respectively. By the time a rider reached the Carthaginians, Scipio would have been within five to seven days' march of New Carthage. The race, if there was one, to New Carthage was already over before it began. Scipio had all winter to lay in supplies, gather animals, repair equipment, put his ships back in the water and make them seaworthy, and prepare his troops to assemble from winter quarters. When Scipio crossed the Ebro, the Carthaginians were still dispersed in their winter quarters. They would have needed at least a month to gather their armies and make the logistical preparations for a march on New Carthage. Even then the journey would have taken at least three weeks. Probably by the time they were ready to march, news had reached them that the city had already fallen to the Romans.

Scipio was probably surprised at the small size of the garrison left to defend the strategically important city of New Carthage. The city was the closest port to

Carthage itself and the main port of embarkation for reinforcements from Africa. It also held the enemy's war treasury, a highly valuable resource to an army that relied so heavily on mercenaries. The city also held the Carthaginians' most important hostages, taken as a means of keeping the tribes obedient. Thus, capturing New Carthage by storm would strike a powerful moral blow against Scipio's enemy and seriously weaken its logistics and resupply capability. Scipio understood that his father's campaign had failed because no Roman base existed south of Saguntum to support an offensive. With New Carthage in Roman hands, Scipio would be able to mount that offensive within a year. The difficulty was, of course, that he had to assume that his attack on New Carthage would spur the Carthaginian armies to react and move to retake it. Caution forced him to presume that the Carthaginian armies were already on the march. If so, he would have no longer than three weeks to overcome the city's defenses and prepare to meet the Carthaginians' relieving attack. In all likelihood the garrison's small size convinced him that the city could be taken quickly by storm. He ordered his army to attack New Carthage.

New Carthage sat on a hill rising from a peninsula that was surrounded by a small bay and connected to the mainland by a narrow, quarter-mile-wide causeway. The city was surrounded by the sea on the east and south and by a shallow lagoon on the north. The perimeter of the city's wall was 2.5 miles in circumference.[25] Scipio established his camp on the landward side and then set about inspecting his forces, including the naval contingents. He was rowed among the ships to ensure the artillery was properly installed on their decks and to urge the captains to be vigilant during the night and guard against surprise attacks. The Carthaginian garrison numbered only a thousand regulars under the command of an officer named Mago (not to be confused with Hannibal's brother). To meet the Roman attack, Mago recruited and armed two thousand of the most able-bodied inhabitants. Scipio ordered his fleet to take up positions on the city's seaward side and, with catapults and ballistae mounted on the quinqueremes' decks, began bombarding it. The naval bombardment must have begun just after dawn, for on the "third hour of the day" Scipio sent a force of two thousand men to attack the city's walls, which ran across the narrow front of the peninsula's width.

Scipio's troops were equipped with scaling ladders, and they began mounting the walls. Mago's force was far too small to defend the entire perimeter. As soon as the attack began, he ordered the gates thrown open and sent his two thousand armed civilians in a bold sally against the Romans. A sharp engagement broke out in which the Carthaginians fought bravely, driving Scipio's troops back toward the Roman camp a quarter mile away. When the Carthaginians had come some distance from the safety of the covering fire from the city walls, Scipio counterattacked. Attacking with a larger force from within his camp, he broke the Carthaginians' momentum and drove the armed citizens back toward the open gate. Many were killed in the rout and others trampled to death, caught in the crush to enter the narrow gate. The Roman counterattack narrowly missed pressing through the open gate. Mago's attack had accomplished nothing and cost him more than half his militia. His attention, however, was now focused on Scipio and his army deployed in front of the city.

Scipio ordered a second frontal attack. With only fifteen hundred or so men at his disposal, Mago could not have hoped to defend 2.5 miles of perimeter wall against an assault by more than twenty-five thousand attackers. But New Carthage was surrounded by the sea and a lagoon on three sides, leaving only the quarter mile of wall that extended across the peninsula vulnerable to ground assault. The narrow front also made it impossible for the Romans to bring their numerical advantage to bear with any great effect. Mago's fifteen hundred troops could defend the 1,320 feet of wall at a density of three men per meter, enough to mount a stiff resistance as long as their courage held.

Scipio's second attack failed. According to Polybius, the reason was that the city's walls were so high that the attackers became dizzy from the height and were easily repulsed by the defenders. The walls' height required long scaling ladders, which broke under the weight of too many men climbing them at the same time. Also, the Carthaginians mounted a vigorous defense, throwing stones and beams from the battlements along with a hail of missiles so thick that they quickly ran short of them. After what could have been no more than a few hours, Scipio broke off the attack.

What happened next is often cited as evidence of Scipio's brilliant planning and ability to use tactical intelligence. Laelius told Polybius the story that even before Scipio had left Tarraco, he had learned that the lagoon protecting the city was shallow and could be easily forded on foot at low tide. During the attack on New Carthage, Scipio told his troops that Neptune would provide help and that the gods had foreordained his victory. This incident seems to have provided the basis for the Scipio legend that he was favored by the gods and that he consulted them on important matters.[26] While it is quite possible, of course, Scipio had learned in Tarraco of the lagoon's depth and tendency to empty in the evening with the tide or wind;[27] however, the claim that Scipio planned his attack through the lagoon to coincide with the ebb tide while he was still in Tarraco is probably

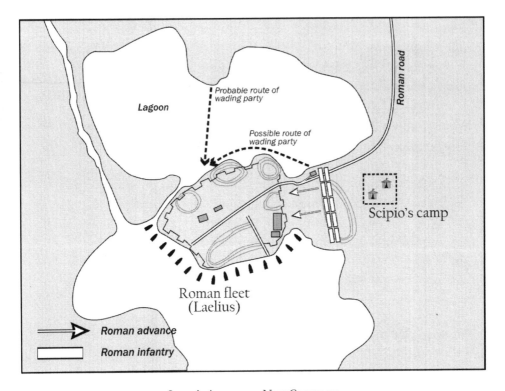

Lagoon

Probable route of
wading party

Possible route of
wading party

Roman road

Scipio's camp

Roman fleet
(Laelius)

Roman advance

Roman infantry

not true. Polybius himself tells us that Scipio "had learned from a number of fishermen who plied their trade there that the whole lagoon was shallow and could be forded at many points, and that the tide which covered it receded far enough every evening to make this possible."[28] Having failed to take the city in two attempts, Scipio could have learned only then from the local fishermen that the lagoon was shallow. In this case, Scipio did not need to await the ebb tide before crossing the lagoon. Scipio's men could have easily waded across at any time events required it.

Scipio set loose a ferocious ground attack against the front walls, drawing the defenders to the point of attack. With the assault under way, he sent a small force of five hundred men with scaling ladders to take up positions on the lagoon's far side. "He bade them [his men] follow Neptune as their guide on the march, and make their way straight across the lagoon to the walls."[29] At this point the water receded "as a strong and deep current setting in through the channel to the neighboring sea."[30]

The figure on page 96 shows that Scipio could have used two different routes to position his forces for the attack. The shortest route was closest to the wall, but the defenders on the wall would have immediately detected the attackers, relinquishing the element of surprise. The second route permitted Scipio's troops to move into position without being detected. Without the element of surprise, the small, five hundred–man assault force would have had no chance of success. As events turned out, the attack was completely successful.

> Meanwhile the force that had crossed the lagoon arrived at the city wall. They found the battlements deserted, and so not only set up their ladders unopposed, but swarmed up them and seized possession of the wall without striking a blow, for the defenders had been called away to other points, in particular to the isthmus and the eastern gate.[31]

After the assault force reached the walls undetected, scrambled over the top, and cleared the battlements of light resistance, the men made their way to the landward gate. There they fell on the defenders from behind and threw open the doors. Ready at the head of his troops, Scipio himself led the assault through the gates. Within minutes the Romans were inside. Mago and his remaining troops fled to the citadel to make a last stand.

The accounts of the attack may have neglected the important role the Roman naval infantry played in breaching the city's walls. After capturing the town, a dispute broke out between a centurion of the land forces and a naval marine over which one of them ought to be awarded the *corona muralis*, an award given to the first soldier to breech the walls. This account suggests that the naval infantry played a significant part in taking the city. Scipio's fierce attack on the city's land side may have forced Mago to shift his forces away from the seaward side, or where the Roman ships had been bombarding the city. If so, this change might have afforded the marines the opportunity to scale the walls on the south side and enter the city simultaneously with the land army.[32]

Scipio had won a quick and painless victory. But with three Carthaginian armies probably marching on New Carthage, he could neither afford a drawn-out siege of the citadel nor risk more casualties on a direct assault. Scipio was not a brutal man by nature, but he accepted the value of brutality as a means to achieve important ends. With time of the essence, he could ill afford to wait until the Carthaginian defenders were starved out. Mostly Carthaginian colonists populated New Carthage. Scipio ordered the slaughter of the townspeople in full view of Mago's holdouts. Polybius describes what happened next:

> Scipio, when he judged that a large enough number of troops had entered the town, let loose the majority of them against the inhabitants, according to Roman custom; their orders were to exterminate every form of life they encountered, sparing none, but not to start pillaging until the word was given to do so. This practice is adopted to inspire terror, and so when cities are taken by the Romans you may often see not only the corpses of human beings but dogs cut in half and the dismembered limbs of other animals, and on this occasion the carnage was especially frightful because of the large size of the population.[33]

The horrific slaughter convinced the Carthaginian commander that further resistance was pointless. Mago and his men surrendered.

The question remains, why did Scipio's wading party take Mago by surprise? If Scipio knew that the lagoon was shallow and easily crossed, surely the local Carthaginian commander charged with defending the city must have known as well. No doubt he did know, but there was little he could do to prevent a crossing. Mago's situation was desperate. The Roman fleet attacked him from the east across the peninsula and from the south. Inadequate to begin with, his garrison had suffered casualties in the two previous Roman attacks. Even if Mago had known in advance about the third attack, from the north across the lagoon, he could only have met it after weakening another sector of the wall that was already under pressure. Perhaps he hoped to shift troops to the threatened sector at the last minute and ran out of time. With only a thousand or so troops to defend the city against Scipio's sizable Roman army, Mago's task was impossible from the beginning.

The Romans took ten thousand prisoners at New Carthage, and all but a handful were civilians. The city's citizens, Carthaginian colonists with their wives and children, were permitted to return to their homes and granted their freedom. Some two thousand artisans, mostly Spaniards skilled in blacksmithing and in manufacturing other war materials, were made public slaves of Rome. Scipio promised them their freedom if they worked diligently. The rest of the male population—the Carthaginians, Libyans, and Spaniards—was assigned to the fleet for Scipio needed rowers. He had captured eighteen ships, bringing his fleet to forty-eight ships.[34] Using his Roman naval crews as petty officers and deck hands, Scipio still needed 270 oarsmen per ship for each of the eighteen ships, or 4,860 oarsmen. Because it would be unwise to outfit the ships completely with impressed men of uncertain loyalties, Scipio mixed the impressed oarsmen with his own Roman oarsmen at a ratio of two Romans to one impressed oarsman.[35] He promised the impressed men their freedom once Carthage itself was finally defeated.

It is interesting to note that Scipio's use of slave-rowers was a departure from the normal practice in which oarsmen were usually free, skilled, and paid workers. Rowing a quinquereme required skill, training, and strength, and the common notion that in the ancient world oarsmen were "galley slaves" is false.[36] In the Second Punic War, however, the evidence that the Romans used slaves as rowers and even as soldiers is clear. Romans suffered terrific losses in the battles with Hannibal, and only after Cannae and the resultant manpower shortage did Rome use slaves on some of its warships.[37]

If Scipio expected the Carthaginians to arrive soon, he also knew that he was outnumbered. In the coming fight, his fleet would be an important asset. Its ability to move unhindered along the coast would allow Scipio to insert naval marine forces behind Carthaginian positions, presenting them with a threat or a surprise attack in the rear or along their flanks. Scipio's forty-eight ships could carry 5,760 marines (120 marines per ship was the normal wartime complement of Roman naval infantry) into battle, or more than a legion of men. They could even transport more than that if necessary. It is not surprising that Scipio paid immediate attention to making the captured Carthaginian vessels seaworthy.

Great quantities of war matériel, foodstuffs, and supplies also fell into Roman hands. But among the more important prizes of war were the three hundred Spanish hostages whom the Carthaginians held as a guarantee against treachery. Scipio assured these family members of important tribal and clan leaders that they would soon be restored to their tribes if their tribes were prepared to become Rome's allies. Having achieved his military objective, Scipio turned to exploiting its political benefits. He understood that Rome would triumph more quickly by gaining the Iberian tribes' respect and support, a task made somewhat easier after the Carthaginians' long, harsh rule over the Spanish. Scipio sent most of the Spanish soldiers back to their tribes, where they carried their tale of Roman victory, fairness, and mercy. Scipio sent Mago on to Rome as a prize of war.

Scipio spent the next few weeks repairing the walls of the city and keeping his men in fighting trim. He introduced a training regimen for his troops based on a four-day cycle. There were, after all, still three Carthaginian armies in the field, and Scipio probably expected them to advance on New Carthage as soon as possible. If they did, Scipio intended to meet them in battle well prepared.

Livy describes the training drill:

> On the first day the legionnaires maneuvered under arms [marched in full battle kit] over a distance of four miles; on the second their orders were to parade in front of their tents [were inspected] and attend to the maintenance and cleaning of their weapons; on the third they had a mock battle all in proper form with wooden swords and foiled [blunted] missiles; on the fourth day they rested, and on the fifth there were more maneuvers in full equipment . . . the oarsmen and marines were sent to sea to test in mock battles the capability of their vessels in rapid maneuver.[38]

Scipio's success did nothing to change his mind concerning the tactical weaknesses of the legions and the Roman method of fighting, all of which he had witnessed firsthand at Cannae. He knew that the Carthaginian armies waiting for him beyond the city's walls could not be defeated with the old system.

It was probably during that summer in New Carthage that Scipio first began training his troops in a new tactical system that required them to execute a number of new maneuvers on command. This revolution in Roman tactical methods made Scipio's later victories over the Carthaginians possible and placed him among the world's great generals.[39]

It was spring, perhaps only the beginning of May, when New Carthage fell. Scipio still had five months before his army would have to return to winter quarters and he would leave for Tarraco, as Polybius tells us. Perhaps it was at the Ticinus or at Cannae, where Scipio had fought Spanish troops, that he had acquired his respect for the Spanish sword. He now directed the captured artisans to manufacture enough of these weapons to equip his entire army. Citing Livy, Diodorus, and Cicero, R. J. Forbes has calculated that a Roman army of eight legions (approximately forty thousand men) required sixteen hundred smiths and fabri (craftsmen) to keep its equipment and transport prepared for battle.[40] Scipio's army, then, may have had as many as eight hundred Roman fabri at its disposal to learn the new technology. The Spanish were first-rate metalworkers, and Scipio likely required them to reveal their secrets to his own smiths. Later, when Scipio invaded Africa, his army was fully equipped with the Spanish sword.[41] Scipio was the first Roman general to equip and train his army in the use of the deadly weapon that, with some later modifications, became the famed gladius.

Meanwhile, Scipio dispatched several detachments to the south and into the interior as a reconnaissance in force perhaps to tempt the Carthaginians into action and to discover their positions.[42] But summer and early fall passed without incident. The Carthaginian generals may have concluded that Scipio's position around New Carthage was too strong to risk an attack. Roman command of the sea made a seaborne attack impossible as well. The Roman victory may also have encouraged some of the Spanish tribes to revolt, forcing the Carthaginians to spend time and effort putting them down. Scipio continued to successfully court the Spanish tribes. In any event if Scipio had planned to draw the Carthaginians into a great battle, it would have to wait for another time.

Probably sometime in October Scipio set out for Tarraco. While no source informs us, certainly Scipio did not repeat the Carthaginians' mistake and leave New Carthage lightly guarded. Scipio would probably have left at least two legions in and around New Carthage because maintaining control of the city was absolutely vital before making any attempt to campaign farther south the next year. He also would have garrisoned small troop detachments for the winter along the southern approaches to the city to act as trip wires. Another large contingent of perhaps a legion's strength would have been positioned at Saguntum, with the rest guarding both the Sucro and Ebro River crossings and only a few small units actually returning with Scipio to Tarraco. The road from Tarraco to New Carthage was vital to maintaining and supplying the city. Without Roman supply convoys building storehouses and depots and moving supplies forward, Scipio's offensive to the south would be difficult. As Scipio traveled the road to Tarraco, he met with the local tribal leaders who had to decide if they should give their allegiance to this Roman officer who held out the promise of freeing them from the Carthaginian lash.[43]

Capturing New Carthage struck the first great blow at Carthaginian power in Spain, and in retrospect the wound was mortal. Losing their main supply base made supporting the Carthaginian armies in the field much more difficult. Having to rely on the countryside and what they could extract from the Spanish villages and towns by force and fear loosened their already tenuous hold on the Spanish tribes' loyalty. News of how Scipio freed the Spanish hostages at New Carthage spread quickly and convinced many tribal leaders that an alliance with

Rome was preferable to one with Carthage. Over the long run the tribal leaders' decision would threaten Carthage's ability to raise troops and make it difficult to recruit sufficient manpower to reinforce Hannibal in Italy. After capturing what was left of the Carthaginian fleet at New Carthage, Scipio strengthened Roman control of the sea and further hindered Carthaginian troop and supply movements by ship. The Romans no longer had to worry about Carthaginian seaborne raids across their line of communications. While the Romans controlled the sea, reinforcing the armies in Spain from Carthage itself became a far riskier proposition. Finally, the fall of New Carthage also delivered its valuable silver mines into Roman hands. The Carthaginians depended heavily on mercenaries, and their main source of payment was now lost. This defeat marked the beginning of the financial difficulties that Carthage would face in sustaining its armies for the remainder of the war.[44]

In time these strategic consequences of Scipio's victory would affect Carthaginian fighting capability. From an operational perspective, however, Scipio's capture of New Carthage had three immediate consequences. First, he had blocked the road to Italy. Major Carthaginian reinforcements could no longer reach Hannibal. Next, Scipio now possessed what his father never had, a great logistics base from which to launch a major offensive to the south and the interior. New Carthage had always been the key to military success in the south, and now it was firmly in Roman hands. Finally, Scipio's victory provided the opportunity to equip the Roman army with new weapons and to train it in new tactical maneuvers and formations, greatly increasing its flexibility and combat effectiveness. After Scipio's innovations, the tactical advantages of the Carthaginian mercenary armies he faced were neutralized. When Roman and Carthaginian troops met in battle again, it would be on equal tactical footing.

THE BATTLE OF BAECULA, 208 BCE

Scipio spent the winter of 209–208 in Tarraco, where he continued to receive the various tribal leaders and tried to win them over to the Roman cause. As soon as he had arrived in Tarraco, Edeco, a prince of the Edetani, came to him and pleaded for his wife and sons, who had fallen into Scipio's hands at New Carthage. The Edetani were a powerful tribe living between the Ebro and Sucro rivers, and Edeco's defection to Scipio would be an important coup and serve as an example to other tribes that the Romans could be trusted. Edeco asked that Scipio release his relatives, and in return he promised to be Rome's loyal friend. Soon other tribal chiefs came to Tarraco, most notably Indibilis, one of Spain's most powerful chieftains, and secretly discussed with Scipio changing allegiances. Scipio's success in convincing these tribal leaders to abandon the Carthaginians reveals his keen awareness of the war's political and moral context. With words and promises, he accomplished what the Carthaginian armies could not, winning the Spanish tribes' genuine loyalty. In the spring Indibilis and his brother, Mandonius, deserted Hasdrubal and defected to the Romans, bringing their troops with them and depriving Hasdrubal of much-needed manpower.

While in winter quarters, Scipio instituted another reform of his army. He knew from his experience at Cannae that the Roman maniples lacked the weight to withstand the shock of tribal infantry and cavalry attacks, especially when delivered to the flank. He had already partially remedied this weakness by training his troops in new tactical formations, including shifting to the flanks on command and maneuvering each of the legion's three lines independently.[45] Now Scipio carried out his most important tactical reform by introducing a new combat formation, the cohort. The manipular formation, with its built-in spaces and quincunx arrangement, provided dispersion and flexibility. It worked well against organized opponents who deployed in their own structured formations. The semi-autonomous maniples were small and easy to control, and their dispersion made an orderly retreat easier. They also afforded some degree of tactical flexibility, as when a few maniples could be hidden in ambush or marched around the line to strike the enemy from behind.[46] However, in Spain the Romans were not fighting organized infantry formations but war bands of Spanish and Celtic tribal infantry. These war bands could rush the maniples with terrific force, breaking them on impact. Their use of the wedge and the Spanish habit of operating in close cooperation with cavalry made penetration of the manipular formation a constant danger. For all these reasons, Scipio and others must have recognized the need for a heavier infantry formation capable of withstanding the war bands' attacks.[47]

Polybius tells us that at the battle of Ilipa the Roman cohorts were comprised of three maniples of heavy infantry, or 360 men, and one of light infantry velites of 60 men, for a total of 420 men.[48] When formed as cohorts, the light infantry deployed to the front to act as a screen for the heavy infantry and engaged the enemy with its missiles before the heavy infantry's attack. Scipio trained his army to change on command from the manipular to the cohort formation and back again if necessary.[49] Scipio first used the cohort formation at Ilipa when "the maniples marched in succession forming up and following in column as they wheeled" into cohort formation.[50] He used these heavier cohorts to fall on the enemy flanks and drive them inward in much the same fashion as Hannibal had used his heavy African infantry phalanxes at Cannae. Later, at the battle of the Ebro River, Scipio used the heavy cohorts to deploy across a narrow valley and block the enemy advance.

But did Scipio first conceive of the cohort? Mention of the *cohortes'* earliest use is found in Livy's description of events in Spain in 210 BCE, after the Scipio brothers' deaths and after Lucius Marcius had established the Roman line at the Ebro. Livy tells us that Marcius deployed "a Roman cohort supported by cavalry" in the woods to guard the approaches to the Roman camp.[51] These events occurred before Scipio arrived in Spain, so it is possible, as M. J. V. Bell suggests, that Marcius first used the cohort in combat. Given that he had seen service against the Spanish tribes and had been present at the destruction of the Scipio brothers' armies, it is not unlikely that this experienced infantry officer realized the need for a heavy infantry formation when fighting tribal contingents. After Scipio arrived, Marcius remained on his staff and possibly brought the idea to his new commander's attention. To Scipio's credit, he recognized a good idea when he saw it and introduced the cohort as one of the legions' combat formations.

To undertake a spring campaign against the Carthaginian armies in the south, Scipio needed every combat soldier he could get. For all its expectations of an offensive campaign in Spain, Rome had not provided sufficient manpower to accomplish it. Scipio was and had been outnumbered from the beginning. Now that he intended to engage the main Carthaginian armies, his shortage of troops made the campaign a risky endeavor. Polybius and Livy tell us that Scipio obtained additional manpower by beaching his fleet of forty-eight ships and drafting the naval marines into the infantry.[52] His Roman quinqueremes each carried 270 rowers, 30 sailors, and 120 combat marines.[53] Scipio had earlier equipped his ships with Carthaginian captives and transferred legion infantry to the boats to act as marines.[54] So, in fact, Scipio had only the original thirty contingents of marines from which he could draw and increase his legions' combat strength.

Drafting the marines into the ground forces provided thirty-six hundred additional troops, or about an additional legion, for the infantry, and all of them were fully equipped with armor and weapons. Roman marines were really seaborne infantry and experts at hand-to-hand combat aboard ship or against shore positions. Using only those rowing crews comprised of Roman citizens who had crewed the original thirty boats, Scipio had another eighty-one hundred men who might be turned into ground soldiers. The blacksmiths of New Carthage and captured Carthaginian stocks would have supplied the weapons and equipment to equip the rowers. By distributing the marines and the yet-untrained rowers throughout the legions' ranks, both groups could be quickly trained in the new tactics. Although Scipio would then have enough new troops to outfit three legions, using them in that manner would have been foolish given their lack of training. Integrating them into the existing six legions, perhaps by distributing the new troops among the maniples, would have been more practical. Used in this way, Scipio would have been able to increase the strength of his legions by more than two thousand men each. Because Scipio could not afford to take his entire fleet out of service, he probably did not transfer the entire complement of available troops to the infantry.[55] Had he transferred only half the men, he would have been able to increase the strength of his six legions from four thousand men to almost five thousand men each.[56]

Scipio now had a large army under his command. The losses at New Carthage had been minimal to Scipio's original force of twenty-eight thousand infantry and sixteen hundred cavalry. If Scipio increased the strength of each of his legions to five thousand men, a total of six thousand additional troops were added to his original strength, bringing his army to around thirty-four thousand men.[57] Howard Scullard suggests that as many as six thousand to twelve thousand Spanish troops also joined Scipio as he marched south, increasing the total number of combat troops in his army to more than forty thousand men. With spring already reaching Tarraco, Scipio began to move south, gathering his troops as he went.

Why the Carthaginian armies failed to concentrate against Scipio remains a mystery. The distances all three armies had to cover to link up in the Baetius Valley were, in fact, shorter than the distance Scipio had to travel to get there. Even making allowances for differences in terrain, there seems to be no good military reason why the Carthaginian armies did not make a common effort against their Roman enemy. The explanation Polybius offered, that the other generals were hostile toward Hasdrubal and would not cooperate with him, remains unconvincing.[58] Moreover, after the disaster at Baecula (modern-day Bailen), the three Carthaginian generals did meet and agreed on a common plan to deal with the Romans. According to Livy, the meeting took place "a few days after the fight,"[59] suggesting that the Carthaginian armies had attempted to join Hasdrubal at Baecula but arrived too late.

It is only under the assumption that the other Carthaginian armies were on their way to join him that Hasdrubal's actions at Baecula make military sense. Both Livy and Polybius tell us that Hasdrubal decided to engage Scipio because he was already suffering serious desertions from the Spanish tribes. Although he knew that Scipio's army was larger than his, Hasdrubal supposedly decided to risk the battle anyway. He made contingency plans that if events turned against him, he would retire to the west, recruiting Spanish tribes as he went, and move northwest over the Pyrenees and into Italy to join Hannibal.[60] But this tale is unconvincing. Why confront Scipio at all under these diminished circumstances? It is important to remember that when the Carthaginian Senate assigned Hasdrubal his command, his strategic mission was to recruit an army, cross into Italy, and reinforce Hannibal.[61] The Senate gave the mission of dealing with the Romans in Spain to Mago and Hasdrubal, son of Gisgo. With Scipio on the move, why did Hasdrubal not just refuse battle and cross the Pyrenees, especially if, as Livy and Polybius suggest, he could expect no help from the other generals? Why, instead, did Hasdrubal move *south* toward Baecula and place himself directly in the path of Scipio's army?

The answer must be he wanted to draw Scipio after him and lure him into a battle against the combined Carthaginian armies that were marching toward Baecula. As noted earlier, all three Carthaginian armies could easily have reached Baecula before Scipio did. Baecula is approximately equidistant from the Carthaginian armies' winter garrisons. In the heart of Carthaginian-controlled Spain, where most tribes were still loyal to Carthage, the farm country could support the armies' logistical needs. Baecula was also the location of the last major silver mines still in Carthaginian hands after Scipio captured those around New Carthage. Concentrating at Baecula would force Scipio to operate far from his base at New Carthage. And by arriving first, Hasdrubal would be able to choose the terrain for battle. If Hasdrubal could entice the Romans into a fight on strong defensive terrain, he could reasonably hope to occupy them until the other armies arrived. Hasdrubal could put about twenty thousand to twenty-five thousand troops in the field, a much smaller army than Scipio's, and encourage Scipio's thinking that he held the advantage. If the trap worked, Scipio would find himself facing the seventy thousand troops of three combined Carthaginian armies.

Scipio moved quickly down the coastal road toward New Carthage, gathering his forces from their winter cantonments as he went. Somewhere along this route the two Spanish chiefs Indibilis and Mandonius defected to the Romans. Livy tells us that Scipio's "route lay through country where all was quiet, and he was welcomed and escorted by friendly peoples as he passed the boundaries of the various tribes."[62] With little need to be cautious, the Roman army made good time. Scipio arrived in the vicinity of Baecula after Hasdrubal but before Hasdrubal had fully deployed his troops and before the Carthaginian armies could join him. Acting as a screen for the Roman van, light infantry ran into Hasdrubal's cavalry outposts guarding the approaches to the valley and "went for them as they came up, straight from the march."[63] The pickets fled and warned Hasdrubal that the Romans had arrived.

That Hasdrubal had not yet fully deployed his lines for battle is clear from both Livy's and Polybius's reports. Not until *after* the Romans had arrived *and* night had fallen did Hasdrubal redeploy his forces to a hill that offered a stronger defensive position behind his original camp, located on the flat land below. Another indication that Hasdrubal was caught unprepared was that he never had time to deploy his elephants in the center of the Carthaginian defensive line.[64] The importance of this failure to the battle's outcome cannot be overemphasized. Livy tells us that the Romans attacking in the center were able to carry the top of the ridge, something "they could never have done over such difficult ground if the enemy line had remained intact with the elephants in the van."[65] Contrary to Scullard's contention that Hasdrubal had prepared his defense carefully, in fact he was forced to choose his terrain quickly and to assemble his forces in the enemy's very presence. That he was able to do so at all was a testament both to his skill and to Scipio's mistake in not attacking immediately. Scipio, instead, waited two days before going into the attack.

Polybius's reason for Scipio's delay was that "he became alarmed at the possibility that Mago and Hasdrubal, son of Gisgo, might arrive, in which case he would find himself surrounded by the enemy on all sides."[66] Undoubtedly, that must certainly have been the case. Scipio's concern, however, is further evidence that the Carthaginian armies were closing on Baecula to link up with Hasdrubal. Scipio must have received information about their whereabouts from Roman cavalry scouts or tribal informants that made him think he could attack Hasdrubal and defeat him before the Carthaginian relief force arrived. Given that Hasdrubal's army was still a considerable force of more than twenty thousand men, he was nevertheless greatly outnumbered. Scipio may have calculated that he could win a quick victory precisely because Hasdrubal was not yet ready to fight. Scipio ordered his army to attack.

Scipio had encamped on ground that commanded the approaches to the Guadalquivir River in the Baetius Valley. Concerned that Mago or Hasdrubal, son of Gisgo, might arrive unexpectedly, Scipio sent two cohorts to block both approach routes to the battle area and to act as trip wires.[67] Meanwhile, Hasdrubal had taken up positions during the night, but his deployment was not yet complete. His camp was in disarray and his defensive positions only partially manned, for shifting twenty thousand men and animals in the dark was no easy task.

Hasdrubal used the two days that Scipio afforded him to arrange his forces. Livy describes Hasdrubal's position as being

> on a hill which had a wide area of level ground at its summit; behind him was the river, in front and on both sides the whole position was encircled by a sort of steep bank. Below him was another stretch of open ground, on a slight slope, and this too was surrounded by a wall-like rim, no easier to get over.[68]

Attacked from the front, the terrain required the Romans to fight their way up a steep ridge. Once they took this ridge, they had to assault another ridge before they gained the hilltop. There the land broadened out into a flat area where the main Carthaginian line, anchored in the center by a line of elephants, would normally have been deployed forward of its camp, which was located to the rear of the hill and protected the avenue of retreat. The hilltop was a strong defensive position if the defender had the time to get his forces into position. But a defender could not prepare adequately both to fight and to withdraw at the same time.

It is unclear from the accounts who began the battle. Livy says Hasdrubal sent his Numidian cavalry, together with his light Balearic and African troops, to the ridge first to block the Roman advance. It was all to Hasdrubal's advantage to play for time, arrange his troops into a proper defense, and await the Carthaginian armies' arrival. Even so, he would have positioned some troops as a covering force on the first ridge early on since he would have expected the Romans to follow their pattern and attack from the front. Polybius is probably correct, however, when he says Scipio attacked first by sending "a picked force of infantry" up the first ridge.[69] But who was this force, Scipio's Spanish allies? Here was a perfect opportunity to put the tribal chiefs' reliability to the test by using them in a bloody frontal assault. Was the "picked infantry" Spanish tribal troops or velites or a combined force of both? Although the sources do not tell us that the Spanish troops fought at Baecula, they may have played some role, because Scipio awarded their chiefs the pick of the captured horses when the battle was done.

Both sides fought well, with the Carthaginians raining a barrage of stones down on the Romans. After some time, Scipio's troops gained the top of the first ridge, at which point the Carthaginians fled uphill to their alternate positions. Scipio immediately ordered a stronger follow-on attack against the center, probably using the rest of the light infantry to reinforce his forward elements. Polybius tells us that in the meantime Hasdrubal was still in his camp, waiting with his main force and "trusting to the natural strength of his position and feeling confident that the enemy would never venture to attack him."[70] But Hasdrubal's positions were already under attack. After the battle for the first ridge began, it is inconceivable that Hasdrubal did not prepare to deploy his main force to the hilltop's edge, assuming, of course, he intended to defend his position at all.

Having focused Hasdrubal's attention on the front with his fixing attack, Scipio divided his army into two large maneuver elements. Scipio himself led one to the right of the hill while Laelius took the other to the left in simultaneous attacks up the hill and against the flanks of the main Carthaginian position.

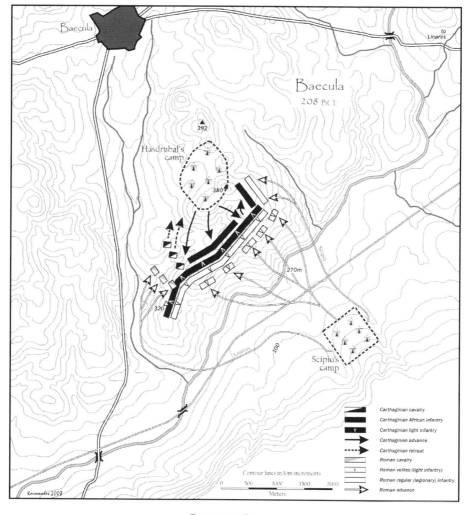

BATTLE OF BAECULA

109

According to Polybius, Hasdrubal and the Carthaginians were taken unprepared because "while this maneuver was in progress Hasdrubal was still engaged in leading his troops out of the camp."[71] Taken in both flanks, the Carthaginians withdrew from the brow of the hill to avoid being cut off in the rear. The Romans trapped a great number of Carthaginian troops between the enveloping pincers and cut them down. Still, the majority of Hasdrubal's army, perhaps as many as two-thirds, escaped.[72]

If true, the tale is one of Hasdrubal's monumental military incompetence. If Kromayer and Veith, both soldier-scholars, are correct in their description of the battlefield of Baecula as presented in their *Schlachten-Atlas zur antiken Kriegsgeschichte*, Hasdrubal's camp was located on a hill 380 meters above the valley floor overlooking the Roman troop deployment.[73] The Roman camp was located on a knoll 100 meters above the valley floor which itself was almost at sea level. The angle of incline of the front ridge was very steep, between forty and forty-five degrees. The distance from the valley floor to the first ridge was approximately 120 meters. Once this ridge was taken, the Roman troops still had to fight their way up to the top, another 420 meters. The total distance to be covered from top to bottom was 540 meters and would have taken at least several hours to traverse against even minimal enemy resistance. Hasdrubal would certainly have detected any major Roman troop movements from this vantage point. Even if he somehow failed to do so because, as Polybius says, he did not expect the Romans to attack, once the Roman attack had begun he would surely have been aware of it. The excuse that Hasdrubal did not deploy his infantry to the brow of the ridge because he did not believe the Romans would attack, and that his position was secure even if they did, is not believable unless Hasdrubal was a rank incompetent, which he was not.

Moreover, the claim that Scipio could divide his army in half, as Polybius tells us, and march behind the entire Roman line and assault the flanking ridges without being detected seems unlikely. The distance from Scipio's line of departure to the bottom of the ridge is 2,300 meters. Laelius had to cover 4,000 meters before he could attack the Carthaginian positions on the Roman left. Surely some Carthaginian officer on the brow of the hill would have noticed that the Roman maneuver elements, each ten-thousand-men strong, were moving across the plain and toward the Carthaginian flanks. Once in position, Scipio's and Laelius's troops would have had to climb a ridge with a thirty-five-degree incline and traverse 662 meters of ground to reach the top before they could begin to engage Hasdrubal's infantry. From beginning to end, Scipio's maneuver would have taken several hours at least. Thus, it is difficult to believe that Hasdrubal was taken by surprise. If Hasdrubal was taken by surprise in *both* flanks, how was most of his army able to escape what must have been a near double envelopment?

To understand what happened at Baecula, we must recall that Hasdrubal had moved from the Tagus River toward Baecula not to engage Scipio but to link up with the other two Carthaginian armies that were also making their way there. He knew full well that Scipio's army was considerably larger than his own and had no intention of fighting Scipio by himself. Scipio's march to the southwest was designed to engage one of the Carthaginian armies, but Scipio did not know exactly where any of them were located. He therefore struck deeply into the Baetius Valley, the heartland of Carthaginian control, hoping to draw one of them into a battle. His movement was more rapid than could normally be expected, and as he struck for the important town of Baecula and its rich silver mines, he encountered Hasdrubal, who had arrived there only a few days earlier. The proof that Hasdrubal did not expect Scipio is that Hasdrubal had not bothered to occupy any defensive position on his arrival. He was waiting encamped on the open plain for Mago and Hasdrubal and thought he was safe in a Carthaginian-controlled area. He moved to a defensive position only after learning of Scipio's arrival.

Outnumbered almost two to one, Hasdrubal must have known that to offer battle was to court disaster. Hasdrubal's brief was not to fight the Romans in Spain but to invade Italy and reinforce Hannibal. To accomplish this mission, he had to conserve his troop strength, which was already somewhat depleted after the disloyal Spanish tribes defected. Once Scipio had arrived, however, Hasdrubal's hope was that the other Carthaginian armies would arrive before Scipio attacked. If they did not, the only realistic course was to break contact with the Romans, withdraw westward from whence he had come, follow the Tagus River, and head over the Pyrenees into Gaul and Italy. Hasdrubal waited for Scipio to attack, hoping that Mago and Hasdrubal Gisgo might yet arrive in time.

Once Scipio began the assault, Hasdrubal sent his light troops into action as a covering force for his main body. When the first ridge fell, he may have sent some of his regular troops to the brow of the hill to contain the Roman attack while holding most of his forces and his elephants back from the battle. As long as he could hold Scipio's fixing attack at the front ridge, there was no need to do anything else. The longer the battle went on, the greater the chance that the Carthaginian armies would arrive to help. But when Hasdrubal saw two large Roman maneuver elements move to the wings of the line, he must have known at once they were moving toward his flanks. At that point he had to either make a stand against Scipio's superior force or follow his original plan, save his army, and withdraw. He probably sent his less valuable light troops to stiffen the front and may have deployed some heavy infantry to hold the flank ridges against the advancing Romans. These troops may have been the ones that Polybius and Livy say the Romans overran. Taking his elephants, his treasury, and two-thirds of his army, Hasdrubal withdrew down the back of the hill with his army intact. Indeed, Livy tells us that Hasdrubal had already sent his elephants to the rear *before* the battle began, which explains why this valuable combat asset was not deployed to block the Romans' advance on the second ridge.[74] While the troops holding the brow of the hill on three sides were overrun, Hasdrubal and his army escaped.

Scipio immediately transferred his camp to the site of the captured Carthaginian camp because it had a much stronger defensive position than his previous location.[75] Polybius is clear that Scipio feared the other two Carthaginian armies would yet arrive and attack him, so he prepared to defend himself on good ground. It was a wise move, indeed, for the Carthaginians did arrive in the vicinity of Baecula and linked up with Hasdrubal "a few days after the fight at Baecula."[76] The commanders held a council of war and decided that Hasdrubal should carry out his original mission and proceed to Italy. Mago's command was transferred to Hasdrubal Gisgo, and Mago was slated to go to the Balearic Isles and hire more mercenaries. The unified forces under Hasdrubal were to withdraw deeper into Spain and avoid any battles with the Romans.[77] Massinissa, the prince of the Numidians, was to be left behind with a force of three thousand light horse cavalry to conduct guerrilla operations in western Spain, support those tribes that were still loyal to Carthage, and punish those that had gone over to the Romans.[78] When the war council concluded, the Carthaginian commanders went their separate ways.

This version raises interesting questions. First, even assuming Livy's inflated figure of ten thousand Carthaginian prisoners taken at Baecula is correct, Hasdrubal's army still had fourteen thousand to sixteen thousand troops. When joined with the two other Carthaginian armies, each numbering about twenty-five thousand men, the combined force had more than sixty thousand troops. Moreover, if the war council meeting took place "a few days after the fight at Baecula," the Carthaginian armies must have been only a short distance from the Romans' position at Baecula. A normal rate of march in retreat over, say, four days placed the rival armies only thirty or so miles apart, meaning they were close enough to concentrate their forces and march on Baecula. So why did the Carthaginians not attack Scipio? Second, if the commanders put greater importance on Hasdrubal's mission of invading Italy, why did they reinforce Gisgo's army and then send it to the rear, where it could not fight, instead of giving Hasdrubal more troops? Third, why did Mago leave to recruit mercenaries when the Carthaginian armies in Spain already outnumbered the Romans? Finally, if blocking Hasdrubal's invasion of Italy was the most important strategic objective for the Romans in Spain, when Hasdrubal began marching toward the Pyrenees, why didn't Scipio attempt to stop him?

Perhaps the reason the Carthaginians did not attack Scipio at Baecula had less to do with manpower issues and more with the tactical capabilities of their respective armies. Carthaginian armies fought best when they could take advantage of their tactical flexibility, could maneuver, and fight from ambush, or where their cavalry could be decisive. Scipio's strong position on the heights at Baecula immediately neutralized these advantages. If the Carthaginians had attacked Scipio, it would have been simple infantry combat, and no one was better at this kind of "bludgeon work" than the Romans. With no tactical advantage to be had, then, the Carthaginian commanders observed their own tactical rule and decided not to fight. The decision to leave the Romans to Massinissa and withdraw deeper into Spain remains puzzling, however, and it makes strategic sense only if the Spanish tribes' revolt was even more extensive than reported in the sources. Livy says that Mago and Hasdrubal, son of Gisgo, were indeed convinced "that the entire Spanish population had been deeply affected, individually and collectively, by Scipio's generosity and that there would be no end to Spaniards going over to the Roman cause."[79] With too few troops to fight the Romans and suppress the Spanish tribes at the same time, Hasdrubal's withdrawal and Mago's recruitment efforts make sense. Their goal was to raise a large army that could suppress the tribes and then return to fighting the Romans. Until then, Massinissa would harass the Romans with guerrilla tactics.

However, the most pressing questions remain: Why did Scipio not pursue Hasdrubal when he had him on the run? Why did he not make an effort to block the Pyrenees passes and prevent Hasdrubal from reaching Gaul? The answer to both questions is because of the Carthaginian armies' proximity—only a few days' march—to Baecula. Scipio had been worried about encountering these armies from the beginning. He probably considered himself fortunate to have driven Hasdrubal off his strong defensive position so quickly. Scipio then occupied it himself in anticipation of the other Carthaginian armies' arrival. Thus, he would hardly have taken the risk of pursuing Hasdrubal for fear that he might collide with the Carthaginian relief force. If the collision happened in open country, where the Carthaginian cavalry could be decisive, the result might have been disaster for Scipio.

Fear of the Carthaginian armies also convinced Scipio not to attempt to block Hasdrubal's movement toward the Pyrenees passes. By the time Hasdrubal was on the move, Scipio certainly knew the other Carthaginian armies were nearby. Any attempt to block Hasdrubal meant exposing his flank and, as the pursuit progressed, his rear to the two Carthaginian armies in the vicinity. Instead, Scipio dispatched a relatively small detachment "to keep watch on Hasdrubal's movements."[80] Scipio was concerned that Hasdrubal might halt, turn back toward Baecula, and attack in concert with the other Carthaginian armies, catching Scipio between the hammer and anvil. He had also to be concerned about exposing the road to New Carthage to a sudden Carthaginian advance. As at Belle Alliance, when Napoleon sent Marshal Grouchy to follow the Prussians and prevent them from returning to the battlefield, Scipio dispatched a force "to keep the sabre in the back" of Hasdrubal, that is, to block his return to Baecula.[81] Scipio was later criticized in the Roman Senate by Quintus Fabius Maximus for failing to prevent Hasdrubal from invading Italy. Other historians have argued that while Scipio won a tactical victory at Baecula, he suffered a strategic defeat in failing to stop Hasdrubal.[82] The criticism is, as I have attempted to show, unfair.

However one judges Scipio's actions from a strategic perspective, Scipio's tactical brilliance was on full display at Baecula. As Scullard notes, "The tactics employed by Scipio at Baecula were a complete break with the traditional movements of a Roman army, and mark a real turning point in military development."[83] The legions that Scipio had armed, strengthened, and trained in new tactical maneuvers made their debut at Baecula. Formerly able to attack only to the front, Scipio's new legions showed their ability to hold the enemy with a front-fixing attack while maneuvering its stronger cohorts to the wings and mounting an independent attack against the enemy's flanks. If there was any tactical shortcoming, it was the Roman center's failure to hold the enemy long enough for the maneuver elements to gain the flanks and close off the enemy's retreat, the tactic Hannibal used at Cannae. But Scipio can be forgiven this circumstance because unlike Hannibal, Scipio did not possess sufficient well-trusted and trained cavalry that could have cut off the Carthaginian retreat or at least closed more quickly with its flanks. Moreover, Hasdrubal never intended to fight unless joined by the other armies, and he moved quickly to escape before Scipio's attack could fully develop. At Baecula, Scipio showed what the reformed Roman legions could tactically achieve when well trained and well led. The new weapons and new tactics had won the day. The later battles at Ilipa, the Great Plains, and Zama were only further developments of the same tactical principles.[84]

Scipio remained in Baecula for the rest of the summer and established good relations with the tribes living in the area before returning to Tarraco's winter quarters. He had freed all the native Spanish troops captured at Baecula without ransom and allowed them to go home. He treated his Spanish allies generously, giving Indibilis three hundred horses and distributing the rest to Spanish soldiers. This largesse we must regard as a diplomatic gesture since no evidence shows that the Spanish took part in the battle (although, as noted earlier, they might have served as shock troops against the Carthaginian center). Several tribal chiefs came to pledge their loyalty to Scipio and addressed him as "king," a term the Roman Republicans despised. Scipio assembled his allies and told them that while he wished to act kingly, he preferred the term *imperator*. Here, then, may be the first recorded example of a Roman general's troops proclaiming their leader as imperator.[85]

THE BATTLE OF ILIPA, 206 BCE

In the spring of 207 BCE, a new Carthaginian commander arrived in Spain. His name was Hanno, and he arrived with a force of ten thousand troops to compensate for the loss of Hasdrubal's army, which left the Spanish theater for Italy.[86] When joined with the army of Hasdrubal, son of Gisgo, near Gades, total Carthaginian strength in Spain was still some sixty thousand troops.[87] Prompted by substantial defections of their tribal allies, the Carthaginians set about to re-cruit more Spaniards from the tribes deep in the country's interior, where they thought Roman influence had not yet reached. Hanno succeeded in raising an additional nine thousand men there.[88]

The size of the Carthaginian army in Spain must have given Scipio reason to be cautious. Rather than risk his entire army in another southern campaign, Scipio decided to send out a reconnaissance in force in advance of his army to locate the Carthaginians, gain an appreciation for their numbers, and test their willingness to fight. A force of ten thousand infantry and five hundred cavalry under Marcus Silanus moved into the Baetius Valley. Scipio himself remained at the valley's northern end with the main body of his army.

Somewhere in the valley's interior Silanus stumbled across Hanno and Mago with their assembled new recruits. Silanus's cavalry discovered their two camps across the main road a few miles to his front. One camp contained four thousand Carthaginian regulars and two hundred cavalry while the other, perhaps a mile or so away, held nine thousand Celtiberian recruits. The Carthaginian camp was properly defended, with outposts, sentries, and the usual military dispositions, while the recruits' camp had no such precautions "in the usual manner of barbarians and raw recruits."[89] Using the woods, glens, and rough ground for concealment, Silanus moved his men to within a mile of the recruits' camp before being discovered. When the alarm sounded, Mago and Hanno rushed to the camp with four thousand men and two hundred cavalry and took up positions in front of it. The Romans emerged from their concealment, formed up their legions, and went into the attack.

Both lines crashed together in hand-to-hand combat. The battlefield's broken ground hindered the Carthaginian troops' usual agility while the Romans stood fast in their formations. Unable to run, the Carthaginians were butchered. The *Punica* describes it "less a battle than a scene of ruthless execution . . . slayers on one side and the slaughtered on the other."[90] That the Romans outnumbered the Carthaginians also contributed to the slaughter. Mago escaped with all his cavalry and perhaps half his infantry, turning up nine days later in Gades to join Hasdrubal's army. Hanno himself was surrounded, taken prisoner, and "dragged through the midst of the throng, his hands bound behind his back; though a captive in bonds, he begged for his life."[91] The Celtiberian recruits were scattered to the surrounding area and eventually made their way back to their homes. Silanus's victory was important because it broke the back of the Carthaginian recruitment effort, at least for the moment. Hasdrubal could count on no more Spanish troops.

Sometime after this skirmish, Hasdrubal moved forward from Gades through the Baetius Valley and encamped about a hundred or so miles south of Scipio, who had also moved into the valley following Silanus's successful reconnaissance. The Carthaginians redeployed to hold their tribal allies fast in their alliances and to prevent further defections to the Romans.[92] It is unclear how much of Hasdrubal's army was with him. In any case he was certainly on the strategic defensive and was not yet ready to force a battle with Scipio, at least not where his allies might desert or even turn on him. So when Scipio began to advance down the valley in force, Hasdrubal retreated toward Gades. As Hasdrubal moved south, he dispersed his army into strong garrisons behind the walled towns along his route of withdrawal. He was determined to avoid the decisive battle that he was certain Scipio sought. By dispersing his troops in walled towns, he forced Scipio to choose between withdrawing and fighting another day or spending weeks and months reducing one town after another. Scipio decided that the prize was not worth the game, and he broke off his march and withdrew to Baecula. There he spent the summer and fall strengthening his alliances with the Spanish tribes.

As a demonstration of force, Scipio sent his brother, Lucius, in command of ten thousand infantry and a thousand cavalry to attack the town of Orongis about a 150 miles southwest of New Carthage.[93] The reason for the attack is unclear, but perhaps the town was still loyal to the Carthaginians. According to Livy, the townspeople tried to flee, holding shields before them and their empty sword hands above their heads. The Romans mistook this attempt to surrender for an attack and slew hundreds of townspeople by mistake. Some two thousand Carthaginian soldiers were also killed.[94] With winter approaching, Scipio withdrew to Tarraco, and his army dispersed to winter quarters.

While these events were transpiring in Spain, the Carthaginian cause suffered a mortal blow in Italy. Hasdrubal had made good his crossing of the Pyrenees and spent the winter of 208–207 BCE in Gaul. He recruited ten thousand Gauls for his army, bringing his total strength to about twenty-five thousand men.[95] He had left Spain with fifteen thousand to eighteen thousand men after the battle at Baecula. In the spring of 207 BCE, he crossed the Alps and arrived in the Po Valley in May. The Romans intercepted a message from Hasdrubal to Hannibal proposing that their two armies link up in Umbria. Two Roman armies under Marcus Livius Salinator and Gaius Claudius Nero caught Hasdrubal on the banks of the Metaurus River and dealt him a terrible defeat. Ten thousand Carthaginians and Gauls were killed compared to Roman losses of two thousand men.[96] Another ten thousand Carthaginians and Gauls were taken prisoner. Hasdrubal himself was killed and beheaded. Hannibal learned of his brother's death when the Romans threw his head into Hannibal's camp. By early 206 BCE, the news of Hasdrubal's defeat had reached Spain.

The defeat at the Metaurus River forced the Carthaginian commanders in Spain to face two unpleasant facts. First, they no longer had any hope that a Roman defeat in Italy would force Rome's strategic withdrawal from Spain. Nor, indeed, could they reinforce Hannibal from Spain. Second, Scipio would now begin reducing one town after another until all the Carthaginian outposts in southern Spain were eliminated. He would then attack their main base at Gades. The choice for Hasdrubal and Mago was either to await Scipio's campaign on the defensive or to take the offensive and meet him in open battle. In the spring of 206 the Carthaginian army set out from Gades to confront Scipio. Hasdrubal and Mago marched to Ilipa, somewhere close to modern Seville, where they selected their ground and waited for Scipio to arrive.[97] Scipio began to concentrate his forces, sending Silanus to collect the three thousand infantry and five hundred horses promised him by the tribal chief, Culchas. Scipio advanced south with his main body and was joined by Silanus and Culchas near Baecula. The Roman army and their Celtiberian allies amounted to forty-five thousand infantry and three thousand cavalry. The Carthaginian army numbered around sixty thousand infantry, four thousand cavalry, and thirty-two elephants.[98] Scipio approached Ilipa and pitched his camp on some low hills directly opposite the Carthaginian positions.

As his army prepared for battle, Scipio was forced to deal with two difficulties, and either might easily have convinced a less confident and imaginative commander to change course. First, he was badly outnumbered. Of greater concern, however, were the contingents of Iberian troops that Scipio's new Spanish allies raised. He could hardly forget that his father and uncle had gone to their deaths because they had trusted their Iberian allies, who deserted them on the battlefield and left both consuls and their legions to a bitter fate. Scipio could ill afford not to use them, but he knew better than to trust them.[99]

Scipio approached Ilipa and found Hasdrubal waiting for him, encamped on the low hills that formed a valley. With Scipio encamped on the near side, the battlefield was set between the two armies. As Scipio's troops set to constructing their camp, Mago, the bold and often reckless cavalry commander, took the opportunity to carry out a harassing attack. Scipio had foreseen this possibility and had placed some of his cavalry under the shelter of a hill to deal with it. When Mago attacked, the Romans took his cavalry in the flank. Scipio sent some infantry units into the fray and drove the Carthaginians back to their camp to lick their wounds. Scipio had won the first round. More to the point, his cavalry had performed well. Polybius notes that the "Carthaginians were disconcerted by the agility of some of the Roman horsemen in dismounting."[100] Generally the Roman cavalry tended to dismount and fight as infantry, a weakness that deprived it of mobility, shock, and the ability to pursue. As Walter Brewitz explains, Polybius depicts their dismounting as a strength and notes that the "Roman cavalry showed the greatest dexterity in leaping from their horses during the battle, holding their manes in one hand, and stabbing the enemy horses in the bellies with the other, and then springing back again."[101]

The two camps faced each other across a valley between two low ridges. Every day for three days, always in mid-morning, Hasdrubal led his army out onto the valley floor to offer battle. Scipio followed suit but always after the Carthaginians had deployed. For hours the armies stood in the sun, neither side making a move to engage the other. Then, as the day turned to dusk, the armies would return to their respective camps, with the Carthaginians always being the first to return. Each day Hasdrubal set out the same order of battle, his center comprised of African and Carthaginian regulars and his wings of Spanish allies and cavalry. His elephants were deployed between the wings and the center but closer to the wings. Scipio, too, displayed his same order of battle each day, with the center comprised of legion heavy infantry and the wings held by his Iberian allies and cavalry.[102] Day after day Scipio formed up his army in this manner until he was convinced that he had baited the trap sufficiently. As Hannibal had done at Cannae, Scipio set the trap in plain sight. And when Hasdrubal did not detect it for three days, Scipio decided that it was time to fight.

On the night before the fourth day, Scipio ordered his troops to rise, eat, and arm themselves before daylight. He instructed the cavalrymen to saddle their mounts and be ready to move before the sun broke the horizon. As the sun came up, Scipio ordered his cavalry and light troops to carry out a harassing attack against the Carthaginian camp. While the attack was in progress, Scipio moved his main units onto the field and deployed for battle. The Carthaginian camp filled with noise and confusion as men stumbled from their beds half-asleep and half-naked. When Hasdrubal learned of Scipio's deployment, he feared Scipio would soon attack in force. Hasdrubal ordered his men to form for battle. None had been fed, and more than a few were only partially armed as they assembled in their usual order and prepared for battle. Scipio ordered the signaler to recall the cavalry and light infantry. Anticipating by more than two thousand years Napoleon's dictum to do nothing to stop a man who was making a mistake, Scipio did nothing to hinder the Carthaginian deployment. Neither Livy nor Polybius tells us what was going through Hasdrubal's mind that day or whether he recognized that he was caught even before the battle had begun. While Hasdrubal's men were arranged as before, Scipio had completely altered his order of battle. Now the heavy Roman infantry were on the wings along with the light infantry deployed behind and to the oblique. In the center Scipio had placed his least reliable troops, the Spanish allies.

Scipio and the Roman troops did nothing for some time, waiting until the

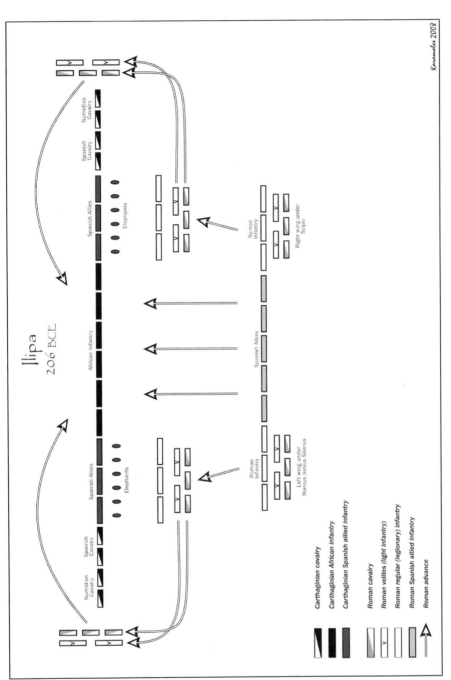

Ilipa
206 BCE

Numidian Cavalry

Spanish Cavalry

Spanish Allies

Elephants

African Infantry

Spanish Allies

Elephants

Spanish Cavalry

Numidian Cavalry

Roman Infantry

Left wing under
Marcus Junius Silenus

Spanish Allies

Roman Infantry

Right wing under
Scipio

Carthaginian cavalry

Carthaginian African infantry

Carthaginian Spanish allied infantry

Roman cavalry

Roman velites (light infantry)

Roman regular (legionary) infantry

Roman Spanish allied infantry

Roman advance

Karumales 2008

BATTLE OF ILIPA

Carthaginians began to feel their lack of breakfast and became fatigued from standing in the mid-morning heat. As the sun rose higher, small skirmishes broke out between the two sides' cavalry and light troops. Shortly before noon, Scipio recalled his skirmishers and moved into the attack. It is a testament to Scipio's daring and confidence in how well he had trained his army that he was willing to risk everything in a battle where he was outnumbered, employing tactics that depended on his army executing complex maneuvers against an army that had already mastered those same maneuvers. Scipio ordered the Iberians into the attack, but he also ordered them to move slowly and to delay reaching the Carthaginian line for as long as possible. With himself in command of his right wing and Silanus of the left, Scipio ordered the legions and the accompanying cavalry to march quickly forward, aiming at the Carthaginian wings opposite them.

Within a few minutes the Roman wings were well forward of its center. As the wings approached the enemy, Scipio and Silanus maneuvered to the oblique and overlapped the ends of the Carthaginian line. Having gained the outside of the Carthaginian line, the legions turned inward and fell on the Carthaginian flanks with great fury. Scipio then brought his cavalry into play. He ordered the cavalry to break from the outside of the legion's wings, ride around the Carthaginian line, and strike it in the rear. He ordered his light infantry to turn inward and take the enemy deeper in the flank.[103]

The success of a flanking attack depends heavily on the ability of the fixing attack to hold fast the enemy troops in the center of the line. When Scipio's maneuver elements moved toward the Carthaginian flanks, his Iberian infantry still had not yet reached the Carthaginian line. Their slow rate of advance had permitted Scipio to "refuse" the center, something no Roman commander had ever attempted before.[104] Although not yet engaged, the Iberians' approach forced the Carthaginian center with Hasdrubal's best troops to remain in place. If they advanced, they exposed their flanks to the Roman maneuver elements and their supporting cavalry. If they remained where they were, however, they were effectively out of the fight and risked being enveloped once Scipio's legions overcame the Carthaginian flanks. The fight was Cannae in reverse. Scipio had carried out a double envelopment. The legions drove the Carthaginian flanks inward and on the center, and the slaughter commenced. The *Punica* describes the horror: "No upheaval of the earth could cost as many lives; and no fearful rage of wild beasts could ever work such carnage in their savage haunts. Plains and valleys soon were soaked, and weapons lost their edge. Africans and warlike Spaniards fell alike."[105]

To his credit Hasdrubal did not panic even after the Roman cavalry had spooked his elephants and routed them into the Carthaginian line.[106] The Romans drove the elephants back through the Carthaginian cavalry posted on the wings, throwing the cavalry into confusion and driving it from the field.[107] To save themselves, the Carthaginians began cutting their way through the back of the Roman envelopment, hoping to gain their camp, and they withdrew in relatively good order. Then Fortuna smiled on Hasdrubal. Polybius says a cloudburst suddenly broke overhead, turning the ground to mud and preventing the Romans from storming the Carthaginian camp.[108] When night fell and prevented further action, Hasdrubal took the opportunity to slip away. Then he discovered that Scipio had placed infantry cohorts across his line of retreat. Still, large remnants of the Carthaginian army fought or slipped through the Roman noose. "Nor would that day have ended the struggle, nor that courage have failed, had not an arrow pierced Hasdrubal's corslet, inflicting a slight wound."

Having brought the enemy to hand, Scipio was not of a mind to let it go easily. He sent his cavalry in pursuit with instructions to attack and harass the enemy and to slow his withdrawal. Scipio ordered his legions to begin a forced march, and with great speed they set out to catch the retreating Carthaginians. The Roman cavalry performed well once more, slowing the Carthaginian march so that the legions could overtake it. Hasdrubal attempted to escape across the Baetis River, but Scipio sent units to block the fords. The Romans finally caught the fleeing Carthaginian army and fell upon it, slaughtering the weary enemy. The remnants of the defeated army were left to Silanus and his eleven thousand men, who dealt cruelly with these wretched souls. Polybius says of this final engagement that "it was no longer a fight, but a butchering of cattle."

With brilliant tactics and battlefield daring Scipio's well-trained army had proved itself superior to the Carthaginians. It had destroyed an army of sixty thousand men. Livy says that Hasdrubal escaped with only six thousand men. The rest were dead, wounded, or taken prisoner and sold into slavery. Hasdrubal reached the Carthaginian stronghold at Gades and boarded a ship bound for Carthage. There is no better example in military history of a battle in which a weaker force gained so complete a victory over a stronger one than the battle of Ilipa. The Romans won with innovative tactics, daring, concentration of force, and the preparation and imagination of a brilliant general. Much of Spain remained to be pacified, but after Ilipa, the Carthaginians could no longer prevent the Romans from gaining control of the country. They held fast to Gades but could not prevent the Romans from pacifying the Iberian tribes with diplomacy or killing them. Spain was no longer a source of Carthaginian military manpower, and Scipio's victories had removed the threat of a second invasion of Italy. Hannibal could fight on. But after Ilipa Carthage's defeat was now just a matter of time.

5

The Strategist

WITH THE CARTHAGINIAN armies in Spain crushed beneath the power of his legions, any other Roman general would have regarded his task complete and his accomplishments sufficient. Not so Scipio, who, as Livy tells us, "looked upon the conquest of Spain as a mere preliminary sketch of the great things which, in his noble ambition, he yet hoped to do. Already his thoughts were on Africa and Carthage."[1] What drove Scipio was probably a quest for personal glory and his disciplined, strategic mind seeking a long-term solution to Rome's security problems with Carthage. Scipio was far beyond the provincial-minded Roman generals of his day in his strategic thinking. Men like Quintus Fabius Maximus and the members of his senatorial faction sought the removal of Hannibal from Italy as their primary strategic objective. In the Fabian view, Hannibal's departure from Italy would allow Rome to resume the important task of increasing its agricultural settlements and finally colonize the north with Roman farmers. Scipio saw this policy as dangerously shortsighted. Rome had suffered greatly during the war, and removing Hannibal's army from Italian soil was meager recompense for such suffering. Moreover, with Hannibal undefeated and Carthage allowed to rebuild its strength, there was nothing to prohibit both from mounting another war against Rome. Fabius's policy conceded the strategic offensive to Carthage and did little to guarantee Rome's long-term security interests.

Scipio's strategic assessment of Rome's security interests was more realistic. Scipio understood that Spain, not Italy, was the critical variable in the Carthaginian power equation. He believed the country's wealth, manpower, and strategic location as a platform of operations against Italy, Sardinia, and Corsica could never again be allowed to fall into Carthaginian hands. Carthaginian power in Spain not only had to be broken, as Scipio had already done with his military campaign, but had to be eradicated altogether. To achieve this goal, Rome would be forced to control the country and ensure that control with Roman troops and garrisons. For a city-state with as yet no foreign possessions, the strategic requirements of undertaking the military occupation of a country the size of Spain were extraordinary and completely novel. Moreover, Scipio saw the occupation of Spain as the beginning of a policy of Roman territorial expansion.

Rome could never be secure until Carthage was defeated and brought to such terms that it could never again threaten Roman security interests in the western Mediterranean. Rome could achieve these objectives only by excercising its military and naval power on the North African littoral and establishing a permanent commercial and diplomatic presence in the western Mediterranean, further increasing Roman strategic military requirements. But Carthage could not be brought to heel unless it was first defeated on the battlefield and Hannibal and the Carthaginian army were destroyed. Carthaginian military power had to be reduced to a level fit only for maintaining domestic order and protecting itself from enemies on the North African mainland. Hasdrubal's defeat at the Metaurus River had ensured that Rome itself would not fall to Carthaginian arms, but Hannibal remained in Italy. Years of military effort had failed to remove him, and the future portended more of the same for similar military efforts in Italy. Scipio saw that the way to remove Hannibal was to threaten Carthage with military attack. Under these circumstances, Hannibal would be forced to return to defend the city. If he chose to remain in Italy, he would become a strategic irrelevancy. Thus, with these national security objectives in mind, Scipio began planning for the invasion of Africa after his victory at Ilipa.

AFRICA

A general who prefers to achieve his ends through diplomacy rather than war is rare, and it is the strategist's challenge to determine whether war or diplomacy is preferable in a given case. For Scipio, both were but means to ends, neither having more worth than the other except as particular circumstances might dictate. Scipio understood that Carthage would ultimately have to be defeated by force of arms. To facilitate that task, he engaged in diplomacy to deprive Carthage of its African allies while gaining their allegiance for Rome before the decisive military confrontation occurred. The Roman victory at Ilipa had changed the strategic equation in Rome's favor. Massinissa, the Numidian prince who had once been Hasdrubal's cavalry commander, understood this shift. While serving as Mago's cavalry commander at Gades, Massinissa secretly approached the

Romans through Marcus Silanus, Scipio's trusted subordinate. Massinissa had been in command of a cavalry detachment at the battle where Scipio's father and uncle had been killed. At Baecula, Scipio had captured Massinissa's young nephew and had returned him to his relatives unharmed.[2] Now Massinissa proposed an alliance with Rome.

To ensure that he could deliver on his promises, Massinissa proposed to return to Africa and make certain his people would follow him in his change of allegiances. Livy tells us that "the reason for this sudden change of sides was not, at the time, entirely clear."[3] The reason seems to have been the death of Massinissa's father, King Gaia of the Massyles, and the usurpation of his throne by a pretender who enjoyed the backing of the Carthaginians and Syphax. King of the Masaesyles, Syphax sought to absorb the Massyle kingdom into his own.[4] Massinissa wanted the Romans' assistance for his attempt to reclaim his father's throne. To secure that help, he offered to support the Romans and supply them with troops. On the one hand, Scipio had been duly impressed with the Numidian cavalry's performance in Spain, and on the other hand, he must have been aware of Massinissa's role in his father's and uncle's deaths. But sound strategic planning left little room for personal grudges. Lacking good Roman cavalry had not been vitally important in Scipio's Spanish campaign because of the rugged terrain; however, on the open North African plains, cavalry could well prove the decisive combat arm. As things stood, Scipio had no counter to the Carthaginian cavalry. The prospect of acquiring the Numidian light cavalry for his army was too important for Scipio to ignore. Massinissa was sent on to Africa with Scipio's promise of support.

At the same time Scipio decided to approach Syphax, Massinissa's adversary in the dynastic struggles plaguing Numidia. The most powerful and important of the Numidian kings, Syphax had been allied with the Carthaginians for years. Scipio's attempt to bring about his defection is testimony to Scipio's understanding of the dictum later formalized by Carl von Clausewitz: "War is the continuation of policy by other means." In other words, there are many ways to win, and Scipio knew the value of politics in such calculations.

The Romans had had prior dealings with the wily Syphax in 214 BCE. Syphax had tried to unite the nomadic tribes of northwest Africa so they could deal with the Carthaginians from a position of strength. That year Hasdrubal suffered a defeat, and Syphax took advantage of this weakness to encroach on Carthaginian lands and strike a deal with Scipio's father. The elder Scipio sent a few Roman centurions to train the Numidians in infantry fighting in return for Syphax's bringing about the

Numidians' desertion from the Carthaginian army in Spain. This defection forced Hasdrubal and his troops to return from Spain to deal with the Numidians. Hasdrubal urged Syphax's neighbor to the east, Gaia of the Massyles, to make war on Syphax. In that war Gaia's son, Massinissa, distinguished himself as a cavalry commander. None of this fighting came to much, and by 212 BCE, Syphax had returned to supporting the Carthaginians and Massinissa was in Spain, commanding Hasdrubal's Numidian cavalry.[5]

Syphax was an important element in Scipio's strategic calculations for his military operations in Africa. Syphax was the wealthiest of the African princes; could raise large numbers of troops, most of them excellent cavalry; had war-fighting experience; and knew the countryside and Carthaginians well. The *Punica* says, "He was the most powerful, save Carthage itself. He was rich in territory and in horses, and in those huge beasts [elephants] that spread terror on the battlefield; he had also an army of picked soldiers [professionals]." His capital at Cirta had a population of two hundred thousand people, and he could put twenty thousand infantry and ten thousand cavalry in the field. Livy also tells us that Syphax's kingdom could produce large quantities of grain to feed the Roman army. Syphax's kingdom was a warrior society established on a strong agricultural base, and he could supply impressive amounts of cavalry, infantry, and almost limitless supplies and logistics. In addition, Livy tells us that his "kingdom was conveniently situated with regard to Spain, being on the other side of a compara-tively narrow strait," thus making resupply of the Roman army that much easier.[6] The value of Syphax's help to Scipio's campaign was enormous, and Scipio showed that he was prepared to run any risk to obtain it.

Scipio sent Laelius across the strait to negotiate with Syphax. Sensing that the strategic tide had already turned, Syphax prepared to abandon the Carthaginians and switch sides again. Syphax told Laelius that he was prepared to accept Rome's friendship, but he would not formally ratify a treaty to this effect except in the Roman commander in chief's presence. Laelius returned to Scipio with Syphax's promise for Scipio's safe passage to Africa if he agreed to ratify the treaty. It was a dangerous gambit, for there was no guarantee that the treacherous Syphax would not deliver Rome's greatest field commander into Carthaginian hands.[7] But if Syphax could be convinced to support Rome, the Carthaginian political and mili-tary position in Africa would be greatly weakened before a single Roman soldier set foot on African soil. Along with the prospect that Massinissa might also be turned to Roman advantage, Scipio reckoned the opportunity was well worth the risk. He placed Marcius in command at New Carthage and Silanus at Tarraco.

Then accompanied by Laelius, Scipio set sail from New Carthage in two quinqueremes for Siga (modern Takembrit), Syphax's western capital.

The two men "made the passage to Africa mostly under oars with a calm sea, occasionally helped by a light breeze."[8] As Scipio's ships approached the African coast, they sighted Hasdrubal with seven triremes already in the harbor. Hasdrubal, too, had come to seek Syphax's support, and here he saw the man who had beaten him at Ilipa was within his grasp. Livy tells us that Hasdrubal's "anchors were down and he was bringing his ships in to the beach" when he spotted Scipio. Despite a great effort to put his ships to sea, Scipio's boats caught a breeze and entered the harbor before Hasdrubal's ships could lift their anchors. Once in port, Scipio was under the protection of Syphax, unless Syphax had planned all along to deliver him to the Carthaginians. But that evening the two generals who had faced each other at Ilipa dined with Syphax in his palace.

Roman historians attribute Syphax's agreement to support the Romans to Scipio's powerful personality, which even impressed Hasdrubal.[9] More likely it was Syphax's cold calculation that the Carthaginians were finished in Spain and that Scipio, whether or not Syphax threw in his lot with him, was determined to invade Africa and bring Carthage to heel. The cunning Syphax was determined to be on the winning side. Scipio's agreement with Syphax struck a great blow to Carthaginian strategic defenses. Carthage was now effectively isolated from Spain and could expect no help from that quarter. Scipio sailed for Spain comforted by the knowledge that he and Syphax had reached an agreement that bound both by their mutual interests.

SPAIN

Scipio's approach to unresolved matters in Spain now changed from the tactical to the strategic. His goal was to prepare the country's people and tribal leaders for what he envisioned as its future as a territorial possession of Rome. He would no longer permit the powerful tribal chieftains in command of independent political and military kingdoms their autonomy. The Spanish tribes' loyalty had to be transferred from their leaders to Rome itself. Instituting this switch, however, turned out to be far more difficult than the Romans expected. Scipio's policy, while successful in the near term, would result in a forty-year guerrilla war, and it was not until Pompey finished the task much later that the Spanish tribes finally accepted Roman rule. Finally, Spain had to be indelibly marked as Roman territory and the first military colonies established. Ridding Spain of the remaining Carthaginians cooped up in Gades remained only a tactical issue since it was already clear that Carthage's influence was finished in the country. Exerting Rome's supremacy, Scipio's policy combined fairness and diplomacy with Roman brutality and force.

Scipio set out to demonstrate that the penalty for defying Rome was terrible indeed. Certain Spanish towns had always opposed Rome's interest while others, once allies, had betrayed their patron after the Scipio brothers had been killed. Conspicuous among the latter was Ilorci.[10] The town had been allied with Rome during the Scipio brothers' time, but it had gone over to the Carthaginians after their deaths.[11] When the Roman survivors of that catastrophe made their way to the town and sought refuge, the townspeople massacred them. Now that the Carthaginian armies were no longer a threat, Scipio could turn his attention to revenge as an instrument of strategic policy while seeking the Spanish tribes' allegiance. Marcius was summoned from Tarraco with a third of the army and sent against the town of Castax, which had defected from Rome in 211 BCE.[12] Scipio himself led the remainder of the army against Ilorci.

In his speech to his men before the attack, as recorded by Livy, Scipio made it clear that the assault against Ilorci was to be extremely brutal. He wanted to make an example of the place as a lesson to all Spain as to what would happen to violators of the loyalty oath to Rome. He divided his forces, giving command of one element to Laelius, and launched an assault against the town's fortifications in two places.[13] Knowing that only death awaited them, Ilorci's inhabitants sought to sell their lives dearly and fought "with so fierce an ardor that the famous army which had conquered the whole of Spain was again and again driven back from the walls by the fighting men of a single town and thrown into disorder in a manner by no means to its credit."[14] The resistance was so fierce that Scipio worried it might demoralize his troops. Thus, Scipio rushed forward, threatening to scale the walls himself if his men did not manage to gain the top.[15] Inspired by Scipio's courage, his presence so close to the walls, and his sharing the danger, his troops renewed their assault. Laelius, attacking from another direction, managed to scale the walls in his sector.

The brutality that followed was almost beyond comprehension. Livy describes the event:

> That it was rage and hatred which had inspired the assault was
> then all too apparant. No soldiers took prisoners or had a thought
> for plunder, though everything lay open to his hands; armed and
> unarmed citizens were butchered alike, women and men without
> distinction; they did not stop short in their beastly blood-lust even

at the slaughter of infants. Then the buildings were set ablaze, and what would not burn was demolished. It was the victors' delight to blot out every trace of the hated town, to destroy the very memory of the place where their enemies had lived.[16]

Scipio and Rome meant to be masters of Spain. Ilorci's destruction was a harsh lesson in the terror that awaited those who resisted. Scipio marched to join Marcius at Castax, which had been withstanding the Roman siege. Scipio's appearance and the news of Ilorci's fate convinced the town to surrender. Having made his point at Ilorci and seen its lesson carried swiftly to Castax, Scipio showed mercy to the inhabitants when the townspeople betrayed the Carthaginian garrison to the Romans. Scipio returned to New Carthage, and Marcius was sent against those tribes that still remained obstinate. The destruction of Ilorci served Scipio well, and most Spanish towns surrendered without a fight.

Challenging Scipio on the very point for which he had destroyed Ilorci was folly. Astapa had always been hostile to the Romans, although the reasons for its hostility are not clear in our sources. The citizens of the town decided to fight to the death. Their armed men made a vigorous sortie through the town gate and almost broke the Roman line. Veteran troops came up, extended the line, and enveloped the townsmen, who were then killed to a man. Inside the town the women, children, and property had been gathered around a pile of wood and logs that was then kindled into a great bonfire. A guard of fifty armed men surrounded the people, began to kill them, and threw their bodies into the fire. Livy tells us:

> Hundreds of weak and defenseless women and children were being slaughtered by their own friends. A fire had been kindled in the market place, and bodies, often still breathing, were flung in the flames, which were almost extinguished by the rivers of blood. Finally the appointed slaughterers, exhausted by their pitiful work, themselves leapt, sword in hand, into the fire.[17]

The tale spread, however, that the Romans had annihilated Astapa just as they had Ilorci and would do it again elsewhere if circumstances warranted. The horror of Astapa was sufficient, and Marcius was able to frighten the surrounding towns into surrendering without a fight before he returned to join Scipio at New Carthage.

The greatest threat to Roman rule in Spain was yet to come, however. Scipio had fallen ill in the summer. The nature of the illness remains unknown, but it was undoubtedly serious. Rumors spread throughout Spain that Scipio had died. The belief that Scipio was dead provoked two serious incidents. First, with their pay in arrears, a garrison of eight thousand bored Roman troops stationed near the Sucro River became demoralized and mutinied. Second, Indibilis and Mandonius, recent allies of Rome's, rose in revolt. The two brothers had once been allies of the Carthaginians, but they had joined the Romans when Scipio appeared to have the upper hand. Their issue was one of tribal independence and political sovereignty. After Hannibal deprived the brothers and their tribe of their status as an independent nation, the brothers had hoped that the Romans would restore their position.[18] When it became clear that Scipio intended to permit no other authority in Spain but Rome's, Mandonius and Indibilis bided their time. Now, thinking Scipio was dead, they revolted, raised an army, and devastated the lands and towns of Rome's allies north of the Ebro River. As luck would have it, the Roman troops' mutiny on the Sucro River blocked Scipio from attacking the rebels assembled inland.

Polybius tells us that Scipio "never felt himself more at a loss how to act or in greater embarrassment" than when he was faced with the mutiny.[19] Scipio must have been deeply hurt as well as shocked. He had just won the greatest battle of his career with men he himself had trained to become an instrument of his own will. He was proud of these troops and the way they had performed in battle. Like all successful combat commanders, he had grown close to his men and regarded them as members of his family. As Scipio himself tells us, he was stunned at the behavior of some of them. "I never thought words in which to address my troops would fail me," he said. "Having lived with the army almost from my boyhood, I know soldiers through and through. But now, in your presence, I do not know what to say or how to say it."[20] He immediately called his senior officers together and asked for their advice. Eight thousand veteran troops were a significant part of Scipio's total force. A misstep in dealing with them could well result in disaster for Scipio's plans for the future of Spain. Indeed, the Spanish tribes' mutiny was probably the most severe in Rome's early history.[21]

Because the immediate cause of the revolt was an arrears in pay, Scipio ordered that the tribute levied on the Spanish towns be collected immediately to pay the troops.[22] But the cause of Roman mutinies was usually not important. As William Messer points out in his definitive study of the history of mutiny in the Roman army,

> Contrary to the usual conception, mutiny and insubordination were surprisingly prevalent in the Roman army. Mutiny was not confined to any particular period of Roman history, early or late. It appears in all periods, when the troops involved were few in number as well as when they reached figures seldom attained before the recent world war.... Every type of soldier is guilty of it. Every type of commander suffers from it.[23]

This being said, it must be kept in mind that Scipio's armies were militia armies filled with part-time citizen-soldiers who were probably more disposed to disgruntlement than the professional soldiers of the later periods of Roman history. The professional soldiers on as his way of life while the militia soldier most wants to return home.

Scipio announced that the troops would be paid if they came to New Carthage either as individuals or as a group. When they were assembled there, Scipio addressed them. And here Livy's and Polybius's accounts differ in spirit. Livy tells us that Scipio won over the mutineers with appeals to patriotism and personal feelings. Polybius says that the troops were impressed and fearful of Scipio's authority to punish them. Dio, writing much later, reports that Scipio threatened the mutineers with death saying, "You all deserve to die!"[24] In this case, Dio might be closer to the truth. Scipio offered the mutineers amnesty if they would take an oath of loyalty to Rome. This deal relaxed the crowd, which had expected to be severely disciplined. Suddenly, Scipio's loyal troops surrounded the mutineers. The thirty-eight ringleaders were "bound to the stake and scourged and beheaded, while their watching comrades stood so numbed with fear that there was no cry of protest against the severity of the punishment, not even a groan."[25] The punishment was draconian even by Roman standards of brutality since, as Messer notes, "contrary to the generalizations of the authorities ancient and modern, usually mutiny went unpunished."[26] Sentencing militia soldiers, one's fellow citizens, to death is neither functional nor wise, for their families are likely to seek revenge once the war is over.[27] The other mutineers accepted the offer of amnesty and came forward one by one to swear their loyalty to Rome. The end of the mutiny restored discipline to the army and removed Scipio's obstacle to taking action against Mandonius and Indibilis.

The punishment meted out to the mutineers convinced Mandonius and Indibilis that they could expect no mercy from Scipio for their treachery. To save themselves, the princes decided to make one more effort against the Romans or die trying. They collected a force of twenty thousand infantry and twenty-five hundred cavalry.[28] Then they crossed into the territory of the Edetani, where they had had a permanent camp at the beginning of the rebellion. By concentrating the rebellious tribes into a single force, Indibilis played into Scipio's hands. Instead of having to spend time reducing the hostile tribes one at a time, Scipio might be able to destroy the single army in one stroke. Quick to grasp this advantage, Scipio ordered his troops to prepare for a forced march. Both Polybius and Livy say that Scipio moved from New Carthage and reached the Ebro River in ten days. There he crossed the river and moved inland and up the valley for four days until coming into contact with the enemy. This rate of movement is, of course, not possible under the best of conditions. Either Scipio took longer, say eighteen to twenty days to reach the Ebro, or he staged not from New Carthage but from the Roman camp on the Sucro River, the former mutineers' garrison. Scipio could have marched from the Sucro River camp to the Ebro crossing in about ten days.

The size of Scipio's army is not revealed by our sources, but it probably was not very large. Polybius and Livy tell us that it was comprised only of Italians; that is, Scipio did not include Spanish allies, undoubtedly out of his concern that the Spanish might not be trusted to fight against their own countrymen.[29] In addition, Marcius had some ten thousand troops and cavalry with him campaigning in the south and trying to force Gades to surrender. Several thousand other Roman troops must have been garrisoning captured towns and guarding river crossings, strategic passes, New Carthage itself, and supply depots. Of Scipio's original army, the Italian troops numbered only thirty thousand men, so Scipio would have been fortunate to have been able to take fifteen thousand to eighteen thousand men into the field against the rebel chiefs.

THE BATTLE OF THE EBRO RIVER, 206 BCE

Four days' march from the Ebro, Scipio met the rebel army encamped on a hill at the end of a narrow valley that was surrounded by steep hills. The Romans camped on a hill at the valley's mouth. Between the two armies lay flat ground tightly narrowed by hills rising on either side. No more than four infantry cohorts were able to deploy abreast between the hills. The following day Scipio drew the rebels into a fight. He gathered some cattle from the Roman supply train and drove them into the valley. When some of the Spanish troops came down from their positions to take the cattle, Scipio sent his velites to skirmish with them. As the fight developed, the rebels sent more troops into the valley. The Romans followed suit until the infantry combat raged. Meanwhile, before the fighting began, Scipio had ordered Laelius to assemble a cavalry force and conceal it behind a spur of hills. When both sides were significantly engaged, Scipio sent more troops into the valley and launched a frontal assault while Laelius, who had made his way behind the enemy, attacked the rear. The Roman infantry, attacking from the front, had a tough time until, as Livy tells us, a section of the Roman cavalry attacked from the front and "rode the Spanish down."[30] By the end of the afternoon most of the enemy had been killed or driven from the field.

The armies' initial clash had been only a skirmish, but it so infuriated the rebels that they resolved to fight a pitched battle. The clever Scipio had drawn the Spanish into a decision to offer battle when the Romans' superior discipline and tactics gave Scipio the advantage. Both sides were about evenly matched in numbers, so the better training and discipline were significant factors. The Spanish were at their best fighting on ground that afforded them ample room for maneuver. Scipio's choice of the narrow valley denied them this advantage. The Spanish could have chosen not to fight and instead withdraw farther up the Ebro and into the highlands. From there they could have conducted a guerrilla war, using ambush and hit-and-run tactics. Had they done so, Scipio might have been forced to spend months in search-and-destroy operations, disrupting any timetable he had for returning to Rome for the consular elections and for gathering political support for his plan to invade Africa. The battle of the Ebro River was an important event insofar as it prevented these delays.

The enemy came down from its camp at mid-morning and deployed for battle. Livy tells us that the battlefield was too narrow to accommodate all the rebel troops so that "two-thirds of their infantry, therefore, moved into line, together with the whole cavalry force; the remainder of the infantry were left straggling up the side of the hill."[31] The troops positioned on the hillside were mostly light infantry. The valley must have been narrower on the Romans' end because Scipio deployed his infantry across a front of only four cohorts, with the cohort at each end of the line anchoring its flank on the steep hillside.[32] The rest of the Roman infantry must have been positioned in great depth behind the front line, for there was nowhere else to put them. With the enemy cavalry deployed foolishly on the front line, Scipio had no concerns about his flanks. Scipio's plan was to draw the rebels into a frontal assault on his infantry, relying on his legionnaires' superior discipline and sword skills and the great depth of the Roman formation to break and contain the Spanish charge. Livy tells us that Scipio engaged quickly to draw the enemy's attention to his front. It is not clear who attacked first. It was to Scipio's advantage to have the enemy come to him and engage across a narrow front, where their numbers' full weight could not be brought to bear.[33]

Scipio watched the rebels deploy across the valley. He ordered Laelius to assemble the cavalry in back of the covering hills behind the Roman camp and out of the enemy's sight. Once the infantry engaged, Scipio sent Laelius on a wide, sweeping turning movement behind the hills. At the same time the Roman velites were sent to attack the rebels scattered on the hillside to the Roman line's left. The rebel cavalry, having been placed on the left of the Spanish front line, was effectively out of the fight once the infantry forces came together. With both sides fully engaged in an infantry battle, Laelius and the Roman cavalry came out from behind the covering hills and took the rebel cavalry in the rear. Caught between the Roman infantry to their front and their own infantry to the right, the

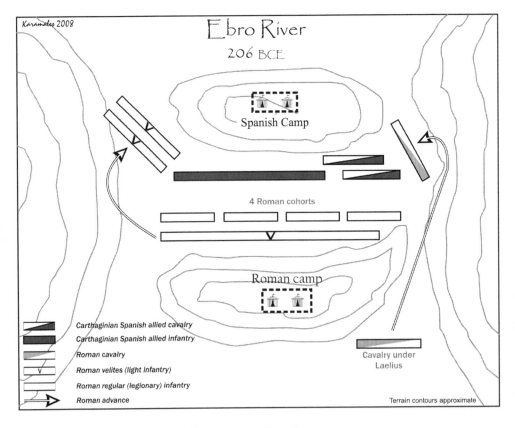

BATTLE OF THE EBRO RIVER

rebel cavalry was unable to maneuver. Livy tells us that "they formed a circle and sat on their horses, trying to defend themselves as long as they could, but in the end they were all killed."[34] The rebel infantry, too, was massacred, although Livy's suggestion that two-thirds of the rebel army was killed is clearly an exaggeration.[35] Along with much of the rebel light infantry posted on the flank, Mandonius and Indibilis survived by running away. The Romans took three thousand prisoners when they captured the enemy camp. Roman losses were twelve hundred dead and three thousand wounded.[36]

The Roman victory dealt the revolt a severe blow. Its leaders and a considerable force were still at liberty, however, and relatively safe in the harsh terrain of the upper Ebro. Dislodging them by force would be a difficult endeavor and take time. The rebel forces' location also presented a threat to the Roman line of communications between Tarraco and Saguntum. Scipio could hardly afford to leave for Italy with the problem of the rebel tribes unresolved. But Fortuna smiled on Scipio, and the Spanish chiefs decided to abandon their rebellion and seek an accommodation with him, putting their trust in "the Roman general's well-tried honor and clemency." They might have trusted as well in Scipio's sense of strategy and self-interest. Scipio pardoned the rebels on the strength of their word that they would not take up arms against Rome again. He permitted them to keep their arms and took no hostages. The rebels were required to furnish an amount of money sufficient to cover the Roman soldiers' pay. Having granted generous terms to the rebels, Scipio raised the threat of future Roman vengeance if they did not observe these terms: "You have known me now both as an enemy and friend: you may choose whether you prefer to have the Romans on your side, or ranged in anger against you."[37] With that agreement, the Spanish revolt died out, at least for the time being.

In the meantime, Scipio had sent Marcius south toward Gades to exploit the promise of some treasonous citizens of the city to deliver Gades to the Romans. Having finished with the rebels, Scipio hurried to catch up with Marcius on the Atlantic coast. Scipio planned to meet with Massinissa, who was still commanding Mago's cavalry at Gades. After his initial approach to Silanus following the battle of Ilipa, Massinissa had presumably gone to Africa and searched for allies to regain his throne. Then he had returned to Gades, where he sought to meet with Scipio and finalize his agreement with the Romans. After convincing Mago that his troops needed some exercise in raiding, Massinissa and a small cavalry troop left Gades and met the Romans on the mainland. During the meeting between the two commanders, Massinissa confirmed that he and his troops would support Scipio when he invaded North Africa, and Scipio vowed to support Massinissa's claim to the Numidian throne. It was excellent strategic thinking: Scipio's command of the Numidian cavalry on North Africa's open plains would greatly enhance his army's combat power, and after Massinissa regained his throne, his loyalty would secure Rome's western flank politically once Carthage had been brought to heel.

The events that finally forced Mago and the remnants of the Carthaginian armies in Spain to abandon Gades are of only minor importance since his army posed no threat and the Carthaginian withdrawal from Spain was inevitable after Ilipa. Mago was, however, a talented combat commander, and the Romans' failure to capture or kill him in Spain would come back to haunt them when he raised yet another army of mercenaries and attacked Liguria (modern-day Genoa) in northern Italy. Shortly after Scipio had put down the mutiny and tribal revolt, Mago attacked New Carthage with a handful of transports and a few warships. While the Roman ground forces beat back the attack, it threw into sharp relief Scipio's failure to use his naval forces correctly. The Roman fleet was still beached in Tarraco where Scipio had left it after stripping its crews and marines for the battle of Ilipa. Thus, Mago was able to sail his unarmed transports into New Carthage's harbor without encountering any resistance from the Roman fleet. Had Mago attacked New Carthage while Scipio was still dealing with the mutiny and the Spanish revolt, Scipio would have found himself in great difficulty without sufficient forces to meet all three challenges.

If Scipio sometimes failed to appreciate the role of naval power in ground operations, so, too, did his successors in Spain. After the raid on New Carthage, Mago retired to the Balearic Islands. There he received orders from Carthage to recruit more mercenaries, sail to Hannibal's aid, and invade northern Italy. In a bold and dangerous gamble, Mago assembled his men and fleet of transports (he had no warships), sailed across the open sea, and landed his force in Liguria. Had the Romans had a greater grasp of naval affairs, they would have easily been able to use their fleet at Tarraco to intercept and destroy Mago's invasion force. The Roman fleet had apparently given up routine patrolling, however, and Mago's ships sailed past Tarraco while the Roman fleet remained on the beach. Mago's successful invasion forced the Romans to redeploy six legions to the north to block his movement south. Mago tied down these six legions for more than a year when they were desperately needed elsewhere.

Of great political significance was Scipio's founding of a settlement for his military veterans at Italica (modern-day Santiponce). By establishing it, Scipio set an imperial precedent and a new departure in Roman colonial history, the founding of Rome's first overseas colony. Scipio gave Spain its first Italian community deep in the heart of the populous Baetius Valley, hoping it would help teach the natives something of Roman thought, methods, and culture. It was Rome's first small attempt at Romanization, what later came to be the civilizing influence of much of the ancient Western world.[38] Italica itself more than repaid its debt to Rome. The little town became the birthplace of Trajan, Hadrian, and Theodosius the Great, three of Rome's great emperors.[39]

RETURN TO ROME

Placing the Spanish command in the hands of Silanus and Marcius in early autumn 206 BCE, Scipio sailed from Tarraco with ten ships and returned to Rome in time for the consular elections for 205.[40] Scipio met the assembled Senate outside the city in the temple of Bellona and presented the formal report of his victories in Spain. No Roman general was permitted to enter the city while still holding his imperium, and according to custom Scipio formally relinquished his military authority.[41] Because no one who had commanded armies without holding a regular magistracy had ever been permitted a triumph, Scipio's request for one was denied, and he entered the city on foot.[42] Scipio deposited 14,342 pounds of silver and a great quantity of silver coins taken from Spain into the Roman treasury.[43] The consular elections were held, and Livy tells us that "a greater crowd of people than any other during the war" turned out to see Scipio and vote for him.[44] Scipio was elected easily along with Publius Licinius Crassus, the *Pontifex Maximus* of Rome. Scipio made no secret that he wished to have the command of Sicily from which he intended to carry the war to Africa. Crassus made no objection to being assigned the command in Bruttium since his religious duties as Pontifex forbade him to leave Italy.[45] However, Scipio's plan encountered significant opposition in the Senate. After some political maneuvering and with the Aemilian-Scipionic faction's support, a compromise was reached in which Scipio was assigned to Sicily and given the right to sail to Africa if the "interests of the state demanded it."[46]

Rome was at the crossroads, and two opposing versions of Rome's national security strategy were in conflict. The debate centered on whether Rome should continue on its traditional path and remain an agrarian-based peninsular power without overseas possessions—the Fabian party's position—or, as Scipio saw it, strike out boldly in a new direction and become a world or great regional power, complete with overseas colonies and dominion over the western Mediterranean basin. The Fabian view was based in the agricultural class, which wished to stem the influence of Hellenistic and other foreign ideas that were beginning to influence Roman life. Its objective was to finish the war quickly and then heal the wounds those in the Italian countryside suffered. To this end they wished to free Italy of Hannibal; reconquer the Po Valley, which had been lost to the Gauls, and colonize it with Italian farmers; and repair the damage to Italian towns and villages.[47] None of these actions required expanding the war to Africa or establishing overseas colonies.

Scipio's grand strategic vision was based in the new Roman class that looked to overseas expansion and commerce for Rome's future. In Scipio's view, Carthage's predations in Spain and Sicily were forcing Rome to become a world power for it was the only way in which its legitimate security interests could be satisfied. Scipio must have foreseen that with Spain and Carthage conquered, Rome would have to govern both or risk the rise of another threat to its security. The sea, traditionally called the *mare clausum*, or that which enclosed and protected Italy, was no longer a sufficient security barrier. With the conquest of North Africa and Spain, one half of the Mediterranean would become *mare nostrum* (our Roman sea).

These contrasting visions of national defense strategy led to different strategic and military views. What Clausewitz later described as the strategy of exhaustion, the Fabian strategy was inherently defensive. It sought to wear out one's enemy with a war of attrition, relying on one's superior will and resources to force the enemy to quit the fight and retire.[48] This strategy may have indeed forced an end to hostilities eventually, but it conceded the strategic initiative to the enemy and could not force a strategic decision. Under the best of circumstances, the Fabian strategy might force Hannibal to retire from Italy, but it could never impose terms on Carthage that would satisfy Roman security requirements. Scipio's strategy, by contrast, aimed at forcing a strategic decision through victory in the field. He deemed defeating Hannibal in Italy as not sufficient, for Hannibal was a creature of Carthaginian power, and that power would continue to threaten Rome even after a Hannibalic defeat. The key to Rome's security, therefore, lay not in the defeat of Hannibal but in the defeat of Carthage itself.

To achieve his strategic vision, Scipio advised a strategy of annihilation, as Clausewitz later described it.[49] The military means to achieve the strategic objective required that he discover and destroy the enemy's main armed force in a pitched battle as a prelude to forcing political concessions on his adversary. Scipio's strategic brilliance is revealed in his awareness that Hannibal had to be defeated in Africa. Had Scipio defeated Hannibal in Italy, the Roman people would have likely regarded the war as finished, and it would have been difficult, if not impossible, to convince the Senate and the Roman people to carry the war against Carthage itself. Thus, a victory against Hannibal in Italy would, paradoxically, vindicate the Fabian strategy and make continuing the war politically impossible. If war is fought as a means to political objectives, then Rome's victory in Italy would do nothing to convince Carthage to abandon its policies. Scipio understood that Hannibal's defeat had to occur on Carthaginian soil so that once the military means for its defense were destroyed, Carthage would have no choice but to yield to Roman security demands. There was, of course, some sense of personal revenge that also influenced Scipio's thinking. In his speech to the Roman Senate to justify the invasion of Africa, Scipio took no pains to conceal his personal desire for revenge:

> Italy has suffered long; let her for a while have rest. It is Africa's turn to be devastated by fire and sword. It is time a Roman army threatened the gates of Carthage, rather than that we should again see from our walls the rampart of an enemy camp. Let Africa be the theater of war henceforward; for fourteen years all the horrors of war have fallen thick upon us, terror and defeat, the devastation of our farms, the desertion of our friends; it is her turn now to suffer the same.[50]

His business with the Senate concluded, Scipio prepared to assume command of his province in Sicily and to plan the invasion of Africa.

6

The African Campaign

IN EARLY SPRING of 205 BCE Scipio began to prepare for the invasion of Africa. Livy tells us that the Roman Senate refused Scipio permission to raise troops for a new army but permitted him to recruit volunteers.[1] Dio, however, says that Scipio was permitted to enroll as large a force as he wished.[2] Brian Caven suggests that Scipio probably left Rome with a newly raised consular army[3] instead of the seven thousand volunteers Livy says were raised among the Romans and allied states.[4] It seems unlikely that after they lost the battle to prevent him from taking the war to Africa Scipio's enemies in the Senate would have possessed the political strength to deny him the ability to raise an army and carry out his plan. Even Roman political partisanship had its limits whenever Rome faced an external threat, and Hannibal was still in the field. P. A. Brunt may be correct, then, that Scipio took a consular army of ten thousand men with him to Sicily instead of an army of volunteers.[5] All that is certain is that Scipio had some difficulty raising the forces for the invasion because of political opposition. The details remain lost.

Livy is likely correct in saying that Rome's allies provided most of the supplies and war materials for the expedition because Rome was suffering serious financial difficulties.[6] The Italian allies had been contributing troops to the Roman effort against Hannibal for decades and had suffered considerable losses. They may have welcomed the opportunity to fulfill their obligations to Rome by providing money instead of men. Among the supplies Rome's allies provided was raw timber. From these supplies Scipio had constructed twenty quinqueremes and ten *quadriremes*. Scipio personally oversaw their construction, relentlessly keeping the workmen at their tasks and completing the ships in only forty-five days.

143

INVASION, 204 BCE

Scipio immediately set about transforming his army into an instrument of his will, equipping it with the Spanish gladius and training the men in the innovative tactics he had developed in Spain. He selected the Fifth and Sixth legions already in Sicily as the core of his army. These troops were the survivors of Cannae who had been exiled to Sicily in disgrace and confined to garrison duty. Scipio himself had barely escaped at Cannae, and as a seasoned soldier he knew that the Roman defeat had not been caused by the legionnaires' cowardice. Like all combat veterans, Scipio preferred to take seasoned soldiers into battle. Livy tells us that "there were no other equally experienced soldiers in the Roman army or men with comparable knowledge of the various sorts of fighting, including siege warfare."[7] However, the long years of war had changed the Roman army. It was no longer comprised of citizen-soldiers, citizen-officers, and citizen-generals as it had been when it first took the field against Hannibal in 218 BCE. Most of Scipio's soldiers, including the officers and generals, had already seen several tours of duty. The army that Scipio assembled in Sicily was almost a professional army, and he and his officers a professional officer corps.

Scipio's reputation preceded him, and it was likely that the men of the Roman Fifth and Sixth legions welcomed the opportunity to redeem their reputation by fighting under the command of Rome's great general. Scipio understood the fighting élan of troops is an important combat asset.[8] He also screened the seven thousand volunteers he had brought with him for their experience as soldiers and transferred some to his army. What happened to the remainder is unclear, but they may have been used in logistical and administrative roles or even formed into a separate legion.[9] Livy tells us that Scipio especially sought out those soldiers who had fought under Marcellus in the long siege of Syracuse (214–212 BCE) because they were skilled in siege and assault operations.[10] Assembling special units, Scipio obviously anticipated the need to reduce Carthaginian towns once in the theater of operations.

The size of Scipio's invasion force is the subject of dispute.[11] Scipio's two Cannae legions were probably brought up to full strength with replacements drawn from his volunteers. Augmented by two legions brought by Marcellus, each with 6,200 infantry and 300 cavalry, Scipio had a total of 26,000 infantry and 1,200 cavalry, or 300 horses per legion.[12] The marines on the warships account for a substantial number of troops as well. Scipio's fleet was comprised of 40 warships, each with a normal complement of 120 marines, or another 4,800 men, along with 400 troop and supply transports.[13] The total invasion force numbered some 31,000 soldiers and marines and 1,200 cavalrymen.

While the force was surely considerable, it is questionable whether it was sufficient to accomplish Scipio's objectives of threatening Carthage, forcing Hannibal to leave Italy, and then defeating him in open battle. On first glance, the force seemed insufficient to its tasks. Later, when word reached Hannibal that Scipio had arrived in Africa, he made no effort to return home on the grounds that the size of Scipio's force was only adequate for harassment but not large enough to effect a strategic decision. Indeed, Scipio was unable to even capture Utica. The defenses of Carthage could not be taken by storm with an army the size of Scipio's. Achieving Scipio's operational objectives seemed to require a considerably larger field force than the one Scipio brought with him; instead, to attain his goals with the force at hand, he would have to rely on brilliant generalship and luck.

On his arrival in Syracuse Scipio ordered the newly constructed quinqueremes pulled out of the water. They had been fashioned of freshly cut timber, and he needed to season their hulls. Scipio discovered thirty ships of the fleet already in Sicily that required repair before they could be put to sea. He promptly put them in fighting trim and sent them off under Laelius's command to harass and reconnoiter the African coast.

Scipio's weakness remained his cavalry. Its insufficient numbers and training and fighting techniques made it an imperfect arm with which to fight the Carthaginians and their Numidian allies, both of whom had superb cavalries.[14] While the cavalry had not been overly important during the Spanish campaign because of the country's rugged terrain, on North Africa's open plains, it might well prove decisive. Given the Roman cavalry's usually uneven quality, Scipio probably planned to rely on the excellent Numidian cavalry of both Massinissa and Syphax, with whom he had already concluded alliances. Should these alliances come undone, however, Scipio would find himself deprived of an essential combat arm.

Laelius landed at Hippo Diarrhytus (modern Bizerta), a Punic colony at the head of the land of the Masaeyles and Massyles, and began to raid the countryside.[15] Laelius was supposed to spread fear, gather intelligence, and establish communications with both Syphax and Massinissa, whose tribal kingdoms were nearby. Laelius was to meet and sound out both princes to ensure that their respective pledges to aid the Romans were still holding. Livy tells us that Massinissa met with Laelius but makes no mention of Syphax. Massinissa had fallen on hard times since meeting with Scipio in Spain. He was an exile reduced to brigandage in his own country, which was in the hands of a pretender who was sustained with Syphax's aid.[16] This news must have filled Laelius with concern. How were two rivals at war with one another going to agree and support the Roman armies after the invasion? In his condition Massinissa could hardly have been relied on for more than a few hundred cavalry troops. And where was Syphax? He was by far the more important of the two for he could provide thousands of infantry and cavalry to the Roman cause. It could not have reassured Laelius that Massinissa urged the Romans to invade quickly, nor could he believe that Syphax would keep his agreement with the Romans. The strategic alliance that Scipio had forged with the African chiefs and on which so much of Roman troop strength, battle planning, logistics, and political advantage depended was in serious jeopardy. Surely Livy is incorrect when he says that when Laelius reported these circumstances to Scipio, "Scipio was impressed by the adjurations of Massinissa."[17]

Laelius's raid provoked a panic in Carthage. News of Scipio's crossing to Sicily and the buildup of his invasion force had already reached Carthage, and many thought Scipio had already landed on the African coast. Laelius's raid, however, lent a new air of urgency to the prospect of a Roman invasion, and the Carthaginians began to prepare for it. The Carthaginian Senate voted emergency funds to raise a local levy within the city and to send the mercenary recruiters into the countryside to secure African troops. The city's walls and gates were repaired, and large supplies of grain, weapons, and armor were laid in. A small fleet was raised, and watchtowers were built along the coast.[18] More important defensive measures were set in motion at the strategic level. A delegation was sent to Syphax and other African tribal princes to strengthen their alliances with Carthage. Special overtures were made to Syphax that ultimately succeeded. Carthage also made a diplomatic approach to Philip V of Macedon, promising financing and other inducements if he would invade Sicily or Italy to draw off Roman strength. Carthaginian commanders in Italy received orders to increase their activities and hinder Scipio in every possible way.

While Scipio was preparing to cross to Sicily, Mago had sailed from the Balearic Islands and arrived unopposed in Italy at Liguria with thirty ships, twelve thousand men, and two thousand cavalry. After Laelius's raid, Carthage sent him reinforcements—twenty-five warships, six thousand infantry, eight hundred cavalry, and seven elephants—along with money to hire Gallic mercenaries.[19] This turn of events created a new strategic threat in Italy itself. Mago forged an alliance with the Gauls and moved south, forcing the Romans to deploy six legions in his path to stop him. Carthage sent a supply convoy of eighty ships carrying grain and military supplies to reinforce Hannibal in Italy, but it was blown off course and fell into Roman hands.[20] The Carthaginian leaders were excellent strategic thinkers, utilizing every element of national power, diplomacy, and politics to undermine the Roman invasion.

Meanwhile, a minor event in the town of Locri played directly into Carthaginian hands and came within an ace of halting the Roman invasion. While in Syracuse, a group of exiles from Locri approached Scipio and requested Roman help to free their town from Carthaginian occupation, promising that their supporters would betray the town from within. Locri was located on the far west side of the toe of the Italian boot, fifty miles directly across from Rhegium (modern Reggio) across the Strait of Messana (modern Messina). Locri was among those southern Italian towns that had gone over to Hannibal after Cannae and was occupied by a Carthaginian garrison.[21] Indeed, Hannibal controlled the whole southernmost boot of Italy. Rhegium itself was isolated and had to be supplied by sea.

Why Scipio agreed to help the Locrian exiles remains a mystery, for he certainly had more important matters to attend to in preparing his army for the invasion. Getting involved in the Locri affair meant that Scipio had to leave Sicily and go to Bruttium, which was the province of his co-consul, Crassus. Lacking authority in Bruttium, Scipio's attempt to exercise authority there would have been a significant violation of Roman law and custom and would certainly have angered his already numerous enemies in the Senate. The commander in Rhegium was Quintus Pleminius, who held the delegated authority of *legatus pro praetore*— that is, governing authority delegated under Scipio's imperium—and thus legally acted on Scipio's behalf. Scipio may have become involved because he was legally (and criminally) liable for Plemenius's actions in the Locri affair. More important, Scipio failed to anticipate the political consequences of failure. He still had many enemies in the Senate who would seize on any failure to undermine his authority and stop the invasion of North Africa. Getting involved was a serious lapse in judgment for the otherwise clear-thinking Scipio. Nevertheless, he ordered two tribunes and a small contingent of troops to accompany the exiles to Rhegium. They carried a letter instructing the commander Quintus Pleminius to assemble a force of three thousand troops and attack the Carthaginian garrison in Locri.[22]

The Roman attack carried one of the two citadels on each side of the city, with the Carthaginians holding the other. Skirmishes continued over a period of days, with both sides drawing reinforcements from the rival tribal peoples of the area.[23] At some point the rumor spread that Hannibal himself was marching to relieve the town. When it reached Scipio in Syracuse, he immediately set sail "as soon as the south-going tide began to run in the Straits" with a squadron of ships and made for Locri. When he arrived, Livy tells us, "there were still some hours of daylight left" so that the troops "disembarked and entered the town before sunset."[24] The size of Scipio's force is unknown, but if he took ten ships with him and each carried the usual complement of 120 marines, Scipio would have had some 1,200 troops with him.[25] It is, of course, possible that Scipio transported a larger number of troops with him by loading them aboard some of the troop transports he had assembled for the invasion. Doing so, however, would have taken a considerable amount of time, and the sense of Livy's text is that Scipio moved quickly. The quinqueremes were already in the water and had their troop contingents available on short notice. Thus it is more likely that Scipio used the warships and their marine contingents.

As Livy tells it, the next morning Hannibal arrived and began to immediately attack the city's walls. Suddenly the gate to the city swung open, and Scipio's men rushed forth to engage the Carthaginians, inflicting some two hundred casualties and driving them away from the walls. In what is clearly a detail added *ad maiorem Scipionis gloriam* (for the greater glory of Scipio), Livy says that when "Hannibal realized that Scipio was present, he withdrew the rest of his army into camp, after sending a message to their comrades in the citadel that they must see to their own safety as best they could."[26] Hannibal then broke contact and withdrew. Later that evening the Carthaginian garrison set fire to the city, escaped under cover of darkness, and joined Hannibal.

Livy's account leaves much unexplained. Hannibal certainly knew that Scipio was assembling an invasion force in Sicily. During the attack on Locri, he learned that Scipio was inside Locri's walls with only a legion of troops—the three thousand dispatched from Rhegium and the twelve hundred Scipio had brought with him by sea from Syracuse—at his disposal. Hannibal was outside the walls with a considerably larger army, certainly several times the size of Scipio's. Here, then, was Rome's most able commander and the commanding general in charge of the pending invasion of Africa trapped inside the city. Under these circumstances it is beyond comprehension that Hannibal did not press the attack on Locri at all costs to capture Scipio, who had committed several errors. Scipio should not have been in Locri in the first place, putting himself at risk, and once there he had no avenue of retreat or any means to summon reinforcements. Indeed, the area around Locri was sympathetic to Hannibal, not the Romans. Given Hannibal's appreciation of strategic intelligence, it is not unreasonable to believe that he also

knew about Scipio's enemies in the Senate and their opposition to his appointment and planned invasion of Africa. Had Hannibal captured Scipio, he would
have had every reason to believe that the Roman invasion of Africa would have
collapsed under the politics of the Roman Senate. Perhaps Hannibal's intelligence failed and he did not know that Scipio was in Locri, although Livy clearly
says that Hannibal knew. All that can be believed reasonably from Livy's account
is that the Romans captured the town after the Carthaginian garrison fled.[27] It is
unlikely that Hannibal attacked Locri.

Because Locri had betrayed Rome by going over to Hannibal, Scipio punished the pro-Carthaginian faction by seizing its property and giving it to the pro-
Roman loyalists before he returned to Messana. He left Pleminius in charge.
Pleminius soon set about plundering the town, even seizing the sacred treasury
of the temple of Persephone. Soon the troops were out of control and fighting
among themselves for loot. Some of Pleminius's men got into an argument with
troops still under the command of Scipio's tribunes. Pleminius ordered the tribunes seized and scourged and Scipio's legate mutilated. When news of these
events reached Scipio, he immediately sailed to Locri to settle the matter.[28] Curiously he supported Pleminius. No sooner had Scipio returned to Messana than
Pleminius ordered Scipio's tribunes and legate tortured and put to death. He next
turned his men loose on the civilian populace of Locri without mercy.

The incident at Locri played into the hands of Scipio's enemies in the Senate.
Locrian envoys arrived in Rome seeking help, charging that Scipio was too busy
with the invasion preparations and too prejudiced in Pleminius's favor for them
to get a fair hearing of their complaints. The Fabian faction was quick to attack
Scipio not only for failing to conduct a thorough and fair investigation of the
Locri incident, but also for his "Greek habits," which, they claimed, threatened
military discipline. Livy describes the charges against Scipio in the following way:

> Apart from the attacks on Pleminius's criminal conduct and the
> miseries of Locri, much was said also against the commander-in-
> chief himself. His dress and bearing were un-Roman, and not even
> soldierly; he strolled about the gymnasium in a Greek mantle and
> sandals, and wasted his time over books and physical exercise; his
> staff and friends were enjoying the amenities of Syracuse no less
> luxuriously, while Carthage and Hannibal seemed completely for-
> gotten. The discipline of the whole army had gone to the dogs, just
> as at Sucro in Spain and again at Locri, so that it was more of a
> menace to its friends than its enemies.[29]

Fabius, no doubt, wished to remove Scipio from his command and end the African invasion plans once and for all, but he lacked the political support to do so. Instead the Senate sent a commission of inquiry to investigate the Locri matter and to report on the condition of the army in Sicily. If it found that Scipio had ordered or had known of the outrages at Locri, he was to be removed from his command and ordered back to Rome probably to stand trial. So serious were the charges considered that if he were found guilty but had already left for Africa, he was to be removed and replaced by two senators in the dual command arrangement previously typical of the Republic. As events turned out, however, the commission found Scipio innocent of all charges. The commission's review of the invasion force found it to be in such excellent condition that when the commission returned to Rome the Senate finally and formally authorized the invasion to go ahead. It also instructed Scipio to take whatever troops from the Sicilian garrisons that he might require.[30] The politics of the Roman Senate had come within a hair's breadth of canceling the most important military operation in Rome's history and punishing its commander by removing him from his command.

The Locri incident illustrates the importance of the political context in which military operations occur. The Carthaginians masterfully used politics to their strategic advantage,[31] and in their approaches to Syphax, they scored a major victory. The Carthaginians had correctly discerned that the key to Scipio's chances for success lay in his alliance with Syphax,[32] and they moved quickly to undermine it. Hasdrubal, son of Gisgo, had noticed during a meeting that Syphax was taken by the beauty of Saphanba'al (Sophonisba), Hasdrubal's daughter.[33] Then "seeing that the king was aflame with desire—the Numidians surpass all other barbarian peoples in the violence of their appetites—he sent to Carthage for the young woman and hurried on the wedding."[34] A political agreement in which both Hasdrubal and Syphax pledged their mutual support in the event of a Roman attack on Africa further strengthened their family ties. At Hasdrubal's and his new wife's urging, Syphax sent envoys to Scipio in Syracuse informing him of Syphax's new agreement with the Carthaginians. Syphax warned Scipio that he no longer considered himself bound by his prior agreement with Rome. It was his wish, he said, that Rome and Carthage should continue their dispute outside Africa, where he would not be forced to become involved. But should Scipio carry the war to Africa, Syphax would be compelled to fight with the Carthaginians and defend his homeland.[35]

In a single political stroke the Carthaginians had seriously weakened Scipio's invasion plan by depriving him of a much-needed supply of troops and logistics.

It "meant the collapse of a high hope and the loss of what might have been a decisive influence in his African campaign."[36] The central pillar supporting Scipio's chances for success was suddenly gone. If word of Syphax's defection reached Rome, the Fabian faction would likely renew its call to cancel the invasion and have Scipio recalled. With his insufficient troops and resources the subject of political debate, the Senate would have probably been forced to acquiesce to the Fabian demand.

Time worked against Scipio. If he went ahead with the invasion he would have to do so with the manpower and supplies he had on hand. He could expect no help from any quarter, not even Rome, once in the field. If he postponed the invasion to build up his force, the information of Syphax's defection might reach Rome. Scipio decided to go ahead with the invasion. Fearing that word of Syphax's defection might leak out (Numidian trade representatives were in Syracuse) and cause morale problems among his troops, Scipio lied to them. He assembled his troops on parade and told them that there must be no more delay "because their allies, the African kings, were insisting that they must make the crossing immediately."[37] No doubt he hoped that his words might reach Rome as well to counter any rumors to the contrary. He ordered the invasion force, the war fleet, and as many merchant ships as could be hired or seized to assemble at Lilybaeum on Sicily's southern coast and prepare for the invasion.

By moving the invasion fleet, his troops, and supplies from Syracuse to Lilybaeum, perhaps Scipio was attempting to create an atmosphere of inevitability that the invasion would go off as planned. Once he set events in motion on Sicily itself, it would be more difficult to stop them for political reasons. Scipio may have had this thought in mind as he appeared daily among his troops, supervising the transfer of men and supplies to Lilybaeum. This said, however, Lilybaeum was also a logical staging point for an invasion of Africa, sitting only sixty-five miles across the sea from Carthage itself or a little more than half the sailing distance from Syracuse.

The invasion fleet was comprised of forty quinquerme warships and four hundred transports.[38] Scipio himself meticulously oversaw the loading of supplies and men. The distance to Africa by sea was less than a single day's sail away,[39] so storing shipboard provisions for the men and the animals presented no problems. The ships were ordered to take aboard sufficient food and water for both men and animals to last forty-five days. Scipio intended his army to be self-sufficient once it landed for at least a month, which was hopefully long enough to capture the Carthaginian port of Utica and turn it into a Roman supply depot.

Shortly before embarkation, Scipio ordered all shipmasters and pilots along with two soldiers from each ship to assemble at his headquarters. At this meeting he asked each shipmaster to swear that the required rations and water were aboard his ship. He instructed the soldiers to maintain order and ensure that the troops did not interfere with the sailors during the crossing.

The logistics of Scipio's invasion are interesting. His shipboard transport capability had to move twenty-six thousand infantry and twelve hundred horses a distance of sixty-five nautical miles. The forty warships could transport the forty-eight hundred marines as their usual troop complements. The transports would be forced to carry the troops themselves, the horses, equipment, and sufficient food to sustain the army after it established a beachhead. In Roman antiquity the most common merchant vessels for carrying cargo could transport 80 to 100 tons burden. While the later Roman grain ships were much larger and capable of carrying some 350 tons burden, in Scipio's day the average entrepôt ship for hire around the Mediterranean was around 80 tons burden.[40] Thus, we might reasonably assume that Scipio's transports could each easily accommodate 80 tons of cargo. Few harbors had unloading piers, so most trade goods were unloaded onto smaller vessels or by beaching the ship and then unloading the cargo.[41]

The size of these ships and how many square or cubic meters of cargo space they afforded are matters of speculation.[42] The Romans and Greeks of the period were capable of constructing ships more than a hundred feet long and twenty-five feet wide (only slightly longer than the quinquereme). An approximate model of a Roman (80 to 100 tons burden) transport can be found in the entrepôt vessels that plied the New England coast in the 1870s. These vessels were ninety feet long, sixteen feet wide, and fourteen feet deep from keel to deck. They were shallow-draft boats, drawing less than two feet of water when empty, and capable of carrying a hundred tons of firewood, lumber, or coal.[43] In antiquity a ship of this approximate size could be configured to carry troops, grain, or horses. Unlike modern vessels, though, these ancient ships were shallow-draft, open-decked, barge-like boats in which men and horses were exposed to the elements during a voyage.

A horse transport required special configuration of its internal hull. Horses require a firm, flat surface on which to stand. An average horse is approximately 90 to 115 inches long and 34 inches wide and weighs about 1,000 pounds.[44] The cargo space of a boat 100 feet long and 20 feet wide would permit the construction of fifty horse tie stalls, each 9 feet long and 3.5 feet wide. A sling in each stall supported the horse and kept it from falling. A rope barrier separated each stall from the one in front of it. Fifty horses would consume some 750 pounds of hay, 275 pounds of barley and oats, and 375 gallons of water per day.[45] Since Scipio had to feed and water the animals for less than a day's travel, the additional space and weight of the animals' supplies were of no concern. Of some concern, however, would have been the loading and unloading of the animals. Horses' legs are fragile, and a stumble can break one. The men probably loaded the animals in Sicily from a pier using ramps. Unloading them on the beach in Africa, however, was probably considerably more difficult. Whether off-loaded from a beached transport tilted at a sharp angle or from a transport swaying in the surf, it is likely that some animals were injured so badly they were useless. In sum, a horse transport ship could carry fifty animals at a weight of 25 tons burden and another 4 tons of animal rations and water for a total weight of only 29 to 30 tons, easily within the carrying capacity of even a small entrepôt vessel of the day. Scipio would have required twenty-four horse transports to move his twelve hundred cavalry horses to Africa.

Troop transports must have been little better than animal transports, at least from the perspective of available space. An average Roman soldier weighed approximately 150 pounds and his equipment another 60 pounds or so; therefore, the boat had to carry about 210 pounds of weight for each passenger. A vessel that was eighty feet long and eighteen feet wide could accommodate forty-eight benches arranged back to front like pews in a church, with a one-foot aisle running lengthwise between the bench rows. A bench twenty inches deep permits sufficient room for an average soldier, with five inches of legroom to spare. Allowing a shoulder width of twenty-four inches leaves him two inches on either side from the men next to him. Under these conditions, each bench could accommodate 4 soldiers in the two aisles of forty-eight rows, or a total of 384 men per transport. With their equipment stowed under the benches or elsewhere on the boat, these 384 men would weigh some 40 tons, which an ancient entrepôt could easily carry. Assuming 26,000 infantry and 1,200 cavalrymen and another 800 or so other personnel, Scipio required eighty troop transports to transport his army to Africa.

If Livy is accurate in that Scipio utilized 400 transports for the invasion, how were the other ships used? He says Scipio ordered that sufficient food for forty-five days be carried aboard the transports. In Roman times, the usual measure of grain was the *modius*, a unit of volume equal to 8.75 liters. Hero of Alexandria tells us in his *Stereometrica* that 7,680 *modii* of grain equaled 58 tons and 12,600 *modii* weighed 95 tons.[46] Thus, a modius of grain weighed about 15 pounds.

Accordingly, a Roman transport capable of 80 tons burden could carry 8,000 *modii* or 160,000 pounds of grain. If, as noted earlier, we calculate the Roman soldier's rations as grain, beans, salt, and dried fruit, weighing together some 2.2 pounds per day, then thirty thousand troops will require 33 tons of rations per day. Thus, a Roman transport could carry sufficient rations to supply the army for two days. To carry enough rations to feed the army for forty-five days Scipio needed 23 ships. We can, therefore, account for 127 transports, leaving 273 vessels unused. If Scipio brought all eight thousand mules assigned to his four legions, he would have required an additional 133 ships. Another 4 ships could transport his siege engines and artillery, and he would still have 136 ships without cargo to transport.

If we take Livy's claim that Scipio ordered a forty-five-day supply of food and water to be carried aboard ship as accurate, why transport forty-five days' worth of water for men and animals for a journey of only sixty-five miles? Armies in antiquity could not carry sufficient water and animal forage to supply even a small force for any length of time, and they were forced to rely on streams, rivers, and local forage. A horse requires five pounds of hard fodder (oats and barley) a day. Thus, twelve hundred horses require 3 tons of hard fodder per day times for forty-five days, or 135 tons. Three ships could easily carry this amount of oats and barley for the horses. At four pounds of hard fodder per day, eight thousand mules will consume 720 tons of hard fodder over forty-five days. Twelve ships would be required to transport this amount of fodder for the mules. Deducting these 15 ships from the total still leaves 121 ships unused. If Livy is correct in his claim regarding Scipio's requirement of a forty-five-day food supply, either these 121 ships were not used at all, or they were used for something else not mentioned in the account.

Scipio's fleet put to sea at dawn sometime in the spring of 204 BCE. Scipio and his brother, Lucius, with twenty warships protected the flotilla on the right while Marcus Porcius Cato and Laelius, the admiral in command during the crossing, with another twenty ships protected the left. Forty warships as protection for the transports would have been adequate only if the Carthaginian navy was in reduced circumstances, as indeed it was. Scipio's capture of the silver mines at Baecula had deprived Carthage of much of its money and therefore its ability to build ships and hire crews. Carthaginian ships had also been sent to aid Mago in his invasion of Italy, and another eighty transports had been lost in the failed attempt to resupply Hannibal. Scipio certainly was aware of these circumstances and may even have possessed some intelligence that led him to trust his transports' safety to the protection of his small fleet of warships.[47] During darkness the warships set out a single light, the merchantmen two lights, and the command ship three lights to reduce the possibility of collisions. Livy tells us that the pilot's orders were "to steer for Emporiae, a strip of coast south of Thapsus."[48]

There was no way Scipio could have prevented the Carthaginians from learning of the invasion fleet's departure. A huge crowd, including the men of the legions left behind, was in attendance and cheered as the ships pulled away from the anchorage. Scipio himself said a public prayer for success and offered sacrifice and "flung the raw entrails of the victim into the sea." If Scipio could not conceal the time of departure from the Carthaginians he could, however, deprive them of the knowledge of where he planned to land. Livy's account that the invasion force planned to land at Thapsus was either an elaborate deception by Scipio or the originally planned location before Syphax defected to the Carthaginians. Thapsus was 180 miles *east* of Carthage in the fertile farming and trading area known as Emporiae and would present only minor resistance to the Roman landing. Once safely ashore, Scipio's army could march west toward Carthage and draw supplies from the surrounding farms.[49] Syphax's kingdom was located to the *west* of Carthage. Scipio had depended on him to raise large numbers of troops and cavalry (as Syphax later did for his Carthaginian relatives) and to march on Carthage from the west. Both armies could have converged on the Carthaginian capital, cut it off from its hinterlands and food supply, and laid siege to it. But once Syphax had defected to the Carthaginians, the original plan had to be abandoned.

Knowledge of the Thapsus landing site had probably been rumored for months among those sailors and troops making the invasion preparations over the winter and spring. When Syphax defected to the Carthaginians that winter, Scipio let the rumor continue. He may even have made it clear at the meeting of his shipmasters and pilots shortly before sailing that Thapsus was still the invasion site, all the while intending to change it once the invasion fleet was under way. Thapsus is an almost three-hundred-mile sea journey from Lilybaeum, and without Syphax's promise of troops and supplies, it no longer offered any military advantage. Indeed, its distance from Carthage would provide the Carthaginians with more time to raise their armies and more strategic depth in which to maneuver. While strategic surprise was not possible, Scipio could still achieve tactical surprise. But to be successful, Scipio had to strike quickly, take the offensive, and maintain the initiative. The only way to achieve this goal was to land as closely as possible to Carthage itself, establish a supply base with his forty-five-day supply of food, and commence offensive operations before the Carthaginians could react.

Livy tells us that after a two-day, fog-bound journey covering just less than a hundred miles, the pilot leading the flotilla reported sighting land five miles off the Promontory of Mercury (modern Cape Bon).[50] Scipio ordered the fleet to pass the cape to the west and stop off the next headland. After passing a foggy night at anchor, the Romans came ashore at first light on the western coast of a small promontory jutting from the mainland sixteen miles northeast of the city of Utica.[51] Obviously no pilot steering for Thapsus could have been so mistaken as to arrive at Cape Bon, even in the fog. Livy's account that the flotilla intended to land at Thapsus may simply have been based on the rumor that Scipio encouraged as a form of deception.[52] A historical parallel, of course, is the 1944 Allied deception meant to convince the Germans that Eisenhower's invasion force would land at Pas de Calais when the real destination was Normandy. As noted, Scipio may have originally planned to land at Thapsus and knew that information may have gotten around as the invasion force made its preparations. But with Syphax's defection just a few months before the planned invasion, the change in the strategic situation forced Scipio not only to choose another landing site but to modify the entire battle plan once the invasion had been accomplished. That Scipio was able to do both is testimony to his military brilliance.

The theater of operations in which Scipio's African campaign took place was a relatively small part of North Africa, consisting of the northern half of Tunisia, which is bounded on the north and east by the Mediterranean and on the west by modern Algeria. A chain of mountains running from deep in the interior north and eastward to Cape Bon divides the area. Most of Scipio's operations took place north of this line. This northern zone is itself divided by the Bagradas River into two interior zones. The terrain north and west of the river is mountainous highland in which it is very difficult to conduct combat operations. The terrain to the south and east of the Bagradas is more hospitable, with small mountain ranges of isolated peaks separated by open plains. In this area stretching from the interior to the bay of Carthage, most of Scipio's battles were fought.[53]

Passing through the mountains and connecting the plains to one another, the river valleys in the area offered the easiest avenues of advance. In the summer the major rivers' tributaries often went dry, becoming lesser obstacles to troop movement and maneuver. The climate was hospitable, and even in the summer the temperature usually did not force military operations to cease, as it often did in Spain. The chief problem of summer campaigning was the lack of water, which often had to be packed overland by mules and donkeys to sustain the armies.[54] In the winter the land was barren, and food supplies had to be packed in as well. Winter was also the season for storms at sea, so supplying the logistics bases by ship was difficult and sometimes forced an end to winter operations.[55] The area's terrain and climatic conditions made the movement of armies within it possible but only in certain well-defined directions.

THE BATTLE AT THE TOWER OF AGATHOCLES, 204 BCE

The Roman landing caused a panic in the immediate countryside, and the local residents fled into the towns. When the news reached Carthage, a great fear gripped the city. Preparations for a siege began immediately, and a general call to arms was issued. Carthage sent Syphax appeals to honor his treaty and send aid to Carthage. The citizens' fear was fed by a stark reality "that they had no military force of any strength in the city and no general to lead the resistance."[56]

Livy is exaggerating the Carthaginian situation, for Carthage had the experienced Hasdrubal, son of Gisgo, at its service. He had earlier gone into the interior to raise a force of mercenaries and, as Appian tells us, already levied some six thousand infantry and six hundred horses from among the Carthaginians and the same number of troops from the Libyans, for a force of some thirteen thousand men and twelve hundred cavalry.[57] Most of these troops, however, were raw recruits and irregulars who were no match for the disciplined and combat-hardened Romans. Hasdrubal was also short of cavalry, and later he made efforts to obtain some four thousand horses from the Numidians.[58] When Scipio landed Hasdrubal's small force was some twenty-five miles inland from Carthage and not in position to disrupt the Roman landing or even place itself between Scipio and his line of advance toward Carthage.[59]

Scipio quickly moved inland for a short distance, occupied the ridge overlooking the sea, and placed pickets and outposts to guard the approaches to the beach, where his army was unloading its men, equipment, and supplies. Cavalry units were sent forward to raid the nearby farms, spread fear, and obtain provisions.[60] The Carthaginians sent a small cavalry squadron of five hundred men along the coast to reconnoiter the Roman positions and cause what disruption and delays they could. They clashed with Scipio's cavalry screen and suffered heavy casualties, including the death of their commander, a young noble named Hanno.[61] Scipio then sent his units farther afield, capturing the nearest town and raiding the countryside. The well-populated area around Utica was agriculturally rich, and Scipio sent large cargos of captured material, including eight thousand civilian captives, back to Sicily on his transports.[62] Meeting no resistance, Scipio moved his whole force closer to Utica and encamped on a line of hills about a mile southwest of the city itself.[63] The Roman fleet moved into position offshore, ready to land marines or bombard the city.

Scipio's attack on Utica was prompted by Roman caution. Without Syphax to supply his army, Scipio was forced to ensure his own lines of supply. Utica was located on the western side of the Bay of Tunis, about one-third of the way down the Promontory of Fair God, and some twelve miles from Carthage. Scipio intended to turn Utica into an operational base from which he could supply his troops and establish their winter quarters. Utica was a major port with a good harbor and piers, something uncommon in the ancient world, and they permitted resupply by sea even during the stormy winter season, when ships could seek shelter in the harbor. Equally important, the city was situated in the Bagradas Valley, an important agricultural region and the main source of Carthage's food supply. From Utica, Scipio could move inland along the valley and live off the land as he cut off supplies to Carthage. With only a forty-five-day supply of food, Scipio had to secure another source. The farms of the Bagradas Valley would serve nicely.[64]

Around this time Massinissa arrived with two hundred cavalrymen. Massinissa's circumstances had not improved in the year since his meeting with Laelius. Still an exile in his own land, he commanded a small band of brigands and had achieved little success in regaining his throne.[65] He was in no position to provide the Romans with the troops and cavalry that Scipio had hoped to acquire from him. Nonetheless, his appearance as a "king" of the Numidians at the head of a "bodyguard" of two hundred horsemen may have been useful to Scipio insofar as it convinced his troops of his earlier claim that the Numidian kings were ready and waiting to support the Roman cause.

As Scipio moved into position to attack Utica, Hamilcar's son, Hanno, received command of a newly raised cavalry force of four thousand troopers, two hundred of which were the sons of wealthy and noble Carthaginian families and the remainder being Numidians. Hanno occupied the town of Salaeca, which was fifteen miles from the Roman camp. Scipio moved immediately to neutralize the threat. He could not permit the Carthaginians to concentrate any significant force within striking distance of his own position, at least not until his army was fully deployed and his ships unloaded. The battle between the two cavalry forces occurred near the Tower of Agathocles, which Appian places at some thirty stades, or about three miles, from Utica. The tower was probably a small ruin that may have been constructed by Agathocles, the warrior prince of Syracuse who attacked Carthage in 310 BCE. The battle itself (whether or not a tower was there in Scipio's day) occurred near the coastal road connecting Utica with Bizerta. Salaeca lay to the west. Here a range of hills forms a broad saddle or narrow neck, with gently sloping ground on both sides formed of firm but not rocky soil, between which Scipio's cavalry could have been hidden. A cavalry squadron could rush from its concealment there and attack along a broad front with little difficulty.[66]

To draw Hanno into the trap, Scipio dispatched Massinissa and his two hundred cavalrymen to demonstrate against the walls of Salaeca. Again and again Massinissa rode up to the gates only to withdraw. Hanno seems to have had some difficulty getting his men mounted and into the fight. When Hanno's troops finally did venture forth, Livy tells us that "their sortie was a badly organized affair and their leader was having a troublesome time of it," suggesting the troops had not been trained.[67] At last Hanno's forces engaged with Massinissa, who gradually gave ground until, pretending to flee, his squadron turned and galloped away. Hanno's men carelessly pursued Massinissa, who led the Carthaginians around the saddle's southern end, where Scipio's cavalry waited in ambush.[68] None of the accounts tell us the size of either man's force. We do not know if Hanno brought his entire force of four thousand with him or if only a part of his force was involved. Scipio had taken twelve hundred with him on the boats from Sicily, and there is no mention of his recruiting any more cavalry in Africa at this time, save Massinissa's two hundred troopers. But Scipio would have been foolish to leave his beachhead unprotected, so some cavalry was probably left behind. If Scipio took three-fourths of his total cavalry force with him, he would have had nine hundred men.

Massinissa drew Hanno toward the hills behind which the Roman cavalry was concealed. As Hanno's column passed the neck of the saddle, Scipio's cavalry rushed to take Hanno in the flank. At the sound of Scipio's attack, Massinissa's men wheeled around and struck Hanno's column from the front. The men in Hanno's front ranks, a thousand according to Livy,[69] were quickly caught between Massinissa and Scipio. Hanno's column was cut in two, and the rear of his column turned and fled. Either Scipio had launched the attack too soon to surround the entire column and block its retreat, or if he was outnumbered, he may have deliberately permitted some of the enemy to escape to even the odds against

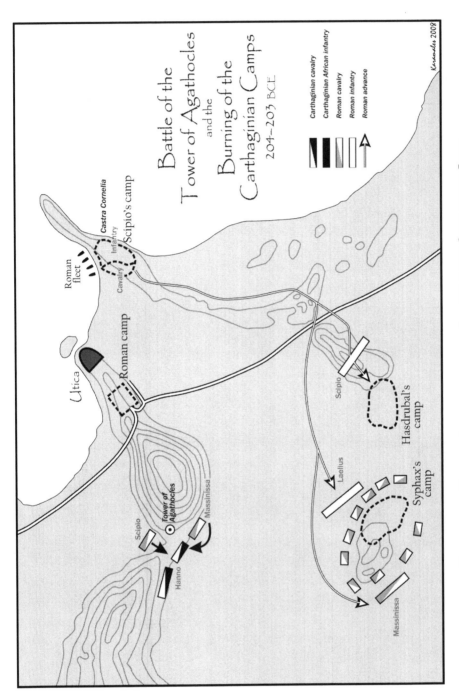

Battle of the
Tower of Agathocles
and the
Burning of the
Carthaginian Camps
204–203 BCE

Kesrandes 2008

Carthaginian cavalry
Carthaginian African infantry
Roman cavalry
Roman infantry
Roman advance

Castra Cornelia
Scipio's camp
Infantry
Cavalry
Roman fleet

Utica
Roman camp

Scipio
Tower of Agathocles
Massinissa
Hanno

Scipio
Hasdrubal's camp

Laelius
Syphax's camp

Massinissa

BATTLE OF THE TOWER OF AGATHOCLES AND THE BURNING OF THE CARTHAGINIAN CAMPS

160

what was left of Hanno's cavalry. If so, Scipio's timing permitted the Romans a numerical advantage over the trapped men and quickly overwhelmed them. Hanno was killed fighting with his troops. Livy says that the Romans pursued the column's remnants for more than thirty miles, "finally killing and capturing some 2,000 more,"[70] but this seems unlikely. Salaeca was only ten miles away and would have provided refuge for the fleeing Carthaginians. Although some Carthaginians were probably overtaken by the Romans and killed or taken prisoner, Livy's claim that the entire force suffered this fate is unlikely.

Next Scipio marched on Salaeca and occupied it. For a week his troops plundered the surrounding area. They returned to their camp outside Utica laden with booty.[71]

Scipio's operations around the landing zone had finally secured the area, and he could now turn his attention to Utica, hoping to capture the city and transform it into an operational base before winter set in. Scipio had brought artillery and siege engines with him and had captured craftsmen manufacture additional artillery in a makeshift arsenal. He received other artillery from Sicily when supplies arrived.[72] It is the first time we hear of Scipio receiving supplies. Perhaps they were transported on the ships that went unused in the original invasion. Scipio was an excellent logistician and may well have planned to assemble extra ships precisely to use some of them as a follow-on resupply capability once he had secured his position in Africa. Livy tells us that Scipio had not only hired transports for the original invasion fleet, but he also had ordered others "seized and brought to Lilybaeum."[73]

Scipio besieged Utica for forty days, but he made little progress against the city's defenses. While Scipio was occupied at Utica, Hasdrubal continued raising troops and guarding the approaches to Carthage against any Roman advance. At some point Syphax arrived from the west with a large army and joined forces with Hasdrubal. Together they marched toward Utica, establishing positions a short distance from the Roman camp and blocking Scipio's avenue of advance inland. It was late autumn, winter was approaching, and Scipio had made little progress against Utica. With the Carthaginian and Numidian armies' arrival, he broke off the siege and retired to winter quarters.

It is difficult to escape the impression that Scipio was not at his best in the months after the invasion and may have made a number of mistakes. His siege of Utica, for example, seems to have been a strategic error, and even with skilled forces, boats, and siege machinery, he failed to take the city. If his point was to break the political will of the Carthaginian leadership, then attacking Utica brought Scipio no closer to his goal. He should have simply bypassed the city. Stopping to lay siege to Utica squandered whatever operational momentum the invasion and the small early victories had afforded the Romans. Scipio had wanted to turn Utica into a logistics base, but as his winter encampment proved, he already had sufficient supplies and did not need Utica at all. Equally troubling is that Scipio seemed to have forgotten his history. The key to Carthage was not Utica but Tunis. Carthage sat at the end of a peninsula whose isthmus was blocked by a range of hills. Tunis commanded these hills. An army on this high ground could cut off Carthage from its hinterlands and source of food and troops. Invading armies in the previous two centuries—Agathocles (310 BCE), Regulus (256 BCE), and the mercenaries of the Truceless War (241–237 BCE)—all seized Tunis as a prelude to moving against Carthage. Capturing Utica would have done nothing to weaken Carthage itself.

Perhaps Scipio thought that Utica would fall into his hands with little effort. Utica was the oldest Phoenician city in North Africa and had been Carthage's ally for centuries. However, it had sided with the mercenaries against Carthage during the Truceless War and in the First Punic War had offered itself to Rome as an ally.[74] Perhaps Scipio believed that politics would carry the day after a brief show of Roman determination and Utica would come willingly over to the Roman side again. If so, he was wrong.

The time Scipio spent at Utica left Hasdrubal free to continue to recruit, train, and equip his army. It also gave Syphax time to put down a rebellion in his own country, gather his army, and march to join Hasdrubal, who was already encamped outside Utica and blocking Scipio's route to the Bagradas Valley. As a result Scipio lost the opportunity to move quickly against Carthage and the interior towns while the Carthaginian forces were of marginal strength and scattered throughout the interior. Thus, the two Carthaginian armies, with a combined strength of thirty thousand infantry and three thousand to five thousand cavalry, linked up and marched against Scipio, threatening to trap him against the defenses of Utica and forcing him to withdraw.[75] Because Scipio had failed to seize the initiative and hold it, he was forced on the defensive. He withdrew his army two miles east of Utica and encamped on a narrow line of raised ground nine miles long that formed a headland to the sea.[76] Along this raised peninsula Scipio established Castra Cornelia, his main camp and supply base, to pass the winter. He had accumulated large food supplies after plundering the local farms and receiving shipments from Sicily and Sardinia. His own ships were beached.

Castra Cornelia was hardly an ideal position. Its only defensive asset was the marshy ground between the camp and Utica itself. Scipio seems to have been unable to strongly fortify the position. Perhaps he lacked suitable materials.[77] Perched on the narrow, rocky peninsula, Scipio was cut off even from the towns he had captured, which were again in the Carthaginians' hands. He had failed to take Utica and had not captured a single port on which he could rely for sustained supply. His sea communications were threatened by storms. With the sea at his back, Scipio was vulnerable to naval attack once the weather calmed, and it could not have been welcome news that the Carthaginians were preparing a fleet.[78] Two Carthaginian armies whose strength exceeded his own were encamped a few miles away, blocking his advance to the interior. The only good news was that at the turn of the year word reached Scipio that Rome has extended his command *donec debellatum foret* (until the war should be finished).[79]

THE BURNING OF THE CARTHAGINIAN CAMPS, 203 BCE

Over the winter Scipio turned to diplomatic stratagems to try and alter his strategic situation. He had always believed Syphax was the key to Rome's success in Africa; therefore, he opened negotiations in the hope of convincing him to abandon his alliance with Carthage. Syphax welcomed the overture but refused to meet directly with Scipio, serving instead as an intermediary between Scipio and Hasdrubal. While Syphax refused to abandon his Carthaginian ally, he insisted that the basis for a just peace lay in Rome leaving Africa and in Hannibal leaving Italy, with each side being allowed to keep those places each already held between the two countries.[80] Strong advocates in Rome and Carthage also wished to see the war end. But Scipio's original strategic plan called for Carthage's defeat in the field so that Rome could dictate a peace that accommodated its security interests. Scipio was not about to abandon it now. As the negotiations dragged on, Scipio came to the conclusion that they would eventually prove fruitless. He began to seek a way of dealing the enemy a major blow.

The Carthaginian armies were camped about ten miles from Scipio's, and Hasdrubal's encampment was about a mile from Syphax's camp. Hasdrubal was camped to the east so he could easily cover and communicate with Carthage; likewise, from his camp to the west, Syphax could maintain communications with his kingdom.[81] During the negotiations Scipio's envoys reported that the Carthaginians had constructed their huts "out of wood and boughs without using any earth, while [the Numidians] had made theirs out of reeds."[82] Scipio devised a plan to destroy the Carthaginian armies by setting their camps on fire. Although Scipio had always rejected Syphax's formula for peace, now he gained Syphax's and Hasdrubal's confidence by suggesting that he might agree after all. His deception drew out the negotiations through the winter. The envoys' meetings became so frequent the Romans could wander unattended through the enemy camps. Polybius tells us that Scipio included among his envoys "men of tried experience and others of military capacity; they would be humbly and shabbily dressed, disguised in fact as slaves, and their task was to examine and explore the approaches and entrances to both camps without interference."[83]

As the weather warmed, Scipio stirred his troops from Castra Cornelia, sending two thousand men to occupy the high ground overlooking Utica. He outfitted his ships with siege engines, launched them, and moved them close as if to blockade the city from the sea. Scipio wanted to create the illusion that he intended to continue his assault on Utica. Meanwhile, as the negotiations continued, Scipio sent a message that while he agreed peace was possible, his own military council opposed it and more talks would be necessary. Throughout this time Scipio continued to issue orders and move his troops about as if they were preparing to attack Utica. One afternoon he called a meeting of his unit commanders and told them his plan. They were to assemble their units for a march after the evening meal. Then he held a meeting of all the spies who had been in the enemy camps and called in Massinissa to evaluate their reports and check their accuracy. Next, he assigned a strong guard to secure the camp while the army was gone. Finally, under cover of night, Scipio moved his army out of Castra Cornelia and in position for a night attack on the Carthaginian and Numidian camps.

Arriving in the camps' vicinity undetected, Scipio divided his army. He placed half the infantry and all the Numidian troops along with Massinissa under Laelius's command and gave the order to attack Syphax's camp immediately. Scipio himself took command of the rest of the army and advanced against Hasdrubal's camp. When Laelius reached his objective, he divided his force into two elements, both of which attacked the Numidian camp. Laelius's men set the first row of huts afire; the flames quickly spread. Massinissa's men took up positions at the various entrances and exits to prevent anyone from escaping. At first the Numidians thought the fire was an accident and rushed from their huts. Many were trampled trying to reach the exits, and others burned in their huts. Those who escaped the flames ran into Massinissa's men blocking the exits and were cut down. The few who did manage to get through were slaughtered by Laelius's legionnaires.

A mile away Scipio and his troops remained concealed behind a range of low hills. The Carthaginians saw the flames and rushed to aid their comrades. Thinking the fire an accident, few grabbed their weapons or armor. Scipio's men rushed into action, falling simultaneously on the Carthaginian camp and those soldiers trapped in the area between the two camps. Roman units ran through the Carthaginian camp, setting it ablaze and creating a terrible conflagration that consumed a great number of lives. Both Syphax and Hasdrubal, now realizing that Scipio was upon them, fled with small detachments of cavalry. Their armies were left to their fate. Polybius captures the horror of the incident, telling us,

> but of all the rest, thousands and thousands of men, horses and mules perished miserably and piteously in the flames, while others of their comrades died a disgraceful and dishonorable death at the hands of the enemy as they strove to escape the fury of the fire, for they were cut down naked and defenseless, not only without their arms but without even their clothes to cover them. The whole place was filled with wails of dismay, confused shouting and cries of terror which mingled in an unspeakable din, while above all this rose the roar of the raging fire and of flames which overcame all resistance.[84]

Livy's account tells us that forty thousand men died in the fire, but the number is not believable.[85] It is possible, however, that close to half the Numidian and Carthaginian forces perished, were injured, or were captured.

Scipio pursued Hasdrubal and caught up with him at a small town. Hasdrubal lost his nerve and abandoned the town, fleeing toward Carthage. Syphax, too, escaped, and "he breathed out savage threats and ground his teeth, to think that his face had been scorched by the fire in the camp, and that he had with difficulty been rescued from the foe, a naked man in the midst of his discomforted soldiers."[86] Scipio returned to Castra Cornelia to resume the siege of Utica.

One cannot help but wonder what Scipio was thinking when he returned to Utica. He had broken out of his confinement on the peninsula, launched a daring attack on the enemy, destroyed it almost completely, and in one bold stroke regained the initiative. He surely knew that there was no significant Carthaginian force between him and Carthage itself. His own well-supplied army was at full strength, and it was early spring, the beginning of the campaign season. Scipio could have marched unopposed against the Carthaginian capital and had his ships equipped with siege machinery and artillery arrive in the city's harbor and ready to go into action. It would have been a bold and decisive maneuver indeed and might have brought Carthage to its knees psychologically in a single blow. At the very least a threatening move against the capital might have convinced the Carthaginians to recall Hannibal from Italy sooner than they did.

Of course, Scipio never had any chance of taking Carthage by storm. The city was one of the largest and best defended in the world. Its fortifications had a circumference of 26,905 meters, or three times longer than those of Rome. The citadel (*Byrsa*) of Carthage was built on a hill near the end of a peninsula that was connected with the mainland by an isthmus three miles broad. Its defense was a triple line of fortifications, the outer wall of which was forty-five feet high with towers at two-hundred-foot intervals. The whole peninsula enclosed some thirty miles in circumference. The city had vast storehouses for food and a great number of horse and elephant stables. Scipio's army was far too small to attempt to storm Carthage, and he had little chance of receiving Roman reinforcements to help with the task. The key to capturing Carthage still required first capturing Tunis and then blockading Carthage by land and sea until starvation and disease forced it to surrender. Scipio, however, made no move against Tunis.

Liddell-Hart says of Scipio's attack on the camps that it was in the best tradition of Napoleon's maxim that "the whole art of war consists in a well-ordered and prudent defensive followed by a bold and rapid offensive."[87] Perhaps so. But Napoleon knew that the key to success was the ability to follow on and exploit success, that is, to build one victory upon another. Scipio's failure to exploit his victory and attack Tunis must be recognized for the error that it was.

THE BATTLE OF THE GREAT PLAINS, 203 BCE

The disaster at the camps plunged Carthage into a panic. Its only army was lost, its control of communications to the interior severed, its food supply was threatened, and the Roman fleet was in a position to blockade the city. The Carthaginian strategy of containing the Romans on the peninsula near Utica and using its fleet to blockade them from the sea now had to be abandoned. Some in the Senate wanted to sue for peace, others wanted to recall Hannibal, and still others, led by the Barcid family, convinced the Senate to continue the fight. But fight with what? Hasdrubal had survived the camps' conflagration with only two thousand infantry and five hundred cavalry. Syphax, with perhaps an equal force, was making his way back to Numidia. As luck would have it, Syphax met a contingent of four thousand Celtiberian mercenaries who had been recruited in Spain and were headed to Carthage. About the same time Hasdrubal's messengers reached Syphax and instructed him to turn around and rejoin Hasdrubal at a location some seventy-five miles south and inland from Utica.[88] Hasdrubal had spent the previous month recruiting new troops, gathering the fires' survivors, and putting together an army of eight thousand infantry and three thousand cavalry.[89] The approximate strength of the combined forces of Hasdrubal and Syphax, including the Celtiberians was perhaps twenty thousand men, including cavalry, which probably numbered between three thousand and four thousand.[90]

The armies concentrated at a place on the upper reaches of the Bagradas River, seventy-five miles inland on a broad plain fifteen miles long and twelve miles wide, now known to history as Campi Magni, or the Great Plains.[91] It had been only a month since the disaster of the camps, and Hasdrubal's army was in no condition to fight. He had chosen the location near the Bagradas precisely because it was far from Utica and Scipio's army. He expected Scipio to occupy himself with continuing the siege of the city while he used the time to gather his strength and make his army ready for battle. When news reached Scipio that the Carthaginians were concentrating their forces, he moved immediately to interrupt their plans. He may have reckoned that with his disciplined and experienced legions, he could exploit the weaknesses of Hasdrubal's untrained force. Leaving behind half his army to continue the siege of Utica, Scipio set out with the rest, perhaps twelve thousand to fifteen thousand men, for Campi Magni.[92] The army was ordered to move in "light marching order" with only a minimum of baggage. After five days' march, Scipio arrived at Campi Magni and encamped on a hill four miles from the Carthaginians' site.[93]

It is interesting to note that Scipio left half his total strength behind to continue the siege at Utica. Why he should have ventured inland with so small an army when he could not have known the Carthaginians' strength seems risky in the extreme. Except for an occasional sortie from the Utican defenders and the remote threat of the Carthaginian fleet attacking by sea, Scipio had little to concern him if he left a smaller force behind and took a larger one into the field. Throughout the entire campaign, Scipio seems to have been focused on taking Utica for reasons that defy military logic. This said, however, Scipio had to regard any possible threat to his base at Castra Cornelia as his first priority and had to defend it, for defeat here meant catastrophe. As a consequence, when Scipio left half his men at his encampment and marched to the plains to offer battle to the Carthaginians, he found himself outnumbered.

Thinking Scipio was occupied at Utica, the Carthaginians must have been surprised by his arrival. Probably because his army was larger and possessed a powerful combat asset in the four thousand combat-hardened Celtiberian mercenaries, Hasdrubal accepted Scipio's offer of battle. It was a grave mistake. A more imaginative commander than Hasdrubal might have realized that with Scipio so far from his base, delay was the better course of action. The Romans had moved without their baggage and probably had rations for only a few days. If Hasdrubal had delayed until Scipio was forced to retrace his march back to his base, the Carthaginians could have harassed him with Numidian cavalry, ambushes, and guerrilla attacks; worn his army down; and caused significant casualties at little cost to themselves. A more imaginative commander might also have maintained his communications with Carthage and convinced the leaders to send the fleet against Castra Cornelia, where the Romans were at half-strength. Together these steps would have seriously weakened Scipio's ability to carry out further operations for the year. Instead, Hasdrubal chose to fight.

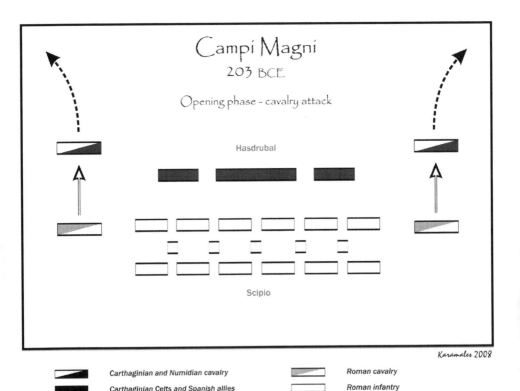

BATTLE OF CAMPI MAGNI: OPENING PHASE—CAVALRY ATTACK

Scipio advanced to battle in the usual Roman manner, drawn up in three lines of hastati, principes, and triarii. The Roman cavalry deployed on the right wing with Massinissa's Numidians on the left. The Celtiberians and Carthaginian levies anchored the enemy's center, with the Carthaginian cavalry on the right and Syphax's Numidians on the left.[94] Scipio opened the battle by sending his cavalry to engage its opposite numbers. It drove both the Carthaginian and Numidian cavalry back, exposing the flanks of the Celtiberians' in the center. This success suggests that Scipio must have taken almost all his cavalry with him, perhaps all but a few squadrons of the twelve hundred cavalry he possessed. In the past, Roman commanders used their cavalry or their light troops to attack an enemy's exposed flanks. But Scipio's army had its new weapons and tactics. On command the front rank of hastati moved quickly forward and heavily engaged the Celtiberian contingent in the center of the line, fixing them fast. Under cover of the first line, the second and third lines of principes and triarii formed into columns, half to the right and half to the left, and marched out from behind the line of hastati and encircled the Carthaginians.[95] Polybius tells us that the Celtiberians fought well, providing time for Hasdrubal and Syphax to make their escape once more: "Hasdrubal, no favorite of Mars and famous for repeated flights, fled once more and gave up the struggle." The rest of the army was "cut down where they stood, except for a few survivors."[96]

Scipio's tactics at Campi Magni were a further development of those he had used at Ilipa and proof that the Roman army was becoming more tactically sophisticated. At Ilipa he had held the enemy center at bay but had not engaged it. At Campi Magni he had held it fast so that it could not turn to the flanks or escape. At Ilipa Scipio had utilized separate units to maneuver and strike the enemy's flanks while at Campi Magni he had used the Roman infantry lines themselves, first as a coherent unit and then to maneuver as independent entities. The lines of principes and triarii were no longer employed only to support the front line of hastati but could now be used to extend the front line or to maneuver independently on command. This revolution in Roman tactics was the logical and next development of the tactical innovations Scipio had first attempted at Ilipa. Now the Roman legions could not only strike at the enemy's flanks, as they had done at Baecula, but they could also encircle the enemy entirely in a more sophisticated and flexible manner than Hannibal had done at Cannae. Hannibal had had to give ground to form a crescent and draw the Romans in before striking them in the flanks. Scipio's formations, however, could encircle the enemy while simultaneously attacking the center of the enemy line.

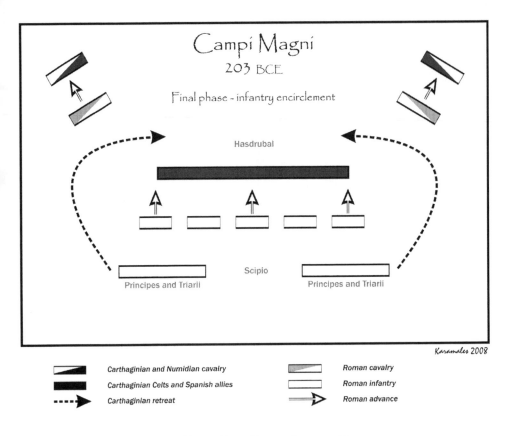

Campi Magni

203 BCE

Final phase - infantry encirclement

Hasdrubal

Scipio

Principes and Triarii

Principes and Triarii

Karamales 2008

	Carthaginian and Numidian cavalry			Roman cavalry
	Carthaginian Celts and Spanish allies			Roman infantry
	Carthaginian retreat			Roman advance

BATTLE OF CAMPI MAGNI: FINAL PHASE—INFANTRY ENCIRCLEMENT

Here, then, we witness the first example of Romans using echelon tactics, which later made the Roman imperial army the master of the battlefield. This tactical revolution is owed completely to Scipio.[97]

With the last remaining Carthaginian field force destroyed, Scipio divided his army and sent Laelius and Massinissa in pursuit of Syphax. While the size of this pursuit force is unknown, it must have included most of Scipio's cavalry and, perhaps, a small number of light infantry for only cavalry had any hope of catching up with Syphax's Numidian cavalry. This operation left Scipio with about ten thousand infantry and a small cavalry detachment for scouting and communications. Scipio then turned his army against the neighboring towns, accepting the surrender of some and storming those that resisted. The booty from these raids was sent to Castra Cornelia in the supply trains that by now had caught up with Scipio's main body.

Scipio's army next marched east toward Tunis. Only fifteen miles from Carthage, Tunis was, as Polybius tells us, "visible from almost every point in the capital." As noted, Tunis commanded the approaches to the city and overlooked the hills blocking the isthmus of the peninsula on which Carthage sat. Given its importance to the defense of Carthage, it is not surprising that Tunis was "a city of great natural strength which has been reinforced by its man-made fortifications."[98]

How curious, then, that Polybius should report "the moment Scipio arrived at Tunis, the garrison took flight and he at once occupied the place."[99] We are to believe that while Utica had held out for almost a year and Carthage had taken to its defenses and was preparing a naval attack against Scipio's base, for some reason one of the most strongly fortified, easily defensible, and militarily significant of Carthage's cities fell to a Roman army of only ten thousand men without offering any resistance. Polybius tells us that "by the time the Romans pitched their camp there, the Carthaginian fleet was already on its way to Utica." He goes on to say that when Scipio saw the ships departing the harbor at Carthage, he immediately broke camp and marched toward Castra Cornelia to intercept the attack on his own fleet.[100] It is likely, therefore, that Scipio did not occupy Tunis at all or that its garrison did not flee.[101] What probably happened was that Scipio camped near Tunis, perhaps on one of the hills that overlooked the bay. When he saw the Carthaginian ships put to sea, he realized they were bound for Utica to attack his base. He broke camp and hurried to its defense. It is improbable that Scipio occupied Tunis before Carthage sued for peace. Afterward, when the garrison left, Scipio occupied the city.

Hasdrubal's defeat and Scipio's march toward Tunis provoked great concern in Carthage, and the Senate met to decide what to do. After considerable debate, it was agreed to fortify the city and prepare for a siege, to send a delegation to Hannibal and order him to return to Africa, and to launch a naval attack against Scipio's positions at Utica. If Polybius's chronology is correct, these decisions were made *before* Scipio arrived outside Tunis. Almost immediately *after* Scipio's arrival there, Carthage sent its fleet against Utica. Scipio must have forced-marched his troops the twenty-five miles from Tunis to Utica because he arrived before the Carthaginian fleet and still had some time to prepare to defend his base. All Scipio's warships had been loaded with siege and artillery weapons to prosecute the attack on Utica and were not prepared for a naval battle in the open sea. Thus he brought his naval combatants close to shore and lashed the supply transports together four deep in front of them. The line of moored vessels formed a barrier against the Carthaginian ships.

171

Livy tells us that what followed had no resemblance at all to a naval battle. Because the supply ships were higher out of the water than the Carthaginian ships were, "it looked, if anything, more like ships attacking walls."[102] The Carthaginians used grappling hooks (what the soldiers called "snatchers") to hook the transports and pull them from the line. Sometimes they ended up dragging away more than one at a time. The Carthaginians broke off the engagement after two days and towed some sixty Roman transports to the harbor at Carthage.[103] The Roman combat fleet, however, was safe. Scipio can be faulted for having converted all his naval combatants to siege service and leaving none configured to defend the transports against attack. He also seems to have misjudged the Carthaginians' morale after his victory at Great Plains and took no precautions to monitor the Carthaginian fleet's status or location. Scipio was fortunate to have been close to Tunis when the Carthaginians sent their fleet against Utica. Had they done it only a few days before, the Roman warships and transports might have been caught unable to defend themselves and destroyed.

SYPHAX'S DEFEAT

Meanwhile, Laelius and Massinissa had marched for fifteen days to reach Numidia. Here the people rose in revolt against Syphax, and several towns opened their gates to Massinissa and accepted him as their king. Syphax set about raising a new army to protect his hold over his kingdom. He assembled "all the men fit for service" and equipped them with horses, arms, and missile weapons from his arsenal, for he was now on his home ground. He raised a force "no less in numbers than the previous one [at Campi Magni], though composed almost entirely of raw and untrained men."[104] Livy says Syphax organized his cavalry in squadrons and his infantry in cohorts just as the Roman centurions had shown him in the early days of the Second Punic War, when Rome made a concerted effort to convince him to abandon the Carthaginians. Livy's anecdote is unlikely, because it would have taken months to reorganize a tribal army accustomed to fighting in clan groups, as individuals, or in loose mobs. If the earlier numbers regarding the strength of Hasdrubal's and Syphax's combined armies that fought at Great Plains are correct, then Syphax was able to raise about eight thousand troops. There is no way of knowing how many of them were infantry, but given the nature of Numidian warfare most were probably cavalrymen. The raw recruits Livy mentions perhaps composed most of the infantry.

Livy's account of the battle raises questions. The battle began with a clash of cavalry in which Syphax's troops in "immense columns sent continually into action . . . were almost irresistible." As noted earlier Laelius's army probably contained less than a thousand Roman cavalry and only a small number of infantry, mostly light infantry, to effectively pursue Syphax. Livy's description suggests that Syphax's cavalry numbers were considerably larger. Massinissa apparently had little success in raising more troops among his own people. The battle was going against the Romans when the Roman light infantry's sudden intervention "stabilized the line and checked the wild charge of the enemy" and brought the enemy "to a standstill." Livy goes on to say that "at this point in the action the Roman legionaries were seen approaching," and one takes "legionaires" to mean the heavy infantry. But where did these troops come from? They are unaccounted for in Laelius's force that left Campi Magni. At the mere sight of these troops Syphax's untested infantry turned and fled. Livy records that casualties were light and "not more than 5,000 men were killed, and less than half that number were captured in an attack on the camp."[105]

Regarding Syphax's fate, Italicus said,

> The first flying spear lodged in the fiery nostrils of the king's charger. With blood dripping from his face, the animal reared up and beat the air with its forefeet; then he fell down in rage and pain, and tossing from side to side the part pierced by the spearpoint, betrayed his rider into the hands of the enemy. They fell upon him [Syphax] . . . then chains and fetters were laid upon him."[106]

The king of the Numidians was felled by a lucky shot that disabled his horse, and he was captured while attempting to rally his men. It was probably seeing their commander wounded and captured and not the Roman heavy infantry's arrival that caused the Numidians to lose heart and flee the battlefield.

Massinissa rode on ahead to Cirta, the capital, bringing Syphax with him in chains. When Massinissa showed Cirta's civic leaders his captive, Syphax, they surrendered. For the next few weeks Massinissa and Laelius dragged Syphax from one town to another, "taking over the remaining communities of Numidia which were still held by Syphax's troops." This story cannot have been entirely correct, for Vermina, Syphax's son and an experienced warrior in his own right, was still at liberty. He must have tried to save what he could of his father's kingdom by ensuring the loyalty of the towns in the interior and by raising troops. While the Romans recovered some towns, they did not seem to advance much beyond Cirta. Still, Numidia had been strategically neutralized, and Carthage could no longer count on any aid from that quarter.

TRUCE

The destruction of Syphax's army and his capture sent shock waves through the Carthaginian leadership. The Senate was called immediately into session. The Senators decided to send a delegation to Scipio and make peace. Envoys had already been dispatched after the defeat at the Great Plains to recall Mago from northern Italy and Hannibal from the south.[107] Scipio had never wished to destroy Carthage; he wanted only to limit its power and thus accommodate Rome's security interests. His victories in Africa had forced Hannibal to withdraw from Italy and Mago from Gaul, a major strategic objective of his campaign. Scipio's ultimate goal was to deprive Carthage of its European empire and to reduce its naval strength to where it could not threaten Roman interests in the western Mediterranean again. Scipio's victories already placed his military reputation beyond question. It was now time for diplomacy.

The Carthaginian Privy Council sent a delegation to Scipio's camp to plead for terms. Scipio proposed the following: Carthage would surrender all prisoners, deserters, and refugees from Roman justice. The Carthaginians would evacuate all forces from Italy and Gaul as well as from all the islands between Italy and Africa. Carthage would evacuate Spain, and all the military action it supported there would cease. Carthage would surrender its entire naval force except for twenty ships. With its fleet gone, Carthage would be in no position to regain or hold any distant territory. It would also have to pay an indemnity of five thousand talents of silver. Until a formal treaty was signed, Carthage would have to furnish double pay for Scipio's troops and provide them with a large quantity of wheat and barley to feed the army.[108]

Scipio's terms were designed to reduce Carthage to a regional African power without an ability to project force beyond Africa itself. Even its status as a regional power would be limited by Roman support for Massinissa in Numidia. Scipio had already recognized Massinissa as king and requested the Roman Senate to ratify his decision. Ten cohorts of Roman infantry and cavalry were placed under Massinissa's command to help him recover the rest of his kingdom and incorporate some of Syphax's kingdom. Scipio gave the Carthaginians three days to accept or reject his offer. They accepted quickly and sent a delegation to sign an armistice. Another delegation was dispatched to Rome to ask the Senate to accept the terms. For the first time in sixteen years, Rome and Carthage enjoyed a respite from war.

7

Scipio and Hannibal

THE CARTHAGINIAN envoys arrived in Rome sometime in the spring of 203 BCE to plead with the Roman Senate to accept the peace terms that Scipio and Carthage had negotiated after the Carthaginian defeat at Great Plains. There was considerable argument and delay in gaining the Senate's acceptance. The main obstacle, Dio tells us, was that the conservative faction refused to accept any peace as long as Hannibal and his army remained on Italian soil.[1] Hannibal had been recalled shortly after the disaster at Great Plains, but he either deliberately made no move to depart or had difficulty assembling enough ships to make the crossing. If the delay was deliberate, he may have wanted to influence the negotiations and secure more favorable terms.[2] Hannibal was a good strategist and realized that Scipio's army was too small to accomplish the strategic conquest of Carthage and its empire by himself. He probably concluded that despite Scipio's capture of Syphax and his victories in the field, he had not made much progress in obtaining his strategic goals. Even after Hannibal arrived in Africa, he seems to have been in no hurry to engage Scipio.

After finally gathering enough ships to transport his army, Hannibal left Italy in the autumn of 203 BCE.[3] J. F. C. Fuller says that Hannibal killed most of his horses before departing to prevent them from falling into Roman hands,[4] but he also might have had too few ships to transport them.[5] If so, this would explain why Hannibal arrived in Africa with only a small contingent of cavalry. Hannibal also culled his army before departing. He took only those soldiers fit for combat and distributed the unfit among the Bruttian towns "ostensibly for garrison duty."[6] Hannibal himself was despondent.

> Seldom, we are told, has any exile left his native land with so heavy
> a heart as Hannibal's when he left the country of his enemies; again

and again he looked back at the shores of Italy, accusing gods and men and calling down curses on his own head for not having led his armies straight to Rome when they were still bloody from the victorious field of Cannae . . . Such were his self-accusations and expressions of distress as he was forced to surrender his long occupation of Italy.[7]

Hannibal arrived at Leptis Minor (modern Lamtah), disembarked his army, and moved to Hadrumetum (modern Susa). Hadrumetum was a farming area with ample crops to support Hannibal's army. It was also far enough out of the way that he could assemble and train a new army. The area covered the approaches to Carthage from the southeast, so if Scipio attempted to move against the city, Hannibal would be in position to attack Scipio's exposed flank.

Mago's army had departed northern Italy earlier and had already arrived in Africa when Hannibal landed at Leptis Minor. Mago had been conducting operations in Liguria when he suffered a minor defeat at the hands of the Romans and was forced to withdraw to the coast. When he arrived there, Carthaginian messengers met him with orders to return to Africa as soon as possible. Livy says that Mago quickly departed because he feared the Romans would press their advantage and move against him.[8] He had suffered a serious wound "when his thigh was pierced" and was eager to be out of the fight. Mago and his army set sail at once, but he died of his infected wound as the ships passed Sardinia.

With the truce in Africa holding while Rome considered the peace terms, the Romans used the time to resupply their armies in the field. In the spring two large ship convoys set out to resupply Scipio. The first of these convoys, comprising a hundred transports and twenty warship-escorts, arrived safely from Sardinia. The second, with two hundred transports guarded by thirty warships, encountered a gale off the coast of Carthage and was scattered.[9] Most of the warships reached safety on the Promontory of Apollo, but most of the transports were driven ashore on the island of Aegimurus (modern Zembra), "an island that closes the bay on which the city is situated," about thirty miles by land from Carthage. The wrecked ships and their cargoes, abandoned by their crews, could be seen from the city.[10] Carthage was suffering from food shortages, probably as a result of Scipio's enforced grain indemnity, and was overcrowded with people from the countryside who sought safety within the city's walls. Here were two hundred Roman transports laden with supplies aground on a nearby island within easy reach.

Hannibal's arrival in Africa had raised Carthaginian morale and breathed new life into the war party in the Carthaginian Senate. At the same time "the envoys had not returned from Rome, nothing was yet known in Carthage of the attitude of the Roman Senate towards the question of peace or war, nor had the armistice expired."[11] The crowds outside clamored for the loot, and the Senate sent Hasdrubal with fifty ships to collect the abandoned cargoes.[12] As this was happening the Carthaginian envoys who were returning with word that Rome had accepted the peace terms were intercepted by Roman ships and brought before Scipio. Having learned of Rome's acceptance of his terms, Scipio permitted the envoys to continue their journey to Carthage and inform the Carthaginian Senate.

Scipio's next move showed diplomatic skill. Although the cargoes had already been taken, Scipio ignored that fact and sent three envoys to warn the Carthaginians that seizing the cargoes would violate the truce. If any had been already taken, Scipio warned, failing to return the cargoes would also violate the truce. Scipio was giving the Carthaginians plenty of room to maneuver. They just had to return the cargoes already in their possession, and that would end the matter. Scipio's envoys put the terms bluntly, but the Senate dismissed them without an answer, probably under pressure from the war party. A crowd had manhandled the Roman envoys outside the Senate on their way to the meeting, and now they feared for their lives. They requested an escort to protect them on their return. The Roman envoys were escorted to their quinquereme. Two Carthaginian triremes escorted their boat up the Macar River where it met the sea, at which point the escort turned back, leaving the Roman ship to continue its journey to its Utica base alone.

Polybius tells us that the war party in the Senate wanted to renew the war and sought to create an incident that would break the armistice.[13] To this end they set an ambush for the ship carrying the Roman envoys. As the Roman ship sailed on alone, "three Carthaginian *triremes* suddenly bore down upon them from their hiding place."[14] The Carthaginians, however, were unable to board the Roman ship. "Instead, they ran alongside and continued to circle round her, shooting at the marines and killing many of them."[15] The quinquereme turned toward shore, hoping to reach the beach, where Roman soldiers were gathering to help. The ship managed to reach safety. The Roman envoys had survived the ambush, but most of the marines had been killed. The incident had flagrantly broken the truce.

By summer Scipio was once more in the field against the Carthaginians. He left behind a strong guard under the command of Lucius Baebius, one of the envoys Scipio had sent to beseech the Carthaginian Senate; set out southwestward; and stormed one town after another. "He no longer accepted the submission of those who offered to surrender, but took each place by storm and sold the inhabitants into slavery, to demonstrate the anger he felt against the enemy because of the treacherous action of the Carthaginians."[16] He sent repeated messages to Massinissa, urging him to keep his promise and join him with an army. Scipio knew that his attacks on the provincial towns would sooner or later force Hannibal to take the field, but he dared not face Hannibal with the small number of cavalry he had at his disposal.

Hans Delbrück argues that Scipio's bold decision to march southwest, thus cutting himself off from his base and the sea and shortening the distance between himself and Massinissa, before he engaged Hannibal, marks Scipio as a great general.[17] This view of events is open to question on two counts. First, it supposes that Scipio knew Hannibal was already in the field and moving westward toward him. Otherwise, there was no risk of a surprise attack and no immediate urgency for Massinissa to join Scipio. But Polybius's account tells us that Hannibal was not yet in the field and that he had received a delegation from the Carthaginian Senate only *after* Carthage learned that Scipio was ravaging the provincial towns. Scipio was certainly in the field before Hannibal, perhaps as much as a month or so earlier.

Second, the move to the west would have been risky if, indeed, it had required Scipio to cut his communications with his base. But Polybius tells us that Scipio was selling his captives into slavery, which would have been possible only if the slave buyers were following the army or, at least, if he had had some way to move the captives to the rear, that is, along the Roman supply chain back to Utica. Polybius does not tell us where Scipio stormed the towns. Delbrück assumes it was along the Bagradas River, but Scipio had taken those towns the previous year, and there is no reason to assume they had reverted to Carthaginian control. Scipio was probably storming the towns farther east of the river in the area around Naragara (modern Sid Youssef), in which case he would not have been cut off from the previously captured towns and their supplies. If his luck turned for the worse, Scipio could always have fallen back on one of these garrisons for defense.[18]

Undoubtedly, Scipio needed Massinissa's help if he planned to take the war to Hannibal; however, some question arises about when this help was required.

If Scipio could send messages to Massinissa, as Polybius says he did,[19] then Scipio's messengers were able to report back on the status of Massinissa's preparations. Common sense dictates Scipio would not have taken the field with so few cavalry unless he had some reasonable expectation that Massinissa could join him in a reasonable period of time. Polybius's account that Massinissa joined Scipio in the nick of time, just two days before the battle at Zama, may not be accurate.[20] It is unlikely that Scipio would have permitted Hannibal to get that close to his army while he still lacked a sufficient cavalry arm, especially on the flat open ground around Zama, where cavalry could be decisive. Scipio was a gambler, but he was not a fool. More likely Massinissa had joined him sometime beforehand, or Scipio had scouting reports that Massinissa was close by.

Scipio's attacks on the provincial towns finally forced Hannibal to take the field. A few days after a Senate delegation urged him to move against Scipio, Hannibal "moved his camp from the neighborhood of Hadrumetum, advanced and then established himself near Zama, a town which lies about five days journey [about 70 miles] to the west of Carthage."[21] While at Hadrumetum, Hannibal had recruited and trained Carthaginian and Libyan infantry levies and attempted to increase his small contingent of cavalry. But even his elephants, as later accounts show, were not sufficiently trained. It is a fair assumption that Hannibal took his army into the field before he was ready. The question is, why? Supported by Delbrück's analysis,[22] the usual answer is that Hannibal could not afford to permit Massinissa to link up with Scipio. His own intelligence may have discovered what Scipio probably already knew from his own messengers: Massinissa was already on the move to join Scipio or at least close to departing his base. Thus, the argument goes, Hannibal hoped to prevent their linkup by getting his army between Scipio and Massinissa and forcing Scipio to battle before Massinissa's cavalry could arrive.[23] If this was Hannibal's plan, it was risky indeed, since nothing would have prevented Scipio from refusing to offer battle and delaying until Massinissa arrived. The plan was flawed insofar as it conceded the tactical initiative to Scipio. There must have been another factor in Hannibal's plan.

A reasonable guess is that the other factor was Vermina, Syphax's son, who had been busy resisting Massinissa on the tribal border and rebuilding his forces in his own kingdom. With the Romans helping Massinissa, Vermina had remained loyal to the Carthaginians, and he had probably sent messengers to Hannibal and promised to join him against the Romans. If so, Hannibal's and Scipio's armies were moving toward one another with the same tactical objective in mind, to be the first to linkup with its respective Numidian ally in order to gain an advantage in cavalry. Both Massinissa and Vermina would have been coming from approximately the same direction, the west, and both armies would have moved in directions that were the shortest distance to the linkup with their allies. Hannibal could expect Vermina's cavalry squadrons to be larger, better trained, and better armed than Massinissa's, for the former's were comprised of the regular units that had formed Syphax's garrisons and had remained loyal to Vermina. Massinissa had made some inroads to retaking his former kingdom, but he had not made significant progress in conquering Syphax's old kingdom. Accordingly, Delbrück may be correct when he suggests that much of Massinissa's cavalry had "come directly out of the Atlas Mountains and from the oases," and that they were as yet ill trained and poorly disciplined.[24]

There is reason to believe that Hannibal was indeed expecting Vermina to come to his aid against Scipio. Livy tells us that for a few days after the battle, Scipio plundered the Carthaginian camp and then made straight for Tunis. He says that "while on their way to Tunis," news reached the Romans that Vermina was coming to help the Carthaginians with "a large force of infantry and a greater one of cavalry."[25] According to Livy, "part of the Roman infantry and all the cavalry were sent to attack the column on the first day of the feast of the Saturnalia [December 17]."[26] Livy's tale implies that Vermina arrived shortly after the battle of Zama, for those Roman troops sent to intercept him were part of Scipio's army, which was marching from Zama to Tunis, but the date given for the troops' battle with Vermina places it two months after the battle at Zama. The precision of the date, one of the few exact dates in Livy's work, renders it suspicious.[27] It may have been that Vermina arrived just a few days too late to help Hannibal. Livy says that Vermina lost fifteen thousand men and twelve hundred captured in his battle with the Romans, suggesting his army was much bigger than the one that Massinissa brought to the battle and was big enough, perhaps, to change the battle of Zama's outcome had Vermina arrived in time. Finally, Vermina's appearance near Zama makes sense only if he was coming to Hannibal's aid. He was occupied with keeping control of his own kingdom in the west and fending off Massinissa's efforts to occupy territory close to his tribal borders. Vermina would have had no reason at all to sally forth against Scipio's army unless it was to help Hannibal.

Hannibal marched west and encamped in the vicinity of the town of Zama, which was about seventy-five miles south of Tunis and about eighty miles from Hadrumetum. Hannibal made the march in five days.[28] Scipio was encamped a short distance west of Naragara. Neither army was yet aware of the other's

Approach to Zama
202 BCE

Carthaginian advance
Roman advance

Promontory of Mercury

Clupea
Neapolis
Nepheris
CARTHAGE
Promontory of Apollo
Tunis
Utica
Hippo Diarrhytus (Bizerta)
Salaeca
Scipio's Route
Great Plains
Sicca Veneria
Zama
Margaron
Hannibal's Advance
Hadrumetum
Leptis Minor
Thala
Naragara
Massinissa's Approach
Vermina's Approach

Miles
0   10   20   30   40   50

Kanonohee 2008

SCIPIO'S APPROACH TO ZAMA

181

position. Hannibal, Polybius tells us, sent three spies "to discover the where-abouts of the Romans and the nature and dispositions of their camp."[29] Both Livy and Polybius tell the tale of the Romans catching Hannibal's spies, but instead of holding them captive or killing them, "Scipio actually detailed a military tribune to accompany them and show them exactly how the camp was laid out."[30] Then he released the spies and sent them back to Hannibal to make their report. This curious tale bears a suspicious similarity to a story Herodotus told concerning Xerxes' army at Thermopylae and is probably false.[31]

Assuming the story is true for the moment, what did Scipio hope to accomplish by permitting Hannibal's spies to observe the camp? They would have learned nothing unusual about a Roman camp except for the estimated strength of Scipio's forces. With the most important element here being the strength of Scipio's cavalry, it raises the question of when Massinissa arrived in Scipio's camp. Polybius says the spies left the day *before* Massinissa arrived.[32] If this was the case, then Scipio may have been attempting to lure Hannibal into a fight by showing him his weakness in cavalry, all the while knowing that his scouts had reported Massinissa was approaching. Livy, however, tells us that the spies left *after* Massinissa had arrived and that they reported his presence to Hannibal.[33] If so, then Scipio may have been showing Hannibal his strength in an effort to weaken Carthaginian morale. As we shall see later, the presence of Scipio's larger cavalry arm forced Hannibal's hand at Zama.

According to Polybius, Hannibal was so "deeply impressed by the courage and the lofty spirit which Scipio had shown" to his spies that he proposed the "surprising idea" that the two should meet.[34] Before answering, Scipio broke camp and moved east toward Naragara, where he encamped within "a javelin's throw" of his water supply. He then sent an envoy to accept Hannibal's offer. Hannibal also broke camp and moved toward Naragara, encamping on a hill less than four miles from the Romans at a place that "was too far away from water, so that his men suffered much hardship from this disadvantage."[35] Why Hannibal would have made such a basic mistake as failing to provide for the watering of his army and animals in the obvious hot and dry climate is not explained. The next day the two commanders met halfway between their respective positions and attempted to come to terms to avoid the final battle. The discussions failed, and both returned to their camps to prepare their armies for battle the next day.[36]

The tale of their meeting is probably a fabrication that serves to explain how the armies moved into position and why Hannibal chose to stand and fight at Zama.[37] If Hannibal's plan all along had been to block Massinissa's arrival and engage Scipio before the two could link up, Hannibal knew his plan had failed when his spies reported that Massinissa was already in Scipio's camp. Even if, as Polybius's contrary report says, Massinissa arrived the day after the spies had left, with the armies only a few miles apart it is difficult to believe that Massinissa's army of six thousand infantry and four thousand cavalry could have arrived in Scipio's camp without being detected by Hannibal's scouts, who by then knew the location of Scipio's army. In either case, Hannibal knew that Massinissa had reached Scipio and that his original plan had failed.

Hannibal's plan had been risky from the beginning and depended on factors over which he had no control. Massinissa had arrived, but Vermina was nowhere to be seen. Now Hannibal had to fight on an open plain against an army that had a superior decisive arm of cavalry. Why, then, fight at all? Why not refuse to offer battle and withdraw? Once more the answer is cavalry. An army is at its most vulnerable when it is in column of march and has its back turned to the enemy. Hannibal's base was eighty miles away across open terrain. If he had turned his back on Scipio and attempted to withdraw, Scipio's Roman and Numidian cavalry would have continually harassed his army with deadly effect during a five-day march to Hadrumetum. If Hannibal had attempted to withdraw, his army would have been cut to pieces by the time it reached Hadrumetum. So despite the unfavorable circumstances in which he found himself, Hannibal stood his ground at Zama because he had no choice.

THE BATTLE OF ZAMA, 202 BCE

The Roman army landed in Africa two years earlier with about thirty thousand infantry and twelve hundred cavalry. Whatever losses it had sustained since then were marginal and probably had been replaced with reinforcements from Italy who came on the supply ships, although not one of our sources mention this possibility. Although it would have been more difficult to replace cavalry, it is a reasonable assumption that Scipio's cavalry may have been resupplied and numbered somewhere around two thousand and, perhaps, even fewer. Polybius tells us that before his battle with Hannibal, Scipio provided for the security of his fleet and transferred command of his base to Lucius Baebius. He would also have left behind a strong infantry guard and some cavalry for scouting and acting as screens for the infantry. While we do not know these forces' strength, they could not reasonably have been fewer than a legion of infantry and a thousand cavalry. Thus, Scipio would have had an army of approximately thirty thousand infantry, or five legions, and a thousand cavalry. Before the battle, Massinissa arrived with six thousand infantry and four thousand cavalry, and Appian tells us a chieftain named Dakamas also contributed six hundred cavalrymen.

Hannibal's army was comprised of three contingents. The first were the troops of Mago's army, which had withdrawn from northern Italy and redeployed to Africa before Hannibal's arrival. Polybius says that Mago's mercenaries totaled twelve thousand men.[38] This figure is almost certainly too low. When Mago's army went to northern Italy in the summer of 205 BCE, he had twelve thousand infantry, two thousand cavalry, and thirty warships.[39] A year later, when Rome was clearly preparing for an invasion of Africa, Carthage sent Mago an additional six thousand infantry, eight hundred cavalry, seven elephants, and a large sum of money to raise troops among the Ligurians.[40] Thus, Mago's army had eighteen thousand infantry and twenty-eight hundred cavalry. It does not seem unreasonable that he raised another ten thousand men from among the Ligurians and brought his force to more than thirty thousand troops. Mago's army must have been of considerable size to prompt the Romans to send six full legions to the north to block his progress. It resulted in a stalemate in which the two armies occasionally skirmished but fought no major battles. In a skirmish that happened just before Mago was recalled from Italy, Mago lost five thousand men and the Romans twenty-five hundred, leaving Mago with twenty-five thousand or so troops. If we assume he left most of his cavalry behind and that most of the Ligurians returned to their tribes, Mago still had more than fifteen thousand mercenaries who could have arrived in Africa to join Hannibal.

The second contingent of Hannibal's army comprised his veterans, the Old Guard. Some of the men had been with him from the beginning, and others came from the southern Italian towns and tribes that had joined him over the years. These were mostly Lucanians and Brutti, and a scattering of others, who had turned their backs on Rome. They had little choice but to leave with Hannibal, since the Romans would have severely punished their disloyalty once Hannibal's army left. Estimates of their number range from twelve thousand to fifteen thousand to eighteen thousand men.[41] A conservative figure of fifteen thousand troops seems reasonable. These were Hannibal's best troops, battle hardened and disciplined, well led, and capable of tactical maneuver on command.

The third contingent comprised infantry recently levied from among Carthaginian citizens and, perhaps, the Libyans. Our sources do not provide estimates of their strength, but Hannibal used them as his second line against Scipio's ten thousand–man front line. Thus, they must have come to somewhere close to this number—between eight thousand and ten thousand men—if they were to perform the tactical mission Hannibal set for them. Given that defeat meant slavery, death, or a Roman occupation, raising this number of troops from among Carthaginian citizens probably was not difficult. The problems with these troops, however, would have been their inexperience and discipline. Perhaps to stiffen these new troops' courage, Hannibal deployed the four thousand veteran Greek phalangites Philip V of Macedon sent in the center of the second line.[42] Taken together, Hannibal's army had approximately forty-four thousand infantry.

Estimating the strength of Hannibal's cavalry is almost impossible. If Hannibal destroyed most of his horses before leaving Italy, as Fuller says, then he arrived in Africa with only a few hundred mounts. Hannibal attempted to raise cavalry from the tribes friendly to Carthage but had only limited success. Polybius tells us that a chief named Tychaeus provided two thousand cavalry, and Appian says another chief, Mesotylus, offered a thousand cavalrymen.[43] It is not unreasonable that Carthage itself, perhaps drawing on its own chora guard, could have raised another five hundred or so. Hannibal's cavalry strength, therefore, would have been around three thousand cavalry, or about half that available to Scipio. Polybius says that Hannibal also had eighty elephants, but Veith is probably correct in reporting the number as only fifteen or twenty animals.[44]

Hannibal's immediate problem was that his army was a collection of diverse elements of varying quality that had never fought together before. Only his veterans could be said to be an instrument of their commander's will, ready and able to respond to commands immediately. His cavalry was not the superbly trained and officered heavy cavalry he had once commanded in Spain and Italy; rather, it was Numidian light cavalry fighting under the command of their tribal and clan officers. Its discipline was uncertain at best. The Carthaginian infantry levies were mostly untrained to any degree of combat discipline, and their reliability under attack was unknown. Even Hannibal's elephants were poorly trained. Only Mago's mercenaries, and undoubtedly the Greek phalangites, could be relied on to perform as professionals. The problem for Hannibal was how to weave these disparate elements into a controllable force that was capable of executing his tactical plan against the best-trained and best-led army that the Roman Republic had ever put in the field.

The manner in which troops are disposed within a combat box reflects their commander's tactical thinking. This was clearly so at the battle of Zama. Scipio deployed his legions in a slightly different manner. As usual, the hastati were

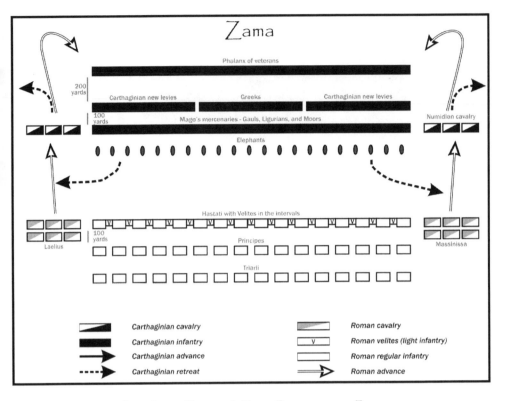

SCIPIO'S AND HANNIBAL'S TROOP DISPOSITIONS AT ZAMA

deployed in maniples across the front, with the velites, or light infantry, filling the gaps between the maniples and each legion presenting a twelve hundred–foot front. The other two lines, the principes and the triarii, were positioned behind the hastati as the second and third lines. Usually these two lines were staggered to cover the gaps between the maniples in the line in front of them, making the famous quincunx, or checkerboard formation. At Zama, however, Scipio arranged the three lines so that the maniples of each line were placed directly one behind the other, leaving uncovered lanes one hundred feet wide running from front to back. Polybius tells us that the principes and triarii were placed "at some distance" behind the hastati, suggesting that they were separated by a greater distance than the usual seventy-five meters from the front line.[45] As usual, Scipio covered his flanks with his cavalry. On his left was the Roman cavalry, perhaps two thousand strong, under the command of the loyal Laelius, and Massinissa "with the whole of the Numidian contingent" was on the right with four thousand cavalry. Most likely Veith is correct when he says that Massinissa's infantry was placed with the Roman velites in the light infantry's role.[46]

The disposition of Scipio's troops permits some insight into his tactical plan. By moving the principes and triarii farther back from his front line by a hundred yards or so, Scipio transformed his army from a phalanx into echelons, thereby changing completely the tactical dynamics of his army. With its lines arranged closely one behind the other, the phalanx's advantages are that it creates mass, allows losses in the front ranks to be replaced by moving the back ranks forward, and instills confidence and psychological cohesion among those engaged in the fight that those men behind them will come to their aid.[47] The disadvantage is that the phalanx can only move forward; it has no ability to undertake tactical maneuvers toward the flanks or to carry out an envelopment. By placing his lines farther apart, Scipio turned his battle formation into echelons and made it possible for his last two lines to maneuver independently. Scipio's echelon formation relinquished the advantages of the phalanx but gained the advantage of being able to maneuver in any direction on command.

There would have been no point in Scipio arranging his troops in this manner if he did not intend to maneuver once the battle began. Scipio seems to have been intent on repeating his tactics of Ilipa and Campi Magni. The lanes left between the maniples were designed to channel Hannibal's elephants harmlessly to the rear and out of the Roman troops' way. Afterward, Scipio's cavalry would attack the outnumbered Carthaginian cavalry and, as Hannibal had done at Cannae, drive it from the field. The hastati were to attack straight on against the Carthaginian front line, become heavily engaged, and hold the Carthaginian center in place. When Hannibal's second line moved forward in support of his first, Scipio intended to order his principes and triarii to march outward toward the Roman line's two ends and sweep around the flanks, enveloping the Carthaginian lines. With the Carthaginians trapped, Scipio hoped his cavalry would return quickly enough to join the battle and annihilate the enemy.

An analysis of Hannibal's troop deployment suggests that he had correctly discerned Scipio's tactical plan and had arranged his troops to prevent its success. Hannibal drew up his infantry in three echelons. The front line was comprised mostly of Mago's mercenary veterans—including Celts, Ligurians, Moors, and Balearics—for a strength equal to the Roman front line, or approximately fifteen thousand men.[48] Most of these troops, certainly the Celts and Ligurians, were heavy infantry. The rest, Moors and Balearics, were light infantry and sharpshooters (slingers). Along with the elephants, the light infantry was deployed to the front of the main line as skirmishers. The second echelon was anchored in the center by the four thousand Greek phalangites with the Carthaginian levies (eight thousand to ten thousand men) placed on either side of the spear phalanx. Like Scipio's second line, Hannibal's second line was placed farther to the rear, perhaps by a gap of a hundred yards or so. Hannibal's Old Guard, about fifteen thousand veterans from Italy, formed his third echelon. These troops were Hannibal's best, and he led them himself. The Old Guard was positioned a full stadium, or about two hundred yards—that is double the distance between the first and second ranks—behind the second line.[49] Hannibal placed his Numidian cavalry on his left and his Carthaginian cavalry on his right.

Hannibal had the advantage in infantry but was badly outnumbered in cavalry. Without enough cavalry, he had no chance of repeating his earlier victories when he used his cavalry as an arm of decision. Obviously he would have to fight an infantry battle. Hannibal's first tactical problem was to neutralize the Roman advantage in cavalry. The solution was to take it out of the fight completely. He would use his own cavalry to draw Scipio's cavalry away from the battle area by ordering his cavalry not to fully engage but to feign retreat and fight a skirmishing rear guard action.[50] With his cavalry engaging, fleeing, turning to reengage, skirmishing, and fleeing again, Hannibal hoped to keep Scipio's cavalry occupied and away from the battle area until he had defeated Scipio's army in an infantry engagement. Hannibal surely knew the Roman cavalry's reputation of lacking discipline. He also understood that to use cavalry to drive off the enemy and then cease its pursuit required a high degree of control and training, which he could assume Massinissa's cavalry, having been recently recruited from the mountain and oases tribes, would not possess. Once on the chase, breaking off and returning to the battlefield would be difficult for them. "And so it happened. On both flanks the Numidian as well as the Italo-Roman cavalry charged away in enthusiasm of their victory behind their enemies and left the point of decision farther and farther behind."[51]

As clever as the ruse was, Hannibal needed time to determine if Scipio's cavalry would take the bait. Suppose they did not and turned instead against Hannibal's flanks? Hannibal's first solution was to fortify his camp to his rear. If the ruse failed and his flanks were attacked, the Old Guard could retire to the redoubt, defend itself, and fight a last battle.

The second solution involved the elephants. As noted, it is unlikely that Hannibal had the eighty elephants that Polybius claims, for that number would have exceeded those employed by any Carthaginian commander during the war.[52] Besides, it takes almost twenty years to train a war elephant, and with the war having lasted for so long, it is unlikely any significant number of trained war elephants were left. Moreover, with Scipio running around the countryside and a civil war waging between Syphax and Massinissa, it is doubtful that the Carthaginians captured and trained substantial numbers of elephants. One clue that Hannibal's army elephants were untrained was that not one of the sources mentions *howdahs*. Like the Greeks, the Carthaginians used these towers strapped to the elephant's back as shooting platforms for archers, javeliners, and spearmen.[53] Their absence at Zama suggests that the elephants were not trained to the noise of war. Untrained elephants are good only for delivering shock, and even then they are highly unreliable.

The ancient armies traditionally used elephants to disrupt enemy cavalry, whose mounts were unaccustomed to the beasts' smell; therefore, the armies usually deployed the elephants on the flanks with the cavalry. At Zama, however, the Carthaginian mounts would have been accustomed to elephants, and those in Massinissa's cavalry would have as well because its army used elephants, also. That left only the Roman mounts, and Scipio probably took the opportunity in the last two years to get his cavalry mounts used to the smell of elephants. If Hannibal was going to employ his untrained elephants to good effect, then, it could only be to deliver shock. Thus, Hannibal placed his elephants in the center of the line to support his light infantry skirmishers and sharpshooters. The idea was for the light infantry to engage the Roman velites for as long as possible, launch the animals against the Roman infantry, and cause the most disruption while consuming as much time as possible until Scipio's cavalry could engage, skirmish, and finally pursue Hannibal's cavalry from the field. At the same time, he could delay the clash of the main lines of heavy infantry as well. If his plan worked and the cavalry left the battlefield, taking it out of the fight, then Hannibal could fight the infantry battle in which he held the numerical advantage.

Scipio had considerable experience with elephants in Spain, and at Zama he combined with complete success almost every known anti-elephant device used in antiquity, lending some credibility to Polybius's claim that a considerable number of elephants took part in the battle. He left gaps in his infantry formations through which the elephants could be diverted without having to break ranks. To conceal the gaps, he stationed light troops in them with orders to give way, either backwards or sideways, into the infantry's main body and permit the elephants to pass. Appian tells us that in front of each cohort Scipio stationed groups of light infantry to act as a screen and to throw iron-shod stakes (probably javelins) at the charging elephants. These light infantrymen were to make every effort at hamstringing the animals as they passed. Scipio's cavalry was posted on the wings and armed with their javelins. To guard against the elephants spooking the horses, Scipio stationed a foot soldier armed with a javelin with each cavalryman to keep the animals at bay. Finally, the legions' trumpets and bugles were put to good use, frightening the elephants away from any area Scipio wished to deny them. With these combined efforts Scipio rendered Hannibal's elephants of little use.[54] However, had the animals been well trained and equipped with howdahs and their accompanying archers and protective infantry screens, the result might have been quite different.

None of the accounts of the battle tell us anything about the terrain except that the fighting took place on a flat plain. A study of Kromayer and Veith's topographic map of the battlefield and its description show it to be exactly that, level ground without any rising or descending terrain of any consequence.[55] The even plain was to the liking of both commanders, each of whom thought it provided him a tactical advantage. If Scipio's plan was as I have described it—to expose Hannibal's flanks with his cavalry, hold the center in place with a fixing attack by his hastati, maneuver his rear infantry echelons to sweep both flanks, and deliver the fatal blow with the returning cavalry—then it could best be carried out on even terrain. As at Baecula, rising or uneven terrain might well prevent the encirclement from being carried out rapidly enough or the fatal blow from being struck at all.

Also, as I have suggested, if Hannibal had detected in Scipio's troop dispositions the potential for echelon maneuver, then he had to counter that movement. To do so Hannibal set a deadly trap for Scipio when he positioned his Old Guard far to the rear of the second Carthaginian infantry line. If Scipio attempted to carry out his encirclement, he would trap only the first two lines of Carthaginian infantry and leave Hannibal the opportunity to attack Scipio's echelons from the rear, crushing them against the Carthaginian infantry lines. By turning his Old Guard into a genuine reserve to be sent into battle independently on command, Hannibal had tactically neutralized Scipio's planned envelopment. For the trap to work, however, Scipio could not learn about the Old Guard's position and strength. Located with his command staff behind and somewhat to the flank of the Roman formation, Scipio's line of sight was blocked by his own infantry lines, two lines of Carthaginian infantry, and a wall of elephants. Chances are that he probably could not completely see the position or strength of Hannibal's veterans across the flat plain from his vantage point more than three-quarters of a mile away. Hannibal, who sometimes rode atop an elephant to obtain a better view of the battlefield, may have been able to see better.

Hannibal's plan was the more sophisticated of the two. If Scipio attempted to carry out the envelopment that his troop disposition seemed to imply, Hannibal's reserve would catch him between it and the encircled Carthaginian second line and crush him. If events forced Scipio to abandon that option and fight a straight-up parallel infantry battle, Hannibal intended to let Scipio waste his strength against the first two ranks, force him to bring up his principes and triarii, and then strike him head-on with the Old Guard. The paradox of Zama was that neither commander was able to carry out his tactical plan in the face of the other commander's countermoves. The result was that both sides were forced into a traditional, parallel infantry battle that neither wanted to fight.

The battle opened with the contingents of Numidian light cavalry skirmishing on both sides, followed by Hannibal's order to the drivers of his elephants to attack the Roman line with the support of the Moors and Balearic light infantry. The Roman velites deployed to the front of the infantry line and went into action, blowing bugles and attacking the elephants with missiles and javelins to frighten them into a panic. Polybius tells us that "some of the animals panicked, turned tail and stampeded to the rear, colliding with the squadrons of Numidian cavalry which had come up to support the Carthaginians."[56] Massinissa quickly went over to the attack, driving the Numidians from the field and continuing in hot pursuit. "Massinissa, hot by nature and hot with youth, hurled his huge frame against the front rank of the horsemen, and dashed round the field with flying javelineers."[57] No doubt the velites made some effort, with only partial success, to force the elephants to run in the open lanes left between the maniples. Polybius says that the "elephants charged the Roman velites in the space between the two armies and killed many of them, but also suffered heavy losses."[58] Killing an elephant with the ancient soldier's weapons was no easy task, and the account of the Roman light infantry inflicting "heavy losses" on the elephants is probably an exaggeration.

At some point the elephant attack became disorganized, and the animals roamed all over the space between the two front lines. Some made their way through the lanes between the maniples, as Scipio had planned, and wandered harmlessly to the legion's rear. Others fled down the space between the two front lines, making their way toward the cavalry posted on the Roman right wing. There they were driven off "with volleys of javelins from the cavalry and in the end [they] stampeded off the field."[59]

Polybius seems to have the sequence of events reversed. Massinissa's cavalry was posted on Scipio's right at the start of the battle and had already gone over to the attack and driven the enemy cavalry from the field *before* Polybius says the cavalry drove off the elephants on the Romans' right wing.[60] More likely Massinissa did not attack until *after* the velites had dealt with the elephants. Also, Massinissa's quick success in driving Hannibal's Numidian cavalry from the field was not because of the stampeding elephants' disruption, but because Hannibal had ordered the Numidians not to engage and instead draw Massinissa's cavalry out of the battle. Having seen the quick success that Massinissa was enjoying against the Numidians, Laelius then attacked the Carthaginian cavalry and "drove them back in headlong flight and pressed the pursuit."[61] The battle's opening phase was over. The first round went to Hannibal, who had succeeded in tempting Scipio's cavalry into a pursuit and taking it out of the fight.

The light infantry on both sides then withdrew to their respective lines, and the two lines of heavy infantry moved slowly toward each other, preparing to do battle. Once within striking distance, the Roman front rank charged.

> The spears were hurled with speed and force, the air was shaken and a fearsome cloud spread over the sky. Next came the sword at close quarters, and face pressed close to face, and eyes blazed with baleful flame. Those who despised the danger and rushed forward to meet the first shower of missiles were all laid low, and the earth grieved as she drank the blood of her sons.[62]

Polybius describes what happened next:

> The whole battle then became a hand-to-hand struggle of man against man. In this contest the courage and skill of the mercenaries at first gave them the advantage and they succeeded in wounding great numbers of Romans. Even so the steadiness of their ranks and the superiority of their weapons enabled Scipio's men to make their adversaries give ground. All this while the rear ranks of the Romans kept close behind their comrades.[63]

This account seems to imply that the Romans' second line had moved closer to the first line to support their comrades, who were taking heavy casualties. The

Carthaginian attack may have forced Scipio to abandon the echelon formation for his second line and revert to a phalanx to contain the pressure from the front. If so, Scipio had lost half his manpower available for maneuver.

As the Romans gained the advantage, the Carthaginian front began to give way until it finally broke. Polybius's explanation is that the Carthaginian second line did not come up and support the first line, as the Romans had done, but "shrank back in cowardly fashion and failed to support the mercenaries," forcing their line to break.[64] The account suggests that Polybius may have confused the difference between phalanx and echelon formations and their different tactical roles.[65] Hannibal had arranged his lines in echelon formation with large gaps between them. The Carthaginian echelons were arranged to crash against the Romans in successive waves and not in one large mass with the rear supporting the front, as in phalanx tactics. The Carthaginian second line did not come forward not because they were cowards but because they were following orders and staying with Hannibal's tactical plan.

Polybius's misunderstanding of echelon tactics leads him to believe that when the first rank saw the second rank was not supporting it, "they retreated and turned upon the soldiers in their rear and began to cut them down."[66] He goes on to say that the second rank was forced to fight the retreating mercenaries and the Romans at the same time, which "forced them [the Carthaginian levies] to die bravely in spite of themselves."[67] Here Polybius adds the charge of stupidity to Carthaginian cowardice, for it is not clear how and why frightened, bloodied soldiers seeking safety in retreat would attack their own comrades. Either the incident did not happen, or Polybius is exaggerating.

Most likely the Carthaginian front gave way under the pressure of the Roman assault. As the hastati pursued the mercenaries to the rear and lengthened the distance between themselves and the principes, the second Carthaginian line went into the attack on Hannibal's order, trapping the fleeing mercenaries between them and the advancing Romans. In the swirling hand-to-hand combat that resulted from the violent clash of the two lines, some mercenaries and Romans inadvertently killed their own men. Polybius may be referring to this melee. That the two Carthaginian lines fought one another while still fending off the Roman assault is not believable.

Polybius seems to contradict his own account of the event when he tells us next that the Carthaginian second line's counterattack "even threw some of the maniples of the *hastati* into confusion." So much so, that when "the officers of the *principe* saw what was happening, they held their own ranks firm, and most of the mercenaries and Carthaginians were cut down where they stood."[68] Put another way, the Carthaginian second line's fierce counterattack pressed hard on the hastati, forcing the principes to come up and engage to stop it. Scipio's echelon deployment was being forced back into a phalanx to hold the front steady. Any hope of using the echelons to maneuver was now out of the question. With both Roman lines engaged, the Carthaginians were significantly outnumbered. They eventually succumbed and "died where they stood." The Carthaginian second line may have been comprised of recent citizen levies, but they appear to have fought well.

What was left of the mercenaries and the second line fled, hoping to find safety behind the line of Hannibal's Old Guard standing ready two hundred yards to the rear. But "Hannibal then barred the fleeing survivors from entering the ranks of his veterans; he ordered his ranks to level their spears and hold the men off when they approached, and they were obliged to take refuge on the wings or in the open country."[69] Hannibal's orders made sound tactical sense. His veterans were fresh and unbloodied, and he intended to use them to deliver the fatal blow against the weary Romans, whose strength had been reduced combating his first two lines. Permitting frightened, wounded, and tired men into his ranks just prior to launching his attack would disrupt morale and discipline and add nothing to his fighting strength. As it was, the remnants of the first two lines found their way to the flanks, regrouped, and went into the attack with Hannibal's veterans later.

The successful Roman attack left Scipio's formations scattered and disorganized. Livy notes that "consequently, the *hastati* of the front line broke up their maniples and ranks to pursue the enemy where they could over the piles of bodies and arms and through pools of blood. Then the maniples of the *principe* also began to break up, as they saw the first line losing formation."[70] The battlefield behind the advanced Roman maniples and the triarii to their rear was "slippery with gore, the corpses lying in blood-drenched heaps, and the spaces between encumbered with arms [weapons and shields] that had been thrown away at random."[71] The field was covered with blood, corpses, and wounded men, creating a physical obstacle to the triarii's advance. The Roman onslaught had carried it beyond the original location of the Carthaginian second line. This placed the scattered Roman maniples some five hundred yards to the front of the triarii, upon whom the maniples relied for support. The triarii had not been committed yet and remained in their original positions.[72] Hannibal's veterans, meanwhile, were only two hundred yards from the front. Scipio's tactical plan for maneuver had been ruined by the dynamics of the battle itself, and he now found himself exposed to Hannibal's counterattack.

At this point Scipio probably realized that he was at great risk. If he was unaware of the Old Guard's position and strength before the battle, he was certainly aware of them and the grave threat facing his army now. And where was the cavalry? His only stratagem was to play for time and hope that Laelius and Massinissa returned with the cavalry very soon. Scipio halted the battle with trumpet calls and stopped his lines' advance. He ordered the triarii to advance and support the forward lines of the hastati and principes. Next, he reassembled his troops just forward of the cluttered battlefield, or just behind the position where the second Carthaginian line had been deployed, and ordered them to form a single infantry line.[73] He positioned the bloodied and weakened hastati in the center of the line "and then sent the *principe* and *triarii* to take up position in close order on both the wings and in line with the *hastati*." He evacuated what wounded he could to the rear and then prepared to receive Hannibal's attack.

But Hannibal did not attack. He accepted the pause in the battle. With fifteen thousand fresh troops positioned only two hundred yards from Scipio's weakened center, why didn't Hannibal go immediately into the attack? One factor may have been Scipio's ability to reassemble and deploy his army into a single line relatively quickly. Because each Roman maniple had a signaler and could respond immediately to trumpet commands, it would not have taken long after Scipio issued the command to redeploy for the army to do it. The result was that after defeating the two Carthaginian lines Scipio's disarrayed troops quickly regrouped and faced Hannibal ready for battle. Whatever opportunity Hannibal may have had to attack during Scipio's redeployment passed quickly.

Scipio's army was now arranged in a single line, with the usual intervals between the maniples closed, so that the Roman line overlapped Hannibal's line on both ends. Scipio must surely have reckoned on this circumstance when he placed his strongest and freshest troops, the principes and the triarii, at the ends of the line. Moreover, Hannibal's initial advantage in infantry when the battle started was now gone. In most battles in antiquity, a victorious army could expect to suffer approximately 5.5 percent killed in action and 6 percent wounded, or approximately 12 percent of its force.[74] A defeated army could expect to suffer horrendous casualty rates of approximately 37 percent killed and 35 percent wounded.[75] These levels of dead and wounded were inflicted usually after the battle formations were broken and the enemy was surrounded or caught in the pursuit. In the case of Hannibal's first two infantry lines, however, many more men would have escaped to the rear either without wounds or with only marginal wounds. If we accept that the casualty rates of these two lines was half of the average rate of 73 percent of combined dead and wounded, then more than 60 percent of these soldiers, or about twelve thousand to fifteen thousand men, would have reached Hannibal's final line alive or with only minor wounds.

If the same analysis of casualty rates is applied to Scipio's force, then he could have expected to lose about 10 percent of his force to casualties in combat against Hannibal's first two lines. Scipio's remaining force would been approximately twenty-six thousand men. Hannibal's Old Guard numbered approximately fifteen thousand men. Had Hannibal attempted to attack Scipio immediately, he would have done so at a considerable disadvantage. Thus, Hannibal accepted the pause in the battle while Scipio redeployed his troops because he also needed the time to gather and reposition his first two lines' remnants to offset Scipio's numerical advantage and cover the ends of the extended Roman line. It is not easy to rouse defeated men to fight again and to assemble them in some coherent battle order under command of their surviving leaders, and it must have taken considerable time to accomplish. Scipio, for his part, would have granted Hannibal all the time he required, for if he was to win this battle he needed his cavalry now more than ever. Thus, Scipio's troops stood in the sun, watching their adversaries organize and prepare for battle.

If we assume that Hannibal was able to assemble only eight thousand of his first two lines' remnants, his army would have numbered some twenty-three thousand men, or about equal to Scipio's army. We have no information regarding how Hannibal formed up his troops. He may have placed his Old Guard in the center to anchor the line and fight opposite Scipio's already bloodied and weakened hastati and then stationed his own weakest troops on the wings. When Hannibal had refused to permit his retreating troops to enter his formation, he had forced them out to the wings. Considerable numbers of them had gathered there after the retreat, and deploying them there now was the simplest way to get them back into the fight. If so, Scipio's best troops would face Hannibal's weakest, inviting the possibility that the flanks would give way and Hannibal's center would be enveloped from one or both directions. It could not have escaped Hannibal's notice that time played to Scipio's advantage. As soon as Hannibal had reformed his army, then, he likely went into the attack.

> The two main bodies hurled themselves upon one another with the greatest ardor and fury. Since they were equally matched not

only in numbers but also in courage, in warlike spirit and in weapons, the issue hung for a long while in the balance. Many fell on both sides, fighting with fierce determination where they stood.[76]

The impression both Livy and Polybius give in their accounts is that neither side was able to gain an advantage in the raging infantry battle. Had the cavalry not returned to the battlefield, the fighting might have continued until both sides were exhausted, and history would have taken a different course. But Laelius's and Massinissa's cavalry squadrons returned at the right moment, and their cavalry attack finally defeated the Carthaginians. Livy tells us,

> Laelius and Massinissa had pursued the routed cavalry for a considerable distance; now at the right moment they wheeled round and charged into the rear of the enemy's line. . . . Many were surrounded and cut down where they stood; many were scattered in flight over the open plain, only to fall everywhere beneath the cavalry, the undisputed masters of the field.[77]

Polybius adds with a more experienced military eye that the "ground was level," permitting the cavalry to effectively pursue those who fled, but that "the greater number of his [Hannibal's] men were cut down in their ranks."[78]

One can only imagine the sight of six thousand horsemen galloping across the Zama plain to smash into the rear of Hannibal's infantry, disrupting it with the power of its impact. But the cavalry at Zama was not the powerful combat arm it would become centuries later. Lacking a firm saddle and stirrups, a Roman cavalryman found it almost impossible to wield his long spear effectively without being knocked from his horse by the force of impact. Nor could cavalry engage at the gallop for the same reason.[79] Mounted on saddlecloths without stirrups and encumbered by the long spear, sword, and shield, most horsemen were unable to remain mounted at any speed. Furthermore, because horses will not charge headlong into a line of soldiers, when the cavalry approached the infantry, many cavalrymen tumbled to the ground and had to continue the fight on foot.[80] Xenophon and Caesar both tell us that the Roman cavalry could achieve little against disciplined infantry.[81] By contrast, Massinissa's Numidian cavalry may have been very effective, especially in the pursuit. The Numidians were experts at riding bareback and armed with several throwing javelins: "The Numidians, riding barebacked according to their custom, had filled the plains and broad valleys alike, and their javelins hurtled in thick clouds through the air and concealed the sky."[82] On the open plain, the fleeing Carthaginians would have made easy targets for these expert horsemen.

Still, most of Hannibal's army died in their ranks as a result of close combat. The initial cavalry attack may have physically and psychologically disrupted Hannibal's line enough that the Roman maniples breached it at several points. The dismounted Roman cavalry, then fighting as infantry, would have forced sections of the Carthaginian line to turn and defend its rear, making more penetrations of the line by the maniples possible. And so the dynamic went until the Roman infantry completely cut off, surrounded, and cut to pieces sections of the Carthaginian line. At some point panic would have overtaken good sense, and soldiers would have begun to flee, only to have Massinissa's cavalry cut them down one at a time on the open plain.

At the end of the day, twenty thousand Carthaginians lay dead on the ground, or nearly the entire force that Hannibal had set to battle that grim day, "and almost as many were taken prisoner."[83] Given that Hannibal's army was approximately twenty thousand to twenty-three thousand men, Polybius is either exaggerating the number of dead or the number of wounded. He places Roman losses at fifteen hundred men, or approximately 5 percent of the force, about average for a victorious Roman army. A similar number would have been wounded.[84] However, Appian says Roman losses were twenty-five hundred men, which, given the heavy fighting between two experienced armies, may be more accurate.[85] He also says that Massinissa's losses were greater than the Romans' losses. If so, the reference must be to Massinissa's infantry and not to his cavalry, which reigned unopposed on the open ground.

PAX SCIPIONIS

Hannibal and a handful of his officers fled Zama and rode headlong for Hadrumetum. Immediately after the battle Scipio stormed and plundered the enemy camp. During this operation a messenger reached Scipio and told him that Servilius Lentulus had arrived at Utica with a force of fifty warships and a hundred transports full of supplies. Scipio repaired to Utica immediately after instructing his army to proceed directly to Tunis.[86] There they established a camp "on the same site as before," when the Carthaginian envoys had arrived to treat with Scipio.[87] Scipio ordered Gnaeus Octavius to march the legions that were guarding the Utican camp to Carthage. Scipio had decided to "strike terror into Carthage from all sides" as a demonstration of force. As his legions marched on

Tunis and Carthage, Scipio himself assembled his fleet and together with the fifty new warships sailed from Utica into the harbor at Carthage. On the way a Carthaginian ship carrying the peace envoys pulled alongside, but Scipio instructed them to go to Tunis once he had established his camp there. He then sailed on and into the harbor. His fleet passed before the city's walls without incident. His purpose, as Livy tells us, was to "humiliate the enemy" before returning to Utica.[88]

Some of Scipio's advisers urged him to attack Carthage at once and bring it to its knees. Scipio wisely decided not to do so. His forces were far too small to storm the well-fortified city. His only alternative was conducting a long siege, which the Roman people might easily tire of and would weaken his hand in the peace negotiations. Equally important was "Scipio's forebodings that a successor to himself was on the way to reap the reward of victory and to appropriate the glory of a war which had really been ended by another's effort and danger."[89] Word had obviously reached Scipio that the newly elected Roman consuls had been squabbling among themselves to see who would obtain Africa as their provinces. Their objective was to replace Scipio and seize the credit for ending the war. These circumstances "brought them all round to the idea of peace."

Before Scipio was willing to formally engage in peace negotiations, he insisted that a number of preliminary conditions be met. First, he granted the Carthaginians a three-month armistice during which they were neither to send envoys to any state except Rome nor to receive any without Scipio's permission and knowledge. With this measure, Scipio prevented further Carthaginian overtures to the Macedonians, who had previously supplied Hannibal with troops.[90] Second, the transports and their cargoes that Hasdrubal had seized causing the first truce to collapse were to be returned. This dictate proved difficult because the cargoes had already been dispersed. The two sides reached an agreement that the Carthaginians should pay the cash equivalent of the lost supplies.[91] Third, Carthage was to support the Roman army with pay and food until a formal peace was ratified.[92] Fourth, the Roman commander would choose a hundred hostages between the ages of fourteen and thirty and take them to Rome.[93]

The conditions of the formal treaty of peace were as follows.[94] The Carthaginians were to live as a free people, and no Roman troops would be garrisoned in their land. They were to be governed by their own laws and customs as before. Carthage was to retain all the cities that it possessed in Africa before the outbreak of the war as well as all its flocks, herds, slaves, and other property. Another clause stipulated that the Carthaginians were to be Rome's friends and allies both on land and at sea, thus essentially giving Rome control over its foreign policy and effectively reducing Carthage to the status of a dependent ally. Carthage was further restricted from making war on anyone inside or outside Africa without permission from Rome. This stipulation did not, however, forbid defensive wars in Africa.

Massinissa was to be restored to his former position as ruler and all lands and properties that had belonged to him or to his ancestors were to be restored to him. Livy tells us that Scipio went somewhat beyond this requirement by holding a formal ceremony in which "Massinissa was presented with the city of Cirta and the remaining towns and lands which had passed from the kingdom of Syphax into the power of the Roman people."[95] All Roman prisoners of war as well as deserters and other fugitives from Roman justice were to be surrendered. Of the deserters and fugitives, those who were Latin citizens were beheaded and the others crucified.[96] Carthage was to surrender all its warships except ten triremes. Scipio ordered that the ships be taken out to sea and set afire. All war elephants were to be surrendered, and Carthage was forbidden from training any new ones. Finally, Carthage was to pay Rome an indemnity of ten thousand talents over fifty years. The annual payment was a concession to Carthage's financial condition and also kept it in Rome's debt for a considerable period. When the Roman Senate formally ratified the peace treaty, all Roman troops were to evacuate Africa within 150 days of its ratification.[97]

It was, by all measures, a reasonable peace, although some of the clauses were more severe than had been set under the original armistice. Thus, the cash indemnity was doubled and the number of ships Carthage was permitted to possess was halved. The limits placed on Carthage's military capabilities reduced it to a Roman client state. Perhaps most ominously, Rome gave no guarantees as to Carthage's future security. Massinissa would keep watch on the great city out of his own interests, and, if necessary, Rome could use Massinissa's presence as both a pretext and means for future aggression. Vermina, meanwhile, was left with some of his kingdom intact as a check on Massinissa. The failure to provide for Carthage's future security would return to haunt Rome. Years later the commercial rivalry between Carthage and Rome would prompt Cato and the Senate to use Massinissa to threaten Carthage. But Rome could not control its former ally, and fearing that he might occupy the great fortified city himself, Rome destroyed Carthage in the Third Punic War. Scipio's treaty contained within it the seeds of Rome's future aggression.[98]

Once the negotiations were complete and the treaty ratified, Scipio and his army set sail for Lilybaeum in Sicily. He sent the greater part of his army on to

Rome by sea while he made his way over land through Italy. "Everywhere he found rejoicing . . . when the towns poured out to do him honor and crowds of peasants to hold up his progress along the roads."[99] He reached Rome and entered the city in a triumph, which Livy describes "as had never been seen before." He awarded his soldiers a bonus and deposited 123,000 pounds of silver in the treasury. Sometime later Scipio acquired the surname *Africanus*. Livy tells us he was not able to determine how the name came about. Perhaps it was "through the army's devotion to their general, or from popular favor; or it may have started with the flatter of his close friends. . . . What is certain is that Scipio was the first general to be celebrated by the name of the people he had conquered."[100]

8

Triumph and Fall

FOR MORE THAN a decade after Scipio returned from Africa in 201 BCE he was the "first man in Rome," the state's most famous and influential person. Although he did not win every political battle in which he became involved and his faction did not always succeed in carrying the annual elections for their candidates, Scipio was an important political player in all the major Roman policy decisions, and he had some share in every important movement or event.[1] With such fame and influence came powerful enemies. Scipio's political opponents plagued him for all his life until they finally brought him down and forced his political exile from the city that he loved and that had once bestowed honor and gratitude on him. In this sense Scipio and Hannibal suffered the same cruel fate, both forced into exile to live out their days far from the center of their past glories and without their countrymen's regard. Livy put it well when he remarked that "the two greatest cities in the world were at almost the same time shown to be ungrateful to their leading citizens; but Rome was the more ungrateful of the two, in that conquered Carthage had expelled the conquered Hannibal, whereas victorious Rome was driving out the victorious Scipio."[2]

SCIPIO'S POLITICAL LIFE

To understand the political life and fall of Scipio Africanus one must understand how the Roman political system of his day worked. In Scipio's day the Roman Senate was the center of political decision making, a position it had gained mostly by custom and its own initiative rather than because of law. The popular assemblies, which represented the people of Rome, could sometimes overturn its rulings. The people did not elect the Senate members; instead, the censors chose them for lifetime membership.[3] The body was comprised of three hundred men drawn mainly from the landed aristocracy, including all the former consuls and magistrates; however, not all senators possessed equal influence. Real power lay with the *nobiles*, an inner circle of senators from a small number of the oldest families. The Scipios were among the most notable of these important families. In practice the Senate's prestige, its individual members' reputations, and the patronage these powerful individuals and their families controlled made the Senate of Scipio's day the Republic's de facto government. The Senate reserved to itself control over foreign policy and the state's financial matters.[4] Therefore, the state's effective management rested in the hands of some twenty or fewer families who supplied the generals, administrators, and provincial governors. By guiding senatorial policy, these men shaped Rome's destiny.[5]

Conflict within the Roman Senate arose from personal ambition, historical enmities, personal alliances, and differences over public policy. It resulted in rival factions that made Roman politics a sea of shifting alliances and coalitions that had to be assembled or placated in order to gain support for a public policy. By the time Scipio returned to Rome in 201 BCE, the years of war and the passage of time had taken a heavy toll on the older senators who had guided the Republic through Rome's troubles. This thinning of the older political ranks opened opportunities for new and younger men with records of military achievement, political skills and connections, and sufficient ambition to try and make their influence felt. Men like Scipio, not yet thirty-seven years old, and Titus Quinctius Flamininus, who was "not yet more than 30" when given command of Roman armies during the Second Macedonian War,[6] were ready to make their influence felt on Roman politics.

Early on, the Romans had a deep distrust of consular power, especially when that power was associated with men who had military reputations and were popular with the public. When Scipio returned victorious from Spain, some in the Senate strongly opposed his appointment to the African command on the grounds that he would become too powerful.[7] That Scipio's appointment to Spain had been as *privatus imperio* in violation of all Roman custom and precedent did little to assuage the fears of Scipio's enemies that one day he would become a danger to Rome's freedoms. Scipio's threat to take the issue to the people when the Senate initially refused his request for the Sicily command only added to their concern. This same fear also drove the opposition to Scipio's lenient peace with Carthage. Scipio's allies in the Senate had protected him during his absence, and the political attacks had come to nothing. His opposition's trepidation over Scipio's great popularity with the Roman people served as the backdrop against which his political career played out over the next decade. As Scullard notes, "even before

Scipio came back from Africa the question was, would the conqueror of Hannibal raise any constitutional issues and how would he meet the challenges of the hostile faction that had been intriguing against him during his absence."[8]

In 199 BCE Scipio was appointed *princeps senatus* over three more senior patrician ex-censors, and his name was placed first on the list of senators. This honor gave him the authority to speak to the issues of the day with great moral standing. The Romans held a man's character in high esteem, and an act of bad character was the primary reason for removing a senator from office. Scipio's appointment made him first among equals, and his political influence grew. More important than his appointment as princeps senatus, however, was his election as censor in the same year. This office was Rome's *sanctissimus magistratus* and was considered the crowning glory of a political career. The *comitia centuriata*, the oldest of Roman popular assemblies, elected two censors who held office only until their functions were performed and anyway for not more than eighteen months. The censors' primary tasks were to revise the list of citizens, register them in proper classes for taxation, let public contracts, and assess property as part of the taxation lists. Most important politically was their authority to review the membership of the Senate; they could enroll new members and remove any they deemed morally unworthy of the office. A censor could not be called to account for his actions as censor, and the office was regarded as the most august of all Roman magistracies. The holders of this office were almost always ex-consuls.[9] Scipio's two high-level offices made him the official leader of the Senate oligarchy. As censor Scipio could have removed some of the senators who opposed him, but he did not do so.

Scipio's first task on returning to Rome in 201 BCE was to care for his veterans. At Scipio's urging, the Senate formed a ten-man commission to allocate some of the *ager publicus* (public land) in Samnium and Apulia for his veterans. In theory Roman soldiers were part-time militia who owned farms to which they would return and earn their livelihood. But the wars had lasted so long and Hannibal had ravaged so much of Italy that many of these farms had been destroyed. The commission awarded two *jugera* of land for every year a soldier served in Spain or Africa. Although during his Spanish campaign Scipio had established the military colony of Italica in Spain on his own authority, awarding land for military service was a new Roman practice. It is particularly noteworthy that Scipio asked the state to award the land so that the compensation was given as an obligation of the state and not the gift of a military commander. Later when the policy changed to a commander's gift, it caused disastrous consequences for the

Republic. Here we see Scipio's democratic and Republican tendencies in evidence. He understood that if, instead of the state, he were to organize the land settlements for his veterans, it would have been widely perceived as a dangerous precedent. Scipio remained to the end a servant of Rome's.[10]

Over the next decade Scipio and his supporters in the Senate exercised important influence on Roman policy, most particularly with regard to Rome's foreign policy toward Greece and Antiochus the Great of Syria. Of the twenty-two consuls elected between 200 and 190 BCE, seven were directly related to Scipio. This total includes his election to a second consulship in 194 BCE, a remarkable honor for a Roman noble in times of peace.[11] Other historians sometimes add six other consuls who were members of the Scipionic faction and supported Scipio's policies, bringing the total to half of all consuls holding office during that period. This support is a remarkable testament to Scipio's political influence and skill in the political arena at a time when Rome was at an important crossroads in its history.

The empire of Alexander the Great fell apart almost immediately after his death in 323 BCE, leaving five powerful states in its wake. By the time of Scipio's victory at Zama in 202 BCE, more than a century of war among these kingdoms had reduced the number of important states in the eastern Mediterranean to three: Syria or Asia under Antiochus III, the Great (223–187 BCE); Egypt under Ptolemy V Epiphanes (205–180 BCE); and Macedonia under Philip V (221–179 BCE). Rome and Carthage had contested for dominance in the western Mediterranean, with Rome emerging as the victor. Philip V's attack on Rome during the Hannibalic war had given Rome reason to doubt his intentions, and with Carthage subdued, Rome turned its attention to the east.[12]

When Scipio arrived home from Africa, Rome was dealing with revolts in Spain and the Gauls' attacks in northern Italy. The key security issue was Greece, where Philip V of Macedon had moved with force to occupy some of the Greek city-states. At the same time the death of Ptolemy IV Philopater in Egypt encouraged Antiochus to march into Syria. The Greek city-states of Pergamum and Rhodes watched the regional balance of power crumble before their eyes and appealed to Rome, a distant and therefore apparently less dangerous great power, for help in checking Philip.[13] The Romans also had to worry about Antiochus, who was asserting his hereditary territorial claims in Asia Minor and Thrace. When Philip and Antiochus signed a pact to partition Egypt's external territories, the Romans saw these powerful states as conspiring to dominate the eastern Mediterranean at Rome's expense. Livy tells us that after the Greek envoys from Pergamum and Rhodes arrived in Rome, "at the first meeting of the Senate called by the consul, there was unanimous demand that the matter of Philip and the grievances of the allies should have precedence over all other business."[14] Scipio probably arrived home in time to take part in the discussions.[15]

Scipio certainly was involved in the discussions to send an army against Philip. There is no evidence that he opposed the war, but he seems to have urged caution. Most likely he objected to issuing an ultimatum to Philip when the door to diplomacy remained open to further discussions.[16] Throughout his career Scipio had attempted to tailor the use of force to achieve clear political objectives, and more than once he had obtained strategic objectives through diplomacy and negotiation. Perhaps it was a question of emphasis. Scipio was too clear a strategic thinker not to recognize the threat Philip posed. He likely considered Philip only part of the difficulty and saw that Antiochus and his enormous empire represented the greater threat in the long run. In this view Rome could not permit Philip to gain a foothold in Greece where he might then form an alliance with Antiochus and present Rome with a complex of power that would be very difficult to match. The problem was probably a question more of means than ends, for Philip had to be dealt with in any event. Scipio urged caution, the mark of a true statesman who possessed a gift for finding political solutions to difficult problems.[17]

Beyond these strategic considerations, Scipio supported the war against Philip for another reason. Scipio and many members of his Senate faction were strong supporters of Greece on cultural and moral grounds. Over rugged Roman simplicity these philhellenists favored Greek customs, values, virtues, and fashions as symbols of civilization to which Rome and its people ought to aspire. Greek influences were already being felt in Rome by Scipio's day. Greek religious rites had been introduced, and the presence of Greek tutors educating the nobility's sons was strongly influencing education. Roman drama drew its origins and themes from Greece.[18] In the realm of military affairs, the example of Alexander's generalship was still the standard against which Roman generals measured themselves, and Greek military prowess was much admired and feared. In the philhellenists' view, Rome was very much a crude, rural, and somewhat uncivilized culture when compared with that of the Greeks, and they "wanted to gain for Rome [from the Greeks] recognition as one of the civilized nations of the world."[19]

On the one hand, the philhellenist view led some Romans to admire their fellow republican regimes among the city-states and independent kingdoms of Greece and their cherished values of self-governance and political freedom. On the other hand, they observed Philip of Macedon's monarchy and the imperial realm of Antiochus of Syria with distrust. Thus, when Philip attacked the Greek states, the philhellenists had both strategic concern and cultural sympathy for the Greeks. When Rhodes and Pergamum sent envoys to Rome to plead for help, their pleas fell on sympathetic ears. In 200 BCE Publius Sulpicius Galba and Gaius Aurelius Cotta were elected consuls. The Roman Senate declared war on Philip and sent Galba to Greece at the head of an army. The Second Macedonian War (200–196 BCE) began.

Sulpicius Galba crossed into Greece at the head of a Roman army. He had commanded troops in Greece during the First Macedonian War and gained a reputation for harshness and cruelty. The Greeks were aware of Galba's reputation and mistrusted him. Within a short time he had once again aroused Greek resentment and was unable to make much headway against Philip. Insignificant military skirmishes and diplomatic difficulty in dealing with the Greeks marked his tenure. When his consularship ended, Galba's command was not extended, but because of his extensive military experience, he was not recalled to Rome. Instead, he was seconded to the new Roman commander, Titus Quinctius Flamininus, who was elected consul in 198 BCE, and took command of the war in Greece.

Regarding Flamininus, Polybius says that "he was exceedingly acute, if ever a Roman was. The skill and good sense with which he conducted public business and private negotiations could not be surpassed, and yet he was quite a young man, not yet more than thirty."[20] In short, he was everything that Sulpicius Galba was not. Flamininus was also a philhellenist, and although he was not a member of the Scipionic faction, Scipio's political support likely aided Flamininus's election to consul and his assignment to command in Greece.[21] Scipio saw in Flamininus a fellow philhellene who possessed the right combination of diplomatic and military skills to convince the Greeks that Rome was the true champion of Greek liberty, wished no territory for itself, and could be trusted. Later the two men became political rivals. For the moment, however, Scipio thought Flamininus the right man for the job of stopping Philip and winning the confidence of the Greek states.

Two events serve as evidence of Scipio's support for Flamininus. First, Sextus Aelius Paetus was elected consul along with Flamininus. A colleague and supporter of Scipio's, Pateus would not have been elected without Scipio's support. Thus, Scipio supported one of his own men to work with Flamininus.[22] Second, probably at Scipio's suggestion, Flamininus had been appointed to serve on the commission that allotted land to Scipio's veterans, permitting him to establish a relationship with Scipio's old troops. In raising his army for Greece, Flamininus "had followed the policy of selecting, in general, soldiers of exemplary courage who had served in Spain or Africa."[23] He took three thousand of Scipio's veterans with him as volunteers, something that would have been impossible if they believed that their old commander did not support Flamininus.

But why didn't Scipio try to obtain the Greek command for himself? The old constitutional system of awarding military commands to the consuls was back in effect since the Carthaginian threat had been removed. Further, Scipio could not hold consular office again until ten years had passed since his last election in 204 BCE. This rule had been overlooked several times during the war with Hannibal, but afterward it was usually enforced. Scipio could have tried to obtain a major command under the new consuls, but he did not do so. The obvious reason seems to be his lack of political support in the Senate. His opposition feared that Scipio could still present a danger to the Republic. Scullard explains this concern:

> The nobility as a whole probably feared to entrust him [Scipio] with a first-class military command which would give him the chance of placing the Roman People once again deeply in his debt. If at the head of a devoted army he was to humble Philip and earn the gratitude of Greece, would he again retire quietly to private life?[24]

Scipio's political sense would have told him that a command was not possible, so he supported Flamininus as the best available man for the task ahead.

Flamininus followed the Scipio model in war by first attempting to achieve his objectives through diplomatic means. He opened negotiations with Philip in which he demanded that Philip withdraw from Greece, release those states he had conquered, and relinquish his claims by inheritance to any others. They were, of course, impossible demands. Rome understood that the freedom of the Greek city-states required that Macedonia's power be broken permanently and its freedom in foreign affairs severely curtailed, as Carthage's had been. Philip refused. The armies met in 197 BCE at the battle of Cynoscephalae (Dog's Head).[25]

The Roman victory at Cynoscephalae may well have owed something to how Scipio trained his men. At a critical point in the battle, the Roman right wing gained superiority over the enemy's left. At the same time the Roman left was being pressed hard by Philip's right, forcing it to give ground. Then "one of the Roman military tribunes conceived a design on the spur of the moment. He took with him the soldiers of twenty maniples, abandoning that part of the line which was obviously getting the better of the enemy, and brought them quickly round to attack the enemy's right wing from behind."[26] Many of Flamininus's men were Scipio's veterans fighting under some of their old officers. The tribune who detached the maniples and attacked the enemy rear may have been one of Scipio's former unit commanders who remembered the tactical lessons he had been taught while under Scipio's command. Until Scipio carried out tactical reforms during his campaigns in Spain and Africa, no Roman legion had demonstrated such tactical adaptability in the heat of battle.[27]

The war between Philip and Rome dragged on, causing important new political developments. Flamininus understood that one of the outstanding features of Hellenistic history was the importance of Greek public opinion in public policy. Even the most powerful monarchs and ruthless tyrants paid heed and deferred to it.[28] Throughout the war Flamininus had cast Roman policy as an effort to free the Greeks from Philip as a way of cultivating public opinion and enticing Greek states and cities to support the Roman cause. After Flamininus's earlier victory at the battle of Aous, the Aetolian League, one of the two strongest powers in Greece, came over to the Romans. Flamininus kept the pressure on Philip, besieging one town after another until the Achaean League, too, declared for Rome.[29] Philip sued for peace, and the two sides met at Nicaea (Nicea) to negotiate an agreement.

Before the war the Greeks had seen the Romans as barbarians, a minor player in the coalition effort against Philip.[30] Flamininus's efforts had convinced the Greeks, however, that the Romans' intention to free the Greeks was genuine. The result was momentous. Rome, only an equal member of the Hellenistic coalition against Macedon, had become the arbiter of the war's settlement. The Greeks had come to trust Flamininus and delegated to him the authority to treat with Philip in their name. Thus, the Hellenistic world had delegated to Rome the authority to pass and maintain the final judgment in settling its business, and it never again exercised to any marked extent independent jurisdiction over its own foreign affairs.[31] The Greeks would learn that Rome intended to guarantee the status quo in Greece, and in trying to do so against Antiochus, Rome would use Greece as the strategic platform to expand its empire in the eastern Mediterranean.

The peace with Philip saw the victory of Scipio's foreign policy over that of the Roman Senate's more conservative factions who had sought to crush Macedonia completely. Both Scipio and Flamininus pressed for a more moderate policy toward Philip. The final terms were those that Flamininus had previously demanded during the first negotiations with Philip. Although Rome deprived Philip of his Greek conquests, his fleet, and the Demetrias, Chalcis, and Corinth fortresses, which he called the "Fetters of Greece" because of their great strategic value, Philip kept his throne, his army, and the kingdom of Macedonia intact. Scipio realized that Macedonia was the only geographic buffer between the northern barbarians, or the Gauls, and Greece itself. In a curious turn of events, Philip was left to protect Greece by preventing these barbarian tribes from moving any farther south. From a wider strategic perspective, Scipio also understood that destroying Macedonia would create a vacuum into which Antiochus of Syria might be drawn, creating an even more serious threat to Roman interests in the East. For these reasons Scipio and Flamininus both used their political influence to secure a more moderate peace for Philip.

The potential threat from Antiochus was also on the Romans' minds when they made peace with Philip. As Polybius notes, it was important to end the Greek war quickly so that Rome could turn its attention to Antiochus.[32] Rome went further, however, and formally declared that "all the rest of the Greeks in Asia and Europe were to be free and governed by their own laws."[33] This message went considerably beyond the stated Roman policy of freeing the city-states that Philip had seized. The claim seemed also to apply to those Greek polities in Asia that were within Antiochus's kingdom. Rome seemed to announce a policy where it regarded itself as the protector of Greek freedom wherever it needed to be protected. The warning to Antiochus was clear: Scipio was already looking to Rome's strategic interests beyond Greece.

The strategy both Scipio and Flamininus championed departed from Rome's usual method of dealing with defeated kingdoms. After the war the Greek states were declared to be Roman *amici*—that is, "friends of Rome," or a status that treated them technically as equals. Usually the Romans regarded former enemies only as *socii* (associates), a term that implied their subordination to Rome that was given effect when the Romans' levied on them obligations to supply troops and supplies in wartime. In both cases, of course, the disparity of power between Rome and its amici or socii primarily determined the nature of the relationship. The peace with Philip did not gain Rome any new members for its federation that were required to support and supply it during time of war. As Haywood notes, "This was a striking liberalization of foreign policy. It made Rome [or would have had it not been too strong for the other Mediterranean republics] not the head of a tightly bound federation, but the friend of the famous Greek republics of the time, a recognized equal among the civilized nations of the world."[34] This, then, was the policy of the Roman Senate's dominant Scipio faction in its support of Flamininus.

We do not hear of Scipio again in the original sources until 195 BCE, when Livy tells us of Scipio's opposition to the Roman delegation sent to investigate charges against Hannibal.[35] In 196 BCE Hannibal had been elected *sufete* in Carthage and introduced financial and democratic reforms detrimental to the ruling oligarchs. They appealed to Rome on the grounds that Hannibal was planning an alliance with Antiochus. The situation played perfectly into the hands of the Roman Senate's conservative faction, which had been looking for an excuse to punish Hannibal ever since the peace with Carthage had not delivered Hannibal into Roman hands. Scipio's opponents used the affair to criticize his lenient terms with Carthage, and by implication the leniency of the terms with Philip, because they had permitted Hannibal to return to power where he might yet be a threat. The Carthaginians pressed rumors that hinted that Hannibal was already scheming with Antiochus. Over Scipio's opposition, the Senate voted to send a commission to Carthage to investigate the oligarchs' complaints. Hannibal was too smart not to realize that the Roman commission was aimed at him, and he fled Carthage. Eventually he found asylum at Antiochus's court, where he was an even greater danger for now he had cause to turn against Rome. The factional infighting of the Roman Senate had delivered Scipio a political defeat, but it also had increased the threat from Antiochus and Hannibal.

Roman troops, meanwhile, were still in Greece and occupying the fortresses of the Fetters of Greece at the beginning of 195 BCE. The Greeks began to doubt the Romans' promise that they had come to save Greek liberty and would withdraw. Scipio and his supporters, on the one hand, urged the continued presence of Roman forces in Greece until Antiochus's intentions became clear. Flamininus and the conservative factions, on the other hand, argued for the Romans' withdrawal on the strategic grounds that if war with Antiochus were to come, Rome would need the Greek states' wholehearted support, which would be forthcoming only if Rome kept its promise and withdrew from Greece. The Roman troops' continued presence, they argued, only made the Greeks more suspicious and weakened their value as allies should a war start. The Senate appointed a commission to go to Greece and make recommendations.

The commission concluded an alliance with Philip that guaranteed his support and the logistical supply of Roman troops should they be required to pass through Greece to confront Antiochus in Asia. A Roman guarantee of support against Philip, should the circumstance ever arise, temporarily pacified the disgruntled and powerful Aetolians. Most important, however, the Senate commission agreed with Scipio and recommended against the Roman troops' withdrawal in light of Antiochus's recent steps to cross into Europe and renew his ancestral claim to the city of Lysimachia. Scipio's strategic vision was much broader than that of his Senate opponents, and he searched for a policy that defined Rome's relations not just with the Greeks but with all the different kingdoms, monarchies, republics, and city-states throughout the eastern Mediterranean, including Asia. In Scipio's view, Antiochus would have to be confronted sooner or later. The Senate also sent envoys to Antiochus to discuss the situation, but they accomplished nothing. Meanwhile, word reached Rome that Hannibal had arrived in Antiochus's court.

In 194 BCE Scipio was elected consul for the second time. His colleague was Tiberius Sempronius Longus, whose father had been consul with Scipio's father in 218 BCE.[36] Scipio was in his early forties and at the height of his political career. Why, then, seek election as consul again? Two reasons suggest themselves. First, Hannibal was afoot again. Scipio knew well Hannibal's hatred of Rome. Whatever part of it had been abated when Rome treated him and Carthage humanely after the war was rekindled when the Roman investigative commission forced him into exile. Hannibal had been no threat in Carthage. Now he was in the court of Antiochus, the most powerful military leader of the day. Scipio feared not only that Hannibal would urge Antiochus into a war with Rome but also that he, Hannibal, would once more take the field. Even more disconcerting was the possibility that Antiochus would equip Hannibal with his own army and fleet with which he could bring Carthage into a new war with Rome.

Antiochus's move into Europe to reclaim his ancestral territories in Thrace persuaded Scipio that Antiochus had designs on Greece itself.[37] Scipio feared that the Senate would not keep the Roman army in Greece in the face of pressure from Antiochus, and in this supposition, he proved right. In Scipio's view, Greece had to be held as a barrier to Antiochus's further encroachments and, if need be, as a strategic platform from which to launch military operations against him. This stand meant, of course, sacrificing the principle of supporting Greek freedom that had been the bedrock of Flamininus's policy, and this point is probably where Scipio and Flamininus parted ways politically. In Scipio Africanus's strategic mind, the value of Greek freedom took second place to Roman national interests.

Scipio likely sought election to the consulship to press his view of Rome's strategic interests in the East. Pressure to withdraw from Greece was growing from the conservatives, and Flamininus himself publicly urged the army's withdrawal. He feared the continued Roman occupation would strain relations with the Greek states, which were growing skeptical of Rome's promise to leave. If a war with Antiochus came, Flamininus argued, Rome would need these Greek states's support and was in no position to anger them. To stop this argument from succeeding, after his election Scipio formally requested that the Senate declare Macedonia a province and assign it to one of the consuls for military command.[38] Of course, nothing would have angered the Greeks more than the Romans' presumption in declaring their nation a Roman province and occupying it with a Roman consular army. Had Scipio gotten his way the Greek leagues might have immediately declared for Antiochus against the suspected Roman invasion. Scipio made a rare but important strategic mistake. He probably thought he could convince the Senate to award him Macedonia in light of his past military record. This position would have given him command of the Roman armies in Greece and, perhaps, one more chance to lead men in battle should Antiochus prove the threat Scipio believed him to be. Instead, Scipio suffered one of the worst defeats of his political career. The Senate refused to follow Scipio's advice. It ordered both the consuls to remain in Italy for the time being and the Roman army to evacuate Greece as quickly as possible.

Having failed to convince Rome of the course of action he thought best, Scipio did what he could during his year as consul to protect Rome from the gathering storm. During his consulship, Scipio founded eight maritime colonies on the Italian coast. Five of these had been authorized in 197 BCE, and Scipio saw to their quick completion. Strategically located on the coast of Campania, these colonies were Puteoli, Volturnum, Liternum, Salernum, and Buxentum.[39] Later Scipio appointed a board of commissioners who approved the establishment of other colonies on the southern shore of Italy at Tempsa, Croton, Sipontum, and two Latin colonies at Copia and Vibo Valentia in Bruttium.[40] These colonies had a dual strategic purpose. In the event Antiochus's fleet or Hannibal from Carthage launched a seaborne attack, the colonies provided for the immediate defense of Italy. As E. T. Salmon notes, the colonists were subject to being called to military service, and significant numbers of them were probably veterans.[41] After Hannibal's invasion of southern Italy, Rome was determined to settle the area against future attacks. Second, because some southern towns had gone over to Hannibal during the war, the new colonies gave Rome an increased presence in the south where it could keep watch on the other towns. The veterans in the Roman settlements would provide a quick reaction or punitive force against any town whose loyalty to Rome might be suspect.[42]

During his second consulship Scipio was also elected princeps senatus for the second time. Unable to affect events in the East, Scipio may have taken part in Sempronius Longus's campaign against the Boii in northern Italy. Livy tells us that "according to some writers Scipio joined armies with his colleague and traversed the territories of the Boii and the Ligures plundering on the way, as far as the forests and marshes allowed them to proceed; others say that after achieving nothing worthy of record, he returned to Rome for the elections."[43] We cannot be certain that Scipio led an army into Gaul, but it is not difficult to imagine that with old age and illness coming on, Scipio may have wanted one more chance to command men in war and did lead his army against the Boii. Even so, his consulship expired with the storm gathering in the East but with Rome still at peace.

Scipio had been Rome's preeminent political figure for the past decade and had been influential in shaping Rome's strategic defense policy. In examining Scipio's political life between 204 and 194 BCE, Haywood is correct when he says that Scipio's influence on the course of events during this period was very important. He promoted the encouragement of Greek culture at Rome and a policy of friendliness toward the Greeks. His most important contribution was his attempt of a sort to liberalize Roman foreign policy, to make it more flexible and accommodating, so that Rome could cooperate with the other Mediterranean states in pursuit of its interests. These achievements during this period were probably as important as those of his earlier service.[44]

THE LAST CAMPAIGN

By 195 BCE diplomatic contacts between Rome and Antiochus had ceased. Over the next two years Antiochus moved farther into Greece by occupying Lysimachia on the European coast of Thrace and by restoring relations with other towns in the area. He then moved to occupy Aenus and Maronea farther west along the coast and established good relations with the Greeks in Byzantium.[45] Rome saw these actions as a prelude to further Syrian encroachment in Europe. The Romans had been mistaken in seeing the earlier alliance between Antiochus and Philip as aimed at them and not at Egypt. By the time Rome attacked Philip, the alliance was already coming apart. In a paradox of policy, Rome had brought Philip to heel only to create a vacuum in Greece that Antiochus seemed intent on filling. Rome now viewed Antiochus with a fear that bordered on the irrational.

In 193 BCE Rome sent Flamininus and ten commissioners to negotiate with Antiochus. Antiochus saw the Romans withdrawing its armies from Greece while he was pushing into Thrace as a sign that Rome wanted to avoid war and believed that the commission was sent to reach a diplomatic settlement. The Roman demands seem to confirm this assessment. Flamininus's position was that Rome was prepared to force Antiochus to abandon his claims to *either* the cities in Thrace *or* the autonomous Greek city-states in Asia Minor. In offering this compromise, Rome had abandoned the policy of protecting Greek freedom. Roman security interests took precedence, and Rome was willing to forgo its position of protecting the Greek states' freedom if Antiochus would withdraw from Thrace.[46] The Scipionic faction in the Senate seems to have supported this policy.[47] Removing any Syrian foothold in Europe was worth the price of reneging on Rome's promises to protect Greek freedom in Asia Minor. Antiochus rejected the Roman position out of hand.

The Romans tried again later and sent a diplomatic mission led by Sulpicius Galba to try and reach a settlement. There is a legend that Scipio was a member of this commission and that he met with Hannibal at Ephesus, giving rise to the famous anecdote in which Scipio asked Hannibal who the greatest generals were. Hannibal replied that he put Alexander first, Pyrrhus second, and himself third. "Scipio burst out laughing at this, and said, 'What would you be saying if you had defeated me?' 'In that case,' replied Hannibal, 'I would certainly put myself before Alexander and before Pyrrhus, in fact before all other generals.'"[48] Livy tells us that Hannibal's reply "affected Scipio deeply, because Hannibal had set him apart from the general run of commanders, as one whose worth was beyond calculation."[49]

As Livy readily admits, the tale is based on the historian Claudius's account of "the Greek work of Acilius" (circa 142 BCE), but as A. H. McDonald notes in his introduction of Bettenson's translation of Livy, it cannot be trusted.[50] The story may have its roots in Livy's understanding of Polybius's view that the Romans' military success, especially against Hannibal, was a consequence of Scipio's superior generalship rather than of Roman arms and tactics. Since Polybius is silent on the meeting between Hannibal and Scipio at Ephesus, Livy may have reported Claudius's account per ad majorem Scipionis gloriam and have Hannibal himself admit that Scipio was the greater general.

Scipio, however, likely did travel to the East, probably on an independent intelligence-gathering mission sometime in 193 BCE and not as a member of Sulpicius's commission. At that time Massinissa was creating trouble over territory both he and Carthage claimed. One of Hannibal's agents, Aristo by name, was also in Carthage, stirring up rumors that Hannibal had asked Antiochus for a hundred ships (Antiochus's entire fleet in the eastern Mediterranean), ten thousand infantry, and a thousand cavalry to convince Carthage to enter the war against Rome.[51] Perhaps Hannibal preferred to die fighting his old enemy than to languish powerlessly at the court of Antiochus, leading him to propose the plan. The idea that ten thousand troops could successfully invade Italy was ludicrous on its face, to say nothing of the difficulty of supporting such an operation from Syrian bases so far to the east. Antiochus rejected the plan. Still, the rumors concerning Hannibal could not be ignored entirely, so the Senate sent Scipio and two others to Carthage. They were there ostensibly to settle the matter with Massinissa but really to assess the political situation there and ensure that Massinissa remained loyal. Rome might need him to check Carthage should it be so foolish as to support Hannibal and Antiochus against Rome.[52]

Scipio's colleagues returned to Rome while he traveled through Greece, learning as much as he could about conditions there. He visited Delos, where he dedicated a golden crown to Apollo, and he is rumored to have visited Ephesus about when the Roman delegation was conducting negotiations with Antiochus and Hannibal. This might have been the time that Scipio met with Hannibal, if he did at all. The trip was short, and Scipio returned to Rome in November 192 BCE for the consular elections. The elections of 192 saw L. Quinctius Flamininus, Titus's brother, elected consul, but the Scipionic candidates did well in gaining other offices. Scipio probably used whatever impressions he had gained from his journey to warn his Senate colleagues of Antiochus's growing threat. The official delegation had not yet returned from the failed talks, so Scipio's words went unheeded as Rome continued to attempt to reach a *modus vivendi* with Antiochus.

The repeated and extended negotiations and Roman attempts at accommodation seem to have convinced Antiochus that Rome wished to avoid war at all costs. In the spring of 192 BCE the Aetolians formally asked Antiochus to free Greece from the Romans and to guarantee their liberty, the same rationale the Romans had employed to justify their war against Philip. Antiochus's maneuver could not have come as a surprise, for the Romans had already moved small troop units into Greece to support Philip in case of hostilities. With Antiochus's intentions now known, Rome moved a substantial number of troops to Tarentum and Brundisium in the south of Italy and redeployed several naval squadrons there in support. In the autumn, Antiochus landed at Pteleum in Thrace at the head of an army of ten thousand infantry, five hundred cavalry, six elephants, and a fleet of forty decked ships, sixty open boats, and two hundred transports.[53] There was as yet no formal declaration of war, but events were already gathering a momentum of their own. In a few weeks Roman troops under Philip went into action, and the conflict was under way.

Faced with these events, the Romans held the consular elections for 191 BCE early. The Scipionic group did well with Nasica, Scipio's cousin, elected consul along with Marcus Acilius Glabro, a *novus homo* (new man) and protégé of the Scipio faction, elected as his plebeian colleague. Four of the praetors were also Scipio supporters. The success of the Scipionic faction probably reflected the fact that events had proved Scipio right about Antiochus while Flamininus's initial policy of accommodation in Greece had failed. Acilius received Greece as a province and prepared to lead the Roman army there. Intriguingly, Lucius Scipio, Africanus's younger brother, was assigned to Acilius's staff "doubtless to gain experience in a theater of war in which he might hope later to have command."[54] Lucius Scipio had accompanied his brother in Spain and Africa but had served only as a staff officer. As far as can be discerned, Lucius had never held a major field command, although he did participate in the skirmish against Hanno.[55] Since Acilius was Scipio's protégé, Lucius's presence on his staff was more likely politically motivated, that is, to ensure that Acilius remained loyal to his mentor's policies. In February, Acilius crossed into Greece with an army of twenty thousand infantry, two thousand cavalry, and fifteen elephants and marched toward Thessaly, where a small Roman contingent was already fighting alongside Philip. Thus, the Romans joined with the Macedonian king to reconquer the land from which they had expelled him six years earlier.[56]

The army with which Antiochus had invaded Greece was meant as a symbolic force for he assumed Rome would avoid war and come to an accommodation. It was too small to obtain his strategic objectives by military force alone. (The Greeks called it "the tiny army.") Now that Rome had called Antiochus's hand, he found himself outnumbered and on the defensive. He quickly withdrew to Thermopylae, seizing the heights and blocking the entrance to central Greece. There he awaited the Romans' attack. Antiochus had chosen his ground well, and although the Romans had the advantage of numbers, they were driven back repeatedly by heavy missile fire. Suffering strong opposition from the Syrian front, the Romans detached two maneuver elements, two thousand men each, to try to make their way up the back side of the Syrian positions. Marcus Porcius Cato, an experienced field commander, former consul, and political enemy of Scipio, led one element. It marched by night, taking Antiochus's flank guard by surprise, and attacked the Syrians from the rear.[57] Antiochus's army broke and fled in headlong retreat with the Roman cavalry hot on its heels. Livy, citing Polybius, says "out of the entire army the only men to escape were the 500 who accompanied the king, a very scanty number even in proportion to the 10,000 soldiers whom the king had brought with him to Greece."[58] Antiochus made good his escape to the coast and sailed for Ephesus. In a single battle the Romans had driven the great king from Greece.

With Philip safely in the Roman alliance, with a Roman army in Greece, with the Romans having demonstrated their sincerity and coming to the aid of Greek freedom, and with Antiochus driven from Europe, Roman strategic objectives were achieved. For Scipio, however, the task remained unfinished. Scipio urged the Senate to follow the same policy he had urged them to pursue against Philip and Carthage, reiterating that Rome's future security was possible only once Antiochus's power was broken and his empire pushed back beyond the Taurus Mountains. He insisted that the war be continued until Antiochus was driven from coastal Anatolia, the Greek independent cities there were freed, and a Roman army was sent to Asia for the first time in history to accomplish these goals. Livy tells us, "No dissent was heard and the policy was adopted."

Scipio's critics can be forgiven if they thought he sought more of an empire and conquest than the Republic's security. Where once Greece and Macedonia had been regarded only as a protective buffer against possible Syrian expansion, they had now been transformed into "heartland" territory, and it had to be defended by moving beyond the borders and creating an additional protective zone in eastern Anatolia west of the Taurus. It was a dynamic driven more by strategic psychology than by geography or by a realistic assessment of enemy intentions and was to appear many times throughout history. Intended or not, Scipio had set Rome on the road to imperial conquest.

The consular elections of 190 BCE resulted in a great victory for the Scipionic faction. Gaius Laelius, Scipio's old comrade in arms who had fought with him in Spain and Africa, was chosen plebeian consular, and Lucius Scipio won the patrician consular post. Both, of course, owed their elections to Scipio. The question arose immediately about selecting the respective consuls' provinces. Livy tells us that both consuls wanted Greece. Usually the selection was by lot, but Laelius is supposed to have suggested that given the war's importance, the Senate should decide instead. Lucius conferred with his brother before the vote. Scipio announced that if Lucius received Greece as his province, he would go along as his legatus. At this offer, Livy tells us, the Senate "decreed almost unanimously that Lucius

Scipio should have the command in Greece, while Laelius should hold the province of Italy."[59]

Cicero, however, tells another story that is probably closer to the truth. He says that the usual lots were cast and that Lucius won Greece, but "because Lucius was not considered to have sufficient energy of body or mind," the Senate was preparing to switch commands and give Greece to Laelius. Then Africanus stepped in and announced that he would go to Greece as Lucius's legate.[60] Africanus had possibly struck a bargain with Laelius before the election in which the price of Scipio's support for the consular post was that Laelius would permit Lucius to have the command in Asia. Whatever was the case, it is obvious that Scipio Africanus intended to lead troops in one last campaign, one way or another.

Undoubtedly, Africanus was in charge of the campaign against Antiochus, and Lucius was mostly a figurehead in its planning and execution. We have only Cicero's word that Lucius was "not sound of body or mind," although some later historians say that "his incompetence was notorious."[61] It is not necessary, however, to attribute such disabilities to Lucius Scipio. Laelius was a much more experienced soldier and field commander on the face of it and would have been the logical choice for the command in Greece. Lucius had served as an officer on Scipio's staff in Spain and Africa, but no accounts show that he ever served in command of troops or that he distinguished himself in battle. Scipio seems to have used him mostly as a messenger to transmit reports back to Rome. Surely Africanus would have known of his brother's inexperience and that his own appointment as legate would have put him in effective command of the army once in the field. Although Lucius signed all communications with the title "commander-in-chief of the Romans," he included the addition "and Publius Cornelius" immediately afterward, indicating that Africanus agreed with the contents.[62]

Even the enemy knew who the real Roman commander was. When the Athenians approached the Romans to propose an armistice with the Aetolians, they approached Scipio, not Lucius.[63] The Aetolians did the same thing, and Scipio, not Lucius, convinced them to agree to the cease-fire.[64] Livy tells us that Scipio chose the overland route through Greece, and that it was his idea to ascertain Philip's support in advance.[65] When the Romans attempted to detach Prusias, the king of Bithynia, from the Syrian alliance, Scipio signed the letter and pledged his word of Roman support to the king.[66] When Antiochus made his peace overture to the Romans, his envoys were instructed to approach Scipio directly and not Lucius.[67] Once diplomacy had failed, the Roman army made straight for Antiochus's army in a bold offensive that only Scipio could have planned.[68] When

Antiochus finally came to terms, he negotiated the peace with Scipio. Scipio Africanus, the aging warhorse, had been able to maneuver his way back into one final war, and all the evidence suggests that he, not his brother, was in effective command of the army when it marched into Greece.

The Scipios arrived in Greece in April 190 BCE with thirteen thousand infantry and five hundred cavalry. They quickly linked up with Acilius's army—twenty thousand infantry, two thousand cavalry, and fifteen elephants—which was besieging Amphissa.[69] The Aetolians had previously sought peace with Rome. However, when the Senate rejected its terms, the Aetolians had gone back to fighting. Scipio immediately grasped that this state of affairs would make it impossible for him to deal effectively with Antiochus. He could hardly spend months reducing one Aetolian city after another, nor could he leave a hostile Aetolia at his back. The Aetolian resistance threatened to derail Roman policy in both Greece and Asia. At this point the Athenians, acting as intermediaries for the Aetolians, approached Scipio with an offer to mediate. After some resistance from Lucius, who twice rejected the Aetolian offer of peace by reiterating the Senate's harsh demands, Scipio intervened. He convinced the Aetolians to accept a six-month armistice during which they would send envoys to Rome for further talks. The Aetolians accepted the truce. Once more Scipio's diplomatic skills were put to good service in furthering his military objectives.

Scipio at first considered transporting his army by sea to avoid the difficult and dangerous march across Thessaly and Macedonia, but the Roman fleet, along with its Rhodian allies, was occupied fighting a series of running sea battles with Antiochus's fleet for control of the Hellespont and the Anatolian coast and could not provide sufficient transport. Scipio was forced to stake the entire game on the risky gamble that he could move his army safely through Greece without Philip interfering. The previous treaty with Philip had made him an ally of Rome's. However, with Antiochus driven from Greece, Philip's fear of Antiochus's larger territorial ambitions in Greece had abated. In fact, Greece was now Philip's for the taking. Only Scipio's army stood in the way. Maurice Holleaux is correct in his assessment: "Philip held in his hands the fate of the Roman army as it threaded the dangerous defiles of Macedon and Thrace on its march to the Hellespont."[70]

Scipio saw the danger clearly and advised Lucius to send a messenger, Tiberius Sempronius Gracchus, unannounced to Philip's court to catch him by surprise and determine if he was prepared to provide the supplies and guides required of him as a Roman ally. The messenger rode from Amphissa to Pella, arriving when the king was at a banquet and full of wine. Philip welcomed the Roman envoy and assured him that he understood his obligations to Rome. On the following day the messenger "saw supplies prepared for the army on a generous scale, bridges built over rivers, and roads made where the route was difficult." Thus reassured, Scipio set the army on the march. When the army reached Macedonia, Philip himself greeted and "escorted them not only through Macedonia, but through Thrace also, and made all preparations for their journey until they reached the Hellespont."[71] At sea the struggle for control of the Hellespont and the coastal waters continued on and off until August, when the Roman and allied fleets dealt a severe defeat to Antiochus's fleet and reduced his naval force to half its former strength. The royal fleet lost control of the sea, and the way was open for Scipio and his army to cross into Asia at the Hellespont.[72]

When the Romans approached Lysimachia, the city threw open its gates. After his fleet's loss, Antiochus had abandoned the place and left behind the city's military stores, which now provisioned the Romans. After a few days' rest and replenishment, the Roman army crossed the Hellespont in the Rhodean and Pergamene fleets and what few ships the Romans could spare from their operations against the Syrian coast. Livy tells us that "they crossed shores that were, one might say, in a state of peace, with no opposition, with no confusion, the ships being brought to various landing places."[73] This was the first Roman army to cross into Asia.

While still in Lysimachia Scipio urged Lucius to attempt to detach Prusias, the king of Bithynia, from the Syrian coalition. Bithynia lay just behind the coast of Anatolia and had a significant army. If its king could be neutralized through diplomacy, Antiochus would be deprived of a strategic ally. Antiochus had been spreading the story that the Romans intended to destroy all the kings in Asia and that to save his throne Prusias should throw in his lot with Antiochus. To counter this propaganda, Scipio sent a letter to Prusias pointing out that Rome did not oppose all kings and that, indeed, he himself had created kingdoms for Rome's allies in Africa, installed tribal kings in Spain, and noted that Philip of Macedon still possessed his kingdom. The king was favorably impressed and was even more so when an envoy arrived from Rome. He pointed out that Rome was likely to win the war anyway and that Prusias would be in a much better position afterward if he possessed "a tie of friendship" with Rome before the war ended. Roman diplomacy succeeded, and Prusias stayed neutral.

The Roman army encamped on the Asian shore for "several days." Antiochus had made no efforts to prevent the Roman crossing and did not bring up forces to engage the Romans here. The Roman march came to a complete halt. Scipio, however, had not crossed with the army and remained on the strait's western side. Livy explains,

> After that, they remained encamped at the Hellespont for several days, since it so happened that the sacred days of the procession of the *ancilia* had fallen within the period of their march. These days had also separated Publius Scipio from the army, since their sanctity touched him especially closely, as being one of the *Salii*. Thus he also caused a delay until he caught up with the army.[74]

Scipio was a Salian priest. Annually in March the Salii bore the ancilia, or sacred shields, through Rome in a ceremony devoted to Mars to initiate the campaign season.[75] If a Salian priest was not in Rome at the time of the ceremony, he was required to stop traveling wherever he was and wait for a month before moving on. If we believe Livy, this observance is why Scipio remained in Europe and let the army cross into Asia without him.

There is no reason to doubt Scipio's piety, although it is curious that in the more than eight years Scipio campaigned in Spain and Greece this is the first time we hear of his being compelled to cease his military movements for religious reasons. Moreover, the campaign season began in the spring of each year, after the ceremony in March. However, the crossing to Asia took place in November, and the campaign season was near its end. One might well question why a spring ceremony held up Scipio in November, lest the delay was deliberate on Scipio's part and the Salii ceremony a pretext. In any case, Scipio's delay did not last a month, as required by the observance.[76]

Perhaps there were other reasons for Scipio's delay. Scipio always tried to achieve objectives through diplomatic means before resorting to force. Perhaps he hoped to accomplish just that by delaying the Roman army's movement. Antiochus had already withdrawn from Greece and Thrace and had even abandoned some of his garrisons on the Asian shore. His fleet was in shambles, and he had offered no resistance to the Romans crossing the Hellespont. Most important, Antiochus did not move militarily to confront the Romans where they were encamped, and no evidence suggested that his army was maneuvering to block the Roman advance. Scipio may have interpreted the lack of enemy military activity as Antiochus signaling that he was willing to open negotiations. Scipio's delay of the Roman army's advance may have been his response in kind, a reciprocal lack of military movement to indicate that he was also amenable to peace talks.

223

Sometime "in the course of those days" an envoy from Antiochus arrived in the Roman camp "with instructions about peace." What is interesting is that Scipio's delay, bringing the Roman army to a halt, seems to have, in fact, been the reason why Antiochus sent his envoy. Livy says of Antiochus that "great hopes that peace was attainable were aroused in him by the delay and hesitation of the Romans; for he had supposed that as soon as they had crossed into Asia, they would make a rush for the king's camp."[77] The envoy had been instructed to approach Scipio—not Lucius—directly because of Scipio's reputation for fairness; "moreover, his son [Scipio's son] was a prisoner in the king's hands." How Scipio's son was captured, Livy says, "is one of the many questions on which there is very little agreement in the authorities."

After learning that Antiochus's envoy was in the Roman camp, Scipio crossed into Asia to meet with him, the thirty-day religious travel restriction having expired at the most propitious time. Scipio assembled a military council to hear the envoy's offer. The envoy observed that Antiochus had already withdrawn from Thrace and Greece, as the Romans had demanded before the war. Moreover, Antiochus was prepared to formally renounce his claims to Thrace as well as to "any other cities which the Romans wished to claim from the king's empire on the grounds they belonged to their side." This proposal would permit the Romans to claim the freedom of the Greek cities on the Anatolian coast, fulfilling another previous Roman demand. Finally, Antiochus offered to pay half the cost of the war.[78] Scipio's strategic concern was not with the present but with Rome's future security. As with Carthage and Macedonia, Scipio wished to reduce Antiochus's power so that he could not reasonably threaten Rome again. To destroy his empire would be a catastrophe, unleashing powerful satraps, kings, tyrants, and ambitious pretenders that Rome could not hope to control. To keep these centrifugal forces in check, Antiochus had to retain a sizable army. The solution was geographic. Antiochus could retain his throne and his army, but he had to withdraw from all cities and fortresses west of the Taurus Mountains. Henceforth, the eastern Mediterranean coast, like Greece and Macedonia, would be under Roman military protection.

The price of the Roman peace was too high, and Antiochus refused to pay it. The envoy asked to see Scipio in private, "to play upon the feelings of Publius Scipio. . . . Then he offered to return his son safely without ransom . . . and promised him an immense sum of money and a partnership in the entire realm, with the sole exception of the royal title, if, through his offices, he succeeded in obtaining peace."[79] Scipio refused but thanked him for the safety of his son if he was eventually returned. As for Antiochus, Scipio said, "In my public character I shall receive nothing from him and I shall give nothing. One thing I can give him at the present moment, and that is my sincere counsel. Go and tell him this from me; tell him to stop the war and not reject any terms of peace."[80]

The negotiations having collapsed, Scipio moved quickly to exploit whatever psychological advantage his refusal had given him with Antiochus. He ordered the army to march directly at Antiochus's forces encamped near Sardis, 150 miles from the Roman positions. The army had covered about half the distance when Scipio fell ill. It is curious to say the least that Scipio, Rome's most competent and famous soldier, was left behind at Elaea while the army moved on under the field command of Lucius, a soldier of little or no experience. Scipio had suffered illnesses before and always recovered. Why didn't the army wait to see if he did so this time? It was already mid-November and a winter battle was assured, so they were not trying to beat the weather. Antiochus was established in defensive positions, so they did not have any possibility of surprising him. There does not appear to have been any pressing *military* reason for the army to leave behind its greatest general and march off to battle without him. One might speculate, however, that Lucius may have chaffed under his older brother's authority for some time and took his opportunity to exert himself while his brother was unable to interfere. It is unlikely that Scipio would have voluntarily chosen to remain behind and lose the chance to lead men in battle one last time.

When Antiochus heard that Scipio was ill and had been left behind at Elaea, he sent his son to him without ransom and wished him well. Scipio was grateful for the gift of his son's life and sent a message to Antiochus. "Take back the message to the king," he instructed the envoy, "that the only way I can express my gratitude is by advising him not to come out to battle until he hears that I have returned to camp."[81] What Scipio meant by this cryptic reply has confounded military historians ever since.[82] Scipio's enemies in the Senate later used this statement to suggest that Scipio may have been guilty of treason in favoring Antiochus.

The charge is, of course, absurd. Perhaps Scipio wanted the fame that would have come from defeating the great king, or he knew that Lucius was not up to the task of leading the army in combat and might be defeated at the hands of the experienced Antiochus. As events turned out, Scipio's fears were not unfounded. Maybe Scipio still hoped that Antiochus might be brought to terms without war if the two old soldiers (Antiochus was fifty years old, Scipio forty-six) could discuss matters face-to-face. Or maybe he just wanted to return the favor of his son's safe return and ensure that Antiochus would not be slain on the battlefield. Scipio may have had all these thoughts in mind.

My view is that Scipio did not trust Lucius's ability to command. Scipio had not been able to stop Lucius from moving the army when he fell ill. Now, perhaps, he was attempting to prevent the battle by convincing Antiochus not to fight. Indeed, as the Roman army moved toward Sardis, Antiochus withdrew to Thyatira. As the Romans moved closer, he moved farther east and took up positions on the Campus Hyrcanius east of the city of Magnesia. These phased withdrawals were odd in that they involved a zigzag pattern of movement and took considerable time. Perhaps Antiochus was hoping Scipio would recover to take command of the Roman army. A more practical reason may have been, however, that the size of Antiochus's army and his squadrons of scythed chariots needed flat, open ground on which to assemble and maneuver, terrain the Campus Hyrcanius afforded. In any event, the two armies met on a misty winter morning in January 189 BCE.

The Roman army under Lucius numbered no more than thirty thousand men, including six thousand Greek auxiliaries, mostly light infantry. Antiochus commanded a force of seventy thousand troops, greatly outnumbering the Romans. Antiochus's army was a typical Seleucid army that had arisen in the wake of Alexander's collapsed empire, however; comprised of heterogeneous elements, it had little discipline, training, cohesion, or leadership. It included regular Greek heavy infantry drawn from the Greek settlements in Asia, Galatian mercenaries, Dahae horse archers from the Caspian area, and Arabs mounted on camels. Antiochus's cavalry numbered twelve thousand, both light and heavy (*cataphracti*), supported by twenty thousand light infantry (slingers, archers, javeliners) and fifty-four elephants. Livy tells us that they were Indian elephants that were far superior to the sixteen African elephants the Romans had because they outmatched the African animal in size and fighting spirit.[83] Scores of scythed chariots also took the field.[84] Scipio would certainly have been aware of the size and nature of Antiochus's army and would have known that his own army would be much smaller if and when things came to combat. Scipio would also have reckoned that his own army would have to rely on its superior discipline, officers, and tactical flexibility if it were to have a reasonable chance of defeating Antiochus. Along with the other factors already noted, these circumstances may also have played a role in Scipio's repeated attempts to reach a political settlement short of war.

Scipio was still in Elaea, so we can be certain that the Roman battle plan at Magnesia was not his. It is a reasonable assumption that as consul and commander in chief, Lucius formulated the plan. It had all the characteristics of an inexperienced field general. Lucius placed the Roman legions in the center of the line and the Latin legions on the left and center. Outside of this "regular battle line" he placed Eumenes' three thousand auxilliary troops on the right. Behind them he placed almost all the Roman cavalry, some three thousand horsemen, giving the wing a strong depth and capability for mounted counterattack.[85] On the left Lucius anchored his line on the river, relying on its steep banks to protect against envelopment. Here he deployed only four troops of cavalry (120 horsemen) and no auxiliaries at all. His auxiliaries were deployed to guard his camp in the rear.[86] It was a basic mistake and a disaster waiting to happen.

Antiochus was an experienced and skilled field general with a practiced eye, what Napoleon called the "coup d'oeil," for assessing a battlefield. He immediately spotted Lucius's error in tactical deployment. Livy tells the tale:

> What had happened was that Antiochus, on the right flank, had observed that the Romans, because of their reliance on the river, had no auxiliaries there except four troops of cavalry and these, in keeping contact with their comrades, were leaving the river back unsecured. He had therefore attacked the Roman cavalry with his auxiliaries and *cataphracti*; and he did not attack them in front only; he outflanked them by the river and kept pressing them hard on that side, until first the cavalry were put to flight and then the infantry next to them were driven headlong toward the camp.[87]

The hero of the day was one Marcus Aemilius, a military tribune in charge of the Roman camp. Seeing the Roman left collapse in panic, Aemilius "met them with his whole guard," some two thousand men, and tried to stop the chaos. First he implored the deserters to stop and then ordered his own men to "cut down the leading fugitives and with blows of the sword to drive back the mob that followed and make them face the enemy."[88] Aemilius saved Lucius from catastrophe. The Roman right had succeeded in breaking the enemy with its first attack and was pressing them back. Then Antiochus lost his nerve "when he saw that the troops whom he had just seen fleeing were returning to the fight, while another throng was pouring out of the camp, and yet another streaming towards him from the battle line, he turned his horse and fled."[89] The Romans pressed the attack on the enemy camp "causing great slaughter," while the "horsemen pursued the enemy all over the plain."[90] Livy says that fifty thousand infantry were slain that day and three thousand cavalry, but those figures may be exaggerations. Fifteen elephants and fourteen hundred men were taken prisoner. Among the Romans only three hundred infantry and twenty-four cavalry were killed, but many more were wounded.[91]

Both Antiochus and the Romans withdrew toward Sardis. Scipio, now well, arrived there a few days later and facilitated an approach from Antiochus's envoys to convince Lucius to begin peace talks. Scipio negotiated terms with Antiochus's envoys in which the Romans offered the same terms that they had offered earlier, "when Mars was still neutral and the issue of war still undetermined." Scipio, however, added one important new demand, saying, "but there will never be any real certainty in our minds that the Roman People has peace in any place where Hannibal is; we demand his surrender before all else."[92] As events turned out, Hannibal (and Antiochus) had anticipated the demand for Hannibal's head, and he was able to escape. He later committed suicide while in exile in a small kingdom on the Black Sea. Antiochus accepted the terms, and a mission went to Rome to plead with the Senate to accept the treaty. Lucius divided his army among winter quarters at Magnesia, Tralles, and Ephesus. Scipio returned to Rome sometime in 188 BCE. The old warhorse had tried his utmost to gain one more opportunity to lead men in battle before the end only to be prevented from doing so by illness.

THE TRIAL OF SCIPIO

What has become known as the Trial of the Scipio remains "among the most confused and uncertain episodes of Roman history."[93] No reliable accounts of the incident exist. Polybius deals with it only as an anecdote, which he admits "has been related to me for the double purpose of enhancing the fame of the departed [Scipio] and of encouraging future generations in the paths of honor."[94] However, Polybius is our most dependable source for Scipio's life. We must take him at his word when he says that "someone took upon himself to bring him [Scipio] to trial before the People in a manner usual at Rome, and produced many bitter accusations against him,"[95] and we can be fairly confident that some sort of trial of Scipio did indeed take place. Livy does not help us fill in the gaps Polybius left because Livy's account is based almost entirely on Valerius Antias's writing, which is mostly unreliable in its details.[96] Scullard, Haywood, and McDonald provide the best attempts to assemble an account of Scipio's trial, but each differs significantly from the other in key details and the sequence of events.[97] In the accounting of the events that follow, I have presented only the major details on which scholars agree.

The attempt to reduce Scipio's power and reputation was part of a decade-long battle in the Roman Senate led by Scipio's old enemy, Marcus Porcius Cato, and his faction of security-minded conservatives. They had opposed the terms of Scipio's peace with Hannibal and with Philip as too lenient, and now they opposed the terms with Antiochus on the same grounds. Behind the policy dispute was Cato's personal dislike for Scipio, which help shaped the less personal but important concern of other members of the Senate that the Scipionic oligarchy was becoming too powerful and that Scipio might not retire gracefully from his most recent success in Asia. Scipio had employed all his influence to secure Lucius the Asian command, and his success at convincing the Senate to agree had frightened some of the senators, who thought it an unprecedented abuse of power. The attack on Scipio began immediately after this incident, when Scipio turned to popular support for his line of policy. His appeal challenged the Senate's accepted prerogatives, and in that challenge lay much of the senators' suspicion regarding Scipio's willingness to abide by their control of the executive.[98]

There were also significant policy differences between the Scipionic faction and the opposition led by Cato. Scipio wished to base Roman policy toward the Hellenic world on the free relationships of alliances with the princes, tribes, and peoples of the West and with the kings, federations, and autonomous cities of the East. His policy was comprehensive and flexible, and it appreciated the constitutional function of all the different elements in the Hellenistic political systems. Rome's policy rested primarily on diplomacy to sustain a balance of power among the more powerful elements, with the use of force or occupation employed as a last resort. Scipio's policy was premised on Rome as the leader of a voluntary confederation in which Rome would act as first among equals. Those who opposed his policy did so on the grounds that Rome did not need a confederation as much as it needed security, and there was no more pressing area in which Rome's security interests required guarantees than in the East.[99] Two different views of Rome's future coincided with two different views of the scope of consular power as properly exercised within Rome's political system. The conflict between Scipio and his opponents surely had a personal dimension, but it also had serious domestic and foreign policy elements as well.

The two consuls elected for 188 BCE, Fulvius Nobilior and Manlius Vulso, were without close ties to either the Cato or Scipio factions. The Scipios requested that the command in Asia be prolonged so that they could see through the implementation of the terms they had proposed to Antiochus. The privilege of prolongation of command had been granted to Scipio after his victory in Africa, and the Scipios had every expectation that it would be granted again. Scipio's opponents saw an opportunity to deal him a defeat, and at the request of the consuls they demanded that the usual system of annual commands be followed. The Scipios were denied an extension, and Manlius Vulso was sent to Asia to assume command. The Senate also sent a ten-man commission to settle the final terms with Antiochus. The erosion of Scipio's political support was further evidenced when the Senate refused to accept Scipio's peace terms and demanded additional harsher terms. Left with no choice, the Scipios returned to Rome in 188 BCE, leaving the formulation of a final peace in Asia to others.

On his return Lucius requested a triumph for his victory at Magnesia. Once again the opposition made its influence felt. Led by Cato, Lucius's enemies argued that the most important victory in Asia had occurred at Thermopylae under Acilius Glabro's command, when he drove Antiochus from Europe, and that the battle of Magnesia merely completed a victory that had already been secured. The argument was nonsense, of course, but it reveals the intensity of the Scipios' opposition in the Senate. In the end, the Senate voted to permit Lucius his triumph. At the same time the new censors, Flamininus and Marcellus, who were not Scipio allies but were respectful of his reputation, appointed Scipio as princeps senatus for the third time in genuine gratitude for his service to the Republic. Affairs in Asia dragged on, and the Senate extended Manlius's command, snubbing the Scipios, whose similar request had been rejected the year before. The extension proved to be a mistake. Manlius had failed to secure Philip's help in crossing Thrace. When he was returning through Thrace with his army and loads of booty, the Thracian tribes attacked him, resulting in terrible losses of men and loot. Given Scipio's close relations with Philip, a slippery character indeed, the disaster would never have happened had he still been in command.

Soon after their return to Rome, the Scipios demonstrated their disagreement with the peace settlements in Greece and Asia by attacking the very generals the Senate had appointed to negotiate them. In 187 BCE M. Aemilius Lepidus brought charges against Fulvius Nobilior's conduct of the military command in Greece. When L. Furius Purpurio returned from the East, he was attacked for his treatment of Antiochus. The accusations' details are not important. It is sufficient to understand that those who brought the charges were members of the Scipionic faction. This public attack on the representatives of official senatorial policy revealed the lengths to which Scipio was prepared to go if his aims were blocked in the Senate. The threat to raise the public against the Senate must have hardened feelings against Scipio in that chamber. When Cato moved against the Scipios later in the year, he probably knew that he would have the support of the Senate for his cause.[100]

Sometime in 187 BCE, Cato attacked the Scipios in a further attempt to discredit them and weaken their influence. He urged two tribunes, both named Petillius, to demand that the Senate investigate Lucius regarding his misappropriation of some five hundred talents he had received from Antiochus as a condition of the armistice and to pay his troops. The charge was mismanagement of public funds. Lucius's view was that the money was *praeda*—booty over which he had complete control—and not *manubiae,* or public funds that had to be accounted for to the praetor.[101] It is important to note that these circumstances did not constitute a trial, because the Senate was not a court of law; however, at its own discretion or at another's urging, the Senate could choose to conduct an investigation (*quaestiones*) of any matter brought to its attention. After some consultation, the Senate refused to investigate. Undeterred, Cato arranged for the same charge to be introduced before the People (in one of the People's elected assemblies). There his agents carried a plebiscite and formally requested that the Senate investigate the matter. The Senate could hardly refuse the people's formal request and appointed a praetor to look into the matter. Scipio's friends were still active, and some senators, angry at what they regarded as popular interference in financial matters best left to their betters, joined to appoint Terentius Culleo, the Scipios' friend and ally, to head the investigation. Culleo delayed for a year until his term was finished, and the matter was dropped.

Two years later Cato raised the charge against Lucius again. What prompted the attack remains unknown, but it is possible that the political atmosphere in Rome was changing, becoming more conservative in foreign policy and cultural issues. Lucius was called before the Senate. Africanus, knowing that the attack was really directed at him, accompanied him to the hearing. According to Polybius, Africanus mounted the defense as if the attack had been made on his honesty and not on that of his brother. When asked for an accounting of the funds, Scipio replied that "he had the ledger [account books], but that he ought not to be called to account by anyone." But when the questioner persisted in asking for the accounts, Scipio ordered his brother to get them and bring them to the Senate. Then, Polybius says, "when the schedule was brought, he held it out in front of him, and tearing it to pieces in the sight of everybody bade the man who asked for it seek it out of these fragments!"

This arrogant act must have shocked even the more moderate members of the chamber and seemed to confirm Cato's accusation that Scipio felt he was above the law and had become a danger to Roman democratic processes. It could not have helped that Scipio next addressed the rest of the members just as arrogantly:

> How could you ask for the items of the expenditure of these three thousand talents, and yet no longer ask for an account of how and by whose agency the fifteen thousand talents which you received from Antiochus came into the treasury, nor how it was that you have become masters of Asia, Libya, and Iberia?[102]

The tribunes had brought these charges against a member of one of Rome's oldest families. It was for this reason, or perhaps, because the Senate did not like interference on such serious matters from the tribunes, that the Senate remained loyal to its princeps senatus and let the matter drop once more. But in destroying the account ledgers, Scipio had destroyed the very evidence he needed to put the matter finally to rest. He had no means with which to vindicate Lucius.

A short time later Cato moved against Africanus himself. Once more Cato convinced the tribunes to bring the charges in one of the People's assemblies.[103] The old charges of extravagance in winter quarters while in Sicily and the incident at Locri were raised again, perhaps revealing Cato's hand behind the accusations. Scipio was also accused of the theft of monies belonging to the state that Antiochus had given him to support his troops. "They alleged that his captured son had been restored without ransom; that in all other matters Antiochus had courted Scipio as if peace or war with Rome rested in his hands alone; that he had been a dictator rather than a subordinate to the consul in his province," and that he had sought to convince Greece and Asia "that one man was the source of Rome's power and the prop of her empire. Thus they assailed with spiteful calumny a man untouched by any ill repute."[104] In what is probably a false tale ad majorem Scipionis gloriam, Livy goes on to tell how Scipio came to the Forum to respond to the charges and delivered a speech in which he noted that the day was "the day on which I fought with good success in a pitched battle against Hannibal and the Carthaginians in Africa. Therefore, it is proper that on this day lawsuits and quarrels should be set aside."[105] Then he said he was going straight away to the temples to offer thanks, so "the assembled crowd with one accord left the forum and followed Scipio."[106]

But, as Livy says,

> this was the last day of splendor to shine on Publius Scipio. He
> foresaw that after that day a prospect of unpopularity and of
> struggles with tribunes; accordingly, after a further postponement
> of the trial, he retired to his villa at Liternum, with the fixed inten-
> tion of not appearing to conduct his defense. He was too great in
> spirit and character, too much accustomed to better fortune, to know
> how to stand his trial and to condescend to the lowly state of men
> who have to plead their cause.[107]

When the assembly reconvened to hold the trial sometime later, Lucius Scipio
appeared and gave illness as an excuse for his brother's absence. To some of the
tribunes his nonappearance was nothing less than another arrogant act that they
had come to attribute to Scipio. A motion was raised to have him brought before
them by force. One of the tribunes, Tiberius Sempronius Gracchus, rose in Scipio's
defense and delivered a powerful speech, saying that to bring such a great man as
Scipio before the rostrum would be a greater shame to Rome than to Scipio
himself. The popular assembly was then dismissed, and in a later meeting of the
Senate, the Senate expressed its support of Gracchus's speech and the sentiments
in it. The matter was permitted to drop as long as Scipio remained in Liternum.
"After that," Livy tells us, "there was silence about Africanus."

Scipio had gone into voluntary exile at Liternum. The town was located on
the coast about five miles north of Cumae on the bay of Naples, just south of
where the Volturnus River empties into the sea. It was one of five maritime colonies established in the area of Campania while Scipio was consul in 194 BCE.
Seneca tells us that Scipio's villa was modest by Roman standards (it had only a
small bath), but that it was well built and "well-defended." He also says that
Scipio used to cultivate the fields "with his own hands like the early Romans."[108]
He was no doubt wealthy by Roman standards, but he seems to have lived a
simple life much like the legendary Cincinnatus.

Scullard notes that Liternum was an unhealthy location and that it seemed a
curious place in which to retire.[109] Perhaps Scipio did so because he was honored
there as its founder and some of the colonists were his former soldiers. Roman
colonies, unlike Greek or Phoenician colonies, were not established for commercial reasons but for defense and control over hostile populations. It was the Roman practice to require of all conquered peoples, including those in southern

Italy, that they relinquish a portion of their land to the Roman state. These parcels became part of the ager publicus, or public land. When it was necessary to establish a new colony, the land was granted to a group of colonists, often former soldiers whose farms had been destroyed, "who marched out as a garrison into the conquered town."[110] The colony thus became a permanent Roman garrison that could act against any hostility by the surrounding towns. The colonies founded under Scipio's consulship were established on land probably taken from the Greeks who had settled around Naples more than a hundred years earlier. The defection of some southern Italian towns to Hannibal was probably also in Scipio's mind at the time, and the new colonies were designed to prevent any defection to Antiochus. It is reasonable to suspect that Scipio came to Liternum to retire because with some of his former soldiers settled there, he could spend the rest of his days among his old comrades, enjoying "the respect from the mouths of the chosen few." It is still an old soldier's habit.

Scipio Africanus, Rome's greatest general, died in 183 BCE in his villa at Liternum perhaps surrounded by the officers and men he had led in battle. Livy says that "when he was dying he gave instructions that he should be buried in that same country place, and that his tomb should be erected there, so that his funeral should not take place in an ungrateful homeland."[111]

9

Scipio's Place in Military History

IN TRYING TO DETERMINE the place Scipio Africanus occupies in the military history of the West, one cannot ignore Basil Liddell-Hart's claim that Scipio was the greatest military commander in all antiquity, exceeding in military skill and ingenuity such luminaries as Hannibal, Caesar, and Alexander the Great. Liddell-Hart goes further to suggest that only Napoleon equaled Scipio in military brilliance. The debate is beyond the scope of this book. It seems to me sufficient to ask, where does Scipio stand in the pantheon of Roman generals? Was he Rome's greatest general?

Military brilliance is not something that one can predict will likely emerge in any general, at least not with any degree of certainty. At the minimum, certain technical military skills and character traits are required, but what is required most is the *opportunity* to display one's abilities. The chance to do so is a function of living in challenging times. Had World War II not occurred Dwight Eisenhower would likely have remained "the best damned clerk I have had," as Gen. Douglas MacArthur once described his former staff officer. John Pershing might have been known only for the disastrous Mexican expedition had not World War I broken out. Ulysses S. Grant might have remained a failed drunk had the U.S. Civil War not provided him with the opportunity to command, and even Napoleon might have lived and died in obscurity had the French Revolution not forced itself on history. Scipio might have faced the same fate had it not been for the Second Punic War, which threatened Rome's existence and killed so many of its senior commanders that Rome was forced to offer younger men like Scipio the chance to lead its armies. Frederick the Great may have been right when he said that the most important quality of a general was *l'audace* (audacity). But it is Fortuna that offers the audacious general the circumstances in which his talents may make themselves known.

SCIPIO AFRICANUS

Few Roman generals held field commands as long as Scipio did and in equally trying times. Under the Republic, military commanders changed every year until the Second Punic War, when the shortage of experienced commanders forced Rome to extend commands for longer periods, sometimes *donec debellatum foret* (for the duration of the war). Of the Republic's generals, only Scipio's father, commanding the armies in Spain from 218 BCE until his death in battle in 212 BCE, held a field command for nearly as long as Scipio. In his turn, Scipio held command from 210 BCE to 202 BCE, the longest period for any Roman general during the Punic Wars.[1]

From Scipio's time until the outbreak of the Roman civil war in 88 BCE, only two Roman generals held extended periods of command while fighting Rome's foreign enemies. The first was Gaius Marius, who led for five years, and the other was Lucius Cornelius Sulla, who commanded for a total of seven years in the field. By 60 BCE the Roman Republic persisted in form only, and its generals were no longer servants of the state but *condottieri* whose private armies fought one another for power. One of these generals, Julius Caesar, held field commands for seven years during the Gallic campaign and another six years while fighting his political rivals in Italy, Spain, Africa, and Egypt.[2]

During the imperial period Rome produced a number of competent field commanders for its new professional armies, but its imperial policy did not permit a commander to remain too long in one position for fear that he and his troops might threaten the imperial house. Frequent appointments and rotations of high-level commanders became the rule, and a man's selection to senior command was conditioned on his demonstrated political loyalty to the emperor. Thus, the empire produced competent generals, not brilliant ones. Under this system Roman expansionism reached its height, and the Roman army assumed a defensive strategic posture, providing fewer opportunities for combat. Most Roman military engagements during the imperial period took place against tribal armies led by untalented commanders, reducing the opportunity for military greatness.[3] On balance, then, Scipio's tenure of command was among the longest of any of Rome's great generals. Only Caesar held military command for a longer period.

Command tenure is an important condition for military competency to emerge in a senior officer. As one of Israel's finest field commanders Gen. Avigdor Kahalani once told me, to be effective an army "must become an instrument of its commander's will," a condition that takes time and the experience of combat under the same leadership to develop.[4] Short periods of command require generals "to train on their troops" and have the effect of institutionalizing amateurism in leadership, as was often the case with Roman armies before Scipio.[5] The troops loved and worshipped Scipio and Caesar because both were in command long enough to earn their men's trust in their wartime judgment and abilities and their fairness and tolerance in dealing with the infractions their troops committed in peacetime. Combat soldiers cannot be managed to their deaths. They must be led. Thus, they must trust their commander not to squander them through incompetence. Troops must believe that their commander cares for them, even loves them, if they are to stand with him when their lives are placed at risk by the commander's own orders. Both Scipio and Caesar were noted (and criticized) for being close to their men, walking among them, and calling them "comrade" instead of the more formal "soldier." If this behavior was only acting on both men's parts, it was necessary acting and could succeed only because Scipio and Caesar held their commands as long as they did.

The militia armies under Scipio's command were more difficult to command effectively than the professional armies Marius established after the Roman disaster at Arausio (105 BCE). Scipio's armies had to be assembled, armed, and trained from the ground up before they could be taken into battle with any assurance of success. At times Scipio formed these armies from the remnants of other commanders' armies, as when he first assumed command in Spain. The force assembled to invade Africa was created around units that had been sent into exile because of their previously poor performance on the battlefield. Motivation in citizen militia armies is usually spotty at best and often poor. Some of Scipio's troops, who were often in the field for long periods, lost their farms and civilian livelihoods; therefore, his militia armies needed constant tending. Scipio's ability to assemble, train, discipline, motivate, and lead his armies required great personal command skills matched, perhaps, only by those of Alexander and Hannibal and by no other Roman general except Caesar.[6]

After the Marian reforms, generals commanded armies of professional quality that did not usually require exceptional command skills to keep them cohesive and in fighting trim. Severe discipline and a sufficient quantity of loot was all they usually needed, especially for the condottieri armies that plagued the country during the civil wars. The soldier's loyalty was to his commander—that is, the source of his pay and booty—and not to the country's government. The imperial period saw the rise of a military establishment that was professional in all aspects except its senior officer corps, which remained for the most part a group of amateurs appointed more out of political loyalty than for military ability.[7] During the empire the imperial system subsumed the Roman soldier's loyalty, and the centurions, who were responsible for maintaining unit cohesion and battle discipline, effectively assumed most leadership responsibilities of small combat units.[8]

The professional army was trained in a complete array of tactical capabilities, with the result that the generals who succeeded Scipio show a distinct lack of tactical imagination and innovation.[9] Even Caesar demonstrated little in the way of tactical imagination and seems to have limited his innovations to trying to attack downhill, putting his most experienced cohorts in the front line to maximize shock, and instructing his light infantry to retrieve thrown pila so that they could be thrown a second time. Alfred Bradford suggests that had other Roman generals' written accounts survived, "we might not be so quick to give Caesar primacy among Roman commanders."[10] Under these circumstances all the professional armies required was adequate senior commanders. For most of the imperial period Rome seems to have produced only a few outstanding generals and these men—Trajan, Germanicus, Hadrian, Domitian, and Vespasian, for example—were all members of the imperial household itself.

The professional armies that came after Marius's reforms in 99 BCE owed much to Scipio. He showed the Romans that an army fielded for long periods could be transformed into a fighting force of almost professional quality. Along with other political and economic factors, Marius may have had Scipio's success with his long-standing army in mind when he opened the ranks of the army to all classes of citizens, enlisted soldiers in military service for periods of sixteen years, and abandoned the militia army entirely. Scipio was also probably the first Roman commander to increase the legion's ability to withstand the shock of barbarian mass attacks by increasing the legion's manpower to sixty-two hundred men and the first to deploy some of this manpower in the form of cohorts comprising three maniples of heavy infantry and one of velites.[11] Although Marius kept the strength of the legion at sixty-two hundred men, he replaced the maniples with cohorts of six hundred men, ten cohorts to a legion.[12]

By Marius's time, all ranks of the new legions had the same standard equipment as the heavy infantry—the same armor and the basic combat weapon, the gladius. Scipio had discovered the gladius in Spain and was the first Roman commander to equip his troops with the new weapon. Scipio introduced arms drill for his troops in the Spanish campaign and established the gladius's basic tactical use as a stabbing weapon, and the Marian legions continued both the use of the weapon and its training method. Additional arms training of the legion's now professional soldiers expanded to include techniques then used in Roman gladiatorial schools. The legion's tactical mobility, which Scipio bequeathed to his successors, seems to have remained largely unchanged to the end of the Republic. Caesar's legions, for example, were organizationally similar to those under Marius a half-century earlier and retained the same three weaknesses: poor cavalry, insufficient light infantry, and no organic field intelligence collection capability. Caesar failed to correct any of these deficiencies.[13] While Marius deserves credit for his reforms, no reforms can be attributed to Caesar. No Roman general, then, had a more decisive impact on the Roman way of war than Scipio Africanus.

The ability of a great general can be measured to some extent by the quality of his opponents, and in this regard Scipio fought and defeated some of history's best-trained and brilliant commanders. Hasdrubal Barca; Hasdrubal, son of Gisgo; and Hannibal were the best field generals Carthage produced. Products of the Barcid military family dynasty, whose only occupation was war, they were heirs to a half-century tradition of combat experience. They commanded armies that underwent years of training, discipline, and experience and possessed a tactical flexibility unheard of in other armies that Roman commanders had ever faced. No Roman general after Scipio faced enemy commanders of this caliber again except, perhaps, when they fought each other during the civil wars. Even then their professional armies fought in mostly identical ways, so tactical brilliance and innovation was not evident. Both Alexander and Caesar fought mostly poorly trained armies led by mediocre commanders, as did the Roman commanders of the imperial period. When judging the greatness of a general by the quality of the commanders against whom he fought and triumphed, Scipio clearly stands apart as the best field commander Rome ever produced.

Scipio was more a modern general than a Homeric hero, and he rightly estimated that his value to the army as a commander was more important than his value as a warrior. He took few chances in battle and never seems to have placed himself directly in harm's way. During the siege of New Carthage he traveled the battlefield accompanied by three soldiers carrying large shields to protect him from missile fire. His soldiers became so accustomed to him remaining outside the critical battle space that when his attack on Locri faltered, Scipio spurred his men on by threatening to attempt to scale the walls himself. Until Scipio showed them otherwise, Roman generals had always fought in the front lines with their men, a demonstration of Roman warrior *virtu*, resulting in the loss of many fine officers to absolutely no military advantage. By Caesar's day, however, the tradition of demonstrating virtue in battle had become the centurion's province; consequently, the senior officer corps commanded by leading and rallying rather than by displaying the heedless bravery of a heroic fighter.[14] This shift in emphasis was the logical result of the increasing complexity of warfare and the politicization of command selection. But Scipio had first identified the problem and devised its solution fifty years earlier.

As long as the legion's tactical repertoire consisted of only frontal and rearward movement, it did not matter where the commander positioned himself, for once the legion was set in motion little else was tactically possible. Scipio's introduction of a new tactical repertoire that could be employed on command *during* the battle required the commander to be able to see the battlefield and to judge when to order a change in tactics. To properly direct the battle now required that the commander remain apart from the fighting as Hannibal usually did in order to coordinate the movements of his highly flexible army. That Alexander fought among his men even though his army was tactically flexible stems from his Hellenic culture, which placed a high value on personal heroism as a necessary requirement for a successful general. Roman society also placed great value on martial heroism, and we may surmise that Scipio personally had to overcome its influence before attempting his new method of field command. Recall that when Scipio's political enemies roundly criticized him for lacking martial virtu, he responded that his mother had given birth to "a general, not a warrior!"[15]

This new method of command caught on slowly, however; after Scipio many Roman commanders continued to expose themselves to battlefield dangers. By Caesar's day, however, most Roman commanders had relinquished their roles as heroic examples. By the time of Augustus (63 BCE–CE 14), who rarely ventured into the crucible of battle himself,[16] Roman generals were mostly appointed aristocrats who directed more than commanded thoroughly professional armies, almost eliminating the heroic model of command leadership. It was Scipio who first introduced the modern method of commanding an army from outside the immediate battle space.

Scipio's skill in military affairs went beyond his demonstrated ability as a field commander. He was also one of Rome's greatest grand strategists. He always assessed the application of military force against its value in obtaining the larger political goals for which wars are fought. For Scipio war was always a means to an end, and the end was the larger strategic concerns of the Roman state. It is, then, no surprise that his victories on the battlefield ultimately shaped the direction of Roman expansion, even if the Roman political establishment took years to realize it. After defeating Greece at Pydna (168 BCE), however, Roman generals seemed to lack any sense of strategy at all. They demonstrated this deficiency especially in the period of the Social Wars and during the civil wars, where generals fought one another for personal power and fame undirected at any national strategic goals. Thus while Caesar was a great operational level commander, he did not seem to possess any strategic vision for Rome that went beyond establishing his own power. Even within the area of operational strategy, Caesar sometimes made terrible mistakes. He failed to pacify Gaul completely before he invaded Britain and precipitated a Gallic revolt, and he lingered long in Egypt after defeating Pompey, allowing Pompey's supporters to gather another army and take up positions in Spain.[17] Rome would have to await Augustus before it possessed a grand strategist of Scipio's caliber again.

Scipio owed his success in shaping Rome's strategic direction in large part to his political skill. In this area, Scipio was similar to a modern general who, in democratic societies at least, must muster some degree of political acumen to succeed in getting their views heard and accepted. Scipio commanded when the Roman Senate was at the height of its political power and when political direction of military affairs was common. To succeed as a strategist Scipio had to contend with the swirling forces of Roman politics at his back. Like modern senior commanders, he had to sustain himself politically to achieve his military goals. On the contrary Alexander had complete command of his political and military establishments and Hannibal was left mostly free of the political influences of the Carthaginian Senate until the very end of his adventures. Scipio not only had to fight Carthaginian generals but also had to contend with Rome itself.[18]

Later, during the civil wars, politics governed all aspects of military activity; consequently, there were no restraints on the condottieri generals' actions. The Roman state's strategic direction disappeared completely, and the Republic was destroyed in the process. Under the empire, Rome was once more able to restrain its generals, and political direction became the primary force in Roman military affairs.[19] Thus, strategy was always decided in the political arena and rarely by those generals, who, in most cases, were selected less for their military abilities than for their political loyalties. No general of the imperial period compares favorably with Scipio as either an operational-level or grand strategist.

Napoleon is supposed to have remarked that an army traveled on its stomach. This maxim was no less true in ancient times.[20] One of Scipio's greatest abilities was as a logistician. He appreciated the importance of ensuring that his army was adequately supplied. In this aspect Scipio was superior to Caesar, who repeatedly failed to attend to his logistics and had to alter his campaign plans to compensate. At times, Caesar needlessly placed his army at risk when he ignored logistical matters.[21] Scipio never undertook a campaign or even a battle without making certain that his army was adequately supplied, and he took great care never to sever his line of supply when engaged in extended tactical operations. Ancient historians record not a single instance of Scipio being required to change his operational plans because he ran short of supplies. Scipio was not only a brilliant operational planner and commander but an excellent logistician and administrator as well.

A word needs to be said about Scipio's humanity when carrying out military operations. For Scipio, force was always a means to greater strategic ends, and he recognized that pointless brutality worked against achieving those ends even when Rome was victorious on the battlefield. He understood that wars were not won by battles alone. Rome's strategic interests lay in stable, voluntarily peaceful relationships with its former enemies. To this end Scipio's military campaigns were accompanied by little brutality. He often took no hostages, preferring instead to rely on their word that they would not take up arms. His troops treated the population of the countryside with respect. Captured populations were not enslaved but turned back to working the land. Local kings were permitted to retain their thrones. Scipio's behavior and that of his troops stand in stark contrast to later Roman generals who often exterminated or enslaved whole populations. Scipio could order brutality imposed when circumstances required it, as when he ordered the slaughter of New Carthage's civilian population until the Carthaginian holdouts surrendered or the destruction of two Spanish towns that had treasonously gone over to the Carthaginians. These events stand out precisely because they were rare in Scipio's campaigns and were carried out as means to the larger strategic end of convincing Rome's adversaries that loyalty to Rome was their only reasonable course. In the ultimate sense, of course, all war is immoral in the application of its means, even when the ends for which it is fought are sometimes moral. But Scipio practiced war in a manner that left room for humane treatment, imposing limits on its accompanying violence. In this light, he was a unique figure in the military history of Rome.

Students of military history find in Scipio a moral and practical example of the successful modern commander serving a democratic state. He was a loyal soldier committed to the safety and security of his country and to its Republican form of government, which he believed was the guarantor of individual liberty. Scipio's commitment to Republican values was absolute, and rather than challenge them he went into voluntary exile. He put his country before himself. A lover of freedom, intellectual and otherwise, he was that rarest of military men with an inquisitive mind always open to new possibilities. In this regard he is the model of what we must require of our own senior military commanders. We must not permit them to become narrow experts in the technical orchestration of violence unhindered by political and moral values. The application of military force always has larger political implications, and victory in the interconnected world of the twenty-first century is rarely won only by defeating the enemy on the battlefield. This combination of military and intellectual skill was what made Scipio a great soldier, strategist, reformer, tactical innovator, administrator, and leader of men in war. Our own military men could do no better than to emulate him. He was, after all, the greatest general that Rome produced.

Notes

PREFACE

1. For an analysis of the source materials and historical accuracy of the *Punica,* see John Nicol, *The Historical and Geographical Sources Used by Silius Italicus* (Oxford, UK: Basil Blackwell, 1936).

2. The distance from New Carthage to Tarraco is a matter of some confusion. Polybius says the distance is 2,600 stades, or 280 Roman miles. In her translation of Polybius's work, Evelyn Shuckburgh gives the distance as 325 Roman miles, while Ian Scott-Kilvert's translation says it is "nearly 500 miles." When string measured on a map, the distance appears to be just over four hundred English miles. If the route is calculated at a 7 percent minimal grade to compensate for the undulations of the ground, however, another 8 to 10 percent of the distance must be added to the distance actually walked. Thus, the distance between the two points is then 440 English miles. The distance from the Ebro River to Tarraco is 40 miles, and from the Ebro to New Carthage is approximately 400 miles.

3. N. Whatley, "On the Possibility of Reconstructing Marathon and Other Ancient Battles," *Journal of Hellenic Studies* 84 (1964): 119–39. Whatley's article on the historical method of reconstructing ancient battles was originally written in 1913, presented at Oxford in 1922, and published in 1964. It is required reading for anyone attempting to write military history.

4. Richard A. Gabriel and Karen S. Metz, *From Sumer to Rome: The Military Capabilities of Ancient Armies* (Westport, CT: Greenwood Press, 1991).

5. In addition I have consulted what the Institute of Classical Studies of the University of London, in Tim Cornell, Boris Rankov, and Philip Sabin's *The Second Punic War: A Reappraisal* (1996), regards as the basic works necessary for analyzing Scipio and Hannibal. They are a subset of the scholarship on the general subject of the Punic Wars. "The glamour and dominance of the two leading protagonists of the War, Hannibal and Scipio Africanus, have ensured that its strategy and military narrative have continued to receive attention, from both professional soldiers and historians, at a time when the genre is seriously out of fashion. Amongst the soldiers, N. Bagnall (1990) is only the latest of a line which includes J. Kromayer and G. Veith (1912), B.H. Liddell-Hart (1926), J.F.C. Fuller (1954) and Viscount Montgomery of Alamein (1968). Amongst the

historians, the fundamental studies in the works of H. Delbruck (1907), E. Meyer (1913), and G. de Sanctis (1917), not to mention the contribution made by F.W. Walbank's *Historical Commentary on Polybius* (1957), have more recently been supplemented by those of H.H. Scullard (1970), T.A. Dorey and D.R. Dudley (1971), D. Proctor (1971), J.F. Lazenby (1978), B. Caven (1980), P. Connolly (1981), and J. Briscoe (1989)."

6. Philip Sabin, "The Mechanics of Battle in the Second Punic War," in Cornell, Rankov, and Sabin, *The Second Punic War,* 61.

1. THE MAN

1. Paul Nicorescu, "La Tomba degli Scipioni," *Ephemeris Daco-Romana* 1 (1923): 1–56.
2. A marble bust that for years had been thought to be of Scipio was revealed to be the bust of a Roman priest of Isis. For a photo of this bust, see John Warry, *Warfare in the Classical World: An Illustrated Encyclopedia of Weapons, Warriors, and Warfare in the Ancient Civilisations of Greece and Rome* (London: Salamander Books, 1980), 115. In 1972 a marble bust long thought to be of Drusus was reexamined and pronounced to be of Scipio. See G. Hafner, "Das Bildnis des P. Cornelius Scipio Africanus," *Archaeologischer Anzeiger* (1972), 474–92. But the fact that the bust is wearing a style of helmet typical of the Thracian auxiliary cavalry of the third century BCE casts doubt on this finding.
3. R. Blatter, "Ein mermutliches Munzbildnis des Scipio Africanus," *Gazette Numismatique Suisse* 24 (1974): 78–79.
4. Silius Italicus, *Punica,* trans. J. D. Duff (Cambridge, MA: Harvard University Press, 1934), vol. 1, bk. 7, 433.
5. Ibid. "Such a display of vigor he gave before the ranks. Often his flying feet outstripped a courser [fast horse] as it flew, cruelly spurred over the open plain; often rising to his full height, he threw stone or spear beyond the limits of the camp."
6. Alexander Allen, "Barba," in *A Dictionary of Greek and Roman Antiquities,* ed. William Smith (London: John Murray, 1854), 196–98.
7. For Greek and Roman education under the Republic, see Erich S. Gruen, *Culture and National Identity in Republican Rome* (Ithaca, NY: Cornell University Press, 1992), chapters 2 and 3.
8. John Boardman, Jasper Griffin, and Oswyn Murray, *The Oxford History of Greece and the Hellenistic World* (Oxford, UK: Oxford University Press, 1991), 393. See also Thomas Gartner, "Die praemilitaerische Ausbildung des Scipio Africanus," *MAIA* 55, no. 2 (2003): 317–19.
9. Polybius, *The Histories of Polybius,* trans. Evelyn S. Shuckburgh (Bloomington: Indiana University Press, 1962), bk. 10, 2. All citations of Polybius in this work are from this translation.
10. Richard M. Haywood, *Studies on Scipio Africanus* (Baltimore, MD: Johns Hopkins Press, 1933), 24.
11. See F. W. Walbank, "The Scipionic Legend," *Proceedings of the Cambridge Philological Society* 13 (1967): 54–69. Walbank argues that once Scipio's troops watched the water drain from the lagoon at New Carthage after he had ordered them to have

faith in Neptune this became the basis for the later exaggerated claims that Scipio had a special relationship with the gods. Polybius may have been trying to make Scipio more admirable to his Greek audience, who would have regarded the religion of third-century Rome as primitive and grounded in superstition.

12. Ibid., 43.

13. E. Meyer, *Kleine Schriften*, vol. 2 (Germany: Halle A. S., 1924), 438.

14. W. W. Fowler, *The Religious Experience of the Roman People* (London: Taylor and Francis, 1911), 364–65.

15. Haywood, *Studies on Scipio Africanus*, 44.

16. Moses and Muhammad, for example, were both excellent field commanders and deeply religious men. Buddha was a prince in India's warrior class and probably an experienced warrior. Indeed, it was probably his bloody experience with Indian warfare that led him to turn away from it and seek peace in contemplation. See Richard A. Gabriel, *Muhammad: Islam's First Great General* (Norman: Oklahoma University Press, 2007); and by the same author, *The Military History of Ancient Israel* (Westport, CT: Greenwood Press, 2003).

17. Polybius, *The Histories of Polybius*, bk. 10, 2.

18. Ibid.

19. Ibid., 3.

20. Italicus, *Punica*, vol. 1, bk. 5, 33.

21. Ibid., vol. 2, bk. 16, 409.

22. Mary Frances Williams, "Shouldn't You Have Come and Talked to Me About It? Democracy and a Mutiny in Scipio's Army," *Ancient History Bulletin* 15, no. 4 (2001): 143–53.

23. K. W. Meiklejohn, "Roman Strategy and Tactics from 509 to 202 BC," *Greece and Rome* 7, no. 21 (1938): 171–73. For Scipio's tactical reforms, see also M. J. V. Bell, "Tactical Reform in the Roman Republican Army," *Historia: Zeitschrift für alte Geschichte* 14 (1965): 404–22. The manipular legion was formed during the Samnite wars (340–290 BCE), when the old Greek-style phalanx proved too brittle and unmaneuverable to counter surprise attacks. The legion's tactical array was formed at the same time and did not change until Scipio altered it during his campaign in Spain. In an analogous sense, Scipio is the Roman Epaminondas, the Greek commander who introduced to hoplite warfare the refused wing, the only significant change in Greek tactics in more than two hundred years.

24. See Thomas A. Dorey, "Scipio Africanus as a Party Leader," *Klio* 39 (1961): 191–98. Dorey argues that Scipio lacked the necessary personality and skills to succeed in Roman politics.

25. Daniel A. Fournie, "Harsh Lessons: Roman Intelligence in the Hannibalic War," *International Journal of Intelligence and Counterintelligence* 17 (2004): 511.

26. Italicus, *Punica*, vol. 1, bk. 4, 202–3.

27. Polybius, *The Histories of Polybius*, bk. 10, 3.

28. The essential details are recorded in Italicus, *Punica*, vol. 1, bk. 4, 203. An alternative tradition exists that attributes the rescue not to Scipio but to a slave. See Titus Livius (Livy), *The History of Rome From Its Foundation: The War With Hannibal*, trans. by Aubrey De Selincourt (London: Penguin, 1965), bk. 21, 46; and F. W.

Walbank, *A Historical Commentary on Polybius* (Oxford, UK: Oxford University Press, 1970), 198–99. All citations from Livy are from Selincourt's translation.

29. William Smith, *A Dictionary of Greek and Roman Antiquities* (London: John Murray, 1854), 952–53.
30. Livy, *The History of Rome From Its Foundation*, ii, 20.
31. Richard A. Gabriel, *The Great Captains of Antiquity* (Westport, CT: Greenwood Press, 2001), 105.
32. For an analysis of the qualifications of the lesser men who may have competed with Scipio for the Spanish command, see Haywood, *Studies on Scipio Africanus,* 51–52.
33. Charles E. Bennett, *Frontinus: The Strategemata* (New York: Loeb, 1925), bk. 4, 7, 4. The work is out of print but may be obtained in full translation online at http://penelope.uchicago.edu/Thayer/E/Roman/Texts/Frontinus/Strategemata/1*.html#1.
34. For the distinction between battle managers and heroic warriors, see Sabin, "The Mechanics of Battle in the Second Punic War," 68.
35. B. H. Liddell-Hart cites Livy in *Scipio Africanus: Greater Than Napoleon* (New York: Da Capo Press, 1994), 11. For an excellent analysis of the military tribune's role as well as that of the legion's other officers, see Smith, *A Dictionary of Greek and Roman Antiquities,* 489–511.
36. For a description of the deployment of cavalry forces at the Trebia, see Polybius, *The Histories of Polybius,* bk. 3, 73.
37. On this implication, see Liddell-Hart, *Scipio Africanus,* 12, and R. T. Ridley, "Was Scipio Africanus at Cannae?" *Latomus* 36 (1977): 110–13.
38. Italicus, *Punica,* vol. 2, bk. 6, 327.
39. Michael Grant, *The Army of the Caesars* (New York: Charles Scribner's Sons, 1974), xxxiii.
40. Livy, *The History of Rome From Its Foundation,* bk. 22, 55.
41. For a detailed examination of Republican Rome's governmental structure and operations, including the office of an aedile, see David Shotter, *The Fall of the Roman Republic* (London: Routledge, 2005), appendix 2.
42. Livy, *The History of Rome From Its Foundation,* bk. 25, 2.
43. See *Punica,* vol. 2, bk. 5, 255. Italicus gives us an account of the Scipio brothers' deaths. Scipio's father comes to his son in a dream and tells him about his death to alleviate his son's grief. "Hasdrubal was crippled by defeat, and I was in victorious pursuit of him, when suddenly the Spanish cohorts, a mercenary rabble whom Hasdrubal had enslaved to Libyan gold [bribed], broke their ranks and deserted our standards. Thus left in the lurch by our allies, we were far inferior in numbers to the enemy; and they formed a dense ring around us. We died not unavenged, my son; we played the man on that last day and ended our lives in glory." This story differs significantly from Livy's account in *The History of Rome From Its Foundation,* bk. 25, 36.
44. Italicus, *Punica,* vol. 2, bk. 5, 233. Scipio himself seems to be telling us that he had already served long tours with the army before being assigned to Spain. In addressing the mutineers in 206 BCE, Scipio said that "having lived with the army

almost from my boyhood, I know soldiers through and through." See Livy, *The History of Rome From Its Foundation,* bk. 28, 27.

45. For an analysis of the problems associated with Scipio's imperium and the resulting legalisms surrounding the assignment of Roman military commands, see Robert Develin, "The Roman Command Structure in Spain, 218–190 BC," *Klio* 62, no. 2 (1980): 355–67. For more on the age requirements of an office, see also Shotter, *The Fall of the Roman Republic.*

46. Howard H. Scullard, *Scipio Africanus in the Second Punic War* (Cambridge, UK: Cambridge University Press, 1933), 41.

47. Livy, *The History of Rome From Its Foundation,* bk. 16, 18.

48. Haywood, *Studies on Scipio Africanus,* 46.

49. Theodore Mommsen, *History of Rome,* trans. William Purdie Dickson (New York, 1891), 189.

50. G. B. de Sanctis, *Storia dei Romani,* vol. 3, *L'eta delle guerre puniche* (Torino: Fratelli Bucca, 1916–17), 452. Volume 3 contains the history of the Punic Wars and is the most useful.

51. Werner Schur, *Scipio Africanus und die Begrundung der römischen Weltherrschaft* (Leipzig, Germany: Dieterich, 1927), 23.

52. Fournie, "Harsh Lessons," 519.

53. J. E. Lendon, *Soldiers and Ghosts: A History of Battle in Classical Antiquity* (New Haven, CT: Yale University Press, 2005), 307.

54. Haywood, *Studies on Scipio Africanus,* 53.

55. James Parker, *Comparing Strategies of the Second Punic War: Rome's Strategic Victory Over the Tactical/Operational Genius, Hannibal Barca.* (Carlisle Barracks, PA: U.S. Army War College, 2001), 5.

56. For a detailed critique of Hannibal's strategy, see B. D. Hoyos, "Hannibal: What Kind of Genius?" *Greece and Rome,* 2nd ser., 30, no. 2 (October 1983): 171–80. See also chapter 2 of this volume, "The Strategic Setting"; and John Lazenby, *Hannibal's War* (Warminster, UK: Aris and Phillips, 1978), 226–27, 255–57.

57. For an analysis of Alexander's influence on Hannibal's tactics, see Giovanni Brizzi, "Hannibal—Punier und Hellenist," *Das Altertum* (1991), 201–10. Hannibal was very much a Hellenistic general in his imitation of Alexander and his use of cavalry as an arm of decision. Hannibal realized, however, that the weakness of Alexander's tactical doctrine was that his infantry was too heavy and incapable of maneuver. Hannibal's major tactical innovation was to increase the maneuverability of his infantry and to use it more in concert with his cavalry than Alexander had used his infantry. For a more complete analysis of Hannibal as a Hellene, see G. C. Picard, *Hannibal* (Paris: C. Klincksiek, 1967), 321–50, and Meiklejohn, "Roman Strategy and Tactics," 176.

58. Carl von Clausewitz, *On War,* trans. Michael Howard and Peter Paret (Princeton, NJ: Princeton University Press, 1989), 28.

59. For a list of Scipio's intelligence successes during the war, see Fournie, "Harsh Lessons," 530–31.

60. Ibid., 529.

61. The Carthaginians and their Gallic allies destroyed six Roman armies in ambushes in a little more than three years. These included Lucius Manlius's operation against the Gauls in 218 BCE, the Trebia River in late 218 BCE, and Lake Trasimene in 217 BCE. Later that year Servilius was ambushed by Maharbal, Municus ambushed at Gereonium, and Lucius Albinus ambushed in the Litani Forest.

62. Hannibal's intelligence service was, by contrast, excellent and utilized commercial agents, advanced scouts, Gallic allies, and political provocateurs to gather strategic intelligence and foment political dissent. It used the Numidian light cavalry extensively to gather tactical intelligence. Perhaps the most important element of the Carthaginian intelligence effort was that Hannibal himself was an enthusiastic proponent of its use.

63. Fournie, "Harsh Lessons," 512.

64. Ibid., 512–13. For material on the role of intelligence in ancient Rome, see Rose Mary Sheldon, "Tinker, Tailor, Caesar, Spy: Espionage in Ancient Rome" (Ph.D. diss., University of Michigan, Ann Arbor, 1987); Rose Mary Sheldon, *Intelligence Activities in Ancient Rome: Trust in the Gods, but Verify* (New York: Frank Cass, 2005); Francis Dvornik, *Origins of Intelligence Services: The Ancient Near East, Persia, Greece, Rome, Byzantium, the Arab Muslim Empires, the Mongol Empire, China, Muscovy* (New Brunswick, NJ: Rutgers University Press, 1974); and N. J. E. Austin and N. B. Rankov, *Exploratio: Military and Political Intelligence in the Roman World From the Second Punic War to the Battle of Adrianople* (London: Routledge, 1995). All reach the conclusion that Rome had no formal intelligence service under the Republic.

65. The great captains of antiquity against whom Scipio can be compared are Thutmose III, Sargon II, Philip of Macedon, and Hannibal. For the comparative analysis of these great captains of antiquity, see Gabriel, *Great Captains of Antiquity*, chapter 8, "On the Origins of Great Captains."

2. THE STRATEGIC SETTING

1. Richard A. Gabriel, *The Campaigns of Hannibal* (Carlisle Barracks, PA: U.S. Army War College, 1992), 4–5.

2. J. H. Thiel, *Studies on the History of Roman Sea Power in Republican Times* (Amsterdam: North-Holland Publishing Company, 1946), 443–45. The Romans constructed a new fleet built around a captured ship of Rhodian design that was renowned for its seaworthiness and speed. Polybius tells us the *corvus* was 36 feet long, 4 feet wide, and had handrails.

3. Polybius, *The Histories of Polybius*, bk. 1, 65–66. The war was so vicious that it was called the "truceless war."

4. John Rich, "The Origins of the Second Punic War," in Cornell, Rankov, and Sabin, *The Second Punic War*, 1–37.

5. Yigael Yadin, *The Art of Warfare in Biblical Lands in Light of Archaeological Discovery*, 2 vols. (New York: McGraw-Hill, 1964), 19.

6. Richard A. Gabriel and Donald W. Boose Jr., "Caesar's Campaigns," in *Great Battles of Antiquity: A Strategic and Tactical Guide to Great Battles That Shaped the*

Development of War, ed. Richard A. Gabriel and Donald W. Boose, Jr. (Westport, CT: Greenwood Press, 1994), 286. See also Peter Connolly, *Greece and Rome at War* (Englewood Cliffs, NJ: Prentice-Hall, 1981), 153.

7. Polybius, *The Histories of Polybius,* bk. 1, 26. The five quinqueremes at the battle of Ecnomus in 256 BCE are recorded as having 300 oarsmen and 120 marines aboard. It is assumed as a matter of course that Roman quinqueremes were outfitted in the same numbers. Warry gives the number of people aboard a Roman quinquereme as 270 oarsmen, 30 sailors, and 40 marines in a normal peacetime complement. In war the number of marines increased to 120 men. See Warry, *Warfare in the Classical World,* 118–19.

8. Carthage possessed only a hundred warships to the Roman's 220 at the outbreak of the war. See Hoyos, "Hannibal: What Kind of Genius?" 172.

9. Ibid. For a contrary view, see John Lazenby, "Was Maharbal Right?" in Cornell, Rankov, and Sabin, *The Second Punic War,* 46.

10. Hoyos, "Hannibal: What Kind of Genius?" 176.

11. Ibid., 179.

12. Polybius, *The Histories of Polybius,* bk. 3, 38. For different strength numbers and how Polybius calculated them, see also Leonard Cottrell, *Hannibal: Enemy of Rome* (New York: Holt, Rinehart, and Winston, 1960), 35–40.

13. Strategists have debated whether Scipio's decision to send the army to Spain and to recall Sempronius from his mission in Sicily to invade Africa was the right decision. Perhaps it would have been better to hold Gnaeus's army in place to check Hannibal and raise more forces while Sempronius carried out his invasion of Africa. Spain was important, but the operational center of gravity was Italy. Even after Rome had conquered Spain, Hannibal did not retire from Italy. Only the threat to Carthage itself forced Hannibal to withdraw from Italian soil. Had Sempronius's invasion gone ahead and Hannibal's line of retreat to Spain been left open, he might have retired to protect Carthage. In that case there would have been no battles at Trebia, Trasimene, or Cannae.

14. Polybius, *The Histories of Polybius,* bk. 3, 71.

15. Ibid., 72–74.

16. Hannibal and the Carthaginian commanders in Spain extensively used the elephant. The military use of the animal was not appreciated by Roman and later Western historians. For a treatment of the elephant in ancient and modern warfare, see John M. Kistler, *War Elephants* (Westport, CT: Praeger, 2006); H. H. Scullard, *The Elephant in the Greek and Roman World* (Ithaca, NY: Cornell University Press, 1974); R .F. Glover, "The Tactical Handling of the Elephant," *Greece and Rome* 17, no. 49 (1948): 1–11; and William Gowers, "The African Elephant in Warfare," *African Affairs* 46, no. 182 (1947): 42–49.

17. For the casualty figures at Trebia, see Polybius, *The Histories of Polybius,* bk. 3, 74.

18. Livy notes that the place was *loca nata insidiis* (born for ambush). As Lazenby notes, "What general in command of an army of 25,000 men expects to be ambushed?" See Lazenby, *Hannibal's War,* 40.

19. Livy, *The History of Rome From Its Foundation,* bk. 12, 4–5.

20. Hannibal sought the same objective after the battle of Cannae when he told his prisoners that "his war with the Romans was not to the death—he was fighting for honor and power." See Livy, *The History of Rome From Its Foundation*, bk. 22, 58. Hannibal's comments also clearly reflect his heroic Hellenistic view of war.

21. Polybius, *The Histories of Polybius*, bk. 3, 113–14.

22. Ibid.

23. Livy, *The History of Rome From Its Foundation*, bk. 22, 49.

24. Lazenby, *Hannibal's War*, 47. Polybius puts the number of Roman dead at seventy thousand, with ten thousand taken prisoner, compared to fifty-seven hundred Punic losses (Polybius, *The Histories of Polybius*, bk. 3, 84–85). See also M. Samuels, "The Reality of Cannae," *Militärgeschichtliche Mitteilungen* 47 (1990): 7–29; and Victor Davis Hanson, "Cannae," in *Experience of War*, ed. R. Cowley (New York: Putnam,1992), 42–49.

25. Livy, *The History of Rome From Its Foundation*, bk. 22, 49.

26. See John Terraine, *The Smoke and the Fire: Myths and Anti-myth of War, 1861–1945* (London: Sidgwick and Jackson, 1980), 45. Terraine says that on the first day of the battle of the Somme—July 1, 1916—the British army's losses "were probably greater than those of any army in any war on one single day." But 19,240 British soldiers were actually killed in action, while another 21,977 were listed as missing or as prisoners. At Cannae, 48,200 Roman and allied soldiers were killed. See Lazenby, *Hannibal's War*, 47, note 56.

27. Livy, *The History of Rome From Its Foundation*, bk. 22, 51.

28. Richard A. Gabriel, "The Carthaginian Empire and Republican Rome," in *Empires at War: A Chronological Encyclopedia*, vol. 2, ed. Richard A. Gabriel (Westport, CT: Greenwood Press, 2005), 401; also Lazenby, *Hannibal's War*, 45.

29. Livy, *The History of Rome From Its Foundation*, bk. 22, 51.

30. For the construction and use of siege machinery, see Richard A. Gabriel, "Siegecraft," in *Soldiers' Lives Through History*, ed. Richard A. Gabriel (Westport, CT: Greenwood Press, 2006), chapter 17. Hannibal's engineers certainly had both the expertise and raw materials to construct siege machinery. One reason for his not making extensive use of this machinery in his Italian campaign was his reluctance to besiege Roman allied cities, knowing the resultant destruction would make it more difficult to win them over to his cause.

31. For the reasons, summarized here, for Hannibal's decision not to march on Rome, see Lazenby, *Hannibal's War*, 85–86.

32. For the argument that Maharbal may have been right, see Hoyos, "Hannibal: What Kind of Genius?" 177.

33. Lazenby, "Was Maharbal Right?" 44–45.

34. Ibid. For a detailed analysis of Rome's allies and their loyalty and disloyalty during the Second Punic War, see J. S. Reid, "Problems of the Second Punic War: Rome and Her Italian Allies," *Journal of Roman Studies* 5 (1915): 87–124.

35. Polybius, *The Histories of Polybius*, bk. 3, 95–96. It is often forgotten that Gnaeus Scipio's victory at the Ebro was a great naval victory and not a land battle.

36. Scullard, *Scipio Africanus in the Second Punic War*, 49–50.

37. Ibid., 52.

3. THE ARMIES

1. Few sources describe the Carthaginian army in any detail, and the information contained in this section is drawn largely from them. See B. H. Warmington, *Carthage: A History* (London: Robert Hale, 1958), 45–49; Terence Wise, *Armies of the Carthaginian Wars: 265–146 B.C.* (London: Osprey, 1982); Richard A. Gabriel, "The Carthaginian Empire and Republican Rome, 814–146 B.C.E.," in *Empires at War,* vol. 2 (Westport, CT: Greenwood Press, 2006); D. Head, *Armies of the Macedonian and Punic Wars, 359 BC to 146 BC* (England: Wargames Research Group, 1982). Other sources include Brian Caven, *The Punic Wars* (London: Weidenfeld and Nicolson, 1980); Lazenby, *Hannibal's War*; and N. Bagnall, *The Punic Wars* (London: Hutchinson, 1990). One can also gather this same material reading through Livy, *The History of Rome*; Polybius, *The Histories of Polybius*; and volumes 7 and 8 of the *Cambridge Ancient History.* The information concerning the military use of the elephant in Carthaginian campaigns is from Kistler, *War Elephants*; Glover, "The Tactical Handling of the Elephant"; and Gowers, "The African Elephant in Warfare." I thought it would be more efficient for the reader to list the main sources pertinent to this section in a single footnote rather than clutter up the section with notes for every small detail.

2. For the tribal contingents of the Roman and Carthaginian armies and their military value as fighters, see Louis Rawling, "Celts, Spaniards, and Samnites: Warriors in a Soldier's War," in Cornell, Rankov, and Sabin, *The Second Punic War,* 81–95.

3. Livy, *The History of Rome From Its Foundation,* bk. 30, 32. Livy tries to cover up the fact that some of the Italian southern tribes had willingly defected to Hannibal by saying that those who fought at Zama "had followed Hannibal of necessity and under compulsion, and by no means of their own free will, when he left Italy." Livy neglects to note, however, that the "necessity" was the certainty of Roman slavery or death for those whom Rome considered traitors. Diodorus goes so far as to say that Hannibal massacred the rest of the Italians who refused to accompany him. Diodorus Siculus, *Diodorus of Sicily,* trans. Francis R. Walton (Cambridge, MA: Harvard University Press, 1937), vol. 8, bk. 27, 1–11.

4. Sabin, "The Mechanics of Battle in the Second Punic War," 62. Sabin says Livy's assertion (*The History of Rome From Its Foundation,* bk. 30, 33) that Macedonian Greeks fought at Zama is "obviously an annalisic fiction inspired by Rome's later war with Philip V."

5. Rawling, "Celts, Spaniards, and Samnites," 91.

6. M. J. V. Bell, "Tactical Reform in the Roman Republican Army," *Historia: Zeitschrift für antike Geschichte* 14 (1965): 410–11.

7. Diodorus, *Diodorus of Sicily,* vol. 5, bk. 18, 4.

8. Ibid., bk. 3, 1.

9. Rawling, "Celts, Spaniards, and Samnites," 87; and Italicus, *Punica,* vol. 3, 340. The heads were embalmed in cedar oil and stored with others in war chests.

10. Rawling, "Celts, Spaniards, and Samnites," 92.

11. Ibid., 82.

12. For a discussion of Hellenic influence on Hannibal's tactics, Meiklejohn, "Roman

Strategy and Tactics From 509 to 202 B.C.," 176; and Brizzi, "Hannibal: Punier und Hellenist," 201–2.

13. As a basic source, the information concerning the Roman army prior to and under Scipio is taken from Polybius, *The Histories of Polybius,* bk. 4, 19–42 ("The Roman Military System"). Livy, for all his ignorance of military matters and his patriotic exaggerations, nonetheless remains a valuable source. For a detailed description of the Roman legion's organization and weapons prior to the First Punic War, see *The History of Rome From Its Foundation,* bk. 8, 8. As is sometimes the case, a detailed and documented source for the subject is found in scholarship drawn from the nineteenth century. See William Smith, *A Dictionary of Greek and Roman Antiquities* (London: John Murrary, 1854), s.v. "Exercitus," 481–511. Informative, too, are F. E. Adcock, *The Roman Art of War Under the Republic* (Cambridge, MA: Harvard University Press, 1940); Lawrence Keppie, *The Making of the Roman Army: From Republic to Empire* (London: Batsford, 1984); Connolly, *Greece and Rome at War*; Warry, *Warfare in the Classical World*; Adrian Goldsworthy, *Roman Warfare* (London: Clarendon Press, 2000), and *The Roman Army at War: 100 BC–AD 200* (Oxford, UK: Oxford University Press, 1996); and C. M. Gilliver, *The Roman Art of War* (London: Stroud, 1999). Absolutely essential to understanding the Roman art of war during the Punic period is Cornell, Rankov, and Sabin, *The Second Punic War.*

14. Smith, *A Dictionary of Greek and Roman Antiquities,* 490–91.

15. Meiklejohn, "Roman Strategy and Tactics From 509 to 202 B.C.," 170–73.

16. "When the number of soldiers in the legion exceeded 4,000 the first three divisions (*hastati, principe,* and *velites*) were increased proportionally, but the number of *triarii* remained the same at 600." Smith, *A Dictionary of Greek and Roman Antiquities,* 496.

17. Richard A. Gabriel, *No More Heroes: Madness and Psychiatry in War* (New York: Hill and Wang, 1987), 79–88. For what killing does to the human psyche, see also Dave Grossman, *On Killing: The Psychological Cost of Learning to Kill in War and Society* (Boston: Little, Brown, 1995); and Charles Ardant du Picq, "Primitive and Ancient Combat," in *Battle Studies* (Harrisburg, PA: Military Service Publishing Company, 1946), chapter 1.

18. I am deeply indebted to Philip Sabin and his recent groundbreaking work on the "mechanics of battle" for the information that appears in this section.

19. Sabin, "The Mechanics of Battle in the Second Punic War," 77.

20. Ibid.

21. Ibid.

22. See Richard A. Gabriel and Karen S. Metz, "Death, Wounds, and Injury," in *From Sumer to Rome,* 83–95. See also Gabriel, "Siegecraft," in *Soldiers' Lives Through History,* chapter 17.

23. This is Sabin's judgment ("The Mechanics of Battle in the Second Punic War," 65), with which I wholeheartedly concur.

24. Ibid., 66.

25. Philip Sabin, "The Face of Roman Battle," *Journal of Roman Studies* 90 (2000): 1–17. See "Models of combat," 8.

26. P. Krentz, "Casualties in Hoplite Battles," *Greek, Roman, and Byzantine Studies* 26, no. 1 (1985): 13–20, argues that the *initial* casualty rates suffered in ancient battles were about 5 percent on the part of the victor and 11 percent for the defeated. Once one side broke or was trapped, the casualty rates would greatly increase. See Gabriel and Metz, "Death, Wounds, and Injury," 83–91; and Goldsworthy, *The Roman Army at War: 100 BC–AD 200,* 222.
27. Sabin, "The Face of Roman Battle," 14.
28. The idea of combat pulses, as developed by Sabin, is taken from Goldsworthy, *The Roman Army at War*, 222. It also squares nicely with Livy's description of the fighting at Zama when he refers to "repeated charges" and steady advances and withdrawals. See Livy, *The History of Rome From Its Foundation,* bk. 30, 34.
29. Sabin, "The Face of Roman Battle," 15.
30. Livy, *The History of Rome From Its Foundation,* bk. 1, 43; see also R. J. Forbes, *Studies in Ancient Technology* (Leiden, the Netherlands: E. J. Brill, 1964), 96.
31. Jonathan P. Roth, *The Logistics of the Roman Army at War: 264 B.C.–A.D. 235* (Boston: E. J. Brill, 1999), 87.
32. The calculations for Scipio's army are based on the rates and weights of logistical supplies provided by Roth, *The Logistics of the Roman Army at War,* 66–67. The food requirements for the Roman soldier are based on the following field ration: 2.2 sextari (1.87 pounds or 850 grams) of grain a day per soldier. In addition the soldier would receive 50 grams of beans, 30 grams of cheese, 40 grams of olive oil, 30 grams of salt (necessary for the body to retain fluid), and perhaps 20 grams of dried fruit for a total of approximately 1,000 grams, or 2.2 pounds, of food per soldier. Rations for the troops alone came to 63,800 pounds *per day*. For slightly different rates and weights necessary to sustain the ancient soldier, see Donald W. Engels, *Alexander the Great and the Logistics of the Macedonian Army* (Berkeley: University of California Press, 1978), table 3, 145.
33. As noted by Josephus, *The Jewish War*, trans. G. A. Williamson (Oxford: Penguin 1959), bk. 1, 395.
34. Roth, *The Logistics of the Roman Army at War,* 83.
35. After the Marian reforms, the number of mules per contubernium was reduced to one, forcing the soldiers to carry more of the logistical load. Under the new system, the soldiers began to refer to themselves as "Marius's mules."
36. Roth, *The Logistics of the Roman Army at War,* 83.
37. Ibid., 126.
38. Ibid., 128.
39. Livy, *The History of Rome From Its Foundation,* bk. 27, 12.
40. Ann Hyland, *Equus: The Horse in the Roman World* (New Haven, CT: Yale University Press, 1990), 92.
41. Roth, *The Logistics of the Roman Army at War,* 133.
42. Livy, *The History of Rome From Its Foundation,* bk. 26, 43.
43. Keith Hopkins, "Taxes and Trade in the Roman Empire, 200 B.C. to A.D. 400," *Journal of Roman Studies* 70 (1980): 15, table 2. See also Donald V. Sippel, "Some Observations on the Means and Costs of the Transport of Bulk Commodities in the Late Republic and Early Empire," *Ancient World* 16 (1987): 37.

44. Roth, *The Logistics of the Roman Army at War,* 182.

45. Ibid., 187.

46. K. D. White, *Roman Farming* (Ithaca, NY: Cornell University Press, 1970), 295.

47. James D. Anderson, *Roman Military Supply in North-east England: An Analysis of an Alternative to the Piercebridge Formula* (Oxford, UK: British Archaeological Reports, Series 224, 1992), 15.

48. Hyland, *Equus,* 71–72.

49. White, *Roman Farming,* 132.

50. Emmett M. Essin, "Mules, Packs, and Packtrains," *Southwestern Historical Quarterly* 74, no. 1 (1970): 54.

51. Gabriel and Metz, *From Sumer to Rome,* 25.

52. Bernard S. Bachrach, "Animals and Warfare in Early Medieval Europe," in *Armies and Politics in the Early Medieval West,* ed. Bernard S. Bachrach (Aldershot, Hampshire, UK: Variorum, 1993), 717.

53. Ibid.

54. Connolly, *Greece and Rome at War,* 135. If Roth is right that the contubernium in the Republican armies were allowed two mules, then the "soldier's load" in Scipio's armies should have been considerably less—perhaps forty to fifty pounds less—than that carried by soldiers of the imperial period.

55. Marcus Junkelmann, *Die Legionen des Augustus: Der römische Soldat im archäologischen experiment* (Mainz, Germany: Philipp von Zabern, 1986), 34.

56. Engels, *Alexander the Great and the Logistics of the Macedonian Army,* table 7, 153.

57. Livy, *The History of Rome From Its Foundation,* bk. 11, 16. It was not the usual Roman practice, however, to encumber its baggage trains with animal herds in wartime. The staple of the Roman military diet was grain and not meat, as it was for the tribal contingents that comprised Hannibal's army.

58. Roth, *The Logistics of the Roman Army at War,* 198.

59. Lazenby, "Was Maharbal Right?" 41.

60. Connolly, *Greece and Rome at War,* 135.

61. Junkelmann, *Die Legionen des Augustus,* 34.

62. See B. D. Shaw, "Eaters of Flesh, Drinkers of Milk: Ancient Mediterranean Ideology of the Pastoral Nomad," *Ancient Society,* 13–14 (1982): 5–32. For the Gauls and their desire for meat, see Livy, *The History of Rome From Its Foundation,* bk. 44, 26; and for the Germans' diet of dairy products and meat, see Caesar, *Gallic Wars* (Whitefish, MT: Kessinger Publishers, 2007), bk. 5, 14, and bk. 6, 22.

63. Bachrach, "Animals and Warfare in Early Medieval Europe," 717.

64. Glover, "The Tactical Handling of the Elephant," 10. See also Diodorus, *Diodorus of Sicily,* bk. 19, 83–84.

4. SCIPIO'S SPANISH CAMPAIGN

1. Livy, *The History of Rome From Its Foundations,* bk. 26, 19. It is important to note that ancient accounts often leave out the transport ships' presence and role in the narrative. Perhaps they are overlooked because warships were government property and had to be accounted for while cargo vessels were hired from private contractors and were thus not accounted for in official records. Scipio's thirty

quinqueremes had nowhere near sufficient room to transport his troops, horses, and the supplies needed to sustain them during the voyage, and therefore they must have sailed on troop and horse transports. For information on the size and tons burden of the Roman quinquereme, see Thiel, *Studies on the History of Roman Sea-Power in Republican Times,* 111, fn. 251; Warry, *Warfare in the Classical World,* 118; A. W. Gomme, "A Forgotten Factor of Greek Naval Strategy," *Journal of Hellenic Studies* 53, pt. 1 (1933): 16–24; and Connolly, *Greece and Rome at War,* 135. I am indebted to Professor David George, chairman of the Department of Classics at Saint Anselm College, for his explanation regarding the absence of information about transports in classical battle accounts.

2. Livy, *The History of Rome From Its Foundations,* bk. 25, 36–37. Marcius was a hero who had led his men in a dangerous retreat after the Scipios were killed. He established the Roman line on the Ebro and held off the attacking Carthaginians no less than three times until Rome could send reinforcements. His men idolized him and elected him their commander.

3. Ibid., bk. 26, 17.

4. Polybius, *The Histories of Polybius,* bk. 10, 7.

5. Livy, *The History of Rome From Its Foundation,* bk. 26, 19.

6. Polybius, *The Histories of Polybius,* bk. 10, 7.

7. For an account of the Roman military logistics system, see Roth, *The Logistics of the Roman Army at War.* See also Richard A. Gabriel, "Logistics," in *Soldiers' Lives Through History.* Also of value is R. Alan Hardemon, *A Study of the Logistics of Alexander, Napoleon, and Sherman* (Maxwell Air Force Base, AL: Air University Graduate School of Logistics, 1998).

8. Italicus, *Punica,* vol. 2, bk. 7, 339.

9. Polybius, *The Histories of Polybius,* bk. 10, 7. Livy is obviously in error when he places Hasdrubal Barca's army near the Ebro and Saguntum, a position that would have made it impossible for Scipio to march to New Carthage without first having to encounter Hasdrubal. For an overview of the Spanish area of operations, see Johannes Kromayer and George Veith, *Schlachten-Atlas zur antiken Kriegsgeschichte* (Leipzig: Wagner and Debs, 1922), map 3.

10. Polybius, *The Histories of Polybius,* bk. 10, 7.

11. Ibid., 10.

12. Howard Scullard agrees that Polybius must be wrong here. See Scullard, *Scipio Africanus in the Second Punic War,* 68. See also Johannes Kromayer and George Veith, *Heerwesen und Kriegsführung der Griechen und Römer* (1928), 350; and H. Droysen, "Die polybianische Beschreibung der zweiten Schlacht bei Baecula," *Rhein. Mus.* 30 (1876): 281.

13. For the rate of injuries ancient armies suffered on the march, see Gabriel and Metz, *From Sumer to Rome,* 106–9.

14. For an analysis of the geographical errors Polybius made in his account of the war, see J. S. Reid, "Problems of the Second Punic War: Polybius as a Geographer," *Journal of Roman Studies* 3, pt. 2 (1913): 191–96.

15. Polybius, *The Histories of Polybius,* bk. 3, 39. See also Walbank, *A Historical Commentary on Polybius,* 371.

16. Polybius, *The Histories of Polybius,* bk. 10, 6. The assumption is that Silanus remained behind to protect the tribes loyal to Rome, something that would not have been necessary had there not been still tribes loyal to the Carthaginians somewhere close by.

17. Goldsworthy, *The Roman Army at War,* 290. See also Kromayer and Veith, *Heerwessen und Kriegsführung der Griechen und Römer,* 314. They make the point that the Roman artillery had its own separate section and transport.

18. Roth, *The Logistics of the Roman Army at War,* 48. Another excellent source for the logistics of ancient armies is Engels, *Alexander the Great and the Logistics of the Macedonian Army.* For the most part I have relied on Roth in this section.

19. Roth, *The Logistics of the Roman Army at War,* 82. This number assumes two mules per contubernium, or twenty mules per century. Another sixty extra mules would be needed to carry cavalry equipment and another sixty for the centurions. At least seventy extra animals would be needed to replace those lost to injury or lameness. On average, a Roman legion had one mule for every 3.4 men.

20. Ibid.

21. Connolly, *Greece and Rome at War,* 135.

22. For the dimensions, see Warry, *Warfare in the Classical World,* 118. For displacement see Boris Rankov, "The Second Punic War at Sea," in Cornell, Rankov, and Sabin, *The Second Punic War,* 51. For a comparison of the quinquereme with the trireme along with other pertinent information on these boats, see J. F. Coates in *The Trireme Project: Operational Experience,* ed. T. Shaw (Oxford, UK: Oxford Monograph, 1993), 78–81; and Robert Gardiner and John S. Morrison, *The Age of the Galley: Mediterranean Oared Vessels Since Preclassical Times* (London: Brassey's Ltd., 1995), 138–41.

23. Scullard, *Scipio Africanus in the Second Punic War,* 65.

24. Ibid., 60–62; Polybius, *The Histories of Polybius,* bk. 10, 7; and Livy, *The History of Rome From Its Foundation,* bk. 26, 42.

25. Polybius, *The Histories of Polybius,* bk. 10, 10.

26. On this point see Walbank, "The Scipionic Legend," 54–69.

27. The debate as to whether it was the tide or wind that caused the lagoon at New Carthage to recede is presented in all its technical complexity in Scullard, *Scipio Africanus in the Second Punic War,* 76–78. The question has, curiously, bedeviled classicists for decades. See, for example, Jack Lovejoy, "The Tides of New Carthage," *Classical Philology* 67, no. 2 (1972): 110–11. He argues that the onshore wind blowing at fifteen to twenty-five knots caused by the heating of the land during the day "piles up the shallow waters of the lagoon in the harbor increasing its depth." The wind reaches its maximum strength during the afternoon. Toward evening, "the winds subside and the piled up waters rush quickly to the sea." Chester G. Starr dismisses tides as a cause because "the Mediterranean itself is generally tideless"; see his *The Influence of Sea Power on Ancient History* (London: Oxford University Press, 1989), 11. Arguing that the lagoon was used to produce salt and was always shallow is Benedict J. Lowe, "Polybius 10.10.12 and the Existence of Salt-flats at Carthago Nova," *Phoenix* 54, no. 1–2 (2000): 39–52. For another take on the lagoon, see Antonio Lillo and Martin Lillo, "On

Polybius 10.10.12: The Capture of New Carthage," *Historia: Zeitschrift für antike Geschichte* 37 (1988): 477–80. They say the lagoon was a fish farm of sorts with the water level controlled by large locks or sluice gates (*schleusentoren*) for raising or lowering the water level.

28. For more on the subject of when Scipio knew about the lagoon, see Polybius, *The Histories of Polybius,* bk. 10, 8. See Meyer, *Kleine Schriften*, 331–462. See also U. Kahrstedt, *Geschichte der Karthager,* vol. 3 (Berlin, 1913).
29. Livy, *The History of Rome From Its Foundation,* bk. 26, 45.
30. Polybius, *The Histories of Polybius,* bk. 10, 14.
31. Ibid.
32. Thiel, *Studies on the History of Roman Sea-Power in Republican Times,* 119.
33. Polybius, *The Histories of Polybius,* bk. 10, 15.
34. See Livy, *The History of Rome From Its Foundation,* bk. 26, 47. Livy says Scipio captured only eight Carthaginian ships. There is no account of a naval engagement at New Carthage suggesting that the Carthaginian ships were on the beach, immobilized for lack of crews. Hiring rowers was very expensive, and this cost, more than that of ship construction itself, plagued the Carthaginian navy throughout the war.
35. John S. Morrison, "Dilution of Oarcrews With Prisoners of War," *Classical Quarterly,* n.s., 38, no. 1 (1988): 252–53.
36. Lionel Casson, "Galley Slaves," *Transactions and Proceedings of the American Philological Association* 97 (1966): 35–44. For the opposite view, that oarsmen were slaves, see L. Wickert, "Die Flotte der Römischen Kaiserzeit,"*Würzburger Jahrbücher für die Altertumswissenschaft* 4 (1949–50): 100–25; and E. Sander, "Zur Rangordnung des Römischen Herres: Die Flotten," *Historia: Zeitschrift für antike Geschichte* 6 (1957): 347–67.
37. Jan M. Libourel, "Galley Slaves in the Second Punic War," *Classical Philology* 68, no. 2 (1973): 116–19.
38. Livy, *The History of Rome From Its Foundation,* bk. 26, 51. See also W. Fischer, *Das Römische Lager,* 134. Fischer argues that this same exercise drill was still used well into the imperial period.
39. Scullard, *Scipio Africanus in the Second Punic War,* 94.
40. Forbes, *Studies in Ancient Technology,* 96. See also Livy, *The History of Rome From Its Foundation,* bk. 1, 43; Diodorus, *Diodorus of Sicily,* bk. 7, 59; and Cicero, *de Republica* (Cambridge, UK: Cambridge University Press, 1995), vol. 2, 39.
41. Wise, *Armies of the Carthaginian Wars,* 20.
42. N. Feliciani, "La Seconda Guerra Punica nella Spagna, 211–208 BCE," *Studi e Documenti di Storia Diritto* (1904): 258, for Scipio's probes south of New Carthage.
43. A tribal leader's personal attachment to another person who was regarded as the greater warrior was often the decisive factor in securing a tribal alliance. Some Spanish tribes came to regard Scipio as their king. See Rawlings, "Celts, Spaniards, and Samnites," 91–92.
44. See Kahrstedt, *Geschichte der Karthager,* 513, for an analysis of Carthage's financial difficulties during the Second Punic War.
45. It is interesting to inquire how commands for the maniples to change formations

might have been given and heard over the din of battle. William Smith says each cohort had two signallers (*signum*) and only one carried the cohort's standard. The other, it might be reasonably presumed, was a trumpeter whose task was to relay trumpet calls from the legion trumpeter to each maniple. It is not known if Scipio was the first to add the second signum to the newly enlarged cohorts, but it is a reasonable guess in light of the complex tactical maneuvers he introduced. On the signum, see Smith, *A Dictionary of Greek and Roman Antiquities,* 489–511.

46. Bell, "Tactical Reform in the Roman Republican Army," 409–10.
47. Ibid.
48. Marius later eliminated the velites and triarii, converting all ranks into heavy infantry. The legion was reorganized into ten cohorts of six hundred men each.
49. Bell, "Tactical Reform in the Roman Republican Army," 416.
50. Polybius, *The Histories of Polybius,* bk. 11, 23.
51. Livy, *The History of Rome From Its Foundation,* bk. 25, 39.
52. Ibid., bk. 22, 17; Polybius, *The Histories of Polybius,* bk. 10, 35.
53. Warry, *Warfare in the Classical World,* 118. See also Connolly, *Greece and Rome at War,* 270, citing Polybius.
54. It was a peculiar Roman propensity to always transform a naval engagement into a ground battle. They had won the First Punic War in precisely this manner by ignoring seamanship and simply closing with the enemy ships, grappling them, and rushing aboard to attack the crews. For the Roman view of naval warfare, see Thiel, *Studies on the History of Roman Sea-Power in Republican Times,* chapter 1, "The Romans and the Sea."
55. Polybius, in *The Histories of Polybius,* bk. 10, 35, says that Scipio "picked out the best crews," which suggests that some rowers were also pressed into the infantry.
56. I am assuming that Scipio's legions contained the usual four thousand infantrymen before he increased their strength to five thousand men. In his treatise on Roman warfare (*The Histories of Polybius,* bk. 6, 20), Polybius says that during the Second Punic War, the legions were increased to five thousand men, but it is unclear when this happened. See Smith, *A Dictionary of Greek and Roman Antiquities,* 496. Scipio may have been the first to strengthen the legion to five thousand men or the first to raise the legion from five thousand to six thousand men. Livy (*The History of Rome From Its Foundation,* bk. 29, 24) tells us that when Scipio invaded Africa, the two legions he took with him each contained 6,200 troops.
57. Kahrstedt, *Geschichte der Karthager,* no. 1, 517.
58. Polybius, *The Histories of Polybius,* bk. 10, 37. In contrast, Carthaginian nobles seem to have been extremely thin skinned and ambitious when it came to military reputation and glory. My colleague Professor Mathew Gonzales, in the Department of Classics at Saint Anselm College, suggests in this regard that Hannibal himself came to his command after his predecessor's assassination. This coincidence reasonably implies that Hannibal might have had a hand in his death.
59. Livy, *The History of Rome From Its Foundation,* bk. 27, 20.
60. Ibid.; and Polybius, *The Histories of Polybius,* bk. 10, 41.
61. Scullard, *Scipio Africanus in the Second Punic War,* 104, citing Livy and Dio, who give different dates.

62. Livy, *The History of Rome From Its Foundation,* bk. 27, 17.

63. Ibid., 18.

64. Ibid., 19, says that the elephants had already been sent ahead in anticipation of the planned Carthaginian withdrawal.

65. Ibid.

66. Polybius, *The Histories of Polybius,* bk. 10, 38.

67. Livy, *The History of Rome From Its Foundation,* bk. 27, 38.

68. Ibid. See Kromayer and Veith, *Schlachten-Atlas zur antiken kriegsgeschichte,* map 8, for the battle of Baecula. For a detailed overview of the terrain, see Johannes Kromayer and George Veith, *Antike Schlachtfelder* (Berlin: Wiedmannsche Buchhandlung, 1912), vol. 4, 503–17.

69. Polybius, *The Histories of Polybius,* bk. 10, 38.

70. Ibid., 39.

71. Ibid.

72. Scullard, *Scipio Africanus in the Second Punic War,* 108. Polybius's suggestion that ten thousand troops were taken prisoner seems exaggerated.

73. See Kromayer and Veith, *Schlachten-Atlas zur antiken Kriegsgeschichte,* map 8.

74. Livy, *The History of Rome From Its Foundation,* bk. 27, 19. The *Punica* certainly suggests that Hasdrubal deliberately broke contact with Scipio at Baecula in order to carry out his primary strategic mission of crossing into Italy. "Hasdrubal was by no means equally eager to fight. . . . The word of command went round in secret: the soldiers were to stop fighting and disperse among the woods and hills, and all who got off safely were to make for the highest peak of the Pyrenees." (Italicus, *Punica,* vol. 2, bk. 7, 359)

75. Dio Cassius, *Bibliotheca Historia* (Cambridge, MA: Harvard University Press, 1947), bk. 57, 48. Polybius and Livy do not mention Scipio's transfer to the enemy's camp.

76. Livy, *The History of Rome,* bk. 27, 20.

77. Scullard, *Scipio Africanus in the Second Punic War,* 112, citing Livy.

78. Ibid.

79. Livy, *The History of Rome From Its Foundation,* bk. 27, 20.

80. Polybius, *The Histories of Polybius,* bk. 10, 40.

81. Walter Brewitz, *Scipio Africanus Maior in Spanien, 210–206 BCE* (Tubingen, Germany: H. Laupp, 1914), 1–32. See also Gaby Lepper-Mainzer, *Das Darstellung des Feldhern Scipio Africanus* (Bochum, Germany: Brockmeyer, 1982).

82. L. Keller, *De 2 punische krieg,* 67–77; Feliciani, "La Seconda Guerra Punica nella Spagna," 266. Liddell-Hart in *Scipio Africanus* takes the view that even Tarraco itself would have been placed in danger because once past New Carthage there were few Roman forces to prevent a further Carthaginian advance to the Ebro.

83. Scullard, *Scipio Africanus in the Second Punic War,* 108.

84. Ibid., 112.

85. Livy, *The History of Rome From Its Foundation,* bk. 27, 19; Scullard, *Scipio Africanus in the Second Punic War,* 113. This view is by no means universally accepted. See R. Develin, "Scipio Africanus Imperator," *Latomus* 36 (1977): 110–13.

86. Kahrstedt, *Geschichte der Karthager,* 530.

87. See earlier estimates in this chapter regarding the size of Carthaginian forces in Spain.
88. Livy, *The History of Rome From Its Foundation,* bk. 27, 1.
89. Ibid.
90. Italicus, *Punica,* vol. 2, bk. 16, 391.
91. Ibid.
92. Scullard, *Scipio Africanus in the Second Punic War,* 122.
93. Orongis's location is only a guess. Its exact location is unknown.
94. Livy, *The History of Rome From Its Foundation,* bk. 28, 3.
95. J. F. C. Fuller, *A Military History of the Western World,* vol. 1, *From the Defeat of the Spanish Armada to the Battle of Waterloo* (New York: Da Capo Press, 1954), 132, citing Polybius.
96. Livy, *The History of Rome From Its Foundation,* bk. 11, 3.
97. For the location of Ilipa, see Meyer, *Kleine Schriften,* 406. The battle's location is in some dispute, with Scullard suggesting it was not where Liddell-Hart says it was, that is, near Seville. Agreeing with Liddell-Hart is C. G. Pope, *The Story of Scipio Africanus . . . from Livy* (London: Fredrick Muller, 1934), xiv. See also F. Taeger, "Zur Schlacht bei Ilipa," *Klio* (1931): 339–47; and A. Neumann, "Ilipa," *Klio* (1932): 255–56.
98. Polybius's figures (*The Histories of Polybius,* bk. 11, 20) suggesting that the Carthaginians outnumbered the Romans follow my earlier strength calculations nicely, although some historians suggest that the armies at Ilipa were approximately equal in strength. Lazenby reckons the Carthaginian force at seventy thousand men.
99. Polybius, *The Histories of Polybius,* bk. 11, 20.
100. Ibid., 21.
101. Scullard, *Scipio Africanus in the Second Punic War,* 129, cites Brewitz, *Scipio Africanus Maior in Spanien,* 17, who, in turn, relies on Appian, *Roman History,* trans. H. E. White (Cambridge, MA: Harvard University Press, 1992), bk. 1, 29, as his source for this bizarre anecdote. Portrayals of this strange exercise, called *apobates,* appear in a numerous Greek and Roman reliefs. It is difficult to see how such a maneuver would have had any value on the battlefield, and it is likely that it was either a cavalry training exercise or one of those demonstrations of horsemanship that was performed at public events or military parades.
102. Polybius, *The Histories of Polybius,* bk. 11, 22. See Kromayer and Veith, *Schlachten-Atlas zur antiken kriegsgeschichte,* map 8 for the battle of Ilipa. Also see by the same authors, *Antike Schlachtfelder,* vol. 4, 517–27.
103. Polybius, *The Histories of Polybius,* bk. 11, 22. Scullard, *Scipio Africanus in the Second Punic War,* 131–34, provides a good analysis of Brewitz's description of the five stages of Scipio's tactical maneuvers at Ilipa. See also Brewitz, *Scipio Africanus Maior in Spanien,* 1–32.
104. Of course, other commanders, including Philip of Macedon, Alexander the Great, and Hannibal, had refused a portion of the line.
105. Italicus, *Punica,* vol. 2, bk. 16, 393.
106. Livy says that "Hasdrubal, son of Gisgo, [was] the best and most distinguished

general this war produced after the three sons of Hamilcar" (*The History of Rome From Its Foundation,* bk. 28, 12).

107. The cavalry's role described here relies on Scullard's excellent analysis. Neither Livy nor Polybius has anything to say about the Carthaginian cavalry's role at Ilipa.

108. Polybius, *The Histories of Polybius,* bk. 11, 24.

5. THE STRATEGIST

1. Livy, *The History of Rome From Its Foundation,* bk. 28, 17.

2. Ibid., bk. 27, 19.

3. Ibid., bk. 28, 26. Italicus, *Punica,* vol. 2, bk. 16, 397 gives us Massinissa's words to Scipio: "I offer you an arm worthy of your acceptance. I have not acted thus from foolish fickleness of mind or instability of purpose, nor is my heart set on the rewards of fictitious warfare; but treachery I cannot bear and a nation that has ever been false [the reference is to Carthage]. Your campaign as far as the Pillars of Hercules is completed; let us now together attack the mother of war herself. With fire and sword you must force back to Libya the man [Hannibal] who for twice five years has been the master of Italy and is now planting his ladders against the walls of Rome."

4. Caven, *The Punic Wars,* 237. For a detailed account of Massinissa's motives and history in dealing with the Romans, see P. G Walsh, "Massinissa," *Journal of Roman Studies* 55, no. 1–2, pts. 2 and 3 (1965): 149–60.

5. Caven, *The Punic Wars,* 181.

6. Walsh, "Massinissa," 153–54. Between 200 and 198 BCE, Syphax's kingdom was able to produce 400,000 pecks of wheat and 200,000 pecks of barley for the Roman army. In 191 BCE Massinissa, who had taken over parts of Syphax's kingdom with Roman help, promised to deliver 800,000 pecks of wheat and 550,000 pecks of barley to the Romans. Livy, *The History of Rome From Its Foundation,* bk. 28, 18.

7. Mommsen, for example, thought Scipio's gamble a "foolhardy adventure" precisely on the grounds that Syphax might easily have been playing a double game. See Mommsen, *History of Rome,* 308.

8. Livy, *The History of Rome From Its Foundation,* bk. 28, 17.

9. Ibid., 18.

10. Citing Pliny, Meyer identifies Ilorci as the town; see Meyer, *Kleine Schriften,* 445. Livy is clearly wrong when he tells us the town was Iliturgi. See also Scullard, *Scipio Africanus in the Second Punic War,* 143.

11. Livy, *The History of Rome From Its Foundation,* bk. 28, 19.

12. Caven, *The Punic War,* 226. See also Walbank, *A Historical Commentary on Polybius,* vol. 2, 305. Scipio covered a distance of about 120 miles in five days.

13. See Liddell-Hart, *Scipio Africanus,* 68. He calls Scipio's assault on Ilorci a "convergent attack" because he assaulted the walls from two different directions. This description seems to me a misunderstanding of at least the modern meaning of the term, which implies two independent forces under one command moving on a single objective from two different directions. The important distinction is that

towns cannot maneuver. The point of a converging attack is precisely to prevent an enemy force that can maneuver from doing so.

14. Livy, *The History of Rome From Its Foundation*, bk. 28, 19.
15. Scullard quotes Dio as saying that Scipio scaled the wall and was wounded. Livy does not record such an incident probably because it did not happen. There is no record anywhere of Scipio having been wounded at Ilorci. See Scullard, *Scipio Africanus in the Second Punic War*, 144.
16. Livy, *The History of Rome From Its Foundation*, bk. 28, 20.
17. Ibid., 23.
18. Caven, *The Punic War*, 226. See also Robert Knapp, *Aspects of the Roman Experience in Iberia, 206–100 B.C.* (Spain: Valladolid, 1977); and John S. Richardson, *Hispaniae: Spain and the Development of Roman Imperialism, 218–82 BC* (Cambridge, UK: Cambridge University Press, 1986). Smith considers these books to be the definitive works on the tribal revolt. Appian (*Iberike*, vi. 38) says that Indibilis was killed during the revolt.
19. Polybius, *The Histories of Polybius*, bk. 11, 25.
20. Livy, *The History of Rome From Its Foundation*, bk. 28, 27.
21. William Stuart Messer, "Mutiny in the Roman Army: The Republic," *Classical Philology* 15, no. 2 (1920): 168–69.
22. It was a common Roman practice to make the enemy pay for the military operations and the general occupation of his country.
23. Messer, "Mutiny in the Roman Army," 162.
24. Dio, *Bibliotheca Historia*, bk. 57, 14; and James Moscovich, "Dio Cassius on Scipio's Return From Spain in 205 BC," *Ancient History Bulletin* 2 (1988): 108. See Walbank, *A Historical Commentary on Polybius*, 308.
25. Livy, *The History of Rome From Its Foundation*, bk. 28, 29.
26. Messer, "Mutiny in the Roman Army," 159.
27. Joshua Lawrence Chamberlin, commander of the 20th Maine Infantry Regiment at the battle of Gettysburg in 1863, was faced with mutinous troops who refused to fight. Instead of punishing them, he convinced them to return to the fight. He refused to have any of them executed because he knew that when the war ended, he would have to live in the same small town in Maine with their relatives.
28. Polybius, *The Histories of Polybius*, bk. 28, 31. Polybius does not tell us the size of the rebel force, but Livy says it was thirty thousand foot soldiers and four thousand horsemen. See Livy, *The History of Rome From Its Foundation*, bk. 29, 2. This estimate would be almost twice the size of Scipio's force and cannot be accepted as accurate.
29. Polybius says it was Scipio's lack of trust in his Spanish allies that led him to employ only Italians in the force. Livy says it was purely for purposes of revenge; that is, Romans should properly avenge an offense against their city.
30. Livy, *The History of Rome From Its Foundation*, bk. 28, 33.
31. Ibid.
32. Polybius, *The Histories of Polybius*, bk. 11, 33.
33. Choosing the terrain to narrow one's front and deprive the enemy of its numerical advantage is an old tactic that the Greeks used with great success at Marathon.

34. Livy, *The History of Rome From Its Foundation,* bk. 28, 33.

35. Ibid., 34. Appian gives twenty thousand for losses, obviously an exaggeration.

36. Ibid.

37. Ibid.

38. Caven, *The Punic Wars,* 228. See also Scullard, *Scipio Africanus in the Second Punic War,* 156–57.

39. Caven, *The Punic Wars,* 228.

40. Polybius, *The Histories of Polybius,* bk. 11, 33.

41. Livy, *The History of Rome From Its Foundation,* bk. 28, 38.

42. Triumphs were governed by strict rules. They were granted by the Senate and often refused. The triumph itself was a processional along the Via Sacra through the Forum to the temple of Jupiter on the Capitol. The procession was comprised of magistrates and senators, spoils of the enemy, white oxen for sacrifice, the principal prisoners in chains, the lictors, and the *triumphator,* who led the march in a four-horse chariot and wore a special embroidered robe (*toga picta*), a laurel crown, and red face paint. With him rode his children and a slave who whispered, "Hominem te memento" (Remember, thou art a man), to ward off the gods' jealousy. The army marched behind the chariot and sang the rudest songs they could think of about the general. T. A. Buckney, *Scipio Africanus: The Conqueror of Hannibal; Selections From Livy, Books 26–30* (London: G. Bell and Sons, 1965), 81.

43. Ibid.

44. See Moscovich, "Dio Cassius on Scipio's Return From Spain," 107. He notes that Dio presents an entirely different picture of Scipio's return from Spain. He says it occurred as the result of the Romans "fearing lest Scipio in his arrogance might become a tyrant, and that therefore they recalled him and sent two praetors to relieve him." The story is obviously false, the result of Dio relying on poor sources that he failed to check.

45. Haywood, *Studies on Scipio Africanus,* 53.

46. See De Sanctis, *L'eta delle guerre puniche,* 645. He suggests that Livy's account of the political maneuvering is probably untrustworthy and may not have occurred at all. Scullard seems to agree when he says, "All that is certain is that the Fabian policy was discredited, and Scipio with his African project won the day." Scullard, *Scipio Africanus in the Second Punic War,* 161.

47. Schur, *Scipio Africanus und die Begrundung der römische Weltherrschaft,* 47. For a similar opinion, see also Scullard, *Scipio Africanus in the Second Punic War,* 162.

48. See Johannes Kromayer, *Roms Kampf um die Weltherrschaft* (Leipzig: B. G. Teuber, 1912), 384–85. He offers an interesting discussion as to whether Roman strategy during the Second Punic War was really a war of exhaustion (*ermattungsstrategie*) or a war of annihilation (*Niederwerfungsstrategie*).

49. Ibid.

50. Livy, *The History of Rome From Its Foundation,* bk. 28, 44.

6. THE AFRICAN CAMPAIGN

1. Livy, *The History of Rome From Its Foundation,* bk. 28, 45.

2. Dio, *Bibliotheca Historia,* bk. 9, 11.

3. P. A. Brunt, *Italian Manpower, 225 BC–AD 14* (London: Clarendon Press, 1971), as cited in Caven, *The Punic Wars,* 236.

4. Livy, *The History of Rome From Its Foundation,* bk. 28, 45.

5. Caven, *The Punic Wars,* 236. But as Philip Smith notes, denying Scipio the ability to raise troops was the conservatives' last chance to stop the invasion of Africa. If so, then why did they permit Scipio to raise volunteers? The answer seems to be that they did not think he could raise sufficient forces this way, which turned out to be correct: Scipio could raise only seven thousand volunteers. Moreover, if the African campaign failed, they could blame the lack of troops on Scipio's failure to raise the sufficient number. See Philip J. Smith, *Scipio Africanus and Rome's Invasion of Africa: A Historical Commentary on Titus Livius, Book 29* (Amsterdam: J. C. Gieben Publisher, 1993), 9–11.

6. Livy, *The History of Rome From Its Foundation,* bk. 28, 45. The list of military matériel is interesting and included iron, sailcloth, grain and timber for keels and garboards, shields, helmets, pikes, javelins, spears, axes, shovels, sickles, basins, hand mills, wheat, wood for ships, and money for the travel allowances of petty officers and oarsmen.

7. Ibid., bk. 29, 24.

8. On the importance of morale in battle, see the classic work by Ardant du Picq, *Battle Studies.*

9. Scullard, *Scipio Africanus in the Second Punic War,* appendix 5, 318. See also Smith, *Scipio Africanus and Rome's Invasion of Africa,* 9–11.

10. Livy, *The History of Rome From Its Foundation,* bk. 29, 1.

11. For the detailed debate concerning the size of Scipio's invasion force, see Scullard, *Scipio Africanus in the Second Punic War,* appendix 5.

12. Ibid., 318.

13. Livy, *The History of Rome From Its Foundation,* bk. 29, 6.

14. Polybius, *The Histories of Polybius,* bk. 11, 21. Polybius says that Roman cavalrymen sometimes jumped from their horses during battle and held their mounts by the mane in one hand while stabbing the enemy horses in the belly with the other before springing back on their mounts. If so, this manner is probably the worst way in which cavalry can be employed.

15. Livy incorrectly says Laelius landed at Hippo Regius, a town much farther west, or ten days' march from Carthage, and later made famous as the seat of the bishopric of St. Augustine. Scipio wanted to provoke fear in the Carthaginians and convince them that he was coming. To do that, Laelius's raid had to take place much closer to Carthage itself. See Smith, *Scipio Africanus and Rome's Invasion of Africa,* 20.

16. For the circumstances surrounding Massinissa's failed effort to retrieve his throne, see Scullard, *Scipio Africanus in the Second Punic War,* 182–83. See also Livy, *The History of Rome From Its Foundation,* bk. 29, 29–33; and Walsh, "Massinissa," 149–60.

17. Livy, *The History of Rome From Its Foundation,* bk. 29, 6.

18. Ibid., 4.

19. Ibid. Mago had sailed his invasion force across the open sea to avoid the Roman fleets at Tarraco and Massilia. The speed of an oar-powered warship and a sail-

powered transport was about the same, five to six knots. However, the transports could sail day and night without stopping while the warships had to put into shore each evening for rest, water, and food. Thus, the warships were usually holding up the transports. Moreover, the warships could not operate for long on the open sea and were vulnerable to rough weather. Transports, therefore, were vulnerable to warships' attack only when they ventured close to the coast, which put them in rowing and fatigue range of the warship crews' ability to catch the transport. As long as the transports stayed away from the shore, they were usually safe. Thus, Mago sailed his transports without any warships for protection. For the speeds of transports and warships, see H. Köster, *Das antike Seewesen* (Berlin, 1923), 125.

20. Livy, *The History of Rome From Its Foundation*, bk. 28, 46.
21. Ibid., bk. 29, 6.
22. Ibid. For the legal basis of Plemenius's authority as *legatus pro praetore,* see Smith, *Scipio Africanus and Rome's Invasion of Africa,* 27–28.
23. Caven, *The Punic Wars,* 232.
24. Livy, *The History of Rome From Its Foundation*, bk. 29, 7.
25. For the number of combat marines normally carried aboard a Roman ship, see Warry, *Warfare in the Classical World,* 118.
26. Livy, *The History of Rome From Its Foundation*, bk. 29, 7.
27. See Liddell-Hart, *Scipio Africanus,* 108–9. He says that Scipio's purpose in going to Locri was to have his troops face the dreaded Hannibal and be "blooded." This claim is curious in that with the exception of the small number of troops Scipio took with him, the troops he commanded at Locri were not his but those of Pleminius's garrison in Rhegium. Moreover, except for the thousand or so volunteers Scipio used to fill out the Cannae legions, all of Scipio's troops were already combat veterans, and many, such as those in Marcellus's legions, had already seen battle against the dreaded Hannibal.
28. Livy, *The History of Rome From Its Foundation,* bk. 29, 9. Livy says that Scipio sailed to the mainland in a *hexere,* a special vessel one grade higher than a quinquereme. With six banks of oars, the hexere was a rare type of boat. During the First Punic War the famous Roman commanders Regulus and Manlius had used this type of vessel for their flagships. Its size was obviously meant to impress. It is possible that the one Scipio used was built by Sicilian Greeks (the Romans did not have the shipbuilding skills to construct such a vessel) or that it had been captured from the Carthaginians. Smith, *Scipio Africanus and Rome's Invasion of Africa,* 32.
29. Livy, *The History of Rome From Its Foundation,* bk. 29, 19.
30. Ibid., 22.
31. This Carthaginian skill was thought by the Romans to be nothing less than lying and treachery, so much so that the phrase *punic faith* (*Punica fides*) became identified in the Roman lexicon with treachery.
32. Livy, *The History of Rome From Its Foundation,* bk. 29, 23.
33. Caven gives the girl's name as Saphanba'al while it is listed as Saphanba in de Sanctis, *L'eta delle guerre puniche,* 532.
34. Livy, *The History of Rome From Its Foundation,* bk. 29, 23.

35. Ibid.

36. Ibid., 24.

37. Ibid.

38. Ibid., 26.

39. Köster, *Die antike Seewesen*, 125. The average speed of a transport was five to six knots. Thus the sixty-five-mile journey should have taken no more than an average day's sail.

40. George W. Houston, "Ports in Perspective: Some Comparative Material on Roman Merchant Ships and Ports," *American Journal of Archaeology* 92, no. 4 (1988): 559.

41. M. Launey, "Inscriptions de Thasos," *Bulletin de Correspondance Hellenique* 57 (1933): 400.

42. The best sources on antique cargo ships are R. P. Duncan-Jones, "Giant Cargo Ships in Antiquity," *Classical Quarterly* 27, no. 2 (1977): 331–36; Houston, "Ports in Perspective," 553–64; and Gardiner and Morrison, *The Age of the Galley*.

43. My thanks to Paul Rollins of York, Maine, a naval architect and shipbuilder, for the information on the New England entrepôts.

44. I also owe a debt of gratitude to my dear friend Alison Gagliadri, an accomplished horsewoman, for the information regarding the weight and dimensions of the horse.

45. Roth, *The Logistics of the Roman Army at War*, 66–67.

46. Duncan-Jones, "Giant Cargo Ships in Antiquity," 331.

47. Caven, *The Punic Wars*, 236.

48. Livy, *The History of Rome From Its Foundation*, bk. 29, 25.

49. For the argument that the land around Thapsus was fertile enough to support Scipio's army, see de Sanctis, *L'eta delle guerre puniche*, 580. Smith agrees, telling us that Emporiae was a general area of farming and commercial trading towns running south from Thapsus. See Smith, *Scipio Africanus and Rome's Invasion of Africa*, 58.

50. The Promontory of Mercury is modern Cape Bon, located on the northeastern end of the Bay of Tunis, about thirty miles from Carthage. Smith, *Scipio Africanus and Rome's Invasion of Africa*, 59.

51. For the distance between the landing site and Utica, see Caven, *The Punic Wars*, 237.

52. See Theodore Zielinski, *Rivista di Storia Antica* 3, no. 1 (1898): 86. He argues that Scipio announced his intention to land at Thapsus to deceive the Carthaginians.

53. For the terrain in which Scipio fought most of his battles, see Kromayer and Veith, *Schlachten-Atlas zur antiken Kriegsgeschichte*, vol. 2, map 11.

54. For the Roman pack supply system, see Roth, *The Logistics of the Roman Army at War*, chapter 2.

55. Scullard, *Scipio Africanus in the Second Punic War*, 177.

56. Livy, *The History of Rome From Its Foundation*, bk. 29, 28.

57. Appian offers this estimate, with which Scullard concurs, in *Roman History*, 5.

58. Livy, *The History of Rome From Its Foundation*, bk. 29, 34.

59. Appian, *Roman History*, 9.

60. Livy, *The History of Rome From Its Foundation,* bk. 29, 28.

61. On the one hand, Livy is well aware that the two stories concerning the defeat of the Carthaginian cavalry under someone named Hanno may be repeating the same event. On the other hand, Hanno was not an uncommon name, and in the second story Hanno is identified as the son of a well-known general. Thus both stories could be valid. See Livy, *The History of Rome From Its Foundation,* bk. 29, 35.

62. Livy's number of eight thousand captives sent to Sicily appears high. Scipio probably did clear out the population from the small area where his army was operating, but it is unlikely that so many people lived in such a small area, especially on a rock ridge near the beach.

63. For the terrain's description, see Kromayer and Veith, *Antike Schlachtfelder,* vol. 3, 579.

64. Buckney, *Scipio Africanus: The Conqueror of Hannibal,* 34.

65. For those interested in the details of Massinissa's attempt to regain his throne from Syphax and the pretender, see Livy, *The History of Rome From Its Foundation,* bk. 29, 29–33; and Walsh, "Massinissa," 150–51.

66. Kromayer and Veith, *Antike Schlachtfelder,* 582.

67. Livy, *The History of Rome From Its Foundation,* bk. 29, 34

68. Kromayer and Veith, *Antike Schlachtfelder,* 582.

69. Livy, *The History of Rome From Its Foundation,* bk. 29, 34.

70. Ibid.

71. Ibid., 35.

72. Ibid.

73. Ibid., 34.

74. Caven, *The Punic Wars,* 238.

75. Livy, relying on Polybius, claims that Hasdrubal had thirty thousand infantry and three thousand cavalry and that Syphax arrived with fifty thousand infantry and ten thousand cavalry. These numbers are impossibly large. Others estimate the total combined force at thirty thousand infantry and, perhaps, five thousand cavalry. I have relied on their estimates. See Scullard, *Scipio Africanus in the Second Punic War,* 318; Kromayer and Veith, *Antike Schlachtfelder,* 674; and de Sanctis, *L'eta delle guerre puniche,* 583.

76. Kromayer and Veith, *Antike Schlachtfelder,* 583.

77. Smith, *Scipio Africanus and Rome's Invasion of Africa,* 68.

78. Caven notes, and Livy agrees, that the Romans put three fleets of forty ships each to sea that summer to guard Italy, Sicily, and Sardinia. Caven, *The Punic Wars,* 239.

79. Polybius, *The Histories of Polybius,* bk. 14, 1.

80. Ibid.

81. Kromayer and Veith, *Antike Schlachtfelder,* 586.

82. Polybius, *The Histories of Polybius,* bk. 14, 1.

83. Ibid.

84. Ibid., 5.

85. In addition to the forty thousand dead, Livy says that many Carthaginian nobles, including eleven senators, were killed. The Romans captured 174 military

standards, 2,700 Numidian horses (presumably kept in corrals outside the camp), six elephants, and a great quantity of weapons. See Livy, *The History of Rome From Its Foundation,* bk. 30, 6. It must also be borne in mind that the camps' residents also included wives, children, merchants, and other civilians. The Romans killed them, too. Not all the dead were soldiers.

86. Italicus, *Punica,* vol. 2, bk. 17, 447.

87. Liddell-Hart, *Scipio Africanus,* 128.

88. For a discussion of the place's name, see Polybius, *The Histories of Polybius,* bk. 14, 7. For its location and terrain description, see Kromayer and Veith, *Antike Schlachtfelder,* 590.

89. The estimate is from Leone Saumagne, *Rendiconti della Roma Accademia Nazionale dei Lincei* (1925), as cited in Scullard, *Scipio Africanus in the Second Punic War,* 207.

90. Polybius, *The Histories of Polybius,* bk. 14, 8. The figure of forty thousand Carthaginian, Celtiberian, and Numidian troops at Campi Magni is too high. See Scullard, *Scipio Africanus in the Second Punic War,* appendix 5. He is more likely correct when he estimates the combined force at no more than twenty thousand men, which included three thousand to four thousand cavalry.

91. Kromayer and Veith, *Antike Schlachtfelder,* 590.

92. This number is Scullard's estimate in *Scipio Africanus in the Second Punic War,* 209. Neither Livy nor Polybius provide numbers for the strength of Scipio's army at Campi Magni. Livy does say, however, that Scipio left only "a small force—enough to create the illusion that the siege was still being maintained by land and sea." See *The History of Rome From Its Foundation,* bk. 30, 7. But Scipio was in difficult straits. If he took the gamble and sent most of his army after Hasdrubal and the Uticans attacked or Carthage attacked by sea, he stood to lose everything. He probably reckoned that the force sent against Hasdrubal was sufficient to despoil Hasdrubal's future plans at the minimum and, with luck, to give him a bloody nose. Weighed in the balance, then, the greater danger was to Scipio's base.

93. Kromayer and Veith, *Antike Schlachtfelder,* 590.

94. Polybius, *The Histories of Polybius,* bk. 14, 18.

95. For the tactics Scipio used, see Kromayer and Veith, *Schlachten-Atlas zur antiken Kriegsgeschichte,* map 8 and accompanying diagram.

96. Italicus, *Punica,* vol. 2, bk. 17, 451. Hasdrubal had saved himself from death by fleeing the battlefield no less than three times, once in Spain and now twice in Africa.

97. In support of the claim, see Hans Delbrück, *Historische Zeitschrift* 51 (1883): 13–23. Also by the same author, *The History of the Art of War,* vol. 1, *Warfare in Antiquity,* ed. Walter J. Renfroe Jr. (Westport, CT: Greenwood Press, 1990), 389–90.

98. Polybius, *The Histories of Polybius,* bk. 14, 10.

99. Ibid.

100. Ibid., 11.

101. Appian seems to imply that Scipio did not take Tunis at this time. See Appian, *Roman History,* 30.

102. Livy, *The History of Rome From Its Foundation,* bk. 30, 10.

103. Ibid.

104. Ibid., 11.
105. Ibid., for Livy's detailed account of the battle.
106. Italicus, *Punica*, vol. 2, bk. 27, 449.
107. Polybius, *The Histories of Polybius*, bk. 14, 9.
108. Livy, *The History of Rome From Its Foundation*, bk. 30, 16. Livy says that Scipio demanded five hundred thousand measures of wheat and three hundred thousand measures of barley. This is a considerable amount of food and, with Carthage cut off from the countryside, would have caused extensive shortages in Carthage itself. Scipio may have intended to give Carthage a taste of the suffering Rome had endured.

7. SCIPIO AND HANNIBAL

1. Dio, *Bibliotheca Historia*, bk. 16, 74. Livy, *The History of Rome From Its Foundation*, bk. 30, 23. Dio, following Polybius, claims that the terms were accepted; however, Livy claims that the terms were not accepted.
2. Delbrück, *History of the Art of War*, 380.
3. Livy, *The History of Rome From Its Foundation*, bk. 20, 30.
4. Fuller, *A Military History of the Western World*, vol. 1, *From the Defeat of the Spanish Armada to the Battle of Waterloo* (New York: Da Capo Press, 1954), 139.
5. While Fuller's argument that Hannibal destroyed his horses before leaving Italy makes sense, the only ancient source that confirms the story is Diodorus, *Diodorus of Sicily*, bk. 28, 8, 1–11, who tells us that Hannibal slaughtered "three thousand horses and innumerable pack animals" before leaving Italy for Africa.
6. Livy, *The History of Rome From Its Foundation*, bk. 30, 20. See also Diodorus, *Diodorus of Sicily*, bk. 17, 8, 1–11. Diodorus says that those former Italian allies who refused to leave Italy and accompany Hannibal to Africa were turned over to his army. Some were taken along forcefully as slaves and the rest, "some twenty-thousand men," were slaughtered. The tale is probably false since there was no good military reason to kill these people. The Romans would have regarded them as traitors in any case and probably would have killed or enslaved them anyway.
7. Livy, *The History of Rome From Its Foundation*, bk. 30, 20.
8. Ibid., 19.
9. Ibid., 24.
10. Ibid.
11. Ibid.
12. Ibid. Polybius says only that the ships were "captured."
13. Polybius, *The Histories of Polybius*, bk. 15, 2.
14. Ibid.
15. Ibid. See also Walbank, *A Historical Commentary on Polybius*, 441–42. He is of the view that the whole incident with the cargo ships is a Roman fiction and that the event never happened.
16. Polybius, *The Histories of Polybius*, bk. 15, 4.
17. Delbrück, *History of the Art of War*, 382.
18. Scullard, *Scipio Africanus in the Second Punic War*, 231. The argument that Scipio was

already in the west is supported by Kromayer and Veith, *Antike Schlachtfelder*, vol. 3, pt. 2, 598–682.

19. Polybius, *The Histories of Polybius*, bk. 15, 4.
20. Ibid.
21. Ibid., 5.
22. Delbrück, *History of the Art of War*, 380–82.
23. Ibid.
24. Ibid., 371.
25. Livy, *The History of Rome From Its Foundation*, bk. 30, 36. Polybius is silent on the battle with Vermina.
26. Ibid.
27. Scullard, *Scipio Africanus in the Second Punic War*, 250.
28. The distance is given in Ian Scott-Kilvert's *Polybius and the Rise of the Roman Empire* (London: Penguin, 1979), 468.
29. Polybius, *The Histories of Polybius*, bk. 5, 15.
30. Ibid.
31. Scullard, *Scipio Africanus in the Second Punic War*, 234, citing Herodotus, bk. 7, 146.7.
32. Polybius, *The Histories of Polybius*, bk. 15, 5.
33. Livy, *The History of Rome From Its Foundation*, bk. 30, 29.
34. Polybius, *The Histories of Polybius*, bk. 15, 5.
35. Ibid., 6.
36. For the substance of the conversation between Scipio and Hannibal, see ibid., 6–8.
37. See Scullard, *Scipio Africanus in the Second Punic War*, 235. Scullard is of the view that the meeting between Scipio and Hannibal may well have taken place; however, as a good scholar, he notes that Delbrück and Konrad Lehmann both disagree and believe that the meeting never occurred. Delbrück, *History of the Art of War*; de Sanctis, *L'eta delle guerre puniche*; and Konrad Lehmann, "Der letzte Feldzug des hannibalishcen krieges," in *Jahrbücher für klassische Philologie*, vol. 21 (Leipzig, Germany: B. G. Teubner, 1984), 556–69.
38. Polybius, *The Histories of Polybius*, bk. 15, 11.
39. Livy, *The History of Rome From Its Foundation*, bk. 28, 46.
40. Ibid., bk. 29, 4.
41. Scullard, *Scipio Africanus in the Second Punic War*, 323; and Wise, *Armies of the Carthaginian Wars*, 23.
42. Scullard, *Scipio Africanus in the Second Punic War*, 323. Some doubt whether Greek troops were at Zama. Buckney suggests they were not. Philip V of Macedon had a treaty with Hannibal but quickly realized he had backed the wrong horse and made peace with Rome in 205 BCE. See Buckney, *Scipio Africanus*, 34. Dorey, however, argues that the Greek troops the Romans captured were taken in Carthage and may have been the remnants of the original Greek contingent. See Thomas A. Dorey, "Macedonian Troops at the Battle of Zama," *American Journal of Philology* 78, no. 2 (1957): 185–87.
43. Polybius, *The Histories of Polybius*, bk. 15, 3; and Appian, *Roman History*, 33.

44. Polybius, *The Histories of Polybius,* bk. 15, 11; and Kromayer and Veith, *Antike Schlachtfelder,* 681.
45. Polybius, *The Histories of Polybius,* bk. 19, 9. For the distances separating the various ranks of the Roman legion, see *Great Captains Before Napoleon: A Teaching Guide* (West Point, NY: Department of Art and Engineering, 1965), figure 6 of the appendix.
46. Kromayer and Veith, *Antike Schlachtfelder,* 673.
47. Delbrück, *History of the Art of War,* 373.
48. Polybius, *The Histories of Polybius,* bk. 15, 11.
49. Professor Linda Rulman, a professor of classics at Saint Anselm College and an expert in Roman history provided the distance of a *stadium* as approximately 190 meters.
50. Scullard, Lehmann, Kromayer and Veith, and Delbrück all agree that the tactical role of Hannibal's cavalry was to draw Scipio's cavalry away from the battlefield.
51. Delbrück, *History of the Art of War,* 371.
52. Kistler, *War Elephants,* 132; and Daniel A. Fournie, "Clash of Titans at Zama," *Military History* 16, no. 6 (2000): 30.
53. Kistler, *War Elephants,* 132. For the need to train elephants to carry the howdah in battle, see also Gowers, "The African Elephant in Warfare," 43–44.
54. Glover, "The Tactical Handling of the Elephant," 8.
55. The detailed topographic and terrain analysis of the battlefield at Zama can be found in Kromayer and Veith, *Schlachten-Atlas zur antiken Kriegsgeschichte,* vol. 2, map 8; and Kromayer and Veith, *Antike Schlachtfelder,* vol. 3, pt. 2, 598–682.
56. Polybius, *The Histories of Polybius,* bk. 15, 12.
57. Italicus, *Punica,* vol. 2, bk. 17, 469.
58. Ibid.
59. Ibid.
60. Polybius has Massinissa posted on the Roman right while Livy has him on the Roman left. See Polybius, *The Histories of Polybius,* bk. 15, 9; and Livy, *The History of Rome From Its Foundation,* bk. 30, 33.
61. Polybius, *The Histories of Polybius,* bk. 15, 12.
62. Italicus, *Punica,* vol. 2, bk. 17, 469.
63. Ibid., bk. 15, 13.
64. Ibid.
65. For the tactical dynamics of the phalanx, see Delbrück, *History of the Art of War,* 377.
66. Polybius, *The Histories of Polybius,* bk. 15, 13.
67. Ibid.
68. Ibid.
69. Ibid.
70. Livy, *The History of Rome From Its Foundation,* bk. 30, 4.
71. Polybius, *The Histories of Polybius,* bk. 15, 14.
72. The distance between the triarii and Scipio's hastati was calculated in the following manner. The distance between the Roman front and the last rank at the start of the battle was 230 yards. The battle space between the Roman front and the

Carthaginian front was 100 yards wide. The distance between the Carthaginian front line and the second line was 100 yards, for a total of 430 yards. Scipio reassembled his army in the "forefront" of the cluttered battlefield, or at least 50 yards beyond where the second Carthaginian line had fought. This line left the hastati in front of the triarii by approximately 500 yards.

73. Polybius, *The Histories of Polybius*, bk. 15, 14.
74. Gabriel and Metz, *From Sumer to Rome*, 90. See chapter 4, "Death, Wounds, and Injury," for the ratios used here.
75. Ibid.
76. Polybius, *The Histories of Polybius*, bk. 15, 14.
77. Livy, *The History of Rome From Its Foundation*, bk. 30, 35.
78. Polybius, *The Histories of Polybius*, bk. 15, 14.
79. Gabriel, *Soldiers' Lives Through History*, 150–51.
80. Sarva Daman Singh, *Ancient Indian Warfare* (Delhi: Motilal Banarsidass, 1997), 55–56.
81. For his views on the weaknesses of cavalry versus infantry, see Xenophon, *The Persian Expedition*, trans. Rex Warner (London: Penguin, 1972), bk. 3, 2. For Caesar's view on the same subject, see Ardant du Picq, *Battle Studies*, 78.
82. Italicus, *Punica*, vol. 2, bk. 17, 443.
83. Polybius, *The Histories of Polybius*, bk. 15, 14.
84. For the typical expected casualty rates of a Roman legion in battle, see Gabriel and Metz, *From Sumer to Rome*, table 4.5, 90.
85. Appian, *Roman History*, 48.
86. While on the march from Zama to Tunis, the Romans learned that Vermina was moving toward them.
87. This point seems to confirm my earlier suggestion that Scipio had not occupied Tunis before the first truce but had camped outside the city, which the Carthaginians still occupied.
88. Livy, *The History of Rome From Its Foundation*, bk. 30, 36. Polybius says nothing about the event.
89. Ibid.
90. Ibid., 38.
91. Ibid., 37.
92. Polybius, *The Histories of Polybius*, bk. 15, 18.
93. Ibid.
94. Scullard, *Scipio Africanus in the Second Punic War*, 253. The peace terms "are not proclaimed in a unanimous voice by the authorities." I have adopted Scullard's version here as the most authoritative insofar as he consults most of the scholarly experts on the problem.
95. Livy, *The History of Rome From Its Foundation*, bk. 30, 44. These territories were presumably taken from Vermina after the Romans defeated him; otherwise, how would Massinissa have obtained them? Along with Scipio's awarding of the city of Cirta, Vermina's capital, to Massinissa, this largesse suggests that Livy's account of the battle between the Romans and Vermina shortly after Zama is

probably true. If so, then my suggestion that Vermina was coming to Hannibal's aid but arrived too late is also probably correct.

96. Ibid., 43.
97. Only Appian reports this clause, but it seems reasonable in that the Romans had already promised not to station troops in Africa.
98. Scullard, *Scipio Africanus in the Second Punic War,* 259.
99. Livy, *The History of Rome From Its Foundation,* bk. 30, 45.
100. Ibid.

8. TRIUMPH AND FALL

1. Haywood, *Studies on Scipio Africanus,* 59. In addition to the original sources, this chapter relies heavily on the following academic sources: Scullard, *Scipio Africanus in the Second Punic War,* by the same author, *Scipio Africanus: Soldier and Politician* (Ithaca, NY: Cornell University Press, 1970); de Sanctis, *L'eta delle guerre puniche;* Francesco Grazioli, *Scipione l'Africano* (Torino: Unione Tipografico-Editrice Torinese, 1946); Luca de Regibus, Il *Processo degli Scipioni* (Torino: V. Bucca, 1921); and A. H. McDonald, "Scipio Africanus and Roman Politics in the Second Century B.C.," *Journal of Roman Studies* 28, pt. 2 (1938): 153–64.
2. Livy, *The History of Rome From Its Foundation,* bk. 38, 50.
3. Shotter, *The Fall of the Roman Republic,* 12. Candidates for the Senate also had to have been elected to a public magistracy of the fourth-highest level of public office and had to meet substantial wealth and property qualifications.
4. Ibid., 13.
5. Scullard, *Scipio Africanus: Soldier and Politician,* 164.
6. Polybius, *The Histories of Polybius,* bk. 28, 12.
7. In this regard, Diodorus says, "because of his great achievements, Scipio wielded more influence than seemed compatible with the dignity of the state." Diodorus, *Diodorus of Sicily,* bk. 29, 19, 21.
8. Scullard, *Scipio Africanus: Soldier and Politician,* 173. As noted earlier, Dio says that some Romans wanted to have Scipio arrested on his return.
9. Shotter, *The Fall of the Roman Republic,* 107.
10. Scullard, *Scipio Africanus: Soldier and Politician,* 179.
11. Michael O. Akinde, "Cornelius Scipio Africanus," www.fenrir.dk/history/index.php?title=History (May 2006).
12. E. Badian, "Rome and Antiochus the Great: A Study in Cold War," *Classical Philology* 54, no. 2 (1959): 81–82.
13. Ibid.
14. Livy, *The History of Rome From Its Foundation,* bk. 31, 3.
15. Haywood, *Studies on Scipio Africanus,* 70, citing de Sanctis, *L'eta delle guerre puniche,* 598–601.
16. Scullard, *Scipio Africanus: Soldier and Politician,* 177.
17. Ibid., 142.
18. Haywood, *Studies on Scipio Africanus,* 64. See also Maurice Holleaux, "Rome and Macedon," *Cambridge Ancient History,* vol. 8 (Cambridge, UK: Cambridge University Press, 1954), 230.

19. Haywood, *Studies on Scipio Africanus,* 63; and Tenney Frank, *Roman Imperialism* (New York: Macmillan, 1914), 149.
20. Polybius, *The Histories of Polybius,* bk. 18, 12.
21. Scullard and Haywood both agree. See Scullard, *Scipio Africanus: Soldier and Politician,* 182; and Haywood, *Studies on Scipio Africanus,* 75.
22. Haywood, *Studies on Scipio Africanus,* 74.
23. Livy, *The History of Rome From Its Foundation,* bk. 32, 9. For Flamininus's deliberate selection of Scipio's veterans for his campaign in Greece, see also Frederick M. Wood Jr., "The Military and Diplomatic Campaign of T. Quinctius Flamininus in 198 B.C.," *American Journal of Philology* 62, no. 3 (1941): 281.
24. Scullard, *Scipio Africanus: Soldier and Politician,* 182.
25. For an account of the battle, see Richard A. Gabriel, "Rome Against Greece," in *Empires at War,* vol. 2, chapter 13. Rich in detail and informative, see Livy's account in *The History of Rome From Its Foundation,* bk. 33, 1–11.
26. Livy, *The History of Rome From Its Foundation,* bk. 33, 9.
27. Scullard, *Scipio Africanus: Soldier and Politician,* 185.
28. Badian, "Rome and Antiochus the Great," 89.
29. Wood, "The Military and Diplomatic Campaign of T. Quinctius Flamininus in 198 B.C.," 282–85.
30. Ibid., 277. It is important to realize at this time Rome was not a world power, only a regional power. To the rest of the Hellenic world, Rome was a barbarian backwater whose influence in world affairs was marginal. With the defeat of Philip of Macedon and then Antiochus of Syria, the situation changed as Rome acquired imperial influence and interests.
31. Ibid., 281.
32. Badian, "Rome and Antiochus the Great," 84.
33. Livy, *The History of Rome From Its Foundation,* bk. 33, 30.
34. Haywood, *Studies on Scipio Africanus,* 79.
35. Livy, *The History of Rome From Its Foundation,* bk. 33, 47. Polybius is lost for the years 195–193 BCE and for the greater parts of 192 and 191 BCE, forcing heavy reliance on Livy for much of what follows.
36. Ibid., bk. 34, 46.
37. For a detailed analysis of the events and missteps leading to the war between Rome and Antiochus, see Badian, "Rome and Antiochus the Great," 81–89.
38. Haywood, *Studies on Scipio Africanus,* 76; and Livy, *The History of Rome From Its Foundation,* bk. 34, 45.
39. Haywood, *Studies on Scipio Africanus,* 76.
40. Scullard, *Scipio Africanus: Soldier and Politician,* 193.
41. On the nature of Roman colonies and how they differed from Greek and Phoenician colonies, especially with regard to their military functions, see Andrew Stephenson, *Public Lands and Agrarian Laws of the Roman Republic* (Baltimore, MD: Johns Hopkins Press, 1891), 12–14. See also E. T. Salmon, *Roman Colonization* (London: Thames and Hudson, 1969), chapter 6.
42. Liddell-Hart, *Scipio Africanus,* 210. Scullard agrees; see Scullard, *Scipio Africanus in the Second Punic War,* 283.

43. Livy, *The History of Rome From Its Foundation,* bk. 34, 48.
44. Haywood, *Studies on Scipio Africanus,* 85.
45. Holleaux, "Rome and Macedon," 199.
46. Scullard, *Scipio Africanus: Soldier and Politician,* 197.
47. Badian, "Rome and Antiochus the Great," 91.
48. Livy, *The History of Rome From Its Foundation,* bk. 35, 14.
49. Ibid.
50. A. H. McDonald, "Introduction," in Bettenson, *Rome and the Mediterranean* (London: Penguin, 1976), 19. Scullard agrees; see also, Scullard, *Scipio Africanus: Soldier and Politician*, 198.
51. Holleaux, "Rome and Macedon," 202.
52. Massinissa was causing a problem. He had encroached on some valuable agricultural land that Carthage had claimed for years as its own. Carthage asked Rome to mediate the dispute. Livy says that Scipio could easily have settled the matter, but the evidence was against Massinissa, so Scipio finessed the issue and put off a decision. Scipio was reluctant to find against Massinissa because for years Massinissa had been supplying Rome with grain and cavalry to demonstrate his loyalty and with important help during Scipio's African campaign. Scipio seems to have warned Massinissa not to take any more aggressive steps against Carthage, and Massinissa took no further action while Scipio was alive. See Walsh, "Massinissa," 149–60.
53. Ibid., 208.
54. Scullard, *Scipio Africanus: Soldier and Politician*, 201.
55. J. P. V. D. Balsdon, "L. Cornelius Scipio: A Salvage Operation," *Historia: Zeitschrift für antike Geschichte* 21 (1972): 224–34. Balsdon is of the view that Lucius was a competent military commander and politician but that the Roman historians' focus on Scipio's accomplishments led them to ignore or minimize Lucius's talents. Regarding military experience, the *Punica* has only one mention of Lucius's combat experience, the skirmish against Hanno in Spain: "But Scipio, the brother of the invincible general, hurled a spear with mighty force at Larus, which cut the plume that fluttered on his leathern cap, for the weapon was aimed too high." Italicus, *Punica,* vol. 2, bk. 16, 391.
56. Holleaux, "Rome and Macedon," 213.
57. Livy, *The History of Rome From Its Foundation,* bk. 36, 17–18.
58. Ibid., bk. 36, 19. Livy cites Polybius on this point, but the latter's text is not extant. See Polybius, *The Histories of Polybius,* vol. 2, 251.
59. Livy, *The History of Rome From Its Foundation,* bk. 37, 3. See also W. Jeffrey Tatum, "The Consular Elections for 190 B.C.," *Klio* 83, no. 2 (2001): 388–401. His view is that Scipio and the others had no agreement to obtain the Greek command before the election.
60. Scullard, *Scipio Africanus: Soldier and Politician*, 202. He quotes Cicero but without citation.
61. Holleaux, "Rome and Macedon," 219.
62. Haywood, *Studies on Scipio Africanus,* 61.
63. Livy, *The History of Rome From Its Foundation,* bk. 37, 6.
64. Ibid.

65. Ibid., 7.
66. Ibid., 25.
67. Ibid., 34.
68. Holleaux, "Rome and Macedon," 223.
69. Ibid., 219.
70. Ibid., 225.
71. Livy, *The History of Rome From Its Foundation,* bk. 37, 7.
72. Holleaux, "Rome and Macedon," 221.
73. Livy, *The History of Rome From Its Foundation,* bk. 37, 3.
74. Ibid.
75. Bettenson, *Rome and the Mediterranean,* 312.
76. Ibid., 311. There are two possible explanations. For one, see Walbank, *A Historical Commentary on Polybius,* vol. 3, 105–6. He suggests that the movement in the Roman lunar ritual calendar resulted in the month of March actually falling between October 20 and November 17, as indicated by the Julian calendar in use when Livy was writing. My colleague, Matthew Gonzales, offered another possibility: the Salii were required to observe the same religious obligations during the Ceremony of the October Horse, which fell in the first half of October.
77. Livy, *The History of Rome From Its Foundation,* bk. 37, 34.
78. Ibid., 35.
79. Ibid., 36.
80. Ibid.
81. Ibid., 37.
82. There is little reason for misunderstanding Scipio here. The Senate had set the Roman terms, and Scipio had no room for maneuver. Scipio hoped, even on the verge of battle, that his personal influence might bring about a peaceful settlement. By asking Antiochus not to go to war until Scipio himself was on the battlefield may simply have been playing for time so that a reasonable settlement could be reached. See McDonald, "Introduction," 159.
83. Livy, *The History of Rome From Its Foundation,* bk. 37, 39.
84. For a detailed description of both armies and their tactical dispositions at Magnesia, see ibid., 41–42. See also Holleaux, "Rome and Macedon," 223–24.
85. Livy, *The History of Rome From Its Foundation,* bk. 37, 40.
86. Ibid., 42.
87. Ibid.
88. Ibid., 43.
89. Ibid.
90. Ibid.
91. Ibid.
92. Ibid., 47.
93. Scullard, *Scipio Africanus in the Second Punic War,* 288.
94. Polybius, *The Histories of Polybius,* bk. 23, 14.
95. Ibid.
96. For the original criticisms of Antias's accounts as they relate to Livy, see Haywood, *Studies on Scipio Africanus,* Antias even gets the year of Scipio's death wrong.

97. For their respective accounts of Scipio's trial, see Scullard, *Scipio Africanus: Soldier and Politician*, 288–89; Haywood, *Studies on Scipio Africanus,* chapter 5; and McDonald, "Introduction."

98. McDonald, "Introduction," 161.

99. Ibid., 160.

100. Ibid., 162–63.

101. Scullard, *Scipio Africanus in the Second Punic War*, 218. For the counterargument that the money was not booty and therefore had to be accounted for, see L. Fraccaro, "I processi degli Scipioni," *Storia per l'antica classica* 4 (1911): 376.

102. Polybius, *The Histories of Polybius,* bk. 22, 14.

103. Rome had four popular assemblies that represented the Roman People by election. The sources do not identify in which of the popular assemblies the charges against Scipio were brought. For more on the People's representative bodies, see Shotter, *The Fall of the Roman Republic,* 14–18.

104. Livy, *The History of Rome From Its Foundation,* bk. 38, 15.

105. Ibid.

106. Ibid.

107. Ibid., 52.

108. Scullard, *Scipio Africanus in the Second Punic War*, 209, quoting Seneca, *Letters*, bk. 86, 4–6.

109. Ibid., 284.

110. Stephenson, *Public Lands and Agrarian Laws of the Roman Republic,* 13.

111. Livy, *The History of Rome From Its Foundation,* bk. 38, 53. As Livy notes, Scipio was probably buried in Liternum. The family tomb, however, was located just off the Via Appia in Rome.

9. SCIPIO'S PLACE IN MILITARY HISTORY

1. For the dates during which Gaius Marius, Lucius Cornelius Sulla, and Caesar held command, see R. Ernest Dupuy and Trevor N. Dupuy, *The Encyclopedia of Military History: From 3500 BC to the Present* (New York: Harper and Row, 1986), 90–94.

2. I have relied on the following sources regarding the strengths and weakness of Julius Caesar as they compare with those of Scipio: Lendon, *Soldiers and Ghosts;* Alfred S. Bradford, *With Arrow, Sword, and Spear: A History of Warfare in the Ancient World* (Westport, CT: Praeger, 2001); Ramon L. Jiménez, *Caesar Against Rome: The Great Roman Civil War* (Westport, CT: Praeger, 2000); J. F. C. Fuller, *Julius Caesar: Man, Soldier, and Tyrant* (New York: Da Capo Press, 1991); Gabriel and Boose, "Caesar's Campaigns," in *The Great Battles of Antiquity,* chapter 10; and Grant, *The Army of the Caesars.*

3. Grant, *The Army of the Caesars,* 236–37.

4. Personal conversation with Gen. Avigdor Kahalani of the Israeli Defense Force at Metulla, Israel, 1983.

5. On the problem of amateurism in armies, past and present, see Richard A. Gabriel and Paul L. Savage, *Crisis in Command* (New York: Hill and Wang, 1978), 72–73;

and Richard A. Gabriel, *Military Incompetence: Why the American Military Doesn't Win* (New York: Hill and Wang, 1985), 9–15.

6. Caesar had a reputation among his men for treating them fairly and even over-looking their transgressions. The result was that his men held him in high regard. Grant, *The Army of the Caesars,* 16–17.

7. Lendon, *Soldiers and Ghosts,* 218–20; B. Campbell, "Who Were the *Viri Militares?*" *Journal of Roman Studies* 65 (1975): 11–31; and B. Campbell, "Teach Yourself How to Be a General," *Journal of Roman Studies* 77 (1987): 13–29.

8. Lendon, *Soldiers and Ghosts,* 218–19.

9. Dupuy and Dupuy, *The Encyclopedia of Military History,* 96; Fuller, *Julius Caesar,* 321–22.

10. Bradford, *With Arrow, Sword, and Spear,* 219.

11. Lendon, *Soldiers and Ghosts,* 426. See also Bell, "Tactical Reform in the Roman Republican Army," 404–22.

12. Both Dupuy and Dupuy and Lendon are probably correct that the transition of the Roman army to an all-cohort force, begun under Marius, probably took years to complete.

13. Fuller, *Julius Caesar,* 315–17.

14. Lendon, *Soldiers and Ghosts,* 219; and Grant, *The Army of the Caesars,* 20–21.

15. Bennett, *Frontinus: The Strategemata,* bk. 4, chapter 7, note 4. The translation (Loeb, 1925) is available electronically in its entirety on the LacusCurtius website at the University of Chicago.

16. Gabriel, *Great Captains of Antiquity,* chapter 7.

17. Fuller, *Julius Caesar,* 308–15.

18. Scullard, *Scipio Africanus,* 226.

19. Fuller, *Julius Caesar,* 318–21.

20. The best works on the logistics of ancient armies are Roth, *The Logistics of the Roman Army at War;* and Engels, *Alexander the Great and the Logistics of the Macedonian Army.*

21. In support of his contention that Caesar ignored his logistics, see Fuller, *Julius Caesar,* 315–16, which cites T. Rice Holmes, *The Roman Republic and the Founder of the Empire* (Oxford, UK: Clarendon Press, 1923), vol. 1, p. 120. Fuller argues that historians have misinterpreted Caesar's writings, taking his frequent comments about supplies as indicating that he was always attentive to logistics. Fuller argues these comments are so frequent precisely because Caesar was always worried about his lack of adequate supplies.

Bibliography

Adcock, F. E. *The Roman Art of War Under the Republic.* Cambridge, MA: Harvard University Press, 1940.

Akinde, Michael O. "Cornelius Scipio Africanus." May 2006. www.fenrir.dk/history/index.php?title=History.

Allen, Alexander. "Barba." In Smith, *A Dictionary of Greek and Roman Antiquities,* 196–98. London: John Murray, 1854.

Anderson, James D. *Roman Military Supply in North-east England: An Analysis of an Alternative to the Piercebridge Formula.* Oxford, UK: Archaeopress, British Archaeological Reports, Series 224, 1992.

Antonelli, Giuseppe. *Scipione l'africano: L'uomo che conquisto Cartagine.* Rome: Newton and Compton, 1999.

Appian. *Roman History.* Translated by H. E. White. Cambridge, MA: Harvard University Press, 1992.

Ardant du Picq, Charles. *Battle Studies: Ancient and Modern Battle.* Harrisburg, PA: Military Service Publishing Company, 1946.

Austin, N. J. E., and Boris Rankov. *Exploratio: Military and Political Intelligence in the Roman World From the Second Punic War to the Battle of Adrianople.* London: Routledge, 1995.

Bachrach, Bernard S. "Animals and Warfare in Early Medieval Europe." In *Armies and Politics in the Early Medieval West,* edited by Bernard S. Bachrach. Aldershot, Hampshire, UK: Variorum, 1993.

Badian, E. *Foreign Clientelae, 264–70 BC.* Oxford, UK: Clarendon Press, 1958.

———. "Rome and Antiochus the Great: A Study in Cold War." *Classical Philology* 54, no. 2 (1959): 81–89.

Bagnall, N. *The Punic Wars.* London: Hutchinson, 1990.

Balsdon, J. P. V. D. "L. Cornelius Scipio: A Salvage Operation." *Historia: Zeitschrift für antike Geschichte* 21 (1972): 224–34.

Beer, Sir Gavin de. *Hannibal.* New York: Viking, 1969.

———. *Hannibal's March.* New York: Dutton, 1955.

Bell, M. J. V. "Tactical Reform in the Roman Republican Army." *Historia: Zeitschrift für antike Geschichte* 14 (1965): 404–22.

Bennett, Charles E. *Frontinus: The Strategemata.* New York: Loeb, 1925.

Bibliography

Bettenson, Henry S. *Rome and the Mediterranean*. London: Penguin, 1976.

Blatter, R. "Ein mermutliches Munzbildnis des Scipio Africanus." *Gazette Numismatique Suisse* 24 (1974): 78–79.

Boardman, John, Jasper Griffin, and Oswyn Murray. *The Oxford History of Greece and the Hellenistic World*. Oxford, UK: Oxford University Press, 1991.

Bradford, Alfred S. *With Arrow, Sword, and Spear: A History of Warfare in the Ancient World*. Westport, CT: Praeger, 2001.

Brewitz, Walter. *Scipio Africanus Maior in Spanien, 210–206 BCE*. Tubingen, Germany: H. Laupp, 1914.

Brizzi, Giovanni. "Hannibal: Punier und Hellenist." *Das Altertum* (1991): 201–10.

Brunt, P. A. *Italian Manpower, 225 BC–AD 14*. London: Clarendon Press, 1971.

Buckney, T. A. *Scipio Africanus: The Conqueror of Hannibal; Selections From Livy, Books 26–30*. London: G. Bell and Sons, 1965.

Caesar, *Gallic Wars*. Whitefish, MT: Kessinger Publishers, 2007.

Campbell, B. "Teach Yourself How to Be a General." *Journal of Roman Studies* 77 (1987): 13–29.

———. "Who Were the *Viri Militares?*" *Journal of Roman Studies* 65 (1975): 11–31.

Casson, Lionel. "Galley Slaves." *Transactions and Proceedings of the American Philological Association* 97 (1966): 35–44.

Caven, Brian. *The Punic Wars*. London: Weidenfeld and Nicolson, 1980.

Ciaceri, Emanuele. *Scipione Africano e l'idea imperiale di Roma*. Napoli: R. Ricciardi, 1940.

Cicero, *de Republica*. Cambridge, UK: Cambridge University Press, 1995.

Connolly, Peter. *Greece and Rome at War*. Englewood Cliffs, NJ: Prentice-Hall, 1981.

Consiglio, Alberto. *Scipione e la conquista del Mediterraneo*. Milan: Fratelli Treves, 1937.

Cornell, Tim, Boris Rankov, and Philip Sabin, eds. *The Second Punic War: A Reappraisal*. London: Institute of Classical Studies, University of London, 1996.

Cottrell, Leonard. *Hannibal: Enemy of Rome*. New York: Holt, Rinehart, and Winston, 1960.

Delbrück, Hans. *The History of the Art of War*. Vol. 1, *Warfare in Antiquity*. Translated by Walter J. Renfroe Jr. Westport, CT: Greenwood Press, 1990.

———. *Historische Zeitschrift* 51 (1883): 13–23.

de Regibus, Luca. *Il Processo degli Scipioni*. Torino: V. Bucca, 1921.

de Sanctis, G. B. *Storia dei Romani*. Vol. 3, *L'eta delle guerre puniche*. Torino: Fratelli Bocca, 1916–17.

Develin, Robert. "The Roman Command Structure and Spain: 218–190 BC." *Klio* 62, no. 2 (1980); 355–67.

———. "Scipio Africanus Imperator." *Latomus* 36 (1977): 110–13.

Dio Cassius. *Bibliotheca Historia*. Cambridge, MA: Harvard University Press, 1947.

Diodorus Siculus. *Diodorus of Sicily*. Translated by Francis R. Walton. 12 vols. Cambridge, MA: Harvard University Press, 1937.

Donauer, Friedrich. *Scipio Africanus: Kampf um das Mittelmeer*. Stuttgart: Thienemann, 1929.

Dorey, Thomas A. "Macedonian Troops at the Battle of Zama." *American Journal of Philology* 78, no. 2 (1957): 185–87.

———. "Scipio Africanus as a Party Leader." *Klio* 39 (1961): 191–98.

Bibliography

Dorey, Thomas A., and Dudley Reynolds. *Rome Against Carthage*. Garden City, NJ: Doubleday, 1972.

Droysen, H. "Die polybianische Beschreibung der zweiten Schlacht bei Baecula." *Rhein. Mus.* 30 (1896): 280–84.

Duncan-Jones, R. P. "Giant Cargo Ships in Antiquity." *Classical Quarterly* 27, no. 2 (1977): 331–36.

Dupuy, R. Ernest, and Trevor N. Dupuy. *The Encyclopedia of Military History: From 3500 BC to the Present*. New York: Harper and Row, 1986.

Dvornik, Francis. *Origins of Intelligence Services: The Ancient Near East, Persia, Greece, Rome, Byzantium, the Arab Muslim Empires, the Mongol Empire, China, Muscovy*. New Brunswick, NJ: Rutgers University Press, 1974.

Engels, Donald W. *Alexander the Great and the Logistics of the Macedonian Army*. Berkeley, CA: University of California Press, 1978.

Essin, Emmett M. "Mules, Packs, and Packtrains." *Southwestern Historical Quarterly* 74, no. 1 (1970): 52–59.

Feliciani, N. "La Seconda Guerra Punica nella Spagna, 211–208 BCE." *Studi e Documenti di Storia Diritto* 1904: 249–65.

Forbes, R. J. *Studies in Ancient Technology*. Leiden, the Netherlands: E. J. Brill, 1964.

Fournie, Daniel A. "Clash of Titans at Zama." *Military Review* 16, no. 6 (2000): 27–33.

———. "Harsh Lessons: Roman Intelligence in the Hannibalic War." *International Journal of Intelligence and Counterintelligence* 17, no. 3 (2004): 502–38.

Fowler, W. W. *The Religious Experience of the Roman People*. London: Taylor and Francis, 1911.

Fraccaro, P. "I processi degli Scipioni." *Storia per l'antica classica* 4 (1911): 370–81.

———. *I Processi degli Scipioni*. Rome: Bretschneider, 1967.

Frank, Tenney. *Roman Imperialism*. New York: Macmillan, 1914.

Fuller, J. F. C. *Julius Caesar: Man, Soldier, and Tyrant*. New York: Da Capo, 1991.

———. *A Military History of the Western World*. Vol. 1, *From the Defeat of the Spanish Armada to the Battle of Waterloo*. New York: Da Capo, 1954.

Gabriel, Richard A. *The Campaigns of Hannibal*. Carlisle Barracks, PA: U.S. Army War College, 1992.

———. "The Carthaginian Empire and Republican Rome." In *Empires at War*, vol. 2, 369–434.

———, ed. *Empires at War: A Chronological Encyclopedia*. 3 vols. Westport, CT: Greenwood Press, 2005.

———. *Great Captains of Antiquity*. Westport, CT: Greenwood Press, 2001.

———. "Logistics." In *Soldiers' Lives Through History*.

———. *The Military History of Ancient Israel*. Westport, CT: Greenwood Press, 2003.

———. *Military Incompetence: Why the American Military Doesn't Win*. New York: Hill and Wang, 1985.

———. *Muhammad: Islam's First Great General*. Norman: University of Oklahoma Press, 2007.

———. *No More Heroes: Madness and Psychiatry in War*. New York: Hill and Wang, 1987.

———. "Rome Against Greece." In *Empires at War*, vol. 2, chapter 13.

———. "Siegecraft." In *Soldiers' Lives Through History*, chapter 17.

Bibliography

————, ed. *Soldiers' Lives Through History*. Westport, CT: Greenwood Press, 2006.

Gabriel, Richard A., and Donald W. Boose Jr. "Caesar's Campaigns." In *The Great Battles of Antiquity: A Strategic and Tactical Guide to Great Battles That Shaped the Development of War,* edited by Richard A. Gabriel and Donald W. Boose Jr. Westport, CT: Greenwood Press, 1994, chapter 10.

Gabriel, Richard A., and Karen S. Metz. *From Sumer to Rome: The Military Capabilities of Ancient Armies*. Westport, CT: Greenwood Press, 1991.

Gabriel, Richard A., and Paul L. Savage. *Crisis in Command*. New York: Hill and Wang, 1978.

Gardiner, Robert, and John Morrison. *The Age of the Galley: Mediterranean Oared Vessels Since Preclassical Times*. London: Brassey's Ltd., 1995.

Gartner, Thomas. "Die praemilitaerische Ausbildung des Scipio Africanus." *MAIA* 55, no. 2 (2003): 317–19.

Gilliver, C. M. *The Roman Art of War*. London: Stroud, 1999.

Glover, R. F. "The Tactical Handling of the Elephant." *Greece and Rome* 17, no. 49 (1948): 1–11.

Goldsworthy, Adrian. *The Roman Army at War: 100 BC–AD 200*. Oxford, UK: Oxford University Press, 1996.

————. *Roman Warfare*. London: Clarendon Press, 2000.

Gomme, A. W. "A Forgotten Factor of Greek Naval Strategy." *Journal of Hellenic Studies* 53, pt. 1 (1933): 16–24.

Gowers, William. "The African Elephant in Warfare." *African Affairs* 46, no. 182 (1947): 42–49.

Grant, Michael. *The Army of the Caesars*. New York: Charles Scribner's Sons, 1974.

Grazioli, Francesco. *Scipione l'Africano*. Torino: Unione-Tipografico-Editrice Torinese, 1946.

Great Captains Before Napoleon: A Teaching Guide. West Point, NY: Department of Art and Engineering, 1965.

Grossman, David. *On Killing: The Psychological Cost of Learning to Kill in War and Society*. Boston: Little, Brown, 1995.

Gruen, Erich S. *Culture and National Identity in Republican Rome*. Ithaca, NY: Cornell University Press, 1992.

Gsell, Stephane. *Histoire ancienne de l'Afrique du Nord*. Vols. 2, 3, 5. Paris: 1913–1920. Reprint, Asnabruck, Germany, 1972.

Hafner, G. "Das Bildnis des P. Cornelius Scipio Africanus." *Archaeologischer Anzeiger* (1972), 474–92.

Hanson, Victor Davis. "Cannae." In *Experience of War,* edited by Robert Cowley. New York: Putnam, 1992.

Hardemon, R. Alan. *A Study of the Logistics of Alexander, Napoleon, and Sherman*. Maxwell Air Force Base, AL: Air University Graduate School of Logistics, 1998.

Haywood, Richard M. *Studies on Scipio Africanus*. Baltimore, MD: Johns Hopkins University Press, 1932.

Head, D. *Armies of the Macedonian and Punic Wars, 359 BC to 146 BC*. England: Wargames Research Group, 1982.

Bibliography

Holleaux, Maurice. "Rome and Macedon." In *Cambridge Ancient History*. Vol. 8. Cambridge, UK: Cambridge University Press, 1954.

Hopkins, Keith. "Taxes and Trade in the Roman Empire, 200 B.C.–A.D. 400." *Journal of Roman Studies* 70 (1980): 81–89.

Houston, George W. "Ports in Perspective: Some Comparative Material on Roman Merchant Ships and Ports." *American Journal of Archaeology* 92, no. 4 (1988): 553–64.

Hoyos, B. D. "Hannibal: What Kind of Genius?" *Greece and Rome,* 2nd ser., 30, no. 2 (1983): 171–80.

Hyland, Ann. *Equus: The Horse in the Roman World.* New Haven, CT: Yale University Press, 1990.

Italicus, Silius. *Punica.* Translated by J. D. Duff. Cambridge, MA: Harvard University Press, 1934.

Jiménez, Ramon L. *Caesar Against Rome: The Great Roman Civil War.* Westport, CT: Praeger, 2000.

Josephus. *The Jewish War.* Translated by G. A. Williamson. Oxford: Penguin, 1959.

Junkelmann, Marcus. *Die Legionen des Augustus: Der römische Soldat im archäologischen experiment.* Mainz, Germany: Philipp von Zabern, 1986.

Kahrstedt, U. *Geschichte der Karthager.* Vol. 3. Berlin, 1913.

Keppie, Lawrence. *The Making of the Roman Army: From Republic to Empire.* London: Batsford, 1984.

Kistler, John M. *War Elephants.* Westport, CT: Praeger, 2006.

Knapp, Robert. *Aspects of the Roman Experience in Iberia, 206–100 B.C.* Spain: Valladolid, 1977.

Köster, H. *Das antike Seewesen.* Berlin: 1923.

Krentz, P. "Casualties in Hoplite Battles." *Greek, Roman, and Byzantine Studies* 26, no. 1 (1985): 13–20.

Kromayer, Johannes. *Roms Kampf um die Weltherrschaft.* Leipzig: B. G. Teuber, 1912.

Kromayer, Johannes, and George Veith. *Antike Schlachtfelder.* 3 vols. Berlin: Wiedmannsche Buchhandlung, 1912.

———. *Heerwesen und Kriegsführung der Griechen und Römer.* Munich: C. H. Beck, 1928.

———. *Schlachten-Atlas zur antiken Kriegsgeschichte.* Leipzig: Wagner and Debbs, 1922.

Launey, M. "Inscriptions de Thasos." *Bulletin de Correspondance Hellenique* 57 (1933): 400.

Lazenby, John. *Hannibal's War.* Warminster, UK: Aris and Phillips, 1978.

———. "Was Maharbal Right?" In Cornell, Rankov, and Sabin, *The Second Punic War,* 39–48.

Lehmann, Konrad. "Der letzte Feldzug des hannibalischen krieges." In *Jahrbücher für klassische Philologie,* vol. 21, 556–69. Leipzig, Germany: B. G. Teubner, 1984.

Lendon, J. L. *Soldiers and Ghosts: A History of Battle in Classical Antiquity.* New Haven, CT: Yale University Press, 2005.

Lepper-Mainzer, Gaby. *Das Darstellung des Feldherrn Scipio Africanus.* Bochum, Germany: Brockmeyer, 1982.

Libourel, Jan M. "Galley Slaves in the Second Punic War." *Classical Philology* 68, no. 2 (1973): 116–19.

Liddell-Hart, B. H. *Scipio Africanus: Greater Than Napoleon*. New York: Da Capo, 1994.

Lillo, Antonio, and Martin Lillo. "On Polybius 10.10.12: The Capture of New Carthage." *Historia: Zeitschrift für antike Geschichte* 37 (1988): 477–80.

Livius, Titus (Livy). *The History of Rome From Its Foundation: The War With Hannibal*. Translated by Aubrey de Selincourt. London: Penguin, 1965.

Lovejoy, Jack. "The Tides of New Carthage." *Classical Philology* 67, no. 2 (1972): 110–11.

Lowe, Benedict J. "Polybius 10.10.12 and the Existence of Salt-flats at Carthago Novo." *Phoenix* 54, no. 1–2 (2000): 39–52.

Marks, Raymond. *From Republic to Empire: Scipio Africanus in the Punica of Silius Italicus*. New York: Peter Lang, 2005.

McDonald, A. H. "Scipio Africanus and Roman Politics in the Second Century B.C." *Journal of Roman Studies* 28, pt. 2 (1938): 153–64.

Meiklejohn, K. W. "Roman Strategy and Tactics From 509 to 202 BC." *Greece and Rome* 7, no. 21 (1938): 170–78.

Messer, William Stuart. "Mutiny in the Roman Army: The Republic." *Classical Philology* 15, no. 2 (1920): 158–75.

Meyer, E. *Kleine Schriften*. Vol. 2. Germany: Halle A.S., 1924.

Mommsen, Theodore. *History of Rome*. Translated by William Purdie Dickson. New York, 1891.

Morrison, John S. "Dilution of Oarcrews With Prisoners of War." *Classical Quarterly*, n.s., 38, no. 1 (1988): 252–53.

Moscovich, James M. "Dio Cassius on Scipio's Return From Spain in 205 BC." *Ancient History Bulletin* 2 (1988), 107–10.

Neumann, A. "Ilipa." *Klio* (1932): 255–56.

Nicol, John. *The Historical and Geographical Sources Used by Silius Italicus*. Oxford, UK: Basil Blackwell, 1936.

Nicorescu, Paul. "La Tomba degli Scipioni." *Ephemeris Daco-Romana* 1 (1923): 1–56.

Oakley, S. P. "Single Combat in the Roman Republic." *Classical Quarterly*, n.s., 35, no. 2 (1985): 392–410.

Parker, James. *Comparing Strategies of the Second Punic War: Rome's Strategic Victory Over the Tactical/Operational Genius, Hannibal Barca*. Carlisle Barracks, PA: U.S. Army War College, 2001.

Patterson, Marcia L. "Rome's Choice of Magistrates During the Hannibalic War." *Transactions and Proceedings of the American Philological Association* 73 (1942): 319–40.

Picard, G. C. *Hannibal*. Paris: C. Klincksieck, 1967.

———. *The Life and Death of Carthage*. New York: Taplinger, 1969.

Polybius. *The Histories of Polybius*. Translated by Evelyn S. Shuckburgh. Bloomington: University of Indiana Press, 1962.

Pope, C. G. *The Story of Scipio Africanus . . . from Livy*. London: F. Muller, 1935.

Proctor, Dennis. *Hannibal's March in History*. Oxford: Clarendon Press, 1971.

Rankov, Boris. "The Second Punic War at Sea." In Cornell, Rankov, and Sabin, *The Second Punic War*, 49–58.

Rawling, Louis. "Celts, Spaniards, and Samnites: Warriors in a Soldier's War." In Cornell, Rankov, and Sabin, *The Second Punic War*, 81–90.

Reid, J. S. "Problems of the Second Punic War: Polybius as a Geographer." *Journal of Roman Studies* 3, pt. 2 (1913): 191–96.

———. "Problems of the Second Punic War: Rome and Her Italian Allies." *Journal of Roman Studies* 5 (1915): 87–124.

Rich, John. "The Origins of the Second Punic War." In Cornell, Rankov, and Sabin, *The Second Punic War*, 1–37.

Richardson, John S. *Hispaniae: Spain and the Development of Roman Imperialism, 218–82 BC*. Cambridge, UK: Cambridge University Press, 1986.

Ridley, R. T. "Was Scipio Africanus at Cannae?" *Latomus* 36 (1977): 110–13.

Rossi, Andreola. "Parallel Lives: Hannibal and Scipio in Livy's Third Decade." *Transactions of the American Philological Association* 134 (2000): 359–81.

Roth, Jonathan P. *The Logistics of the Roman Army at War: 264 B.C.–A.D. 235*. Boston: E. J. Brill, 1999.

Russell, W. H. *Polybius on Hannibal and Scipio Africanus*. Annapolis, MD: Academic Fellowship, 1963.

Sabin, Philip. "The Face of Roman Battle." *Journal of Roman Studies* 90 (2000): 1–17.

———. "The Mechanics of Battle in the Second Punic War." In Cornell, Rankov, and Sabin, *The Second Punic War*, 59–80.

Salmon, E. T. *Roman Colonization*. London: Thames and Hudson, 1969.

Samuels, M. "The Reality of Cannae." *Militärgeschichtliche Mittelungen* 47 (1990): 7–29.

Sander, E. "Zur Rangordnung des Römischen Herres: Die Flotten." *Historia: Zeitschrift für antike Geschichte* 6 (1957): 347–67.

Sann, Georg. *Untersuchungen zu Scipios Feldzug in Afrika*. Berlin: Eberling, 1914.

Schulten, Adolf. *Die Lager des Scipio*. Munich: Bruckmann, 1927.

Schur, Werner. *Scipio Africanus und die Begrundung der römischen Weltherrschaft*. Leipzig, Germany: Dieterich, 1927.

Scott-Kilvert, Ian. *Polybius and the Rise of the Roman Empire*. London: Penguin, 1979.

Scullard, Howard H. *The Elephant in the Greek and Roman World*. Ithaca, NY: Cornell University Press, 1974.

———. "A Note on the Battle of Ilipa." *Journal of Roman Studies* 26, pt. 1 (1936): 19–23.

———. *Roman Politics, 220–150 B.C.* Oxford, UK: Oxford University Press, 1973.

———. *Scipio Africanus in the Second Punic War*. Cambridge, UK: Cambridge University Press, 1933.

———. *Scipio Africanus: Soldier and Politician*. Ithaca, NY: Cornell University Press, 1970.

Shaw, B. D. "Eaters of Flesh, Drinkers of Milk: Ancient Mediterranean Ideology of the Pastoral Nomad." *Ancient Society* 13–14 (1982–83): 5–32.

Shaw, T. *The Trireme Project: Operational Experience*. Oxford, UK: Oxford Monograph, 1993.

Sheldon, Rose Mary. *Intelligence Activities in Ancient Rome: Trust in the Gods, but Verify*. New York: Frank Cass, 2005.

———. "Tinker, Tailor, Caesar, Spy: Espionage in Ancient Rome." Ph.D. dissertation, University of Michigan, Ann Arbor, 1987.

Shotter, David. *The Fall of the Roman Republic*. London: Routledge, 2005.

Bibliography

Shuckburgh, Evelyn S. "Punic War in Spain Between 211 and 206 B.C." *Classical Review* 6, no. 9 (1892): 381–85.

Singh, Sarva Daman. *Ancient Indian Warfare*. Delhi: Motilal Banarsidass, 1997.

Sippel, Donald V. "Some Observations on the Means and Costs of the Transport of Bulk Commodities in the Late Republic and Early Empire." *Ancient World* 16 (1987): 12–19.

Smith, Philip J. *Scipio Africanus and Rome's Invasion of Africa: A Historical Commentary on Titus Livius, Book 29*. Amsterdam: J. C. Gieben Publisher, 1993.

Smith, William. *A Dictionary of Greek and Roman Antiquities*. London: John Murray, 1854.

Starr, Chester. *The Influence of Sea Power on Ancient History*. London: Oxford University Press, 1989.

Stephenson, Andrew. *Public Lands and Agrarian Laws of the Roman Republic*. Baltimore, MD: Johns Hopkins Press, 1891.

Taeger, F. "Zur Schlacht bei Ilipa." *Klio* (1931): 339–47.

Tatum, W. Jeffrey. "The Consular Elections for 190 B.C." *Klio* 83, no. 2 (2001): 388–401.

Terraine, John. *The Smoke and the Fire: Myths and Anti-myths of War, 1861–1945*. London: Sidgwick and Jackson, 1980.

Thiel, J. H. *Studies on the History of Roman Sea-Power in Republican Times*. Amsterdam: North-Holland Publishing Company, 1946.

Toynbee, A. J. *Hannibal's Legacy*. London: Oxford, 1965.

Valori, Francesco. *Scipione l'Africano*. Torino: Societa Editrice Internationale, 1955.

von Clausewitz, Carl. *On War*. Translation by Michael Howard and Peter Paret. Princeton, NJ: Princeton University Press, 1989.

Walbank, F. W. *A Historical Commentary on Polybius*. 3 vols. Oxford, UK: Oxford University Press, 1970.

———. "The Scipionic Legend." *Proceedings of the Cambridge Philological Society*, 13 (1967): 54–69.

Walsh, P. G. "Massinissa." *Journal of Roman Studies* 55, no. 1–2, pts. 2 and 3 (1965): 149–60.

Warmington, B. H. *Carthage: A History*. London: Robert Hale, 1958.

Warry, John. *Warfare in the Classical World: An Illustrated Encyclopedia of Weapons, Warriors, and Warfare in the Ancient Civilisations of Greece and Rome*. London: Salamander Books, 1980.

Whatley, N. "On the Possibility of Reconstructing Marathon and Other Ancient Battles." *Journal of Hellenic Studies*, 84 (1964): 119–39.

White, K. D. *Roman Farming*. Ithaca, NY: Cornell University Press, 1970.

Wickert, L. "Der Flotte der Römischen Kaiserzeit." *Würzburger Jahrbücher für die Altertumswissenschaft* 4 (1949–50): 100–25.

Williams, Mary Frances. "Shouldn't You Have Come and Talked to Me About It? Democracy and a Mutiny in Scipio's Army." *Ancient History Bulletin* 15, no. 4 (2001): 143–53.

Wise, Terence. *Armies of the Carthaginian Wars: 265–146 B.C.* London: Osprey, 1982.

Wood Jr., Frederick M. "The Military and Diplomatic Campaign of T. Quinctius Flamininus in 198 B.C." *American Journal of Philology* 62, no. 3 (1941): 277–88.

Xenophon. *The Persian Expedition.* Translated by Rex Warner. London: Penguin, 1972.

Yadin, Yigael. *The Art of Warfare in Biblical Lands in Light of Archaeological Discovery.* 2 vols. New York: McGraw-Hill, 1964.

Zielinski, Theodore. *Rivista di Storia Antica* 3, no. 1 (1898): 84–92.

Index

Index

Index

Index

Index

Index

Index

About the Author

RICHARD A. GABRIEL is a distinguished adjunct professor in the Department of History and War Studies at the Royal Military College of Canada in Kingston, Ontario, and the Department of Security Studies at the Canadian Forces College in Toronto. He was a professor of history and politics at the U.S. Army War College and held the Visiting Chair in Ethics at the Marine Corps University. He is a retired U.S. Army officer and the author of forty-three books and sixty-five published articles on military history and other subjects. Dr. Gabriel's most recent books are *Subotai the Valiant: Genghis Khan's Greatest General* (2006) and *Muhammad: Islam's First Great General* (2007). He lives in New Hampshire, where he flies his antique open-cockpit airplane.